www.wadsworth.com

www.wadsworth.com is the World Wide Web site for Thomson Wadsworth and is your direct source to dozens of online resources.

At *www.wadsworth.com* you can find out about supplements, demonstration software, and student resources. You can also send email to many of our authors and preview new publications and exciting new technologies.

www.wadsworth.com
Changing the way the world learns®

UNDERSTANDING GENDER AND CULTURE IN THE HELPING PROCESS

UNDERSTANDING GENDER AND CULTURE IN THE HELPING PROCESS

Practitioners' Narratives from Global Perspectives

CLAIRE LOW RABIN, EDITOR
Tel Aviv University, Israel

THOMSON
WADSWORTH

AUSTRALIA • CANADA • MEXICO • SINGAPORE • SPAIN • UNITED KINGDOM • UNITED STATES

THOMSON

WADSWORTH

Publisher/Executive Editor: Lisa Gebo
Assistant Editor: Alma Dea Michelena
Editorial Assistant: Sheila Walsh
Technology Project Manager: Barry Connolly
Marketing Manager: Caroline Concilla
Marketing Assistant: Mary Ho
Advertising Project Manager: Tami Strang
Project Manager, Editorial Production: Cheri Palmer
Print/Media Buyer: Emma Claydon

Permissions Editor: Kiely Sexton
Production Service: Ruth Cottrell
Copy Editor: Steven Summerlight
Cover Designer: Ross Carron
Cover Image: © SW Productions / gettyimages
Composition & Illustration: International Typesetting and Composition
Printer: Malloy Incorporated

For more information about our products, contact us at:
Thomson Learning Academic Resource Center
1-800-423-0563
For permission to use material from this text or product, submit a request online at
http://www.thomsonrights.com.
Any additional questions about permissions can be submitted by email to thomsonrights@thomson.com.

Library of Congress Control Number: 2004105086

ISBN 0-534-51389-1

Thomson Wadsworth
10 Davis Drive
Belmont, CA 94002
USA

Asia
Thomson Learning
5 Shenton Way #01-01
UIC Building
Singapore 068808

Australia/New Zealand
Thomson Learning
102 Dodds Street
Southbank, Victoria 3006
Australia

Canada
Nelson
1120 Birchmount Road
Toronto, Ontario M1K 5G4
Canada

Europe/Middle East/Africa
Thomson Learning
High Holborn House
50/51 Bedford Row
London WC1R 4LR
United Kingdom

Latin America
Thomson Learning
Seneca, 53
Colonia Polanco
11560 Mexico D.F.
Mexico

Spain/Portugal
Paraninfo
Calle Magallanes, 25
28015 Madrid, Spain

CONTENTS

CHAPTER 2

**Globalization of the Human Services: Exporting
High-Cultural Artifacts and the Selling of the Therapy
Industry as a Form of Neocolonialism   31**
Elaine Leeder, United States

CHAPTER 3

**Gender and Culture in the Narrative Approach
to Helping   46**
*Jill Freedman and
Gene Combs, United States*

PART II | **GENDER, CULTURE, AND STRESS: MULTILEVEL HELPING PROCESSES**

A. Individual and Family Level Helping

CHAPTER 4

Mental Health Practice for the Muslim Arab Population in Israel 68
Alean Al-Krenawi, Israel
John R. Graham, Canada

CHAPTER 8

Helping Immigrant Women From the Former Soviet Union   129
Roni Berger, United States

CHAPTER 9

Posttraumatic Experiences of Refugee Women   149
*Hurriyet Babacan and
Narayan Gopalkrishnan, Australia*

B. Group Level Helping

CHAPTER 12

Restructuring Social Identity Through Self-Categorizing Groups: The Interface of Group Dynamics, Gender, and Culture 208
Tamah Nakamura, Japan
Cathy Collins, United States

CHAPTER 13

Facilitating Telling of Stories Through Psychodynamic Groups: Traumatized Women in the Former Yugoslavia 230
Doris Gödl, Austria

C. Service and Community Level Helping

CHAPTER 14

**Immigrant Women, Abortion, and Preventive
Intervention in Italy   247**
Mauro Gonzo, Italy

CHAPTER 15

**Violence Against Women in the Family: Immigrant Women
and the U.S. Health Care System   267**
*Susan L. Ivey,
Elizabeth Kramer, and
Marianne Yoshioka, United States*

FOREWORD

PHYLLIS CHESLER
UNITED STATES

Although this is both an academic and a clinical work, its origins are also sacred and personal. According to Claire Rabin, this work is the living intellectual child of two women: Rabin and her deceased colleague, Dr. Amith Ben-David, with whom she wrote a previous book and whose personal and professional memory she wishes to honor. This anthology takes us to the next clinical, theoretical, and political level, in which cultural biases are seen as important as gender, class, or racial biases. In addition to revealing our sexist or racist biases, this book can heighten the professional helpers' awareness of cultural biases and show us ways of integrating culture and gender issues.

Although there has been enormous progress, the clinical biases I first wrote about in 1972 in *Women and Madness* still exist today in the 21st century. Many clinical judgments remain clouded by classism, racism, anti-Semitism, homophobia, ageism, and sexism. I have reviewed hundreds, possibly thousands, of psychiatric and psychological assessments in North American and European matrimonial, criminal, and civil lawsuits. The clinical distrust of mothers simply because they are women and the eagerness to bend over backward to like fathers simply because they are men is of great concern. As was noted in the 1970s, sexism in clinical evaluation remains evident, although perhaps less so than 30 years ago. For example, reports of divorce cases reveal that mothers are still routinely accused of alienating a child from the child's father if that child would prefer to live with the mother.

Other examples of continuing sexism in the helping process include five important areas: (1) women with medical illnesses are often overly psychiatrically diagnosed and medicated; (2) women who allege sex discrimination, harassment, rape, incest, or battery are being ordered into therapy or diagnostically pathologized at trial; (3) people with no insurance cannot afford therapy; (4) people of color face clinicians' fear and hostility; and (5) helper–patient sexual abuse still exists.

Thus, it seems that just because I and many other mental health professionals have continued to challenge the diagnostic pathologizing of women, poor people, people of color, and gay people does not mean that such practices have disappeared. Double and triple diagnostic and treatment standards still exist. Native American, African American, Hispanic American, and Asian American women have good reason to mistrust helping systems. They suspect they are often seen as inferior, although they are doing their best and are commendably as self-sufficient as possible in overwhelming circumstances. Accordingly, many women of color in North America are deeply suspicious of receiving psychiatric medication and of the helping professions within mainstream institutions. Although they are more likely to be raped than white women, they may be less likely to report it to the police or to their families and, with dire consequences, less likely to seek help. If a woman in the United States is poor or speaks no English, her chances of getting the psychological help she may need are minimal. If she is also a lesbian and angry—or actually freaking out—she'll probably be diagnosed as more seriously ill than her white heterosexual counterpart. The cumulative effect of being forced to lead circumscribed lives is toxic. The psychic toll is measured in anxiety, depression, phobias, suicide attempts, eating disorders, and such stress-related illnesses as addictions, alcoholism, high blood pressure, and heart disease. This book demonstrates the universal results of discrimination in the helping process regardless of whether it is by gender, race, ethnicity, or class. It is exactly because this book presents examples from outside the United States and also at times outside the Western world that it can sensitize U.S. and Western readers to outsiders' perspectives on their own professional lives.

Feminist activists, theorists, and therapists have contributed a great deal to professional helpers' growing awareness of discrimination in practice. We now understand that women are not "crazy" or "defective" when, in response to trauma, they develop posttraumatic symptoms, including insomnia, flashbacks, phobias, panic attacks, anxiety, depression, dissociation, a numbed toughness, amnesia, shame, guilt, self-loathing, self-mutilation, and social withdrawal. Trauma victims may attempt to mask these symptoms with alcohol, drugs, overeating, or extreme forms of dieting.

We understand that chronic, hidden family or domestic violence is actually more, not less, traumatic than sudden violence at the hands of a stranger or by an enemy during war. We understand that rape is not about love or even lust but about humiliating another human being through forced or coerced sex and sexual shame. We now understand more about what trauma is and what it does to people. The effects of terror on men at war and in enemy captivity are equivalent to the trauma suffered by women at home in violent "domestic captivity."

There is a literature on feminist therapy and a literature on therapy that is sensitive to culture. Few books do both. My own experience has been in feminist therapy, and to this I speak. I think that many of the principles of feminist therapy resonate with culturally aware therapy, but there are places where these views conflict. This book looks at both the convergence and divergence between feminist and culturally aware therapies.

Although much of what I describe here describes what a feminist therapist does, I also believe that it is the basis of any good practice. There is much in common between basic social work values, narrative therapy practices, and feminist therapies. Thus, I believe that in addition to attending to issues of justice, the helper who is sensitive to both culture and gender is in effect more helpful and probably also more likely to include postmodern methods of helping.

For example, much of what a feminist therapist calls for involves trusting the wisdom of the person who is seeking help. Thus, a feminist therapist tries to believe what women say instead of diagnosing it. Given the history of psychiatry and psychoanalysis, and its reliance on the medical model, this alone is a radical act. A feminist therapist believes that a woman needs to be told that she's not crazy; that it's normal to feel sad or angry about being overworked, underpaid, underloved; that it's healthy to harbor fantasies of running away when the needs of others (aging parents, needy husbands, demanding children) threaten to overwhelm her. A feminist therapist does not label a woman as mentally ill because she expresses strong emotions or is at odds with her tamed, subordinate, feminine role. She or he may also believe that healing and recovering requires political literacy or a spiritual vision as part of the helping process, or both.

A feminist therapist listens, attends to, and focuses on the stories of the client, not the discourse of the therapist. For example, in *Trauma and Recovery* (1992), psychiatrist Judith Lewis Herman models a new vision of therapy and of human relationships, one in which we are called upon to "bear witness to a crime" and to "affirm a position of solidarity with the victim." Herman's ideal therapist cannot be morally neutral but must make a collaborative commitment and enter into an "existential engagement" with the traumatized. Such a therapist must listen—really listen, solemnly and without haste—to the factual and emotional details of atrocities, without flight or denial, without blaming the victim, without identifying with the aggressor, without becoming a detective who "diagnoses" ritual abuse after a single session, and without "using her power over the patient to gratify her personal needs."

Imagine Herman at work in Israel among both Arabs and Jews who have emigrated there from every continent on earth; imagine them at work in Australia, Ireland, Italy, Japan, Mexico, the United States, and the former Yugoslavia—and you have an idea of the ground this book covers. But, although Herman may not be thinking about how her ideas and techniques may work in many different cultures, Rabin and her associates are. Thus, in addition to gender violence per se, Rabin and her contributors also look at how women of different cultures respond to such violence. And they try to understand and model ways to help them.

For all those clinicians and mental health professionals who believe that systems of prejudice such as racism, sexism, classism, homophobia, and other social realities may affect individual psychology as much as one's childhood or genetic factors do, this book makes it clear that culture is as important as gender and that mental health professionals must factor it in if they wish to help anyone, certainly someone who has grown up in or who lives outside of a North American or European city. The pieces in this book show us how gender, class, race, birthplace, one's generation, clan, tribe, religion, and status as an immigrant must all be factored into understanding any living being, especially one in trouble and in pain.

There are reasons why helping in the West privileges the individual over the context in searching for the etiology of problems. Western psychoanalysis and psychotherapy tend to idealize the individual as the major source of problems and their solutions and does not view social systems such as racism, sexism, malnutrition, and unemployment as equally important causal factors because the individual is supposed to know how to overcome adversity. Rabin and others in this volume reject this individualized medical model, which focuses primarily on pathology, not on strengths—and not on the powers of elders or of the community to help one of their own. This volume proposes the involvement of the helper with the social context, expanding the non-Western view of what constitutes professional boundaries. The suggestions to rely upon non-Western traditional elders as mediators and conflict resolvers and on holistic and indigenous healing methods are exciting and sound. Western clinicians are also doing this.

Rabin and others make the excellent point that the "traditional self" is "embedded in community." Western concepts of privacy, individuality, and freedom are not valued as highly as group cohesion and stability. Thus working with traditional non-Western peoples may require nontraditional (and old-fashioned) social work helping approaches. For example, helpers may need to meet in their clients' homes, not in offices, and wake up clients for job interviews and sometimes accompany them, too. Helpers may need to talk to women at home, while the women are cooking or caring for children. Yet feminist thinking also alerts us not to take this too far so that the universal rights of women, even in a highly patriarchal community, are violated. This is a difficult balancing act and will demand continued reflection and discussion. Many of the chapters here demonstrate the ways in which the helpers struggle with the occasionally conflicting demands of universal individual rights with community cultural norms, a central issue for most helpers who are working with oppressed groups in any society.

The contributors to this collection also highlight that establishing a warm and empathic relationship with the client is of primary importance. They also understand that internalized oppression must be addressed. The contributors understand that bearing witness to the sorrow and grief coming from traumatic life situations is important and that being supported instead of punished for doing so is important. Putting one's suffering to use through educating and supporting other victims is important; drafting, passing, and enforcing laws is important. By the very act of helping, the helper can also engage in social protest. Allowing a survivor of violence to testify—creating the listening conditions that make testimony possible—is also a way of taking a moral stand against human rights atrocities. Social injustice may also be confronted by listening carefully and allowing silenced stories to emerge. The boundaries between individual helping and social activism blur, making it clear that these were professional concepts to begin with and that healing is a process of telling one's story in a variety of ways.

In this light, the choice of the narrative approach to highlight the importance of stories told without superimposing professional discourses, concepts, metaphors, and understandings fits perfectly and creates a link between the ideological basis for the helping proposed here and the methods that are more fitting with that ideology. Narrative methods can be combined with other forms of helping as is demonstrated in this volume, such as expressive therapies, dream analysis, and use of mediators. As this book shows, we do not have to be locked into a Western view that embraces an "either–or" dichotomous view of helping but a more holistic "and–and" view that fits other cultures. This book will enrich our work in a variety of settings, including health and mental health clinics, community work in the field, sex clinics, universities, and workplaces by demonstrating the wide range of methods and settings that can benefit from the thinking proposed here. The book will help practitioners from all disciplines move toward more flexible practice with a wider range of populations, allowing them to offer help to people previously marginalized, ignored, and even hurt by the helping professions.

References

Chesler, P. (1972). *Women and madness.* New York: Doubleday.

Herman, J. (1992). *Trauma and recovery.* New York: Basic Books.

INTRODUCTION

A Narrative About This Book

CLAIRE LOW RABIN
ISRAEL

I once heard that the books we read choose us. Like any narrative, the story of a book has a life of its own. Our stories are then like ripples in a pond, in which others are affected and come to affect others in widening circles of influences. In my case, this story reflects my professional development and thus those of the students I teach and the clients I work with.

A fleeting conversation at a professional conference in Israel was the initial impetus of this book's conception. I was talking with a colleague about our work. Dr. Amith Ben-David, a social work teacher specializing in cultural sensitivity, and I, a social work teacher specializing in gender sensitivity, discussed the lack of integration between our two fields. As both teachers and practitioners, we were at that time caught up in the excitement of the narrative revolution coming out of the philosophic postmodern thrust away from abstract concepts and toward more individual, unique stories as the basis for helping. Intuitively we felt that gender and culture were of the same fabric, and that narrative therapy could be an important breakthrough in weaving together these previously separated threads.

In the weeks and following months, I found the conversation coming back to me, bringing a feeling that something needed to be created. We corresponded and eventually developed an idea for a Hebrew book that would bring Israeli case examples with different cultural, ethnic, and racial populations. We believed we could show the similar underlying gender issues in each situation while hoping that the narrative of each helper would highlight the unique dilemmas that each professional faces.

Amith and I had become friends through the work on the Hebrew book (Rabin & Ben-David, 1999). We had shared numerous discussions on the interface of gender and culture, on the sociopolitical politics that underlies our clients' problems, on sexism, on discrimination and prejudice in Israeli society, and, like most women, we shared our own lives with each other as well. I knew that Amith was discouraged about the lack of awareness, sensitivity, and caring of the plight of ethnic minorities in Israel, especially the Arab population. As many women before, she felt that to actualize her own potential she had to leave her family in Israel. Sadly, the week of her departure, she died suddenly in strange and still unexplained circumstances. Her death in her forties was a great shock for anyone who knew her.

At the time of her death, our book was yet to be published. I was left immobilized, not having the heart to look through her papers and finish the work we had started. In time, I came to realize that finishing our Hebrew book and eventually developing the concept to include helper's experiences from outside Israel would be a way to continue our dialogue even further. This book is a continuation of my conversations with Amith.

As an American in Israel, I had always been aware of culture; as a feminist, I was always aware of gender. But it is through these chapters that I found my own understanding of the connection between the two strengthened and clarified. Now I have come to see that the separation of gender and culture is not only artificial but also can distort both and even replicate oppressive processes in the helping endeavor.

This book is first and foremost a book for practitioners and students of the helping process. It draws on a multidisciplinary literature from diverse helping professions in different social contexts. The juxtaposition of "diversities" can offer common insights across the spectrum of work with different populations, using different methods in different social contexts.

Although this book celebrates the rich tapestry of diversity in culture, it also allows us to understand the fundamental gender issues in all cultures. It also posits that men and women need a positive social identity. A common theme is how personal identity is socially constructed and how complicated and challenging it is to develop and maintain a positive identity under conditions of unfair distribution of power. Racism, poverty, and sexism interweave to create oppression that can easily be replicated in the helping process through the privileging of certain dominant values (such as individual achievement and autonomy) and worldview assumptions. These chapters give numerous examples of practitioners who are working to help overcome negative social identity. All types of helping (psychotherapy, counseling, preventive work, group work, and community organization) reflect the helpers' resistance to oppression and a thus freeing of the mind, both in the client and the practitioner.

Narrative therapy was chosen to demonstrate one way to achieve this. The narrative approach involves a questioning of fundamental principles of a scientific medical and deficit-driven view of helping, which focuses on diagnosis and cure. It means learning to think on several interconnected levels: the personal, the community, and the wider social economic and cultural context. This book aims to help the practitioner become aware of how gender and culture are already present in the helping process in both their own assumptions and the problems they are addressing.

Women and culturally oppressed populations have suffered from a loss of what Gilligan (1982) has called "voice." By seeking to enrich and cultivate local knowledge through stories without imposing our own categories of labels, we allow for a process of self-definition to occur. When the professional community becomes audience rather than expert, oppressed people move into the role of experts in their own lives. Their new stories of resistance can be told, retold, and circulated.

Indeed, the reader may notice that regardless of the methods being discussed, most of them include opportunities for clients to tell their stories. Narrative listening can occur when the practitioner is aware of social context, regardless of the theory base the practitioner was trained in. Through nonjudgmental telling of stories with a listener who sees the universal oppression involved, clients become heroes and heroines in the process of coping with almost overwhelming challenges.

As a textbook, this book proposes that the narrative framework can help students also listen better for issues related to gender and culture while also allowing the utilization of a wide variety of helping methods. Others have begun to see the potential in narrative. Kerl (2002) has promoted the teaching of narrative methods as an outstanding way to help students incorporate multicultural principles. She notes that rather than thinking of power in an abstract way that is "out there," concepts related to power will become familiar and personal to students through the use of their own stories of gender and culture. As students reflect on their own gendered, racial, and ethnic identities through stories, they can connect to universal themes of power, domination, marginalization, and oppression of their clients. This book aims to help students move fluidly between abstract concepts related to the "isms" of oppression, and personal stories that link people, themselves, and others. These chapters demonstrate how, by anchoring our thinking in culture and gender, the practitioner is challenged to develop a way of viewing the helping process that links the social context with the individual problem. This overarching goal is to foster a creative search for different models that promote linking of the personal and the political and give clients more of a say in the process.

An edited book of invited chapters similarly struggles with the issue of similarity and differences. To foster continuity, most chapters were written according to a similar outline of:

- an overview
- a discussion of the problem, the population, and the helping process
- a case study to demonstrate helping methods
- personal reflections of the author
- key concepts
- questions that can be used for students and self-awareness, and
- references

Some of the chapters have included exercises that the authors have found useful to increase awareness and understanding of their topic, yet a certain flexibility has also been allowed to include a diversity of voices. The reader is asked to view this multiplicity as an example of the rich possibilities that open up when we view the social context and listen for real-life stories.

OVERVIEW OF THE BOOK

This book is organized into two parts. Part I offers the reader the conceptual and theoretical basis on which the book is based. Chapter 1, written by the editor, is a reflection of my personal and professional journey to include gender and culture in my work and teaching, and the way my journey mirrors the helping professions development in becoming sensitive to gender and culture. It will tie in this change with the narrative revolution and show why narrative is a major change that opens the door to having the social context in the room.

Chapter 2, "Globalization of the Human Services," by Elaine Leeder lays out the foundation for thinking about the exportation of Western therapy as a form of neocolonization. This chapter intends to sensitize us to the way in which the idea of "therapy" was developed within a certain social context and how it can unwittingly become another form of cultural domination rather than help. It then shows that taking the idea of helping beyond medicalized concepts and toward more holistic and indigenous healing methods allows the helper to use a variety of methods, such as mediation and group work, for prevention and education.

Chapter 3 on narrative therapy by Jill Freedman and Gene Combs is offered to introduce the reader to the basic concepts of this form of helping and to demonstrate its potential contribution to more gender- and culture-sensitive practices. It focuses on some of the fundamental methods—such as an analysis of social discourse, externalization, and reauthoring conversations—that can be used in addition to other forms of helping. The authors show how narrative therapy is especially relevant for practitioners who wish to incorporate understanding of power, domination, racism, sexism, and oppression in their practice with individuals and families.

Part II includes contributions from practitioners from around the world who deal with social changes and the upheavals caused by immigration, war, and refugee and minority status. Gender and culture are the basic tools of conceptualization that offer an understanding of women's and men's vulnerability to additional stress and heightened risk in specific cultural populations. The practitioners chose to present their stories work in diverse contexts—from primary health care, mental health, group, and community settings. Their methods include counseling, group work, mediation, prevention, and other forms of helping. Not all use narrative therapy specifically in their work. Yet all incorporate the social context as an overarching viewpoint, all show the practitioner as respectfully listening to stories without focusing on individual pathology or labels of dysfunction, and all demonstrate that hearing clients' stories is a major vehicle in overcoming the effects of oppressive social contexts in their everyday lives as part of the helping process.

Chapter 4 by Alean Al-Krenawi and John Graham explores the Arab population living in Israel and focuses on the way in which conflict affects mental health. They show how a context that includes the domination and oppression of the Arab population together with traditional patriarchal attitudes that oppress women makes it difficult for women to get the help they need. This chapter offers a case in which respected elders in the community are used to help women, an example of working with cultural structures as a resource.

Chapter 5 compares differences and similarities between male and female survivors of sexual assault in Israel. Sheri Oz has reviewed the literature on gender differences and cultural differences in sexual abuse, and she comes to the conclusion that gender is far more predictive than culture. The case shows how a male and a female young person were helped to overcome the trauma of sexual attack within the context of gender-sensitive helping.

Chapter 6 by Yvonne Jacobson shows how sexual problems are related to religious and cultural factors in Irish society. Social change moving from religious domination to the domination of the medical profession shows that social discourses continue to oppress. The case study follows the helping process using narrative therapy to demonstrate how externalizing social problems stemming from oppressive attitudes helped a man overcome the shame and guilt that resulted in sexual impotence.

Chapter 7 was written by Eleanor Pardess of Israel and explores the many unique issues and challenges in helping gay and lesbian clients develop a positive identity in a society in which prejudice and discrimination are highly prevalent. This chapter also offers an example of how the narrative approach, within a postmodern framework, sheds new light on the complexities of the coming-out process on homophobia and heterosexism. Understanding same-sex love differs across cultures and is constantly changing within cultures, thus making awareness of the cultural context imperative. Combining the expressive arts with narrative therapy opens a new possibility for practitioners. By opening lines of communication and transcending culture barriers, the expressive therapies can be a form of giving voice and of helping to overcome dominant oppressive discourses. This combination is innovative and offers new ideas about integrating different forms of therapy that can enrich each other in dealing with gender- and culture-related issues.

Chapter 8 by Roni Berger is on helping immigrant women from the former Soviet Union. This chapter shows that problems can arise from the meeting of two divergent cultures and the shifts of role structure in the family that occur during such a transition. The chapter includes information on the stages of immigration, the ways in which women immigrants are affected by migration, and the problems they experience in the acculturation process. The case study is of a young Russian girl who stopped studying and became depressed. It demonstrates especially the importance of knowing how to join with a foreign culture and how to reach out to women who do not regularly use services.

Chapter 9 on refugee women in Australia by Hurriyet Babacan and Narayan Gopalkrishnan continues the discussion on immigration in a different social context. The similarities and differences can be noted with the Australian social context, including a great deal of racism that impinges on the process of acculturation and assimilation. The authors show the isolating effects of racism and how helpers need to understand the interaction of gender and racial oppression in helping immigrants. The case study discusses the importance of understanding how these social processes result in trauma that may look like mental illness but is more socially induced.

Chapter 10 takes a look at immigration and minority status issues for Mexican women in the United States. Jeanne Hinkelman focuses on cultural attitudes toward women and how these affect the way in which Mexican women experience their absorption into the dominant culture. Helping within a college setting is the focus (that is, the backdrop and setting) of the case study, with an emphasis on using behavioral cognitive methods to empower a young woman who is conflicted about male authority in her life, gender roles and her own achievement, conflicts that resulted from dual loyalty to her patriarchal culture, and her own wish to integrate with a more egalitarian culture.

Chapter 11 demonstrates the intersection of gender and racism in the risk of emotional problems experienced by African American men. Previous focuses on gender have been primarily on women. We generally know less about women because of sexism, which has silenced women's voices in every field of study. Most gender-related discussions try to redress the imbalance by focusing on women. In the last 10 years, a renewed interest in men has emerged because of a growing understanding of how men are also harmed by gendered sex roles. African American men are especially vulnerable due to their position in a white, competitive, and market-oriented society such as that of the United States. Expectations that the male should be the primary provider, the defining characteristic of the traditional male role in the dominant culture, has not suited the African American culture, where couples tend to be more egalitarian. But oppressive welfare laws that marginalize black men and a sexist economy that further disadvantages them has resulted in increasing distress in this population. This chapter focuses also on black male adolescents, who are an especially high-risk group.

Chapter 12 offers a new concept: empowering "self-structuring groups" in both Japan and the United States that offer oppressed women an opportunity to gain a positive social identity with which to return and create social change in oppressive social groups. Tamah Nakamura and Cathy Collins have developed a model that proposes that groups can help overcome discrimination and oppression by offering an opportunity for silenced members to have a voice. Case examples from diverse settings show that self-structuring groups, which allow for increasing voice in their members, are a promising method for overcoming negative self-esteem and silencing in a wide variety of situations.

Chapter 13 continues to show how groups can offer a place for the development of voice by using psychodynamic methods. Doris Godl is a psychoanalyst who traveled from Austria to the former Yugoslavia to work with women in the peace movement on their own traumatized experiences during wars in the 1990s. She shows how, in the context of a group experience, story sharing can be facilitated through the telling of dreams and their analysis. Several cases are offered of women who shared their traumas via dream analysis with a group that offered a safe place for healing.

Chapter 14 by Mauro Gonzo from Italy shows how immigrant women use the health services of their new environment to have abortions at an unusually high rate. His chapter looks at the cultural and gender factors that lead to this form of contraception and the way this is handled in a Catholic country such as Italy. The chapter especially focuses on enriching and increasing information using systemic questions to introduce cultural stories that can be heard by professionals in the health system through interviews and questionnaire. Two case studies show how the health provider can use questions to open up issues that normally would not be dealt with in interviews to decide upon abortion. This chapter shows that even one session that is sensitive to culture and gender can help make service more accessible and useful to immigrant women.

Chapter 15 by Susan Ivey, Elizabeth Kramer, and Marianne Yoshioka shows how immigrant women in the United States are especially vulnerable to violence in the family and how this problem often goes unnoticed by health workers because of cultural factors that sanction and hide family problems. This chapter illustrates how traditional family roles promote violence against women in immigrant groups and how they clash with gender equality and the protection of women in families where the woman is isolated and hidden from public view. Two case studies show how services can become more attuned to the needs of these vulnerable women. This chapter shows how services can reach out and offer help while understanding that removing the woman from her home to a shelter can in some cases cause her even greater harm and lead to isolation and rejection by her own community.

Chapter 16 by Melissa Stone and Vjosa Dobruna on their activism with Kosovar Albanian women shows how the development of a postwar women's human rights culture in Kosova contradicts traditional custom law defined by the Kanun. The authors compare specific provisions of the United Nations Convention on the Elimination of All Forms of Discrimination against Women with those of a widely available version of the Kanun. They describe how traditional gender roles harm women in Kosova rather than provide them with adequate rights and protections for both sexes as defined in international human rights law.

In Chapter 17, Nava Arkin from Israel shows how supervision can be culturally sensitive to minority students who can be silenced within the dominant culture by racism and internalized oppression. This chapter explores the results of either minimizing or maximizing cultural issues in supervision and the results on students helping their clients. The chapter especially focuses on power and authority in the supervision process with students from traditional hierarchal and authoritarian cultures. She offers multicultural methods for increasing voice in supervision and shows how awareness of culture can make the student better able to work with their own clients in a culturally sensitive manner. This chapter also offers a model for training supervisors in cultural sensitivity through focus on awareness, knowledge, and skills.

Two more chapters are available on this book's Web site and are primarily for teachers. A chapter by Vikki Dickerson of the United States suggests that any helping model is a metaphor and shows how students can become not only more aware of the metaphor they are using but also of the narrative metaphor and what it can offer. This chapter is rich in exercises for use in the classroom, workshops, and supervision, allowing the learner to move from modernist paradigms to a postmodernist understanding that the problem is found in the social context and not within the individual.

The second chapter on the Web site is by Toni Zimmerman and Shelley Haddock of the United States and shows how an entire teaching program can become gender- and culture-sensitive through attention to multilevel aspects of the learning context. They demonstrate how course content, research, and clinic and community outreach can be devised with gender and culture consciousness in mind. This chapter is a case study that shows how attention to detail and heightened awareness by the faculty can make a coherent learning experience for students that promotes justice as a primary concern for the helping process.

References

Gilligan, C. (1982). *In a different voice: Psychological theory and women's development.* Cambridge, MA: Harvard University Press.

Kerl, S. (2002). Using narrative approaches to teach multicultural counseling. *Journal of Multicultural Counseling and Development, 30*(2), 135–145.

Rabin, C., & Ben-David, A. (1999). *Being different in Israel* [in Hebrew]. Tel Aviv: Ramot.

GENDER AND CULTURE IN THE HELPING PROCESS

A Professional Journey

CLAIRE LOW RABIN
ISRAEL

CHAPTER I

OVERVIEW

This chapter will present some of the basic concepts involved in moving from the intrapsychic medical model of helping to a form of helping based on viewing the social context as crucial in the process. By tracing the author's professional development and changes through her work in Israel, the limitations of the scientific medical model are described. The journey from a universalistic, essentialism view of methods to a specific culture and gender context view is not without difficulty. One of these limitations is the split within the professional literature between feminist gender and multicultural sensitivity texts. The similarities between these models is presented, as well as some inherent clashes between egalitarian feminist goals and respect for often patriarchal and community-bound goals. Different ways of combining gender and cultural variables are reviewed. Narrative therapy, which makes a conceptual leap from modernist to postmodernist thinking is proposed as one way that allows not only the integration of gender and culture but also of all social contextual aspects that affect clients' problems. The chapter ends with the rationale for using both postmodern narrative and modernist methods of change.

A PROFESSIONAL JOURNEY

When I studied social work in the United States in the 1970s, much of the literature assumed that the same methods for helping individuals and families were applicable to anyone, regardless of culture, class, race, ethnic group, or gender. This assumption was communicated more by what was not said than by what was said. In our practice courses and texts, there was a lack of attention to the ways in which power, domination, oppression, marginalization, and social identity enter into the helping process (i.e., Pincus & Minahan, 1973; Fischer, 1978; Compton & Galaway, 1975). Often the focus was on different theoretical orientations (e.g., Roberts & Nee, 1970). The psychodynamic, cognitive–behavioral, and family systems theories and others were rivals for our loyalty, and much class effort was spent in comparing and contrasting. In the context of the society in which we were studying—Western, capitalistic, individualistic, and competitive—it is not surprising to find an atmosphere of consumerism in which the trainee was invited to think about which "brand" of helping was better.

Future research on the outcomes of different theoretical models would show no greater benefits from one theoretical approach compared to another (Miller, Duncan, & Hubble, 1997). Rather, future studies would clearly show that client-specific factors predict change more than those related to the helper (Beyenbach, Morejon, Palenzuela, & Rodriguez-Aris,1996; Prochaska, DiClemente, & Norcross, 1992). Miller et al. (1997) call clients "the unsung heroes" in the helping process. A warm empathic relationship with clients is apparently more important than any specific method (Lampert, 1992).

I had been taught concepts that reflected the individualistic capitalistic era that situated helping within the context of science and assumed that people could overcome their own inner pathologies on their own. Because the helping process was viewed as a scientific endeavor, it was therefore seen as a universally valid process (much like the laws of physics). Problems in living were defined as similar to diseases of the body. The medical model is deficit-driven: It focuses primarily on pathology rather than on strengths, on treatment rather than on cure, and on the individual rather than on the social context. It was assumed that the helper is the expert in the diagnosis of these problems, just as the medical doctor diagnoses the patient. This view generated tests and measurements that proposed to help in diagnosis and assist the researcher in evaluating the outcome. Concepts such as "diagnosis," "patient," "treatment,"" compliance," and "resistance" all fit within the scientific worldview.

This worldview of helping was taken for granted and not challenged. When I immigrated to Israel at the age of 24, imbued with the enthusiasm and the anxieties of the beginning expert helper, I quickly found myself swept up into practicing and teaching social work in Israel's dynamic melting pot society. Clients from Western countries and Israelis who came from European backgrounds were much like the clients in the United States and responded well to the methods I had studied. But many of the clients who came for help to public service agencies were from non-Western countries and did not resonate with our focus on talking, on the individual, and on abstract concepts such as social skills, differentiation of self, and the enmeshment or disengagement of their families. Many of the models I came with were not helpful enough for clients from countries where strangers are not approached for help, where help is seen as concrete and instrumental and comes primarily from elders, the extended family, or the community. Many of these clients did not share my democratic egalitarian vision of what constitutes healthy relationships. Instead they came with collective, patriarchal worldview assumptions about time, authority, gender roles, and communication. These assumptions did not fit with ideas related to individual rights (i.e., assertiveness) and the bounded autonomous self (i.e., self-esteem) but rather saw the self as bound intricately to family and community.

My students were finding that their "expert" assumptions were challenged when clients did not keep appointments or felt uncomfortable with the open self-disclosure of problems, weakness, and feelings that underlie all of our helping methods. Clients often did not go along with our suggestions. Clearly, concepts such as resistance and lack of motivation just didn't fit when so many clients were rejecting interventions.

Over the years, I experimented in a random trial-and-error manner with modifications to meet the needs of the many diverse cultures that make up Israeli society—and with my clients as my teachers. Together with colleagues and students, new methods for working in the homes of poor young Israeli couples on welfare were developed (Rabin, Rosenberg, & Sens, 1982). Many of our clients came from families on welfare, and from Arabic-speaking countries that are highly influenced by traditional Muslim culture. In their countries of origin, the family and community were the authorities, while professionals were distrusted as agents of the government. It seemed important for our workers to get out of the office and to meet and work with clients in their homes and communities— and to be willing to do hands-on work that appeared to cross professional boundaries such as attending family events, waking clients up to go to work, and meeting with community elders to influence other people.

Because these clients came from patriarchal, traditional, and collective cultures in which men and women played different and separate roles in the family and community, we learned that the helping process was quite different for men and women. The maintenance of traditional gender roles was important to gaining entry. In these cultures, gender differences are distinct and important to uphold, so we needed both male and female workers who could join the sexes in their different areas of living. Often we used nonprofessionals to help us. Workers accompanied men to job interviews and to meet with friends and neighbors who were influential and who could find work for the clients, as well as hang out with them in their leisure-time activities. For the women, female workers took part in the cooking, talking over issues in the kitchens, helping to baby-sit, or keeping the women company in the local parks. Together, with entire families, we went to weddings and to bar mitzvahs. We created informal groups of clients helping other clients that had the sense of a social group in which problems were handled.

The surrounding Israeli culture was more egalitarian, however, and their own traditionalism kept these couples apart and oppressed. The men resented the women's working; the women tended not to consult with the men about money; and the couple shared little intimate conversation. The couple's primary focus was on continuing their deep connections with their extended family and parenting their children. Our dilemma was how to help these young couples adapt to a culture that promoted more equal partnership while still honoring their traditional ways. As a feminist especially, I was challenged to be culturally sensitive in a culture where violence was an accepted and, for some, a desirable mode of legitimizing male authority.

During the 1990s, I continued to be intrigued by the impact of gender and power on families in diverse cultures, classes, ethnic groups, and races (Rabin, 1996) and thus developed methods of helping that took power relationships in the family into account.

Feminist family therapy was developing during this period that made gender the central variable of interest for work with families (Goodrich, 1991; Walters, Carter, Papp, & Silverstein, 1988). Feminist therapy (Burstow, 1992; Brown, 1994) placed gender and sexism as the central focus of the helping process. Although a major site of cultural influences is the family, the gender family texts do not mention cultural diversity.

Eventually, globalization influenced feminism, making feminist practice more aware of diversity and cultural differences. As Lips (2002) stated:

> Because of the economic dominance of the United States in the world and sheer power of the American media, the voices of U. S. women often drown out those of their sisters in other countries. And in the United States and elsewhere, most of the women who are in a position to make their voices heard in public discussions about the status of women, what women are like and the barriers faced by women, are professionals . . . (who) are of European American ancestry, were raised in middle-class families and have lived a relatively privileged life. . . . Just as the power relations between men and women have tended to provide men's points of view about human experience, so too the power relations among cultural and ethnic groups have tended to privilege White middle-class American women's views on women's experiences. (p. 14)

These social changes have resulted in a rapidly growing literature on the role of culture in the helping process, with gender issues intersecting in various ways. Culturally competent family therapy (Ariel, 1999) and practice (Lum, 1999), multicultural counseling (Sue, Ivey, & Pedersen, 1996), culturally responsive psychotherapy (Vargas & Koss-Chioino, 1992), intercultural therapy (Kareem & Littlewood, 1992), cultural diversity and human services (Diller, 1999), ethnically sensitive social work (Devore & Schlesinger, 1996), and social work practice with people of color (Lum, 2000) are only some of the examples of multidisciplinary approaches to culture and helping. All of these mention gender but do not integrate gender directly as an integral part of their models.

Thus, recent literature that relates to the social context focuses on either culture or gender. Through my work with different ethnic minorities in Israel, it became increasingly clear that gender and culture needed to be considered together. It was impossible for me to see gender issues outside of class, race, and cultural factors. Similarly, there were no cultural facts that did not also relate to gender. Being a woman is simply different in different cultures, and to ignore that makes the idea of "woman" some kind of essential universal quality, which is far from true. Being a family and couples therapist, it appeared to me that a major (although not only) site of culture is actually in the relationship between the sexes, and that interaction often occurs in the family. It is here that gender interacts with culture to create lived experiences that can either empower or oppress people. As Julia (2000) states:

> Because ethnicity and gender are simultaneous, interconnected, inter-determining processes rather than separate systems, discussing them separately requires an artificial construction. Therefore, to determine what it means to be socialized in a particular culture, one must inquire about the salience of gender as an organizing principle and how cultural factors outside of the control of members of a particular group shape internal experience. (p. 3)

In thinking about ways to conceptualize gender and culture, we need to understand the similarities as well as conflicts between these different concepts. This will then lead to a discussion of narrative therapy and how it is one way to successfully integrate social context—including gender, culture, ethnicity, class, and race—in the helping process.

GENDER AND THE HELPING PROCESS

The feminist agenda looks at the uses of power and how status hierarchies deprive women of their freedom and equality. Feminist therapies do not offer any one theoretical method for helping, nor do they offer a new type of intervention. Instead, they promote the conceptualization of all problems within the framework of gender and society. Methods that help empower women, that reduce the hierarchy between the therapist and the client, that link women together, and that view problems as induced by social processes can all be utilized. Worell and Remer (1992) have proposed that any helping that takes a feminist position needs to include the following goals:

1. to recognize that the politics of gender are of central concern and are reflected in women's lower social status and women's oppression in most societies
2. to seek equal status and empowerment not only for women but also for all oppressed minority groups
3. to value and seek knowledge about women's experience
4. to understand that values enter into all human enterprises and that neither science nor practice can be value-free, and
5. to commit to action for social and political change

In attempting to meet women's specific needs in helping, there needs to be an understanding of the issues that generally concern women, including family role shifts, violence in the home and outside, the importance of the body, the prevalence of depression and multiple stressors, the high prevalence of sexual abuse of girls and of women in the home and at work, and the overwhelming and unfair workload expected from women because of work and home demands.

Practitioners who base their work on feminist principles often include a sex-role analysis in their work in which both men and women clients are helped to become more openly conscious of their socialization into rigid and harmful stereotypes that also constrict their interaction with the other sex. Hare-Mustin and Marecek (1994) point out that even though there are many different approaches to feminist counseling, they all include an element of consciousness rising around sex roles and about sexist societal structures for both the helper and the client. They all have a strong educational and information-giving component. All promote an egalitarian relationship between the client and the helper to minimize replicating society's power differentials and instead replacing them with shared power. Feminist-informed helping encourages women to value themselves and to focus on their strengths. In general, feminist helping fosters pluralism by validating different experiences of women from culturally diverse backgrounds, but when culture and gender clash and a woman's empowerment is limited by patriarchy, then feminism takes a clear stand on the side of the woman. Perhaps for this reason, only a minority of feminist therapy texts include material on family and couples work, and they tend to think more in terms of individual and group help for women.

Feminist family therapies tend to be concerned with the relationship between gender and power in intimate relationships within the family. One of the most important functions of this literature has been to critique the existing method of family therapy practice. Bogard (1984) and Wheeler (1985) have shown how family therapy tended to blame mothers for family difficulties. For example, Caplan and Hall-McCorquodale's (1985) study of nine major clinical journals in psychiatry, psychoanalysis, psychology, and family therapy found 72 different types of child problems attributed to mothers by therapists. In 1975, the American Psychological Association (APA) Task Force on Sex Bias and Sex-Role Stereotyping in Psychotherapeutic Practice found the following biases in the helping process:

1. assuming that remaining in a marriage would result in better adjustment for women;
2. demonstrating less interest in and sensitivity to a woman's career than a man's;
3. perpetuating the belief that a child's problems and child rearing are primarily women's responsibilities;
4. exhibiting a double standard regarding a wife's versus a husband's extramarital affair; and
5. deferring to a husband's needs over those of a wife's.

Avis (1996) later reviewed the field and found that although decades passed since the task force identified these biases, they continue to be dominant in the culture and to affect practice.

In addition to a critique of traditional family therapy, feminist therapists have promoted new forms of work with women such as the relational model of the Stone Center (Jordan, Kaplan, Miller, Stiver, & Surrey, 1991) which is based on the writing of Jean Baker Miller's *Toward a New Psychology of Women* (1976).

This work proposes that women's development occurs within connection to others, that helping women must maintain that connection and even strengthen it, and that patriarchal helping strategies that focus on independence and autonomy often neglect women-centered values and needs. Miller and Surrey (1997) also note the importance of anger in women as a resource. They say that:

> Once any group in society establishes itself as dominant, it would have to utilize aggression as a disproportionate part of its way of acting in order to maintain its dominance and simultaneously, it cannot develop fully the cultural forms which threaten its dominance. Relationships among people are the key forms which potentially threaten dominance. They are absolutely essential for human life and development and relationships formed in mutuality and based in empathy and responsiveness are inevitably incompatible with systems of dominance. In such a system, anger, a powerful emotion with the potential to right wrongs and play a valuable role in changing hurtful relationships, would likely be suppressed and distorted. (p. 204)

Feminist-informed helping also focuses on the ways that men have paid a high price for their privilege. This literature emphasizes helping male clients understand the way their culture views masculinity and male socialization, and it is especially concerned with working with violent and abusive men. (Jenkins, 1990; Meth & Pasick, 1990; White, 1992; Dienhart & Avis, 1990).

What we see here, and what is evident in all helping that focuses on gender, is an understanding that the "political is the personal." In other words, helping is a personal as well as a political process that helps to overcome gender-oppressive social scripts as individual problems are anchored in their social context. Because women have been less valued than men, for women these scripts have been internalized as low-self-esteem, lack of self-worth, and a lack of assertiveness that inhibits their own growth and development. In general, helping women involves linking them with other women and strengthening their existing links. This can involve referring clients to support groups, community action work, and other relevant community projects. Linking women can also take place in the helping conversation through pointing out the common sex-role biases against women and the effects of sexism. This information generally is shared through self disclosure about the way that the helper's own experiences reveal gender issues rather than in taking an expert stance and "teaching" about gender oppression.

CULTURE IN THE HELPING PROCESS

As diversity theories of helping proliferated in the 1990s, different writers focused on different aspects of culture. Lum (1999) differentiates between ethnicity, culture, minority status, and social class, although all are intertwined and interrelated. According to Lum:

> *Ethnicity* involves ancestry and racial origin, present membership in an ethnic family and community group and future participation in generations of ethnic offspring. . . . *Culture* deals with prescribed ways of conduct, beliefs, values traditions

and customs and related life patterns of a people or community. . . . *Minority status* relates to the inferior and unequal rank in power and access to resources of subordinate and disadvantaged groups in relation to the superiority in power and resources of the dominant majority. . . . *Social class* addresses social stratification or the social hierarchical arrangement of persons based on economic power and status differences, and thus reflects degrees of social inequality based on economic (wealth, income, consumption, occupation) social (influence, community power, group identification) and family status. (Lum, 1999, 100–101)

In this book, "culture as context" is loosely used to denote a variety of social environmental factors related to ethnic, racial, and class factors. These include poverty, racism, generational differences in sexual mores and behavior, immigration and resettlement, and acculturation. Cultural content in the helping process refers to the specific meanings through which these social phenomena appear, including patterns of individual behavior, interpersonal interactions, and emotions. Cultural content includes assumptions about gender roles, attitudes about sexuality, identity, and world and self-views that run through an almost infinite number of guidelines for daily life behaviors.

Assumptions regarding what constitutes normal behavior can be quite different among different ethnic, racial, and class groups and therefore can also be quite different from assumptions of the helper. Chin (1993), for example, shows that Asian and Western cultures differ significantly in their help-seeking behaviors (generalist versus specialists), their definition of help (healing versus self-actualization), their interpersonal relationships (equal versus hierarchal), their emotional openness (catharsis versus self-regulation), their patterns of communication (indirect versus direct), their use of language (meaning versus fluency), what constitutes a mature person (interdependence versus independence), the importance of belongingness (social versus individual), type of desired identity (self-denigration versus modesty), focus of parent–child relationships (importance of mother–son dyad versus father–son dyad), and use of time (fluid versus precise).

Babacan and Gopalkrishnan (2003) point out that behavior that is quite normal in a different culture can be misunderstood and mislabeled in the process. This has negative impacts in the helping process. These writers point to some of the worldview assumptions that often differ between clients and their helpers. For example, dependence on abstract words on the part of the helper is a culturally linked assumption that leads to lack of understanding on the part of the client. Overemphasis on independence is also a culturally based concept, one that can be completely inappropriate and exacerbate conflict. Neglect of the clients' support system is a problem where those support systems play a key role in the client's cultural context. These support systems often replace the role played by the counselor in Western societies, and neglecting them could mean the nonuse of a highly valuable resource. Another assumption is related to dependence on linear thinking, which directly links cause and effect in the traditional scientific method. This assumption can lead to disregarding evidence because it does not fit the expected box, or it could lead to erroneous conclusions because possible effects are disregarded because the direct link is not seen. Neglect of the history of oppression is of particular significance when working with cultures that have a long history of discrimination and that have found their own ways of dealing with it. Often the oppression is based on racism.

Racism is the limiting of opportunities or privilege to one social group while perpetuating privilege to members of another group by viewing one group as not equal to the other. It can be found at the individual and at the institutional level and can be overt or covert in nature. Lum (2000) also adds cultural racism, which refers to the beliefs, feelings, and behaviors of members of a cultural group who assert the superiority of the groups' accomplishments, achievement, and creativity and attribute this claimed cultural superiority to genetic composition. In symbolic racism, there is a rejection of racial inferiority, but there are beliefs that people of color demand too much and that they want success but aren't willing to work for it; people of color are also negatively linked to welfare, urban riots, crime in the streets, affirmative action, and quota systems. McConahay and Hough (1976) see this kind of racism as lumping people of color with negative elements in society. Ethnocentrism is another concept (Lum, 2000) in which the individual's ethnic group forms his or her central point of reference and to the exclusion of other groups. This can result in simply not seeing beyond what is valued by one's own group.

Anthropologists spend months or years studying cultures to gain a true appreciation of them, but professional helpers typically have neither the opportunity nor the time to observe their clients interacting within their cultural environments. Chin (1993) has stated that more critical than knowledge of ethnic content are whether the worldviews that helpers bring to the helping situations facilitate work on diversity. It is necessary to have a framework that values differences, that integrates cultural values into the process, and that views cultural values as not good or bad but which looks to see whether they facilitate helping the client.

COMMONALITIES BETWEEN APPROACHES FOCUSING ON GENDER AND ON CULTURE

Gender and culture link personal problems with political and social realities. Helping thus includes an aspect of liberation from restrictive labels, internalized oppression, and the effects of discriminating social processes that marginalize people because of some social category. Those who work with diversity in mind are aware that there have been systematic attempts to ignore, incapacitate or destroy diverse cultures, such as the culture of women, homosexuals, and any less powerful group. Thus, the helper is involved in what is known in Latin America as *una terapia comprometido* (a bond of commitment), a relationship where the political, social, and psychological alliance between therapist and client is explicit. (Becker, Lira, Castillo, Gome, & Kovalskys, 1990). This is an ethnically non-neutral attitude toward the clients' problems (De La Cancela, 1993).

A focus on both gender and culture reveals the need for social action to remedy situations that extend beyond the individual. Both are aware of the powerlessness of either women or a specific cultural group, and the feelings of helplessness that oppression creates. Both tend to see the connection between an individual's self-esteem and the devaluing of one's group of identity by society. This is called low *social esteem* (Jenkins, 1993), and it results when the dominant society does not have the same values as one's group; objectifies and reduces one's group to a mindless commodity; devalues the group's standards of beauty; rejects the group through stereotypes, exclusion, isolation, and invisibility; and targets the group with violence. Although feminist practice looks primarily at sexism and cultural practice is more concerned with racism and classism, the actual processes and their effects on the individual are quite similar.

Both approaches believe that helping has to be careful not to replicate these oppressive social processes; it therefore promotes taking an egalitarian and nonexpert stance with regard to the client and using empathy for oppressive histories and current realities as a major vehicle. The helper needs to assume that no one method fits everyone and needs to match the method to the client rather than the client to the method.

The need for helper self-awareness and heightened consciousness cannot be understated, as the unaware helper can easily make subtle assumptions based on sexist or racist ideas. McMahon and Allen-Meares (1992) analyzed 117 articles in social work journals and found that much of the literature is naive in that it decontextualizes clients, views oppression as natural, emphasizes individual adaptation to oppression, and encourages a status whose practice adversely affects people of color. It would appear that the helping professions still have a way to go in becoming both gender- and culture-sensitive; because of that, they may still replicate many of the oppressive patterns of society in the helping context itself. A chapter by Toni Zimmerman and Shelley Haddock that describes an entire family therapy program that focuses on both gender and multicultural diversity and equality can be accessed on this book's Web site at http://wadsworth.com/helping_profs/ by searching for this book's specific Web page.

Both frameworks focus primarily on client strengths in their personality, family, and gendered cultural group. Clients are seen as strengthened when they are linked to others and when they can utilize a range of helping methods, including indigenous, local, and nonexpert help. The literature on women calls for a focus on intuition, journal work, expressive therapies, group work, and healing rituals. Similarly, the literature on multicultural practices opens the door to spiritual and native healers and their healing methods.

GENDER AND CULTURE: CLASHES AND CONFLICTS

Despite their numerous similarities, a focus on either gender or culture without integrating the other results in marginalization through universalistic assumptions. This could perpetuate the very problems the helping literature proposes to solve. For example, in studies of "gender," white women were positioned as the universal female subject; in studies of "race," men of color stood as the universal racial subject. In both cases, women of color were left out and rendered invisible.

Lum (2000) has called women of color a "double minority" because they live in a society that is both racist and patriarchal. Helping texts unintentionally continue this. Lum points out the large number of negative controlling images that cultural minority women are subject to: For African American women, it is the mammy who is the faithful obedient servant, or the matriarch who is overly aggressive and unfeminine, the breeder of children, the welfare mother dependent on the welfare state, the jezebel, whore, or sexually aggressive woman. Latino women are often cast as Madonnas—virtuous, self-sacrificing mothers—or as the spitfire, volatile, and sensual. Asian women have been stereotyped as the China doll or the dragon lady, while Native American women are depicted as Princess Pocahontas or the Indian squaw. Green (1994) has pointed out that this type of stereotyping has been used to blame women for their own oppression.

The women's movement has been criticized for representing white, middle-class women's interest, a criticism that started early on. For women of color, issues related to racism can seem more pressing than the issues of sexism. In some cases, white women were oppressors of women of color, such as when maids had to abandon their own children to take care of white women's children. Women of color are often more sensitive to the racist effects on their male partners than they are interested in their own liberation from sexism.

Some feminist writers believe in focusing more on culture than on gender so as not to marginalize minorities. For example, Brown (1990) calls for a deemphasis on gender issues for women of color, poor women, and women from non-Western cultures and for the inclusion of multicultural female socialization experiences, which may vary according to ethnic and cultural gender social factors. She calls for the study of how women in patriarchal ethnic groups accept culturally defined roles and yet transcend them to become liberated persons in their own cultural society.

Other writers (Taylor, Gilligan, & Sullivan, 1995) worry that the discord and conflict within the feminist movement around issues of racism has only served to divide women among themselves and thus serve the patriarchal status quo. This view has resulted in urgent calls for unity and cooperation between women across racial and ethnic lines.

There exists a certain tension between the thrusts for gender awareness and multicultural sensitivity. The idea of gaining strength as a woman within the context of cultural groups that are oppressive to women can be contradictory. Bryan (2001) points out that the multicultural ideal of not severing ties with a cultural group may well conflict with the feminist movement toward self-actualization and breaking free of the bonds of traditional forms of authority perceived as damaging to women. Some cultural traditions have negative implications for women who seek help. McGoldrick, Giordano, and Pearce (1996) have given examples, such as: It is acceptable for upper-class Jamaican men to have mistresses; covert communication is used in Mexican families in the interest of family harmony; Asian Americans tend to express emotional problems through physical symptoms; and Iranian parents value boys more than girls. Many cultural customs fly in the face of women's rights and basic needs, such as female genital circumcision, bride burning, and the abortion of female fetuses.

Helpers are thus often faced with the dilemma of whether to support the culture or the woman in a particular situation. Some authors suggest respecting the values of a client's culture but challenging them when they are not functional (Nichols & Schwartz, 1995), such as when the dominant culture does not support traditional cultural values. My example in this chapter of Israeli poor couples shows how patriarchal patterns in the home led to less opportunity and access to resources for the minority couple. McGoldrick et al. (1996) gives another example of Hispanic families in the United States in which rigid adherence to machismo behavior and attitudes ceases to be adaptive for the family as a whole in overcoming poverty. Still many serious questions about what constitutes "functional" values and whether "indoctrination" into the dominant values isn't another form of oppression, albeit by the helper.

In her provocative book *Is Multiculturalism Bad for Women?*, Okin (1999) makes the point that discrimination against females and the control of their freedom are practiced by virtually *all* cultures, past and present, but especially by religious ones and those that look to the past, to ancient texts, or to revered traditions for guidelines. Home is where much of culture is practiced, preserved, and transmitted to the young. The more a culture requires or expects from women in the domestic sphere, the less opportunity they have of achieving equality with men in either public or private spheres. Thus, ironically, in many cases the defense of cultural practices is likely to have much greater impact on the lives of women than on those of men. Okin gives examples in which the servitude of women is virtually synonymous with preservation of tradition, such as a recent news report about a small community of Orthodox Jews living in the mountains of Yemen. There the elderly leader of this small polygamous sect is quoted as saying that the community refuses to go to Israel because the sect would lose its hold over its women. In other words, acceptance of cultural traditionalism almost *by definition* includes the subjugation of women.

May (1998) exhorts helpers not to hide behind the "cultural mask" by not challenging family gender roles because they are part of a traditional culture. We can easily slip into cultural relativism, in which we defend practices that violate human rights because they are culturally acceptable. Often the "clash" of cultures is felt during immigration, when there are claims from minority immigrant groups for special legal treatment because of their cultural differences. Almost all of the legal cases discussed in an article about group rights by lawyer Sebastian Poulter (1987) concerned gender inequalities in immigrant cultures: child marriages, forced marriages, divorce systems biased against women, polygamy, and clitoridectomy. The majority of the cases he cites were based on women's and girls' claims that special treatment in the law for their own culture violates their human rights. Examples include the Hmong men who claim that kidnap and rape are part of their cultural practice of *zij poj niam* ("marriage by capture") and wife murder by Asian or Arab immigrants to Western countries who claim that family honor can be upheld only by special treatment in situations when women have committed adultery or have treated family members with lack of respect.

For the helper, one major question is how to help when a woman's *own* identity is strongly influenced by her cultural affiliation and her need to continue her ties to her cultural community—even when this connection is oppressive to her. There are no easy answers to the conflict, and no writer has any one solution. Okin (1999) urges us not to romanticize culture, but to take a hard look at culture's inequalities to women. She says that

> because attention to the rights of minority cultural groups must ultimately be aimed at furthering the well-being of these groups, there can be no justification for assuming that the groups' self-proclaimed leaders (invariably composed of their older male members) represent the interest of all the groups' members. (p. 24)

Making these dilemmas visible is one important direction. Bryan (2001) suggests that helpers clarify their ethical commitments about values such as *autonomy* (the recognition that all people have the right to make decisions), *beneficence* (calling on the helper to actively benefit the client), *nonmaleficence* (doing no harm), *justice* (treating all people equally), and *fidelity* (principles of honesty and loyalty). There are times when these values clash, and the helper must be aware of these dilemmas and make them transparent. Thus, the helper needs to question whether promoting a woman's autonomy might actually endanger her when the helper leaves, violating the principles of nonmaleficence. Helpers often have to deal with the tension between what is best for a family and what is best for an individual. When the culture clearly opposes equality for women, there is more potential for violence against a woman when a man feels himself to be powerless. Thus, empowering women in these kinds of cultures can expose them to real danger (Balswick & Balswick, 1995). We are obliged to inform clients of our ideology if it will challenge their traditions.

Helpers can try to find creative solutions to these tensions. May (1998) describes a case of an Asian American woman having difficulty with her husband's family; she was not able to correct the problem herself because of the cultural norms prohibiting direct confrontation. Her helper worked within the cultural system of values to help her find a respected male family member to plead her case. Others such as Almeida, Woods, Messineo, and Font (1998) have proposed models that include *sponsorship,* the idea that former clients from a cultural community help each other; *socioeducational orientation,* in which film clips and readings are used to raise consciousness regarding gender, race, and class; and *cultural circles,* or gender-specific, open-ended groups that provide an opportunity for their members to tell and hear stories.

Most of the chapters in this book exemplify the struggle of practitioners to work with gender and culture to find creative solutions that respect both aspects of social context while not sacrificing women's equality. Examples from this book involve using key people in the community as go-betweens, the development of women's groups that intermediate between gender and culture, the training of professionals so that they are sensitive to issues of both gender and culture, and supervising new students of the helping professions to explore their own minority experiences in light of gender.

INTEGRATING GENDER AND CULTURE

Models that attempt to unify gender and culture take on a real challenge. The attempt to simultaneously address such a rich tapestry of variables is complex. An approach that attempts to integrate gender and culture is the *empowerment model*, which offers an overarching method for thinking about any form of oppression. Gutierrez, Parsons, and Cox (1998) propose that gender is viewed as one source of oppression and ethnic minority status or color are viewed as another. Both are dealt with similarly by empowerment principles that stress understanding the role of power in people's lives at the personal, interpersonal, and environmental levels. Overcoming a sense of powerlessness on different levels is facilitated by the helper sharing power with clients by offering numerous choices in helping methods and goals.

In reality almost all texts that attempt to integrate factors really treat each factor separately. This is a result of a scientific worldview and a resulting reductionism into abstract concepts. The modernist view of helping can only conceptualize gender or culture as separate variables. Unfortunately, a lot of the complexity, richness, contradictions, and conflicts is lost in this process.

THE POSTMODERN NARRATIVE REVOLUTION

A paradigm shift that allows for thinking of both gender and culture in a more integrated and simultaneous manner is the postmodern worldview that has resulted in social constructivism and narrative therapy (White & Epston, 1990). Reality is viewed as socially constructed through language. Language itself is derived from social discourses about gender, race, ethnicity, sexuality, and other aspects of diversity. Thus, the stories we tell are *already* incorporations of gender, class, race, ethnicity, and culture. Power inequality is not policed through coercion by higher authorities but by each person internalizing the oppressive social discourses in her own understanding of herself and her world. This is a kind of "subjugation of the mind" in which untested assumptions about people seem to be obvious, essentialist, and universal truths. For example, the idea that women are just naturally more adept at parenting small babies is one such untested assumption. The idea that poor people are somehow responsible for their poverty is another.

Helping theories that come out of the postmodernist "revolution" are organized under the umbrella concept of *social constructivist* and include different forms such as *narrative therapy* (White & Epston, 1990), *collaborative therapy* (Madsen, 1999), and *psychodynamic narrative* therapies (Roberts & Holmes, 1999). Unlike the "objectivity" and reductionism into abstract concepts of the modernist worldview, postmodernists believe that there are no fixed essential truths separate from the social context. Where modernist thinking is concerned with facts, postmodernist thinking is concerned with making individualized meaning out of the social discourses of society (Freedman & Combs, 1996). People are seen as able to author their own lives only once they free themselves from the stories about themselves that they have internalized from oppressive social scripts about their gender, race, ethnicity, or other characteristics. The liberation comes through questioning conversations with clients in which the helper becomes the audience and not the expert, and the client is the expert on his or her own life stories. The helper is curious about how social discourses (about gender, race, class, ethnicity, and culture) have filtered through to this particular person and searches for ways in which this person has already shown signs of liberating herself from oppressive discourses.

McLeod (1997) proposes that the postmodern narrative turn is actually what has been really happening anyway in the helping professions, even as helpers continue to adhere, at least outwardly, to the scientific modernist paradigm they were taught in universities:

> It is as though the rational, evidence-based scientific side of therapy represents an outer shell that faces the rest of the world. The inner core of therapy is quite different. The construction of psychotherapy as an applied science conceals the true cultural foundations of therapeutic practice. Underneath the theoretical overlay and scientific gloss, psychotherapy is a kind of *conversation, a type of meeting place, a form of social drama.* In a traditional or pre-modern culture, the encounter between the person priest, healer, or shaman can be seen as an event through which a personal story becomes realigned with and assimilated into the story of the community. A similar process occurs in modern psychotherapy but is now much more individualized and framed in scientific terminology. The result is that psychotherapy offers a particular type of narrative reconstruction, one that is embedded in the (largely American) cultural milieu of late twentieth-century industrial society. (pp. 16–17)

Freedman and Combs (1996) propose that narrative helping is a shift in thinking and not just "more of the same."

White (1992) points out that dominant social discourse about how to be a man or women as well as how to be part of a social group determines the shapes of our individual life narratives. People make sense of their lives through stories, both the cultural narratives they are born into and the personal narratives they construct in relation to the cultural narratives. In any culture, certain narratives will come to be dominant over other narratives.

A good example of this comes from *Between Voice and Silence,* the Taylor et al. (1995) study of teenage girls from various ethnic and class backgrounds. Hispanic, African American, and other minority group girls express many of the cultural stories that inform their lives. On the one hand, the authors show how the harsh social and economic realities of many of these girls place them in contradiction to the dominant culture's ideals of family life, such as the fantasy of the perfect mother who is ever-present, devoted, and self-sacrificing. In addition, they point out that the lack of access to education and adequately paid employment has resulted in a change in the meaning of previously positive cultural concepts such as machismo. Originally, machismo included courage, honor, and respect for others, as well as protection and provision for one's family. Men in poor ethnic minority communities cannot live out these cultural stories, and instead machismo is now associated with the actual results of oppression, poverty, and low self-esteem such as violent, sexist, and aggressive behaviors.

On the other hand, these authors found that cultural stories did offer alternative sources of strength for many girls from single-parent, female-headed families. For example, the role of the mother in Latino families is revered and associated with *aguante,* meaning fortitude, endurance, patience, and resilience to toil or fatigue. African American girls described rejecting the white idealized mother images they saw on television and focusing instead on the uniquely close relationships with their own mothers that included both mother and daughter talking openly about problems. These girls talked about femininity as independence and strength and how their mothers did not shield them from the realities of racism but instead prepared them by being open about their own lives.

Postmodernist narrative helping sees these gender and culture discourses as outside the person, which alleviates blame and shame and counters the isolation that comes with feeling personally ineffective and inadequate. Jill Johnson (1973), a feminist author, claimed that identity is what you can say you are, according to what "they" say you can be. Much of narrative helping then becomes the task of enriching those stories that fall outside the constraining effects of dominant social discourses. In this form of empowerment, people are invited through conversation to attend to all those moments and events in which they resisted the effects of power and acted in ways that contradict "what they say you can be."

THE USE OF BOTH MODERNIST AND POSTMODERNIST PRINCIPLES IN PRACTICE

Those of us who wish to work with issues related to gender, oppressed minorities, with immigrants, and with diverse cultures know that helping has to include working to create concrete changes in the environment of the person. People need to be linked to resources, and services must be developed that are sensitive and responsive to diverse needs. Often change has to occur in the service delivery process, in groupwork, and in policies. Conversations can empower people to feel entitled to resources, but helpers also need to be proactive in creating equality as they provide needed resources.

We need to think in terms of a variety of methods to challenge deep-seated discrimination and its effects. The oppression of people because of gender and culture is so massive and real that it takes utilizing all the methods we have to help. We cannot afford to dismiss real knowledge and practices that may be helpful even if they developed out of a modernist, scientific worldview that has been used to oppress people. Rather than thinking in an either–or manner, which privileges postmodern thinking over modernist methods, we need to search for a way to integrate and maximize our ability to help.

In describing work with multiproblem families, Madsen (1999) shows a way in which both postmodern and more instructive directive helping practices can be integrated. His work developed out of the need to help those in especially difficult clinical situations: families beset by overwhelming problems and crises. Many of these multistressed families are marginalized by society because of mental illness, poverty, social class, ethnic and racial background, and, of course, gender. Madsen renames helping as a form of "cultural anthropology" in which we helpers move away from instructing, directing, teaching, and changing people and toward learning how to collaborate with people to change their situations. Seeing clients as experts on their own experiences allows the helper to seek to understand the development of beliefs and practices within the context of gender and culture. He states that such an anthropological stance does not entail an abandonment of our professional and personal knowledge as helpers. Many ideas, observations, and distinctions may prove valuable for families. The helpers' intention in sharing is to offer them ideas that might be useful rather than attempt to get clients to embrace the ideas.

This framework validates both the knowledge of the client and the knowledge of the professional helper. The client's own stories are foremost, while the helper's own knowledge and practices are used to complement, enrich, and enlarge the client's vision of what is possible. The helper's knowledge of problems, processes, and solutions become another resource in the client's empowerment.

For example, the helper who is knowledgeable about the immigration process is able to make suggestions for externalization based on prior knowledge of normative processes. Knowing that immigrants can feel disoriented or isolated, the helper might suggest "disorientation" or "isolation" as externalized problems, and would search for factors in the environment that promote disorientation or isolation, as well as times when the client has overcome disorientation and isolation. In reauthoring their stories to include resistance to the marginalizing process involved in immigration, the client fights accepting the labels that society puts on her and can enter the mainstream of the new culture more quickly. This process, combined with concrete reaching out help in the community to increase access to needed resources, can be a powerful way of helping.

In this way, we can incorporate knowledge, skills, ideas, stories, practices, solutions, and methods that we think might be offered to clients as a resource. As helpers, we do not assume to know what is best nor do we diagnose the client. We do have knowledge about social contexts and their impact on people, which allows us to be at all times sensitive to issues of power and privilege. We also need to be continuously watchful for instances when as careful helpers we are invited into labeling, stereotyping, or discriminating in ways that invalidate clients' own knowledge and skills. We are accountable to our clients, open about our thinking, and willing to use any resource that might help. These resources might include former clients, community people, groups, or intervention in service and policy.

CONCLUSION

This chapter opened with my own story and my own awakening of consciousness through immigration to a new country. It shows how a personal story of increased understanding of the role of gender and culture parallels the helping field's own development. Gender awareness came first as a result of the revolution for the advancement of women's rights in Western countries. The effects of this awareness on the helping process are reviewed here. Later on, the awareness of cultural diversity resulted in a separate literature for helping professionals that heightened their consciousness of the role that culture plays in creating individual problems as well as the way in which culture needs to be respected within the helping process. The similarities of these two developments are described. Their divergences and conflicts are equally important to understand because the major site of gender interactions is within the culture and most noticeably with the family. When they clash, cultural dictates have often won out, leading to oppression of women not only by the community but also by the helper who is caught in the same dilemma as the woman. As women's identity is so strongly linked to their familial relationships, any attempt to liberate her thinking can be perceived as a threat to her ties to her cultural roots. The postmodern and especially narrative approaches are offered as one possibility for integrating gender and culture. These approaches assume that the client is fundamentally a teller of stories, related to both gender and culture, and that the helper empowers her best by being a respectful audience to these stories. The need to integrate narrative and more directive approaches is proposed here as often helping traumatized minority women go beyond witnessing their suffering and developing a new and more positive self-image and actively engaging with their families and community.

KEY CONCEPTS

- scientific modernism
- gender-informed therapy
- gender bias
- culture as race, ethnicity, social class
- viewing cultural context
- conflicts in using gender- and cultural-context models
- models of integration
- narrative therapy
- combining postmodern narrative and modernist helping methods

QUESTIONS FOR REFLECTION

1. Thinking back on your family of origin, can you outline some of the cultural context variables that had an impact on your family?
2. What were the gender roles in your family and how were they connected to power, hierarchy, and decision making?
3. What does your cultural context (ethnicity, race, class) promote as the ideal gender structure for families?
4. In what ways did your family follow these cultural rules?
5. In what ways did your family resist these cultural rules?

6. Think of a real incident in which someone in your family did something that was outside the prescription for your culture's gendered roles. Write or tell this story. In what way might this story indicate a site of resistance to cultural scripts? What was the result of this resistance?

7. What would you hope your children would keep and what would you hope they would change in your culture's gendered scripts?

EXERCISE

Divide the group into smaller groups of four students with one storyteller, one interviewer, and two listeners in each group. The storyteller tells of an incident that typifies her family in its gender roles and social context—ethnic, racial, social class, and so on. The questioner asks about the effects of the social context on this incident and the ways in which people handled the incident. Then the storyteller tells of an incident in which her family resisted gendered roles proscribed by her cultural context and what the results were. The questioner probes for the strengths that are revealed in this story. Finally, the listeners share their reactions to these two stories, describing similarities and differences in their own families, and incidents of resistance that came to mind.

References

Almeida, R., Woods, Messineo, T., & Font, R. (1998). The cultural context model: An overview. In M. McGoldrick (Ed.), *Revisioning family therapy.* New York: Guilford.

American Psychological Association Task Force (1975). Report of the task force on sex bias and sex-role stereotyping in psychotherapeutic practice. *American Psychologist, 30,* 1169–1175.

Ariel, S. (1999). *Culturally competent family therapy: A general model.* Westport, CT: Praeger.

Avis, J. (1996). Deconstructing gender in family therapy. In F. Piercy, D. Sprenkle, & J. Wetchler (Eds.), *Family therapy sourcebook* (2nd ed.). New York: Guilford.

Babacan, H., & Gopalkrishnan, N. (personal communication, 2003).

Balswick, J., & Balswick, J. (1995). Gender relations and marital power. In B. Ingoldsby & S. Smith (Eds.), *Families in*

multicultural perspective. New York: Guildford Press.

Ballou, M. (1996). MCT theory and women. In D. Sue, A. Ivey, & P. Pedersen (Eds.). (1996). *A theory of multicultural counseling and therapy.* Pacific Grove, CA: Brooks/Cole.

Becker, D., Lira, E., Castillo, E., Gome, E., & Kovalskys, J. (1990). Therapy with victims of political repression in Chile: The challenge of social reparation. *Journal of Social Issues, 46*(3), 133–149.

Beyenbach, M., Morejon, A., Palenzuela, D. L., & Rodriguez-Aris, J. (1996). Research on the process of solution-focused therapy. In A. E. Miller, M. A. Hubble, & B. L. Duncan (Eds.), *Handbook of solution-focused brief therapy.* San Francisco: Jossey-Bass.

Bogard, M. (1984). Family systems approaches to wife battering: A feminist critique. *American Journal of Orthopsychiatry, 54,* 558–568.

Brown, L. (1990). The meaning of a multicultural perspective for theory-building in feminist therapy. In L. Brown & M. Root (Eds.), *Diversity and complexity in feminist therapy*. New York: Haworth.

Brown, L. (1994). *Subversive dialogues: Theory in feminist therapy*. New York: Basic Books.

Bryan, L. (2001). Neither mask for mirror: One therapist's journey to ethically integrate feminist family therapy and multiculturalism. *Journal of Feminist Family Therapy, 12*(2–3), 105–121.

Burstow, B. (1992). *Radical feminist therapy: Working in the context of violence*. Newbury Park, CA: Sage.

Caplan, P., & Hall-McCorquodale, I. (1985). Mother-blaming in major clinical journals. *American Journal of Orthopsychiatry, 55*, 345–353.

Chin, J. (1993). Toward a psychology of difference: Psychotherapy for a culturally diverse population. In J. Chin, V. De La Cancela, & Y. Jenkins, *Diversity in psychotherapy: The politics of race, ethnicity, and gender*. Westport, CT: Praeger.

Compton, B., & Galaway, B. (1975). *Social work processes*. Homewood, IL: Dorsey Press.

De La Cancela, V. (1993). A progressive challenge: Political perspectives of psychotherapy theory and practice. In J. Chin, V. De La Cancela, & Y. Jenkins, *Diversity in psychotherapy: The politics of race, ethnicity, and gender*. Westport, CT: Praeger.

Devore, W., & Schlesinger, E. (1996). *Ethnic-sensitive social work practice* (4th ed.). Boston: Allyn & Bacon.

Dienhart, A., & Avis, J. (1990). Men in therapy: Exploring feminist informed alternatives. In M. Bogard (Ed.), *Feminist approaches to men in family therapy*. New York: Harrington Park Press.

Diller, J. (1999). *Cultural diversity: A primer for the human services*. Pacific Grove, CA: Brooks/Cole.

Fischer, J. (1978). *Effective casework practice*. New York: McGraw-Hill.

Freedman, J., & Combs, G. (1996). *Narrative therapy: The social construction of preferred realities*. New York: W. W. Norton.

Goodrich, T. (Ed.). (1991). *Women and power: Perspectives for family therapy*. New York: W. W. Norton.

Green, B. (1994). Diversity and difference: Race and feminist perspective. In M. Mirkin (Ed.), *Women in context: Toward a feminist reconstruction of psychotherapy*. New York: Guilford Press.

Gutierrez, L., Parsons, R., & Cox, E. (1998). *Empowerment in social work practice: A sourcebook*. Pacific Grove, CA: Brooks/Cole.

Hare-Mustin, R., & Marecek, J. (1994). Asking the right questions: Feminist psychology and sex differences. *Feminism and Psychology, 4*(3), 531–537.

Jenkins, A. (1990). *Invitations to responsibility: The therapeutic engagement of men who are violent and abusive*. Adelaide, Australia: Dulwich Center Publications.

Jenkins, Y. (1993). Diversity and social esteem. In J. Chin, V. De La Cancela, & Y. Jenkins, *Diversity in psychotherapy: The politics of race, ethnicity, and gender*. Westport, CT: Praeger.

Johnson, J. (1973). *Foucault live: Collective interviews, 1961–1984*. New York: Semiotext.

Jordan, J., Kaplan, A., Miller, J., Stiver, I., & Surrey, J. (1991). *Women's growth in connection: Writings from the Stone Center*. New York: Guilford Press.

Julia, M. (2000). *Constructing gender: Multicultural perspectives in working with women*. Belmont, CA: Wadsworth/Thomson.

Kareem, J., & Littlewood, R. (2000). *Intercultural therapy* (2nd ed.). Oxford, England: Blackwell Science.

Lampert, M. (1992). The effectiveness of psychotherapy. In A. E. Bergin & S. L. Garfield (Eds.), *Handbook of psychotherapy and behavior change* (4th ed.). New York: Wiley.

Lips, H. (2002). *A new psychology of women: Gender, culture and ethnicity* (2nd ed.). Boston: McGraw-Hill.

Lum, D. (1999). *Culturally competent practice: A framework for growth and action.* Pacific Grove, CA: Brooks/Cole.

Lum, D. (2000). *Social work practice and people of color.* Pacific Grove, CA: Brooks/Cole.

Madsen, W. (1999). *Collaborative therapy with multi-stressed families: From old problems to new futures.* New York: Guilford Press.

May, K. (1998). Family counseling: Cultural sensitivity, relativism and the culture defense. *The Family Journal: Counseling and Therapy for Couples and Families,* 6(4), 296–299.

McConahay, J., & Hough, J. (1976). Symbolic racism. *Journal of Social Issues, 32,* 23–45.

McGoldrick, M., Giordano, J., & Pearce, J. (Eds.). (1996). *Ethnicity and family therapy* (2nd ed.). New York: Guilford Press.

McLeod, J. (1997). *Narrative and psychotherapy.* London: Sage.

McMahon, A., & Allen-Meares, P. (1992). Is social work racist? A content analysis of recent literature. *Social Work, 37,* 533–539.

Meth, R., & Pasick, R. (1990). *Men in therapy: The challenge of change.* New York: Guilford Press.

Miller, S., Duncan, B., & Hubble, M. (1997). *Escape from Babel: Toward a unifying language for psychotherapy practice.* New York: W. W. Norton.

Miller, J. B. (1976). *Toward a new psychology of women.* Boston: Beacon Press.

Miller, J., & Surrey, J. (1997). Revisioning women's anger: The personal and the global. In J. Jordan (Ed.), *Women's growth in diversity: More writings from the Stone Center.* New York: Guilford Press.

Nichols, M., & Schwartz, T. (1995). *Family therapy: Concepts and methods* (3rd ed.). Boston: Allyn & Bacon.

Okin, S. (1999). *Is multiculturalism bad for women?* Princeton, NJ: Princeton University Press.

Pincus, A., & Minahan, A. (1973). *Social work practice: Model and method.* Itasca, IL: F.E. Peacock Publishing.

Poulter, S. (1987). Ethnic minority customs, English law, and human rights. *International and Comparative Law Quarterly, 36*(3), 589–615.

Prochaska, J. O., DiClemente, C. C., & Norcross, J. C. (1992). In search of how people change. *American Psychologist, 47,* 1102–1114.

Rabin, C. (1996). *Equal partners: Good friends—Empowering couples through therapy.* London: Routledge.

Rabin, C., Rosenberg, H., & Sens, M. (1982, October). Home-based marital therapy for multiproblem families. *Journal of Marital and Family Therapy,* 451–459.

Roberts, G., & Holmes, J. (1999). *Healing stories: Narratives in psychiatry.* Oxford, England: Oxford University Press.

Roberts, R., & Nee, R. (1970). *Theories of social casework.* Chicago: University of Chicago Press.

Sue, D., Ivey, A., & Pedersen, P. (1996). *A theory of multicultural counseling and therapy.* Pacific Grove, CA: Brooks/Cole.

Taylor, J., Gilligan, C., & Sullivan, A. (1995). *Between voice and silence: Women and girls, race and relationship.* Cambridge, MA: Harvard University Press.

Vargas, L., & Koss-Chioino, J. (Eds.). (1992). *Working with culture: Psychotherapeutic interventions with ethnic minority children and adolescents*. San Francisco: Jossey-Bass.

Walters, M., Carter, B., Papp, P., & Silverstein, O. (1988). *The invisible web: Gender patterns in relationships*. New York: Guilford Press.

Wheeler, D. (1985). *The theory and practice of feminist-informed family therapy: A Delphi study*. Unpublished doctoral dissertation, Purdue University, West Lafayette, IN.

White, M. (1992). Men's culture, the men's movement, and the constitution of men's lives. *Dulwich Center Newsletter, 3–4*, 1–21.

White, M., & Epston, D. (1990). *Narrative means to therapeutic ends*. New York: W. W. Norton.

Worell, P., & Remer, J. (1992). *Feminist perspectives in therapy: An empowerment model for women*. New York: Wiley.

GLOBALIZATION OF THE HUMAN SERVICES

CHAPTER 2

Exporting High-Cultural Artifacts and the Selling of the Therapy Industry as a Form of Neocolonialism

ELAINE LEEDER
UNITED STATES

OVERVIEW

This chapter is aimed at helping the student understand the process of globalization and its impact on the human services. The process of globalization is described and the transfer of "cultural artifacts" is explained. Colonization, both external and internal, is described as the exploitation of resources and human labor; it was the method by which the West moved into other parts of the globe. Although colonialism previously related primarily to these resources, today "neocolonialism" involves colonization of the mind. This process, first described by Franz Fanon, inculcates inferiority and dehumanization through everyday relationships and cultural practices of the colonized.

This chapter explores the idea that therapy is a form of neocolonization of the mind. The tendency toward ethnocentrism is viewed as an outcome, and as part of this process it results in a kind of theoretical blindness and elitism. Several examples are given of how Western psychological theories, even feminist theories, have suffered from ethnocentrism because of ignoring power differences. The case for cultural relativity is made, with examples from the authors' own practice. This has led to the valuing of indigenous healing practices and the search for alternative therapy modes such as psychoeducational methods. Examples from the author's own experience through meditation and the use of psychoeducational methods are described.

INTRODUCTION

Years ago, I was walking down a street in Manila, the Philippines, in a middle-class neighborhood with fancy boutiques, cafés, and other signs of wealth and upward mobility. As I sat in a café, I noticed a shingle hanging outside a fancy apartment building with the name of a local person and the word PSY-CHOTHERAPIST in English. I entered the building and visited the office, where I found an elegant woman of my approximate age, fluent in English and eager to chat after I introduced myself as a visiting therapist from the United States. I was there to train Filipino social workers in practices used to treat domestic violence in the United States. I was surprised to learn that this woman had an MSW from a reputable social work school in the United States and had gone home to practice in Manila after finishing her clinical work. Her practice was booming, with primarily middle-class families, couples, and depressed women. Her office looked much like many I had seen in the United States, and I felt that I had gone around the corner rather than traveling 36 hours to another country. I could have been visiting a therapist in any city at home. In fact, her therapy modalities were the very ones that I was teaching at my own university.

I left the office pleased at having made a new friend far from home but with little understanding of the implications of what I had inadvertently come upon. Years later, while visiting other countries—including Malaysia, Vietnam, South Africa, Kenya, Zimbabwe, and Venezuela—I found the same phenomenon: psychotherapists practicing in many parts of the world, all using Western treatment modalities. Some had trained in the United States or with teachers who had studied in the United States. Or they trained in their own countries but were employing approaches learned from the books and ideas transferred from the West.

I began to realize that psychotherapy had become a commodity for export, with unintended consequences that were not simply benign. As I investigated further, I realized that this process was, in fact, the globalization process taking place in the field of therapy. On one hand, it looked normal, perhaps even inevitable, given the strength of the global economy. On the other hand, it can also be seen as a form of neocolonialism, a major form of Western imperialism. In the guise of merely passing information from highly advanced, technological societies to those that are developing, we may be seeing a transfer of knowledge that could undermine indigenous and local cultures. Let me explain.

THE PROBLEM: GLOBALIZATION AND ITS EFFECTS IN HUMAN SERVICES

There are debates raging as to whether or not globalization is a good or a bad phenomenon. No matter where you stand on the matter, the world is becoming even more connected, and an unprecedented level of world trade, a global economy, connects all of us. It is a worldwide structure of cultural, social, political, and economic networks that dominate movements of capital and information around the world (Mosler & Catley, 2000). Instantaneously, an event that occurs in one part of the world is broadcast to the rest of the world. For example, movies are widely exported. And so are sneakers, which may be assembled in one part of the world with parts imported from another and then sold worldwide so that young and old look alike wherever you are on the globe. Surely this process has existed since the time of nomads and the time of Marco Polo, but it gained impetus under British expansionism and then escalated dramatically as a result of technological developments over the past century.

Globalization is not just about economics; it is also about every detail of daily life. It permeates the everyday aspects of life such as the TV we watch or the clothes we wear, the so-called low-cultural artifacts as opposed to the more sophisticated aspects of society such as philosophy, art, religion, and technology—the so-called high-cultural artifacts. Some of the more visible types of low-cultural artifacts are Coca-Cola, Marlboro cigarettes, and McDonalds, which one can find in every country in the world. High culture might be seen in classical Western music, Eastern philosophy, or computers. Needless to say, both high and low artifacts are part of the global economy and are being transferred around the world almost instantaneously.

Certainly, this process seems impossible to stop. And not many people seem interested in doing so. In fact, globalization is a *fait accompli,* although there have been protests about the resulting inequities. We know that richer countries are getting richer, while poorer ones are getting poorer. Increasingly, wealth is becoming unevenly distributed. The share of the poorest fifth of the world's population in global income has dropped from 2.3% in 1989 to 1.4% in 1998, and the proportion taken by the richest fifth has risen (Giddens, 2000, p. 33).

One social thinker, Immanuel Wallerstein, has presented us with the world systems theory in which he argues that there is a core, a periphery, and a semi-periphery of countries. The West (including the United States, Great Britain, France, Germany, Canada, Japan, and Italy as the G7—and the G8 if you count Russia) is the core, while the less-developed countries are the periphery—countries in Africa, Latin America, and Asia. The semiperipheral countries are those that seem to be industrializing and moving forward in their process of development (examples would be Venezuela, Brazil, and Israel). Wallerstein argues that the core needs the labor, the resources, and the markets of the periphery and that the poorer countries will never catch up with the others because of the nature of the world system (Wallerstein, 1974, 1992). This system, established centuries ago, makes it virtually impossible for any changes to occur because it is so deeply entrenched. As a result, the periphery will always be dependent on the core.

There is also the concept of *internal colonialism,* which is useful to understand at this point. This term means that there are colonies here in the United States, places where the poor live and work in an environment much like that of developing parts of the world. Often poor people live in inner cities, places where there are few jobs and inadequate education and housing. As a result, their lives are similar to those who live in the peripheral countries. The argument is that industry needs these workers as cheap labor, people who can be the last hired and the first fired, when the economy cannot sustain employing them.

People who write about internal colonialism argue that capitalism must have an expandable and contractable workforce, one that can be surplus labor to serve the corporations. In other words, it pays to have an unemployed labor force that can be hired and fired as the economy needs them. It pays to have poor people.

There is a parallel process that takes place with regard to gender. Women are often used as semiskilled workers as well as temporary office workers to fill positions when they are available and expelled back into unemployment when the jobs disappear. Some theorists (Eisenstein, 1979) have argued that there is a connection between capitalism and patriarchy: Each is a system of domination with people in subordinate and superordinate positions. With patriarchy, men dominate women; in capitalism, owners dominate workers. These theorists argue that capitalist patriarchy is a structural arrangement in which both the individuals and the whole system of interactions is predicated on this unequal situation.

However, globalization can be influenced, as we have seen from the protests at the World Trade Organization (WTO) in Seattle, Washington, and Milan, Italy. Large groups of concerned citizens, including many students, indigenous peoples, labor activists, environmentalists, and others have made their concerns about the inequities of globalization known and have had some impact on the international policies of corporations and the WTO.

Now, you might ask what this has to do with therapy and the work you will be doing in the human services. I would argue that therapy and the human services are high-cultural artifacts that are being exported to developing parts of the world. I believe therapy is high culture because it impacts the standards of behavior, habits, and norms of a society. If something influences how a society does business, its values, and its operational norms, then it reaches deep into the fabric of that society, just as religion does. Therapy and its impact on a social order are far more important than the sneakers one wears or the movies one watches.

Therapy and the human services are formative in the transnationalization of culture. By this I mean that by selling the human services as a commodity, like movies or travel, you are taking the ideas, the values, and the ways of doing business in one society and transferring them to another. In the case of therapy and the human services, we are saying that Western ways of healing and helping people are better than those of less-developed countries. Given that many of you will be working with people who come from countries of the periphery, many of your clients will be trying to attain the American dream and to emulate those of us in the West who have "made it." Whether you work here or in other parts of the globe, what is Western, or American, is often seen as better: It is the West that others want to emulate.

COLONIALISM AND NEOCOLONIALISM

English is now spoken in almost one-fifth of the world; it continues spreading and being adapted everywhere. Some people argue that this is neocolonialism and that the world is being taken over by Western language, technology, and ideas, and that it will lead to cultural genocide—that is, the destruction of valuable culturally specific practices and groups of people (Mies, 1999). According to Mies, wars are fought for economic reasons—to promote globalized free trade—and they trigger conflicts between groups of people who once lived in peace. She adds that this form of neocolonialism emulates the colonialism of past centuries; but now, colonialism is taking new forms. I would argue that some of those new forms of colonialism are therapy and social services.

Colonialism was the method by which the West moved into other parts of the globe and gradually impacted the social orders, politics, and economies of those regions. As industrialization took hold in the West during the 19th and early 20th centuries, European nations began to view Latin American, Asian, and African societies as sources of industrial raw materials as well as markets for Western manufactured goods (Duiker & Spielvogel, 1994, p. 857). Surplus produced in the West began to be exported in return for oil, tin, rubber, and other raw materials needed to fuel Western industrialization.

It became important for the West to find new sources of materials and new outlets for its products. Some people began to call this process "imperialism," as Western nations began to seize markets, extract cheap raw materials, and invest capital in underdeveloped countries, often taking their profits home without reinvesting in their colonies. Colonial countries thus expanded their markets and spheres of influence and vanquished their economic rivals. They used the political and social elite of the countries who received advantages from the colonists in return for helping them increase their economic power over their colonies.

Resistance to this process grew, particularly in countries with long traditions of national cohesion and independence. In such countries, the Western colonizer made every effort to eradicate resistance and obliterate local traditions and cultures. Some of the current hotspots, such as India and Pakistan, are complications resulting from colonialism.

Neocolonialism is the new colonialism. It means that more contemporary forms of imperialism are being created. These forms may not actually take over a country in the way that old nation-states would conquer weaker countries. Today this neocolonialism has all but taken over in the export of high-cultural artifacts. Therapy and human service methodologies are now exported commodities, like TVs or sneakers. Westerners are often unaware of the insidious effect of neocolonialism on indigenous cultures, believing that how we do business in the West is the way it is done everywhere.

COLONIZATION OF THE MIND

Colonization often involved the physical conquering of a population. The insidious form of neocolonialism now taking place seems focused on one aspect of colonization: colonization of the mind. Whereas in the past, a colonized population might have relinquished control to the oppressors, they also could maintain their inner resistance in their thinking. Today, the insidious passing on of Western culture through media and telecommunications expresses a kind of brainwashing about what is and is not desirable. This is a more subtle exploitation.

In fact, one author has called it a "global pillage" versus a global village (Giddens, 2000, p. 34). For example, transnational corporations might sell goods that are controlled or banned in the West such as poor quality medical drugs, destructive pesticides, or cigarettes that are high in tar and nicotine.

There is a vast body of literature on the "colonization of the mind," a term first used by Franz Fanon and built upon by later students of the colonial experience. Fanon was a black middle-class psychiatrist and revolutionary who was born in Martinique in the Caribbean and practiced in Algeria. He wrote on the experience of colonial domination and how it was maintained by systematic and institutionalized violence (Moane, 1999). He argued that violence was the tool that kept the colonized inferior and that it was created to make the colonized see the world as black and white, good and evil, right and wrong, us and them. Naturally, the colonized were the inferiors in this racist ideology and the inferiority was maintained by "colonizing the mind." By inculcating inferiority and dehumanization through everyday relationships and cultural practices of the colonized, they were taught to hate themselves and to fear the undercurrent of violence that permeated their daily life experiences.

For example, blacks have been taught to divide themselves, to try to pass as white in the white man's world, but to behave differently "with one's own kind." The message is unremitting that the white man is superior and induces a desire for the black man to want to be white. That means adopting the cultural practices of the colonizers and speaking like them as well. It creates a split in identity. There is also a hatred of blackness, associated with the negative stereotypes of a group. This leads to a devaluation of the self, a basic insecurity, and feelings of self-contempt and alienation from one's own culture.

However, just as the black person is enslaved by his or her inferiority, it is the white man who is enslaved by his superiority. It is a form of self-delusion and self-aggrandizement. Other theorists have argued that this develops a "postcolonial personality" (Moane, 1999). The idea is that a colonized person becomes more and more constricted, or draws in the outer boundaries, becoming more limited in interests, and moving in smaller and smaller spheres of influence because of the social and personal withdrawal. A colonized person may engage in superficial compliance with the oppressor, while still looking as if there is a resistance or evasion at the same time. It is a complex psychology that develops whereby the colonized turns away from the self and turns away from the reality of his or her condition to become despairing, helpless, and withdrawn.

One of the most famous writers on the colonization of the mind is Paulo Freire, who wrote about his own experience as a poor person in Brazil. He believed that both the oppressed and the oppressor are not able to self-affirm because both are submerged in the oppressive situation. "The oppressors develop a focus on possessing and controlling, leading to dehumanization and objectification of the oppressed" (Moane, 1999, p. 81). Freire writes of the alienation that the oppressed feel and a loss of sense of hope for the future. He is concerned with the "submerged state of consciousness" of the oppressed, with a state government that controls the forms of education the poor receive. He believed in the "pedagogy of the oppressed," which meant that the poor could educate themselves, in their own indigenous ways, without resorting to the "banking model" of education. That form of education uses an expert to impart knowledge, rather than appreciate the indigenous forms of learning. There is a clear distinction between the expert who imparts his or her knowledge and the students themselves, who see themselves and are seen as uneducated and unable to think independently. What it does is to control the thinking of the student, and not allow for his or her own creativity or power in the learning situation.

In this submerged state of consciousness, the person is unable to stand back from the situation and evaluate it. Nor is he or she able to trust his or her own perceptions or to deal with the confusions and contradictions that are being experienced. Because one is powerless to change the situation, there is a sense of being in a world that is controlled and hopeless and without an exit. Freire describes this as a state of resignation and fatalism.

POWER

All of the issues discussed so far relate to the concept of power: who has it and who does not. Power is the ability to get someone to do something that the person would not ordinarily do. It is also the control of resources. Colonizers are powerful, and the colonized are not. Power is manifested in all relationships and is reflected in language, space utilization, and many nonverbal representations. Power is seen in psychotherapy as well, in how far or near a therapist sits in proximity to one's client and in the language that one uses to communicate with a client. Often a therapist inadvertently conveys a sense of being powerful, somewhat the way the colonizer did to the colonized. The phenomenon is based on a sense of superiority and is rooted in one's own ethnocentrism.

ETHNOCENTRISM AND CULTURAL RELATIVISM

Historically, colonialism utilized the ideology of the "survival of the fittest" and justified the use of force through the philosophy that "might makes right." A moral argument was given to justify colonialism: Societies should adapt in order to survive, and the West is morally obligated to help backward nations adapt to the challenges of the modern world (Duiker & Spielvogel, 1994). This was a form of social Darwinism in which the colonizers used moral, scientific, and religious arguments to justify their behaviors; they did not try to assimilate with the cultures of their subjects but instead lived as if they were still in their home countries.

Moral righteousness is a type of ethnocentrism. *Ethnocentrism* is judging another culture by the standards of one's own culture, assuming that one's own culture to be superior. The opposite of ethnocentrism is *cultural relativism,* evaluating any culture by its own standards. Cultural relativism means walking in the shoes of another, understanding their reasons for doing things, and not projecting one's own value system onto them. As we work in the human services, it is imperative that we suspend judgments and understand how and why things are done as they are. This is especially important when one works in a healing profession in another country or with someone from another culture who is residing here.

When we export high-cultural artifacts of Western therapy and human services, we engage in ethnocentrism. Those who teach the Western methods of therapy and those who practice in the human services need to develop a sense of cultural relativism to assist clients in other parts of the world. We need to see that every culture has its own indigenous forms of healing that might be as effective as our Western methods. Unfortunately, Westerners are often jingoistic in their beliefs, broadcasting a chauvinistic patriotism that is almost warlike in nature. This is an extreme form of intolerance that can lead people to war, defending their belief systems, and seeing others as the enemy. Unfortunately, jingoism is rampant in the United States at this time.

It would be helpful to illustrate exactly what I mean about ethnocentrism and neocolonialism being perpetrated in the human services. In September 1996, I attended a lecture by a feminist psychoanalyst whose specialty is gender differences in psychoanalysis. In that lecture, she discussed a case on which she had consulted that involved a Bosnian woman who had been raped during the recent war. The woman had not fought her rapists and was later in treatment to deal with the trauma. The scholar argued that the woman had not fought against her rapists because of her transference with her father, who was big and overpowering as a male. She believed that the woman's problem was psychological in nature, stemming from early childhood trauma in her parental relationships. Having internalized her relationship with her father, she was now acting it out in her response to the rape.

I was surprised at this analysis, waiting for other colleagues to challenge her rather provocative interpretation. Instead, many professors asked deeper, more probing questions about the psychodynamic relationship. In none of the discussion was there any thought given to the structural conditions under which this woman was living: What about poverty, or living in a war-torn country, or being a woman who was powerless against multiple rapists? What might her religion have taught her about dealing with such a situation? What about considering the lack of power that this woman had? Rather, they were looking intrapsychically, blaming the victim and tying it to her early childhood trauma. Instead we saw an ethnocentric interpretation of the woman's problem with an exportation of a Western treatment modality to treat a woman who lived in a completely different place and condition. This is what I mean about neocolonialism and Western high-cultural artifacts being exported. This is also an example of imperialism by Westerners. In this case, even a progressive, feminist psychoanalyst was judging another culture and imposing her treatment modality.

In working with this woman, if you were her therapist perhaps you could try to understand her submerged state of consciousness and her postcolonial personality: She might feel confined by her life experience, with a narrowness and hopelessness based on the external constraints. She could well be living in fear, as a woman, a powerless victim, and a member of an ethnic group who was a victim of both genocide and other war atrocities.

Normality is highly contextual. A practitioner must look at the structural considerations under which a client lives: What are the race, ethnicity, class, and sexual orientation of the person under consideration? What are the cultural constraints and cultural values under which this woman was living? These are important considerations before one suggests a treatment. In this example, we see a Western therapist colluding with the victimization of a woman. In fact, this is double victimization: first the rape and then the diagnosis and treatment.

ETHNOCENTRISM IN WESTERN PSYCHOLOGICAL THEORIES: EXAMPLES

Recently, there have been good efforts in the helping field with teaching cultural competence. This book is but one excellent example of educating students about their own value systems, attitudes, and beliefs, as well as their understanding of groups of people other than their own. Not all practitioners are culturally arrogant, and many are trying to learn to be culturally competent and aware of their own ethnocentrism. Cultural competence also includes using culturally appropriate techniques and communications (Sue, 2001, p. 798). Most practitioners now know that this is a goal and the right way to practice in a postcolonial world. Nonetheless, skilled professionals often inadvertently engage in ethnocentrism and are now receiving criticism for their myopic vision.

For example, attachment theorists (Sue, 2001, p. 798) have long argued that cultural differences are relatively minor and that the theory is applicable universally. They suggest that culture only influences a child's specific behaviors, not the core of attachment, which is immune from cultural influence. Attachment theory looks at the prolonged period of helplessness in human infants, and the baby's need to obtain protection and nurturance from his or her caretaker. The theory says that infants become secure or insecure based on the caretaker's ability to be sensitive to the child's signals. There are different interpretations of why this security, or lack of it, occurs. One theory argues that it is because of the sensitivity of the mother; another argues that a child becomes secure as a result of the social competence of the child; yet a third approach suggests that it is the secure base that is provided by the mother that leads to a child's sense of competence (Rothbaum, Weisz, Pott, Miyake, & Morell, 2000).

However, recent studies (Rothbaum et al., 2000) indicate that these attachments are actually not universal. There are "different ways that people around the world think about and engage in close relationships" (Rothbaum et al., 2000, p. 1101). For example, sensitivity is expressed differently in Japanese society, including how close the parents are when the child is exploring, and the level of skin-to-skin contact with the infant. What counts as social competence also differs from culture to culture, with Western children acting with autonomy, exploring their environments, and showing sociability; Japanese children value preservation of the social harmony, dependency, and emotional restraint (Rothbaum et al., 2000, p. 1099).

In essence, the recent studies of Rothbaum and his colleagues indicate that a theory that once seemed universal is now being questioned and is challenging the dominant assumptions of a whole discipline of study. The challenge leads researchers to argue that future research needs to involve indigenous psychologists in assessing the usefulness of the studies and their applicability to cultures to which they are being exported. This is the essence of what I am arguing in this article: The context of assessing theories and methods must be critically questioned and a more postcolonial analysis must be part of the framework in working with people.

Another example comes from the Stone Center for the Study of Women at Wellesley College in Massachusetts. This is quite a famous program where the leaders have created the relational school of feminist psychology. Dr. Jean Baker Miller and her colleagues articulate the "self-in-relation" model, arguing that "our fundamental notion of who we are is not formed in the process of separation from others, but within the mutual interplay of relationships with others. In short, the goal is not for the individual to grow out of relationships, but to grow with them" (Miller & Stiver, 1997, p. 22). They are particularly concerned with the relational model as it relates to women, arguing that women's relationships and a therapeutic relationship with women can be the source of healing for all relationships, from the dyadic to the larger community (Kaschak, 1998, p. 17). This theory has been quite popular and well studied, being taught in courses in most schools of psychology.

The problem with this theory is that it is "acultural": The authors do not take into context the client's race, class, age, ethnicity, sexual orientation, or country of origin. They propose an essentialist quality of women as connected to others and necessarily suffering from disconnections. This is not always true, and women can benefit from disconnections, especially from patriarchal, oppressive institutions. Kaschak argues that these characteristics must be taken into consideration and "incorporated consistently in any model that hopes to understand and every example that hopes to illustrate the lives of women in particular and people in general" (p. 18). In other words, any theory and model of therapy should not just apply itself without deeply understanding the cultural context of the peoples to whom it is being applied.

Another example comes from the journal *The Counseling Psychologist.* Two recent editions (July and November 2001) were devoted to multicultural psychology and multidimensional facets of cultural competence. In the first issue, topics focus on how people develop their social identities by being placed in their contexts, and the authors suggest using an ecological model for understanding people from different cultures. By this they mean that a person's psychological adjustment is influenced by the social structural conditions under which he or she lives. The authors liken the factors that influence peoples' lives as concentric circles surrounding them, with the microsystem of family, school, home and work being the first one to impact. Next is the mesosystem, which is the interactions of the individual with two or more of those systems such as work and school. The third system is the ecosystem, which are the linkages between individuals and policy levels such as health policy, legal systems, and ethics. The final macrosystem reflects the general norms and values of a society (Neville & Mobley, 2001). The rest of the journal looks at specific examples of attaining cultural competence with different ethnic groups.

Unfortunately, many of these articles tend to be apolitical. They do not look at aspects of colonialism and the resultant internalized remnants of that system as they begin to assess other peoples. Multiculturalism is a fine goal, but unfortunately therapists who argue for cultural competence do not look at issues of power and the role of the West in exporting its paradigms or ways of seeing. Instead, multiculturalism assumes that all peoples are on an equal playing field. However, we know that there is gross inequality in the world, and a postcolonial world is not an equal world in terms of access to resources or ability to command respect in the global market. In other words, once again in a neocolonial world the colonizers are viewing the world through their own lenses rather than appreciating the positions of people coming from periphery or semiperiphery countries.

One may liken this to the dynamics between women and men, where there are power differentials that are neither acknowledged nor understood. Some have argued that men and women are just different from each other and that each must learn to respect and understand those differences. This approach is typified by John Gray's book on men and women, stating that men are from Mars and women from Venus (Gray, 1992). That phrase does not fully comprehend the power dynamics between the genders. It assumes the same playing field and that essentially men and women are "just different." The argument goes "Just understand the differences and learn to get along." It is similar to the argument about multiculturalism: "Just understand each culture and learn to live together." That kind of thinking is quite naive and does not take into account the structural inequalities that are historical and deeply rooted. An argument based on this rationale does not understand power differentials, the structural differences between men and women, and the resultant inequities. In fact, it "essentializes" men and women as different, without the comprehension of the complexity of the roots of those differences. It dangerously creates new stereotypes about men and women and is insensitive to issues of power, difference, and oppression.

PERSONAL REFLECTIONS

For years, I practiced as a psychotherapist, working with couples, individuals, and groups of women, all victims of domestic violence, sexual abuse, and psychological trauma. I believed that psychotherapy was a solution to individual problems. However, after quite awhile in practice, I found that I was dissatisfied because I believed that the work I was doing was a "band-aid on a cancer." I saw social inequities and grave social problems not being dealt with on an individual basis. I was so dissatisfied that I began to seek other methods of reaching people. I also decided to work on myself in a new way. I took up meditation, yoga, and alternative forms of healing, including breathing techniques, acupuncture, herbs, and psychic readings. At first I found them bogus, thinking that I was using "witch doctor"-like practices. I had internalized the imperialistic attitude that anything non-Western did not have anything to teach me.

However, after seeking for a long time, I began to do meditation. I went on four or five silent, weeklong retreats on mountaintops at retreat centers. There I found the kind of healing that I had heretofore never experienced. I felt deep calm after horrific encounters with my own demons. Through meditations, with a trained guide, I felt whole and healthier than I had with years of therapy. This path has served me well for almost 15 years now. In fact, I have given up my own psychotherapy practice because I see now that there are many ways of healing, with therapy being only one of the paths. But what I also saw was that the West had appropriated Eastern forms of healing, turning them into commodities that were brought from other parts of the world and turned into another product to be sold and exported, now in a Western package.

The other example of healing that does not fit the traditional mold of therapy is psychoeducation. I got into this kind of work because I was dissatisfied with the Western psychotherapy models and because I knew that therapy was not always the best approach to changing people's lives. I have worked for the past 7 years in maximum-security prisons for convicted male felons, first in New York and now in California. In those classes, I taught the inmates sociology and writing skills in hopes that they would receive bachelor's degrees upon their release. In one such class, I taught a book I had used in a number of my college classes, a book on batterers. The inmates I was working with were quite fascinated with my presentation on a typology of two types of batterers: Cobras and Pit Bulls. Pit Bulls are offenders who are tenacious, hold tight to the women they abuse, fear loss of their loved one, and are frightened, although appearing to be tough guys. The Cobras are men who are cold on the outside, do not get agitated while they are abusing their victims, and are distant personalities.

I asked the prisoners which they were and why. The men were fascinated with the typology but argued that it was not one type or the other. They argued that one first became a Pit Bull and then transitioned into Cobras after years of victimizing women. They used this information to look at their own lives. They wrote journals on the typology, applying it to their own lives and using it to develop insight into their own behaviors. This was not a therapy session, but the psychoeducation served good purposes in bringing about change.

CONCLUSION

As students training to work in the human services, there are many skills on which you will have to work. A student has to learn specific techniques in diagnosis, treatment planning, assessment of effectiveness, as well as appropriate listening skills and intervention strategies. To that repertoire, nascent human service providers should consider adding awareness of power differentials between themselves and the client as well as an awareness of nonverbal dynamics.

In this article, I have suggested that there is yet another important variable to take into consideration, especially when working with people of cultures other than one's own. I believe that practitioners must understand their own ethnocentrism and the sense of superiority that many of us in the West carry, without even being aware of it as unseen baggage. Cultural competence is more than understanding where another person is coming from and seeing them in their own context. It is being aware that there is often a judgment that is being made: That Western treatment techniques are superior and that these techniques should be exported like movies and TV shows. Even if there are some useful tools that we have acquired here, there are equally useful tools available to indigenous practitioners from other cultures. These need to be valued equally to our own techniques. I urge students to remember to be culturally relative, to avoid being a Western imperialist, and to appreciate and respect others' healing practices. The following chapters of this book go a long way in helping you gain cultural competence. We have to remember that our way is just one way of seeing. There are many ways of seeing and doing the business of helping others. There is no one truth; there are many truths. Perhaps those indigenous healers have much to teach us about how we practice in the helping professions.

Many thanks to Maureen Buckley, Ellyn Kaschak, Zoe Sodja and Abigail Leeder, for their assistance in writing this article.

KEY CONCEPTS

- globalization
- global pillage
- low-cultural artifacts
- high-cultural artifacts
- world systems theory
- core
- periphery
- semiperiphery
- colonialism
- neocolonialism
- submerged state of consciousness
- pedagogy of the oppressed
- ethnocentrism
- cultural relativity

QUESTIONS FOR REFLECTION

1. What is globalization and what is its relevance to the human services?
2. What is colonization of the mind?
3. Describe multiculturalism? What are the pros and cons of this approach?
4. Do you disagree or agree with Leeder's premise about the globalization process and its impact on non-Western peoples? Why or why not?

5. What is the relevance of neocolonialism to your work in the human services? Do you have an example from your own practice?
6. What is essentialism, and how does it relate to men and women?
7. What is power? Why do therapists have it? How does it get shown in the therapy session?
8. Are you ethnocentric? Have you ever engaged in culturally relative thinking? Give examples of both.
9. Do you see any relevance for the concept of "colonization of the mind" for your own work?
10. Does the pedagogy of the oppressed have any relevance to your own experiences in school?
11. How would you have worked with the rape victim in Bosnia?
12. How does submerged state of consciousness relate to the rape victim in Bosnia?
13. What types of experiences have you had that were not psychotherapy, but still brought about change and growth in you?
14. What is the main piece of learning that you gained from this article?

EXERCISE

Take one concept that you have learned that helps you to diagnose and assess problems of clients you work with. It can come from any theory you have studied in individual, family, couples, and group settings. Now think of a client you are working with currently, or who you have worked with in the recent past. Briefly assess this client using the concept you have chosen. Now list some inherent values that are covertly assumed by this concept. For example, "differentiation of self" values autonomy, independence, and self-reliance. Then think of an aspect of the client's gender and cultural context that might clash with the values embedded in the concept you have chosen. How would you have to modify something you did to make your work with this client more relevant to cultural and gender issues? Finally, reflect on how your own mind might have been "colonized" by professional concepts that reflect Western capitalistic thinking. Share all of this process with another student.

References

The Counseling Psychologist. (2001, July). Multicultural psychology: Creating a contextual framework [Special issue], *29*(4).

The Counseling Psychologist. (2000, November). Multidimensional facets of cultural competence [Special issue], *29*(6).

Duiker, W., & Speilvogel, J. (1994). *World history VII: Since 1500.* St. Paul, MN: West.

Eisenstein, Z. (1979). *Capitalist patriarch and the case for socialist feminism.* New York: Monthly Review Press.

Giddens, A. (2000). *Runaway world: How globalization is reshaping our lives.* New York: Routledge.

Gray, J. (1992). *Men are from Mars, Women are from Venus: A practical guide for improving communication and getting what you want in your relationships.* New York: HarperCollins.

Kaschak, E. (1998, March). Growing pains. *Women's Review of Books, V. XV*(6), 17–18.

Mies, M. (1999, November). *Globalization as genocide* (draft of presentation). Ithaca. NY: Cornell University.

Miller, J. B., & Stiver, I. P. (1997). *The healing connection: How women form relationships in therapy and in life.* Boston: Beacon Press.

Moane, G. (1999). *Gender and colonialism: The psychological analysis of oppression and liberation.* New York: St. Martin's Press.

Mosler, D., & Catley, B. (2000). *Global America: Imposing liberalism on a recalcitrant world.* Westport, CT: Praeger.

Neville, H., & Mobley, M. (2001, July). An ecological model: Multicultural psychology: Creating a contextual framework [Special issue]. *The Counseling Psychologist, 29*(4), 471–486.

Rothbaum, F., Weisz, J., Pott, M., Miyake, K., & Morell, G. (2000, October). Attachment and culture: Security in the U.S. and Japan. *American Psychologist, 55*(10), 1093–1104.

Sue, D. W. (2001, November). The superordinate nature of cultural competence: Multidimensional Facets of Cultural Competence [Special issue]. *The Counseling Psychologist, 29*(6), 850–857.

Wallerstein, I. (1974). *The modern world-system: Capitalistic Agriculture and the origins of the European world economy in the 16th century.* New York: Academic Press

Wallerstein, I. (1992). America and the world: Today, yesterday and tomorrow. *Theory and Society, 21*, 1–28.

3

CHAPTER

GENDER AND CULTURE
IN THE NARRATIVE
APPROACH TO HELPING

**JILL FREEDMAN AND
GENE COMBS
UNITED STATES**

OVERVIEW

In this chapter, we will review the basic tenets of an approach to helping that is organized around the narrative metaphor and a poststructural worldview. We work with people of all sorts—rich and poor, conventionally gendered and transgendered, from "mainstream" American culture and from many other cultures. To make this chapter relevant to the overall theme of this book, we have given clinical examples of people dealing with problems concerning gender and culture. We begin with a theoretical overview, describing how people's sense of identity is continually constructed, deconstructed, and reconstructed through the stories that circulate in the larger culture. We then describe how, in our view, problems arise in political contexts. This leads us to seek ways of working that see problems as located in cultural discourses, not in individual persons. We describe how we assist people in developing rich, thickly described lives that are less limited by discourses such as those surrounding gender and culture.

In the second part of the chapter, we focus on some of the more common practices of narrative work: witnessing, listening, externalizing problems, attending to the discourses that support problematic stories, developing preferred stories, and creating an audience for the preferred stories. We conclude with personal reflections and an exercise.

IDENTITY AND SOCIETY

Ten years ago, we met a physician from New York City in a workshop on eulogies. The physician had witnessed an incomprehensible number of young men die in the AIDS epidemic. He had watched as, during their hospital stays, the young men's partners and friends surrounded and cared for them. He told about attending more funerals than he could remember where these same partners and friends were delegated, sometimes literally and almost always symbolically, to the back of the church or synagogue or funeral home.

At death, the biological families of the young men took ownership of their legacies, so it was the biological family members and *their* old friends who provided the eulogies, not the young men's gay partners and friends. According to the physician, the stories told at these funerals ended at about the age of 14—before the young men had publicly claimed any sexual identity. Although some of the stories were, no doubt, familiar to the men's partners and adult friends, the truncated, sexless lives that the family members described, the outmoded identities of the people they mourned, were not.

We found the physician's description heartrending and fascinating. As practitioners of narrative therapy*—an approach first developed by Michael White and David Epston (White, 1988–89; White & Epston, 1990)—we thought about the physician's words in terms of the narrative metaphor (J. Bruner, 1986). His story spoke to us of the power of narrative to define and construct identity. It showed how the sharing and circulation of different stories can build different communities. It vividly illustrated the power of stories to give meaning to lives and relationships—to privilege some people while making others invisible.

THE NARRATIVE METAPHOR

The narrative metaphor suggests that we organize and experience our lives through stories—not stories made up and told by therapists to illustrate particular points, but stories that we live. Although countless events occur in our lives every day, only those that are given meaning through stories shape our lives, identities, possibilities, and futures. Obviously, eulogies are not the only opportunity for storying lives, but unless alternative stories of the young men the physician spoke of lived on in other ways, only their prepubescent identities would be remembered. The physician suggested that the trend toward making videos to play at one's own funeral shows how people want some choice over which stories will be privileged as their friends and family members celebrate their lives.

---

*We understand that the term *therapy* is controversial; for many readers of this book, it might have neocolonialist overtones. However, this is the most common way of naming our approach, so we would feel dishonest not using it at least once. We invite you to reflect on what choice you might make in such a situation. Would you attempt to change the terminology? Would you use the term but comment on it? Would you do something else?

We think about narrative work as a process through which people choose the stories of their lives by which they prefer to be known.

The stories that we are referring to begin with lived events. But different aspects of particular events are prominent for different people, and how meaning is made of those events can vary greatly. For example, as a teenager, I (Freedman) belonged to an encounter group. After five meetings, the leader of the group went on vacation and the group decided to meet once without him. As the youngest member of the group, I had said little up to that point. But at the leaderless meeting, I spoke out and took risks that seemed significant to me—significant enough that I reported them to several of my nongroup friends. When the group met again, the leader asked about the meeting that he missed. One of the members summarized it, leaving out my part completely. He didn't even mention the issue that, for me, was everything the group had been about that week. I was shocked. It was as though he and I had been at completely separate events, and, in a sense, we had. Each of us had storied the experience through different particular moments and details. For both of us, all other events had dropped out of awareness.

Even if the same moments and details of an event are storied, they can have different meanings to different listeners.

Clinical Example

I (Combs) recently interviewed a heterosexual couple. They described a disagreement. Each concurred with the other's description of how the conflict started and who said what. When I inquired about the *meaning* of the event, Erika said she felt wonderful about the conflict. She saw it as an indication that she and Harold could hold and express different opinions. For her, it meant claiming her voice and not giving in to fear. Harold, on the other hand, felt horrible about the conflict. For him, the disagreement meant that they were not getting along.

We give relatively few events in our lives story status. I (Freedman) once was on the faculty for a personal growth seminar that met one weekend a month for 9 months. The format included many exploratory exercises. Exercise instructions often required that people pick a memory and explore that memory in some way. I noticed that people would pick the same memories over and over again throughout the 9-month seminar. Although countless things had happened in each of the participant's lives, relatively few had become important memories. This is true for us all. The memories that do become important are the ones that get storied. The others seem not to count, or may even be forgotten.

People often generalize about the quality of their lives and the possibilities open to them. These generalizations are based on the life stories they remember up to the point from which they are generalizing. Anyone's stories, taken together, imply a particular direction in life. The already-remembered, canonical stories influence people to story other events that support that direction in life and not to make so much meaning of events that would suggest different directions. Conversely, once people begin living out new stories, they can almost always find roots for those new stories in past experience (White, 1997;

FIGURE 3-1

The narrative
metaphor

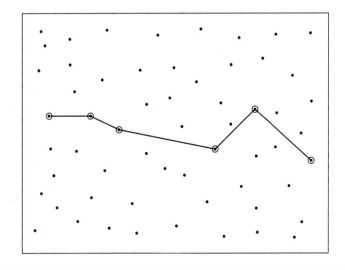

Zimmerman & Dickerson, 1996). In other words, once an event is storied in such a way that its meaning is different than that of the usual stories of a person's life, other memories that support that meaning become accessible.

We find it helpful to pictorially represent how we think about the narrative metaphor (see Figure 3-1).

Any person's life has countless events. The dots in this picture stand for some of those events in the life of one person. The circled dots stand for events that have been storied. These are the memories that the person easily reflects on. They are the stories that he or she tells and retells. They form the basis for how that person approaches and experiences his or her life. One implication of our life stories being constructed like this is that they can be deconstructed (and reconstructed differently).

We have noticed that when people come to see a therapist, their life stories tend to be few in number and to focus predominantly on negative events. However, there are always many, many events that lie outside of, and would not be predicted by, the problematic storyline. By asking questions that invite people to make meaning of those events, we help people add new strands of meaning to their stories and thus to *thicken* them. In this process, the problematic story does not disappear, but people usually have a different perspective on it because it reflects only one strand of a more thickly described life. (See Figure 3-2.)

Three points are particularly useful in shaping our thinking as we approach our work through a narrative lens:

1. We have choice about which life events we give story status.
2. Events can have a variety of meanings.
3. Problems occur in political contexts.

FIGURE 3-2

The metaphor of a
"more thickly
described life"

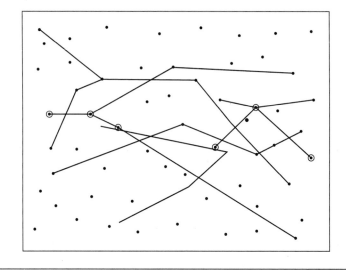

Up to this point, for the sake of simplicity, we have been writing about individual stories. However, we actually think about life narratives in a more complex way. We believe that each of us is born into cultural stories that are so taken for granted that they are invisible. For us, a *cultural story* is more or less equivalent to what poststructuralist writers refer to as a *discourse* (Madigan & Law, 1992; Hare-Mustin, 1994). A discourse is a system of words, actions, rules, and beliefs that brings forth and supports a particular worldview. We might even think of a discourse as a worldview in action. Whether it is through media or other cultural institutions, through myths, or through traditions, all of us are exposed to discourses. These discourses influence what we take for granted as "reality." They shape our experience of the way things are or should be. For example, the meaning of the word *men* in the phrase "all men are created equal" in the United States Declaration of Independence has changed as the discourses involved with who can own land, vote, and hold political office have changed. It originally referred to adult, white, male landowners. It now refers, legally at least, to adults of all genders and skin colors whether or not they own property.

Cultural stories or discourses help pass on traditions and hard-won knowledge. It can be very helpful to have agreed-upon notions of how to do things and of what constitutes a good life. However, when we internalize these cultural stories or discourses, we run the risk of taking on their associated values and then measuring ourselves against the standards set by those values as if they are the only standards that exist. When we do not or cannot measure up to the dominant discourses, they become problematic. People who don't fit the dominant discourses are marginalized. As Foucault (1980) so richly illustrated, and we will discuss this in more detail shortly, discourses and power are intimately interrelated.

A distinguishing characteristic of narrative approaches is that they consider people's problems in the light of discourses and power. Narratively informed helpers inquire into the ways that certain cultural stories, through their unquestioned dominance, contribute to power inequities in our society—to those feelings of not measuring up or not belonging that often bring people to consult with us.

Two examples of discourses that are prevalent in North America are the cultural stories that promote particular norms for success and beauty. We have a saying that "One can never be too rich or too thin." The equation of success with wealth has created an epidemic of people working longer hours, buying more things, and leaving less time to experience the joys of life. It has also led us to assume that poverty equals failure. The equation of beauty with thinness has led to an epidemic of anorexia as young women measure themselves against the impossible standard set by fashion magazines and other popular media.

There are other standards that particular people, because they belong to a nondominant culture, can never match. Last December, I (Freedman) went to a shop to buy a basket of soap for a friend who was in the hospital. A man came in to make a delivery. He said to the person behind the counter, "I really don't like having to hear Christmas carols everywhere I go for more than a month. I'm not Christian, but I have no choice. This music is everywhere!" The woman behind the counter signed for the packages and did not respond to the comment. When he left, one of the customers said, "What a grump." The others concurred. Although it was only with his comment that I had become aware of the music, I said, "I think he has a point." No one responded. This is just an everyday example of how particular beliefs, ways of doing things, and norms permeate the fabric of our lives, promoting some cultures at the expense of others. Some people can take access to resources and participation in society for granted while others have little or no place.

Gender-role socialization limits the possibilities for both genders. Patriarchy promotes power and privilege for males and continues the gender inequity in our society. Although people may not directly refer to discourses such as these when they consult us, we can ask questions that bring forth awareness of the part that discourses play in supporting problematic stories.

To summarize, when people come to consult with us, we listen to what they say as stories. We think of the stories, not the people who consult us, as being problematic. We ask questions that invite people to situate their problematic stories within larger cultural stories or discourses. Through this process, by keeping in mind that stories construct people's realities, we can help them have at least some degree of choice about which stories they allow to influence the meaning of their lives.

POSTSTRUCTURALISM AND IDENTITY

We want to focus for a moment on the different conceptions of identity in structuralist and poststructuralist worldviews. In structuralist notions of identity, each person has an authentic core identity. Structuralist approaches focus on peeling back layers of denial or ignorance in a search to discover this authentic core identity.

The metaphor that is used proposes surface structures and deep structures. A structuralist consultant's expertise is in interpreting surface structure—behaviors, actions, thoughts, dreams, and the like—as clues to a person's deep structure (their authentic core identity). And the goal of structuralist approaches is to assist people in becoming authentic, or who they really are, which can only be known through expert interpretations that reveal their deep structure.

Poststructuralism does not propose a core identity. All the experiences of life are viewed as having effects that we can trace on our sense of identity. We know ourselves through relationships and through the stories of our lives. This brings forth a fluid sense of identity.

Poststructuralist anthropologists and psychologists have identified a shift, often referred to as the *interpretive turn* (Geertz, 1983; J. Bruner, 1986). Before the interpretive turn, anthropologists observed people in particular cultures and made generalized anthropological meaning of what people in those cultures did. This was a structuralist way of working; anthropologists observed surface structure and, through their expert interpretations, identified deep structure. The interpretive turn came about when researchers began to value the meaning people themselves made of their experiences. Anthropologists began to invite people to define their own cultures. A poststructuralist anthropologist, rather than observing and interpreting, asks people in different cultures about the meaning of their rituals, activities, and so on, and tries to render an experience-near account of those local meanings.

In our work as poststructuralist consultants, we can think of each person as a culture of one. We can also think of a family as a culture. Then, rather than interpreting people's experience to reveal their authentic selves, we can ask people the meaning of their experience. We also ask which experiences they prefer. We are interested in helping people develop "thick descriptions" (Geertz, 1973; Ryle, 1990) of their lives. The metaphor is no longer surface and depth, but thick and thin. We think of problematic stories as involving thin conclusions. The question changes from "How can I become my true self?" to "How are we becoming other than who we have already been?" (White, 2000).

With this different description of identity and the different project that is proposed by poststructuralism (becoming other than who we have already been), our job description as helpers changes. We are no longer responsible for helping people learn who they really are. We are responsible for creating a context in which people can decide which of the many stories available to them they prefer, and for helping to develop those stories into thick descriptions of interesting lives.

Our job as helpers, then, is to see through the problematic stories that are coloring people's lives, identities, and relationships, and to believe that other possible stories exist. We don't know what those stories are going to be or which questions will be most useful in beginning to author them, but we do know that every person has life experiences that contradict the dominant plots.

Poststructuralism, especially as it is expressed in the late work of Michel Foucault, is an important influence on how we work with the stories that circulate in people's cultures. Foucault studied, among other things, the various ways that people in Western society have been categorized as "other." He examined madness (1965), illness (1975), criminality (1977), and sexuality (1985) as concepts around which certain people have come to be labeled as *insane, sick, criminal,* or *perverted,* and described various ways they have been separated, oppressed, or enrolled in self-policing on the basis of that labeling.

Foucault described two types of power: traditional power and modern power. Traditional power emanates from a center—typically, from a deity or a monarch—and is enforced in public through harsh external means. It establishes social control through a system of moral judgments that invite people to look to representatives of the god or king for approval based on their moral worth.

Modern power develops and circulates in widely dispersed and shifting communities. It is based on norms and scales, and it is enforced largely through self-policing and the normative judgments of peers. It invites people to look to themselves and each other for approval based on their normative worth.

Modern power is carried in the stories we tell each other about what is worth pursuing and what is not worth pursuing, what constitutes success or failure, who is "in" and who is "out," and where we place ourselves on this or that continuum of normality. As we stated in the previous section, we believe that those stories are roughly equivalent to discourses, and that stories and discourses, through the workings of modern power, tend to be invisible.

We find Foucault's way of thinking clinically relevant. If we can trace how problems gain power by getting people to measure themselves against internalized cultural norms, then we can assist people in identifying those norms (standards, scales) and invite them to value themselves differently. We study the workings of modern power so that we can develop awareness of the discourses that support people's problems. This makes it possible for us to interact with people in ways that invite them to see the effects of different discourses. With this knowledge, they are in a position of greater choice from which they can imagine, experience, and live out more satisfying life stories.

Foucault (1980) was especially interested in how the "truth claims" carried in the "grand abstractions" of reductionist science constituted a discourse that dehumanized and objectified many people. He was interested in finding and circulating marginalized discourses—stories that exist but are not widely circulated or powerfully endorsed—that might undermine the excessive power of the reductionistic scientific discourse. He wrote of the "amazing efficacy of discontinuous, particular, and local criticism" in bringing about a "return of knowledge" or "an insurrection of subjugated knowledges" (1980, pp. 80–84).

Following Foucault, we believe that even in the most disempowered of lives, there is always lived experience that lies outside the dominant stories. Narrative helpers have developed ways of thinking and working that bring forth "discontinuous, particular, and local" stories so that people can inhabit and lay claim to the many possibilities for their lives that lie beyond the pale of norms and standards set by dominant narratives about gender, culture, class, and the like.

NARRATIVE PRACTICES

In the rest of this chapter, we hope to acquaint readers with some of the more usual and "characteristic" things we might do in our day-to-day work. We value our ways of working, and we are interested in letting other people know about them. However, we hope that readers will bear in mind that in a written work of this length, anything we say takes on an unfortunate solidity and definiteness. More than any of the practices we describe here, we value a perpetual deconstruction of our work and its effects.

Witnessing

In our work, we are interested in opening space for new conversations. One way problems thrive is by promoting "the same old same old," ensnaring people in the same arguments, positions, and conclusions over and over again. We have found the process of witnessing (Freedman & Combs, 2002, 2002a; Weingarten, 2000)—or listening from a reflecting position rather than from a directly interacting position—to be useful in promoting fresh perspectives and new conversations. Particularly when we are working with more than one person, speaking with one person at a time and asking the others—partners, friends, or family members—to *witness* that person's story (rather than immediately talk with that person about it), it has become possible for them to hear the story in new ways.

The kind of listening and reflecting that we hope to promote through witnessing is unusual in contemporary Western culture. It is not the dominant way of doing things. We in the West are taught either to listen subserviently to a boss or an expert or criticize and compete for who has the "best" idea when we are allowed to talk. It seems to us that the kind of respectful, curious, patient listening we hope to promote happens more often in some traditional and non-Western cultures.

To facilitate witnessing, we interact with one person at a time, asking the others to listen without talking. We try to be thoughtful about the posture we propose for each person in the witnessing position. For example, with a particular person we might say, "Would you be willing, as I talk with Vernon, to listen as you would to a friend? With friends, sometimes you can suspend your own point of view and listen just to understand. Would that be all right?"

After we have reached a certain point in interviewing one person, we ask the person(s) in the witnessing position to reflect on what they have heard. We ask, directly or by implication, that each person interact only with us while the others who are present now assume or remain in a witnessing position. We might be open in how we request reflections, or we might ask highly specific questions to promote the development of preferred stories. A question such as "What were you thinking about as you listened to your partner?" may bring a quite different response than "What did it mean to you to hear that your partner could put aside your differences enough to recount that memory of you that he treasured?"

In using a witnessing format, we can suggest that those in the witnessing position imagine what it would be like to be in the shoes of the person we are interviewing. In so doing, we hope to begin unmasking differences in power and privilege. Sometimes this happens when a person gets a glimpse of how different the world feels in the other person's shoes. At other times, it happens only when we begin to unpack the things that make it difficult for one person to really step into the other's shoes. By asking each person to speak directly with us while the others listen, we hope to avoid supporting gender or cultural arrangements that give particular people lots of space to speak while silencing others.

Witnessing is as much an attitude as it is a technique. It partakes of a rhythm that permeates our work, an alternation between acting and reflecting on the effects of that action, between talking and listening, between focusing on individual persons and focusing on groups or cultures. This attitude doesn't require the presence of a group. If we are working with an individual, we can ask the person to step back and witness the conversation we have just had from different points of view. For example, we can ask, "Thinking back on our whole conversation, what stands out as most important?" or "If your third grade teacher knew what you've accomplished since you were in her class, what would she learn about you?"

As we have described more extensively in other places (Freedman & Combs, 1996a; Combs & Freedman, 2002), we also cultivate reflection on the effects of our own work. This requires us to cultivate reliable witnesses to our work and to find respectful, safe ways of making our work more public. Without the witness of our "better selves" and that of informed others, we will surely become lost in the very discourses and workings of modern power that we seek to assist others in escaping.

Beginning

The poststructuralist concept of identity proposes a particular role for narrative consultants. Helpers who use structuralist approaches generally believe that people have an authentic core self that can be understood through expert interpretation. This idea contributes to the structuralist consultant's role as an expert. Conversely, in using narrative approaches, we are thinking about ourselves as collaborators rather than as expert interpreters. Following the ideas of the interpretive turn, we are interested in privileging the meaning that people make of their own experience rather than the conclusions we might draw. This calls for a different kind of relationship. We hope to introduce this difference from the beginning.

We greet people as people. We do not start by asking them to fill out forms or describe "symptoms." We might ask people on their first visit if they had any difficulty finding our office or whether they would like some tea. We ask them about themselves outside of the problem and about their relationships outside of the problem. With these practices, we are hoping to convey that we understand that their identities are reflected by many experiences and stories, not just the problematic ones. We do not want to mistake people for the problems that bring them to consult with us. We ask about people's interests, pleasures, and work. Sometimes we ask partners or family members about each other. We may ask questions such as. "What could I count on about your partner if we were stranded together on a desert island?"* or "What do you appreciate about your daughter that he or she probably doesn't know you appreciate?"

Before we begin talking about problems, we ask people if they would like to ask us anything. We think it is important that people have a chance to understand at least a little about our lived experience and where our ideas come from. This fosters collaboration and allows people to decide how to take our ideas. In these beginning conversations, in addition to questions about our professional credentials, we have been asked what books we like to read, whether we believe in God, and what we really love. One thing we really love is questions such as these.

Listening

The discourses we are immersed in profoundly affect how we listen. Because most therapists are educated in terms of structuralist ideas about people and problems, they tend to make sense of what people tell them in terms of those ideas. They listen for symptoms that support a diagnosis or for surface clues that will help them interpret deep meaning.

We endeavor to listen from a different perspective. We listen with the following beliefs:

- People consulting us are not the problem. Their partners or supervisors or children are not the problem. The problem is the problem.
- Many stories lie outside of the problematic story.

This second belief aids us in noticing events that would not be predicted by the problem or that stand outside of the problem. These may constitute important openings that it will be important to ask about later. But first, we keep listening long enough to understand people's experience of the problematic story.

Doing this work has made us profoundly aware that if we were in the situations that many of those who consult with us face, we would not deal with those situations nearly as well as they do. Listening from a so-called objective or expert perspective supports "othering," which can keep therapists from this kind of appreciative awareness. Listening so as to understand people's lived experience of problems, as though it were ours, is humbling. It infuses us with awareness of the privilege people afford us in opening their lives to us.

Naming Problems

We are interested in separating problems from people, or *externalizing* them (White, 1988–89; Zimmerman & Dickerson, 1996). If we separate problems from people, then people can be in relationship with them and thus in a position to negotiate different relationships.

---

*We first heard this question in a workshop with David Epston.

To externalize problems, it is helpful to name them, and it is important to find a name that fits and resonates. This often requires much listening and careful discussion. With some people, the name chosen in the beginning remains constant throughout the work. With others, the name shifts as their relationship with the problem shifts.

Clinical Example

For example, one member of a lesbian couple at first identified her partner as the problem. She thought that her partner was asexual, or sexually troubled. This was her initial understanding of why their relationship lacked sexual intimacy. Later in that conversation, in response to questions about how the problem came between them, she and her partner began to talk about the problem in a different way. They agreed that it was problematic that one of them was more interested in sex than the other. In our conversation, we externalized this problem, calling it "difference in sexual interest." However, it quickly became clear that this description did not capture the whole problem. In talking about the effects of "difference in sexual interest," they described how, for at least one of them, "anger" was a greater problem than "difference in sexual interest." As we talked about "anger" and "difference in sexual interest," each partner became more and more aware of how both of these problems were keeping them from delighting in each other and in the relationship. As this conversation progressed, the couple eventually named "homophobia" as the problem that intruded into their relationship. They traced how it created fear, inhibition, and self monitoring, particularly for the one member who believed that she would lose her job if her sexual orientation became known.

Careful naming helped externalize the couple's problems in a way that allowed the partners to work together in defining their relationship rather than allowing homophobia to control it. Externalizing problems in this way creates room for people to consider their relationships with problems. It allows creative reflection on how they can affect those relationships. They can begin to notice what supports problems and what supports less problematic directions in life.

THINKING ABOUT THE DISCOURSES WITHIN WHICH PROBLEMATIC STORIES ARE SITUATED

As we described earlier, we think that cultural stories and discourses create taken-for-granted ideas about reality. They set our expectations and encourage us to look to certain people as role models while ignoring others. As participants in a culture, we can't help but internalize some of the ideas implicit in the dominant discourses of that culture. The couple in the previous example didn't radically invent the homophobia that threatened their relationship. Intellectually, they didn't agree with it. However, because it was so present in the larger culture, they couldn't avoid internalizing it to some extent, and it had unwelcome effects. Some version of a story such as this is true for all of us. All of us have the experience of thinking, feeling, and acting in ways that don't really match our most precious beliefs and commitments. Even though it is against our better judgment, we find ourselves at moments acting like a teacher who affected us badly or like people we see in the media but don't really value. We sometimes embody our parents' least lovely habits or pick up unwelcome phrases from political leaders, living out roles that our teachers, parents, and political leaders also did not make up.

We all swim in a sea of discourses. Many different discourses may support a particular problem that particular people find themselves caught up in. We don't want to rush to judgment about which discourses are at play in any given situation. We want to stay open to thinking together with people about how to relate the sea of discourses in which they swim to the problems they are struggling with—to the expectations they experience themselves as not living up to, to beliefs that keep their problems alive, and to mismatches between their dreams and the life they actually live. We think about gender socialization, patriarchy, racism, heterosexual dominance, classism, and normative ideas about families and success, but we don't want to get in the habit of thinking that these are the only discourses that affect people in negative ways. Part of our ongoing work is to keep wondering and learning about new discourses and new ways of describing and understanding discourses.

We work to expose problematic discourses and to understand how they work. How explicitly we do this and how much detail we go into varies tremendously. Our conversations vary a great deal, depending on people's particular situations and interests. We don't lecture, and we don't argue that people should follow a particular code of behaviors or beliefs. However, we do think that situating the problems that people struggle with in cultural ideas that may have previously been invisible creates more room for people to construct their lives and relationships in ways that really suit them. This practice of situating problems in cultural discourses helps minimize the possibility of unthinkingly falling back into lives and relationships that are supported by the prevailing norms and standards.

Although our description here may sound intellectual and dogmatic, the conversations we engage in are usually rather free-flowing and down-to-earth.

Clinical Example

Several years ago, John, a man in his mid-20s who earned his living delivering medical equipment, came to consult with me (Freedman). He came to talk with me because a buddy suggested it after—for a third time—John had dated a woman and become engaged only to have her call off the wedding. As John described his situation, I asked what each of the women said when they ended the engagements. He sighed and told me that they all said pretty similar things. They complained that he took them for granted. He seemed to find time for whatever *he* wanted to do but not what *they* wanted to do. They all said he really didn't talk to them, although he seemed to talk to his buddies. He expected them to always be eager to have sex, but he seemed to want to do most other things with his male friends, even though before the engagement they had lots of other kinds of fun together.

I asked John about what it would feel like to be treated the way these women described being treated. At first, it was difficult for him to find an answer. When he really stepped into the experience their words implied, letting go of his perspective on the relationship, John said it would feel pretty bad. I asked where he might have gotten the idea that this was an appropriate way to treat women. He said that was not descriptive of the whole relationship. I acknowledged that, and asked if it described part of the relationship. He said it did. I asked again where he might have gotten the idea that this was an appropriate way to treat women. He thought for several minutes and then said, "Beer commercials." Throughout the ensuing conversation, I focused on asking small, detailed questions. I did not lecture John or instruct him. I just invited him to think things through, experiencing them from a different perspective and examining the effects of looking at things that way.

John was a sports fan, and at that time there was a popular beer commercial that was aired frequently on sports shows. John would have seen it many, many times. This commercial featured two men lazing on a deserted beach. Then two women in skimpy bikinis walk by. One of the men is holding a remote control. As the women pass, he clicks the remote and they back up. The man clicks the remote again and the women walk past them. He clicks the remote again and they back up. This goes on for some time. John and I discussed this commercial and others like it. I asked him to think about how it would feel different to watch it as a woman than it did as a man. I asked about the model of relationship that the commercial was built on, and what that must be like for women.

I asked John if he would want his sisters to be in the kind of relationship that beer commercials modeled. He adamantly stated that he would not. We never used terms such as *objectification* or *power differential* or *discourse*, but this was surely a conversation that exposed discourses. After the conversation, John thought about women and relationships differently than he had before.

We all are participants in culture—both local culture and larger cultures—and none of us is free of the effects of discourses. This means that one way to be able to bring new ideas about discourses into our work is to think about their effects in our own lives. As an aid to this, we highly recommend Rachel Hare-Mustin's (1994) article "Discourses in the Mirrored Room."

DECONSTRUCTING PROBLEMATIC STORIES

We are interested in deconstructing problematic stories. Deconstruction helps people sense that the stories that shape their lives are *constructions* of reality, not direct representations. Deconstruction involves asking questions that trace how problematic stories are constructed, as well as questions that seek to expose gaps in their construction. Our experience is that once people see that a story is constructed, they can see that it might be possible to construct it another way. Recognizing contradictions and gaps in a problematic story makes it possible to engage in conversations that bring forth stories of events that are implied by the gaps. For instance, with the lesbian couple in our earlier example, it was fortunate (but, from a narrative perspective, not surprising) that homophobia was contradicted by many other aspects of the couple's life: They considered themselves to be feminists, they had a great deal of political savvy, and so on.

We have already described how we seek to name problems, to situate them in larger sociocultural discourses, and to engage in conversations that externalize problems. These are all ways of deconstructing problematic stories. Other ways are to ask about how the problem operates and to map the effects of the problem.

Michael White (2002; also see Mann & Russell, 2002) has developed a highly useful format that he calls "mapping a statement of position." It elegantly combines many of these possibilities for deconstruction. To map a statement of position, he uses the following four-part format:

1. Ask questions to negotiate an experience-near definition of the problem.
2. Ask about the effects of the problem on the life and relationships of the person and collaboratively generate a list of these effects.
3. Ask questions that invite the person to evaluate the listed effects.
4. Ask questions that invite the person to justify the evaluation or to fill in what they would prefer instead of the effect.*

The list of effects is generated before moving on to parts 3 and 4. The questions for the third and fourth parts are then asked in concert about each effect in turn. For example, with the couple struggling with homophobia, one of the many effects was self-monitoring. When we came to this effect on the list, we might have asked one of the following questions to invite evaluation of it (part 3): "You may think this is obvious, but what has the self-monitoring been like for you?" or "Do you think the self-monitoring has been helpful, or not helpful, . . . or maybe mixed?" Then, in response to whatever answers we heard, we could ask questions that invited each partner to justify the response or we could ask what each partner might prefer (part 4). Questions such as "Why has the self-monitoring not been helpful?" or "What would you prefer instead of the self-monitoring?" would be useful here. We would then go on to ask similar questions about each of the effects on the list.

When we thoroughly map a statement of position, we invite deconstruction of the problematic story in several ways. It is such a clear and useful format that we often follow it closely. However, there are times when following any kind of set protocol would not feel appropriate. Even then, we believe that familiarity with this format helps us act so as to deconstruct problems rather than solidifying them.

---

*White's format suggests justifying the evaluation in this step. We have found that asking people what they would prefer instead of the effect is also useful.

DEVELOPING PREFERRED STORIES

We are not interested in negating or getting rid of the problematic stories that bring people to consult with us. Rather, we are interested in storying other events so that each person's life narrative becomes more multistranded, affording many possibilities. To do this, we listen and watch for anything that would not be predicted by the problematic story. Variously called a *unique outcome* (White, 1988), a *sparkling moment* (White, 1995), and an *opening* (Freedman & Combs, 1993), an event that would not be predicted by the problematic story can be the starting point for an alternative story.

A sparkling moment may be an exception to the problematic story, but it is not limited to that. It can be anything that would not be predicted by the problematic story. It could even happen concurrently with the problem

Clinical Example

Maryann lost custody of her daughter in a vicious divorce. She had initiated the divorce to protect her daughter from her partner's abusive actions, so the judge's decision was heartrending.

Years later, she sought help because of a growing distance from her daughter. As a teenager, her daughter was no longer interested in visiting, and Maryann felt more and more shut out. This growing distance had many effects. One was that she did not socialize with colleagues at work. Her colleagues assumed that her daughter lived with her, and she did not want them to find out that she was a "bad mother." A unique outcome involved having lunch with a colleague. Even though it did not affect the distance between Maryann and her daughter, the guilt and worry, or even the belief that she was a bad mother, having lunch with a colleague constituted a unique outcome. Her social life had been controlled to some extent by the problematic story. The new relationship at work offered an alternative story about Maryann. It held out new possibilities for connection.

Once we collaboratively agree that an event is indeed a unique outcome, we ask questions that invite the person to develop its story. I asked about details of how Maryann had decided to accept the lunch invitation and what it was like to spend an hour getting to know someone and letting that person know her. As she answered, Maryann described not just a new relationship, but an alternative way of knowing and appreciating herself. As she remembered and arranged the details of the lunch story, they connected with earlier life experiences, which became part of the history of this new one. The lunch story did not take away or solve the problem of distance with her daughter, but it did contribute to changing her relationship with herself. In the long run, the threads of this plot-line did support changes in her relationship with her daughter.

As we work to develop alternative stories, we listen for events and examples that fit with people's preferred directions in life. We endeavor to ask questions about details, steps, and turning points so that people remember and relate more and more examples of preferred stories in experientially vivid ways.

THICKENING PREFERRED STORIES

As people begin to enter preferred stories about their lives and relationships, we work to thicken those stories—to keep them present and growing. Stories become important in people's lives through telling and retelling. Each time it is told, a story is treated as meaningful, as worth repeating. In our poststructuralist worldview, stories have meaning only when they are *performed* (E. Bruner, 1986; Myerhoff, 1986; White, 1997). This notion informs our work in a variety of ways.

We document the stories that people tell us, taking careful notes in their own words. We often begin interviews by reading our notes from the previous meeting. Both the documentation and the reading back of the document are performances of meaning that thicken the texture and the significance of the story.

From time to time, we also make more formal documents to record accomplishments, stands in life, and steps that people have taken, and this formal documentation serves to thicken the meaning of preferred stories. When, as described in the section on deconstructing problematic stories, we map a statement of position, we are bringing forth the story of a problem, the effects of that problem, and a person's stand in reference to that problem. This serves to memorialize and thicken the story of that stand. When we record the stand in a formal document (suitable for framing and available for re-reading), we further thicken its memorableness and meaning.

Similarly, we can replay a tape of a meeting, allowing people to witness their own stories. We sometimes send letters between meetings so that we can retell preferred stories and ask questions that might develop the stories even more (Epston, 1998). People have told us that they experience these letters as worth many face-to-face meetings.

CREATING AN AUDIENCE

People's relationships are critical to their sense of identity. An audience for a preferred story offers an opportunity for heightened performance of meaning. Tellings and retellings within a community strongly shape one's sense of identity. As helpers, we are an audience of one for preferred stories. Through questions such as those that follow, we can help identify a larger audience—one that a person can hold in his or her heart and mind—which, through their witnessing, will thicken the meaning of any new story.

1. Who in your life would have predicted that you could have taken this step? What have they witnessed that would have led to this prediction?
2. Who else do you know who stands for _____, like you stand for it? If there were a _____ team that you belonged to, who else would be on it?
3. Who most appreciates this new direction you are taking?

We may also invite other people to really join in. The witnessing format we have described earlier helps people be an audience for each other's preferred meanings. When we have the permission of the people who consult with us, we may invite others to witness the work, either by joining our conversation in a witnessing position, or, more formally, as members of an outsider witness group (White, 1995, 1997, 2000; Freedman & Combs, 2002).

An outsider witness group can be made up of therapists or of people with personal knowledge of particular problems. They listen to a conversation, often from behind a one-way mirror. At a point in the session, often about two-thirds of the way through the allotted time, everyone switches places so that the people who originally sought consultation can witness the outsider witness group's reflections. In their conversation, the outsider witness group retells stories told in the interview, acknowledging the reverberations the stories have in their own lives and raising questions that they have about further details and ramifications of the stories. After the outsider witness group's conversation, the consultant interviews the people who have sought consultation about what has most interested them in the outsider witness group's conversation.

CONCLUSION

We'd like to end with a brief summary of the helping process we have just described. Please remember that, in practice, it is much more improvisational and ever-changing than any brief description can convey.

First, we listen to the stories people tell us as stories, not as symptoms in need of diagnosis or as surface clues to deep meaning. We keep in mind that there are always other stories, and that other stories would offer different possibilities. We work to deconstruct problematic stories by locating them in larger cultural stories and by exposing how they have been constructed and examining the effects of those constructions. We ask questions that facilitate the storying of events that wouldn't be predicted by the problematic stories. We endeavor to thicken those stories. We think, together with the people who are consulting us, about who might form an audience for the alternative stories. As it seems appropriate, we encourage and facilitate the circulation of preferred alternative stories.

The primary tool that we use in this work is questions. We use questions not to gather information, but to *generate experience* (Freedman & Combs, 1996a). We are interested in helping people reexperience and relive the preferred stories of their lives, so we ask questions about details, sequences of events through time, other people, other perspectives, and meaning—the kinds of things that writers use to make events into stories.

Most important, through it all we believe that there are always alternative stories. We endeavor to see through the problematic stories that are coloring people's identities and relationships and to believe that there are other possibilities. We don't know from moment to moment what those possibilities will be; we don't know which questions will be most useful in beginning to author them; but we do know that each person has a life full of experiences that contradict the dominant plots of their lives.

PERSONAL REFLECTIONS

In the days before narrative therapy had a name, we met Michael White, witnessed his work, and heard about his ideas. Having been political activists since the 1960s, we recognized and delighted in the opportunities this way of working provided. It helped us to recognize more fully politics in people's situations and to strive more consistently for social justice. What we didn't recognize at the time was that the worldview was more important than the practices. We now see the world and our own lives—not just our work lives—through the dual lenses of the narrative metaphor and poststructuralist ideas. This has been tremendously enriching and important for us. These ideas guide us in how we try to contribute to our communities. We hope that readers of our chapter will be inspired to learn more about narrative ideas and practices.

KEY CONCEPTS

- reductionistic scientific discourse
- deconstructing problematic stories
- narrative metaphor
- witnessing
- externalizing
- poststructuralism
- modern power
- developing preferred stories
- thickening preferred stories
- creating an audience
- social discourses

QUESTIONS FOR REFLECTION

1. What are some of the major differences between the scientific modernist view of problems and the narrative postmodernist view of problems?
2. How are problems embedded in the social discourses of society?
3. How might gender and culture be reflected in social discourses that support our clients' problems?
4. How does a narrative conversation open up new possibilities for resisting social discourses?
5. How might you incorporate narrative ideas into your practice?

EXERCISE

Questioning Modern Power and Its Operations

In our quest to unmask discourses and make visible some of the workings of modern power in domains such as gender and culture, we have found it helpful to read widely in poststructuralist literature, to participate in discussions among people of different genders and cultures about power and privilege, and to reflect on the workings of modern power in our own lives. We offer the following set of questions as an example of how we invite people who attend our workshops to enter into this sort of discussion and reflection.* We recognize that people live with different degrees of privilege and marginalization. With this exercise, we do not intend to equate one person's experience with any other person's.

Although one person can fruitfully consider the questions on his or her own, we have found they are especially effective in a group, especially if each person in turn responds to each question before the whole group moves on to the next question. This facilitates an interweaving of the threads of each person's individual experience, producing a rich tapestry of the discourses that shape the stories. Because we believe it is useful for people to stay experientially involved as their stories unfold, we ask participants in such groups to wait until the end to respond to each other's stories.

1. You have probably already reflected at some time or other on how your culture (if not at home, then at school, in the neighborhood, in religious institutions, in media, and so on) has modeled norms, standards, ideals, values, hierarchies, and the like for you. The stories you saw being lived out within the influence of these norms showed you who was a legitimate member of society; they told you whether and how you did or didn't qualify for positions of power and influence in the world. What *specific incident* can you recall in which you got the message that you didn't "measure up" or belong (as an individual or by virtue of race, class, gender, and so on)?

    We believe that you will get the most from this exercise if you revisit the story of a particular incident rather than a generalization. Perhaps your experiences of marginalization were not extreme, or maybe you experienced such extreme marginalization that it is difficult to talk about in a group. These are important considerations and need to be treated with care if this exercise is being done in a group. Nevertheless, the experience will be more compelling if you can find a specific incident that you can safely consider.

2. What was the meaning of this incident to you? What generalizations did incidents such as this one invite you to make? Did you draw conclusions about who "counts" and who doesn't? about who has a voice and who doesn't? What conclusions did the incident invite you to make about the possibilities for your future? What paths were open to you and what ones were closed? (*What did the incident teach you about power and privilege?*)

3. What have been some of the effects of the lessons in step 2 on your life and your relationships?

4. Even though this marginalization occurred, what is an example of a time you were able to act outside of its limits? (To experience voice, agency, choice, freedom to act according to your own values, and so on.)

    Again, you will get more from this exercise if you find the story of a particular incident.

---

*We (Freedman & Combs, 1996b) have previously published an earlier version of this exercise.

5. How were you able to transcend the stories and the models offered by the marginalizing events? What does it mean that you were able to act as you did in this new incident? What person or people stood by you through this or went before you and thus let you know this was possible? What abilities does it show that you have? What did you learn in the process that might help people who come to you for help transcend similar models?

6. What possibilities might it open for your future if this way of being becomes even more available to you? How would relationships between people who consult with you be different if this way of being was part of the dominant societal norms and values?

References

Bruner, E. (1986). Ethnography as narrative. In V. W. Turner & E. M. Bruner (Eds.), *The anthropology of experience* (pp. 139–155). Chicago: University of Illinois Press.

Bruner, J. (1986). *Actual minds/possible worlds.* Cambridge, MA: Harvard University Press.

Combs, G., & Freedman, J. (2002). Relationships, not boundaries. *Theoretical Medicine, 23,* 203–217.

Epston, D. (1998). Expanding the conversation. In D. Epston, *Catching up with David Epston: A collection of narrative practice-based papers published between 1991 & 1996* (pp. 95–110). Adelaide, Australia: Dulwich Centre Publications. (First published in *Family Therapy Networker,* Nov.–Dec., 1994.)

Foucault, M. (1965). *Madness and civilization: A history of insanity in the age of reason* (R. Howard, Trans.). New York: Random House.

Foucault, M. (1975). *The birth of the clinic: An archeology of medical perception* (A. M. Sheridan Smith, Trans.). New York: Random House.

Foucault, M. (1977). *Discipline and punish: The birth of the prison* (A. Sheridan, Trans.). New York: Pantheon Books.

Foucault, M. (1980). *Power/knowledge: Selected interviews and other writings, 1972-1977* (C. Gordon, Ed.). New York: Pantheon Books.

Foucault, M. (1985). *The history of sexuality, vol. 2: The use of pleasure* (R. Hurley, Trans.). New York: Pantheon Books.

Freedman, J., & Combs, G. (1993). Invitations to new stories: Using questions to explore alternative possibilities. In S. Gilligan & R. Price (Eds.), *Therapeutic conversations* (pp. 291–303). New York: Norton.

Freedman, J., & Combs, G. (1996a). *Narrative therapy: The social construction of preferred realities.* New York: Norton.

Freedman, J., & Combs, G. (1996b). Gender stories. *Journal of Systemic Therapies, 15*(1), 31–44.

Freedman, J., & Combs, G. (2002). Using reflecting teams. In A. R. Roberts & G. J. Greene (Eds.), *Social workers' desk reference* (pp. 417–420). New York: Oxford University Press.

Freedman, J., & Combs, G. (2002a). Narrative couple therapy. In A. Gurman & N. Jacobson (Eds.), *Clinical handbook of couple therapy* (3rd ed.) (pp. 308–334). New York: Guilford Press.

Geertz, C. (1973). *The interpretation of cultures.* New York: Basic Books.

Geertz, C. (1983). *Local knowledge: Further essays in interpretive anthropology.* New York: Basic Books.

Hare-Mustin, R. (1994). Discourses in the mirrored room: A postmodern analysis of therapy. *Family Process, 33*(1), 19–35.

Madigan, S., & Law, I. (1992). Discourse not language: The shift from a modernist view of language to the postmodern analysis of discourse in family therapy. *Dulwich Centre Newsletter,* (1), 31–36.

Mann, S., & Russell, S. (2002). Narrative ways of working with women survivors of childhood sexual abuse. *International Journal of Narrative Therapy and Community Work, 3,* 3–21.

Myerhoff, B. (1986). Life not death in Venice: Its second life. In V. Turner & E. Bruner (Eds.), *The anthropology of experience* (pp. 261–286). Chicago: University of Illinois Press.

Ryle, G. (1990). *Collected papers: Critical essays and collected essays 1929–68.* Bristol, England: Thoemmes Press. (Originally published 1971.)

Weingarten, K. (2000). Witnessing, wonder, and hope. *Family Process, 39*(4), 389–402.

White, M. (1988). The process of questioning: A therapy of literary merit? *Dulwich Centre Newsletter,* Winter, 8–14.

White, M. (1988–89). The externalizing of the problem and the re-authoring of lives and relationships. *Dulwich Centre Newsletter,* Summer, 3–20.

White, M. (1995). *Re-authoring lives: Interviews and essays.* Adelaide, Australia: Dulwich Centre Publications.

White, M. (1997). *Narratives of therapists' lives.* Adelaide, Australia: Dulwich Centre Publications.

White, M, (2000). *Reflections on narrative practice: Interviews & essays.* Adelaide, Australia: Dulwich Centre Publications.

White, M. (2002). Workshop notes published on Dulwich Centre Web site. Available at www.dulwichcentre.com.au/articles/mwworkshopnotes.

White, M., & Epston, D. (1990). *Narrative means to therapeutic ends.* New York: W. W. Norton.

Zimmerman, J., & Dickerson, V. (1996). *If problems talked: Narrative therapy in action.* New York: Guilford Press.

CHAPTER

4

MENTAL HEALTH PRACTICE FOR THE MUSLIM ARAB POPULATION IN ISRAEL

ALEAN AL-KRENAWI AND
JOHN R. GRAHAM
ISRAEL AND CANADA

OVERVIEW

Muslim Arabs in Israel, like other postcolonial populations, have reason to be ambivalent toward modern mental health services. On the one hand, certain forms of intervention, particularly medicinal, may improve the lives of many in the population (Al-Krenawi & Graham, 1996). On the other hand, mental health services, as part of the colonial process, continue to have limited cultural sensitivity toward the Arab population, as they do to other non-Western communities as elaborated in a wide body of literature on services for various populations, including African, Asian, Australian and North American Aboriginal, and South American (Al-Krenawi & Graham, 2000; Al-Issa, 1990; Chakraborty, 1990; Ilechukwu, 1991; Kilonzo & Simmons, 1998; Madu, 1998; Ng, 1998; Waldram, 1997; Weaver, 1998). Indeed, one observer describes psychiatry's relationship to culture as "ambiguous." According to Littlewood (1996), "Contemporary clinical understandings of culture derive from imperial medicine, which had applied the accepted distinction between the biological form and the cultural content of psychopathology to local illnesses that could not easily be fitted into the European nosology" (p. 245). Moreover, mental health services are widely understood to have consequences and motivations that are political. Delivery systems in some instances—such as in China (Lee, 2002) and the Soviet Union (Bloch, 1991; Gluzman, 2001)—have explicitly served political regimes that oppress populations whose ideologies are contrary to or perceived as threats to the ruling regimes. In other instances, the psychiatric–political relationship may be less overt but still significant in carrying out social control and in defining deviance and social exclusion (Jablensky, 1992; Furedi, Barcy, Kapusi, & Novak, 1993). We will argue that it is impossible to appreciate services for Arab Muslims in Israel without reference to the geopolitics of the Middle East—particularly the relationship between Arabs and Jews in Israel.

This chapter asserts that mental help service delivery for Muslim Arab population in Israel is inextricably linked to Arab religious and cultural identity as experienced through the prism of politics, gender, and social marginalization. Effective knowledge, intervention, and methods are important to intervention; but so too are the political and cultural contexts in which they are conceived and executed.

THE ARAB ISRAELIS IN CONTEXT

Since the 1948 establishment of the Israeli state, populations of Arab descent have experienced oppression, trauma, social exclusion, and related socioeconomic and political problems. Indeed, 1948 is described by Arab population as "Al-Nakba" (the Catastrophe). Arabs made up the majority of inhabitants of Palestine before 1948. As a result of the war and the establishment of the state of Israel, 84% of Palestinians were exiled and became refugees (Kanaana, 1992). Those Palestinians who remained found they were a minority in what had become a Jewish state. Of a pre-1948 Palestinian population of 950,000, two categories of Palestinian refugees—external and internal—were created. Approximately 800,000 Palestinians were expelled from the country and were forced to become refugees in the Arab states; 150,000 Palestinians remained within the boundaries of the new state of Israel. Close to 25% of those who remained within the state were displaced from their homes to other locations, thus becoming internal refugees (http://www.arabhra.org/; Wakim, 1994).

Since the establishment of Israel, Zionist ideology precipitated state confiscation of a large amount of land owned by the Israeli Arabs (Lustick, 1993; Yiftachel, 1996, 2000). The psychosocial and economic consequences have been severe: Members of the population lost their homes, livelihood, and political power; families were displaced and separated; and communities were destroyed. Between the establishment of Israel in 1948 and 1967, the Arabs in Israel were under a military regime. The traumatic impact of this social exclusion continues to the present time as reported by Israeli and other scholars (Ghanem, 1998; Lustick, 1980; Yiftachel, 2000).

Palestinians are now a minority within Israel, constituting 1 million, or 18% of the country's total population of 6 million. The vast majority resides in all-Arab towns and villages located in three main areas: the Galilee in the north (where Palestinians make up approximately 50% of the population), the "Little Triangle" in the center, and the border that separates Israel from the occupied West Bank (Central Bureau of Statistics, 1998, Table 2.1). More than 700,000 Palestinians are Muslims, roughly 150,000 Christians, and almost 100,000 Druze, Circassian, or other groups (Aviram, 1996). Of the 18.5% of the non-Jewish population in Israel, 81.8% is Muslim, 9.4% is Christian, and 8.8% is Druze (Israeli Government, 2002).

The Arab population is discriminated against in multiple respects. There continue to be huge gaps in the quality of life between Arab and Jewish Israelis (Israeli Government, 2002). More than 100 Palestinian Arab villages in Israel lack official government recognition. More than 70,000 Palestinian Arab citizens live in villages that are threatened with destruction, prevented from being developed, and not shown on any map (Central Bureau of Statistics, 1998, Table 2.1). More than 36% of Arab children are under the poverty line, compared to 18% of Jewish children. A study by ADVA (the Center for Information on Equality and Social Justice in Israel) notes that between 1990 and 1999 the average annual per capita income of Arab localities in Israel was 2.4 New Israeli Shekels (NIS), compared to 3.8 NIS across Israel (http://www.adva.org/settele/settel.htm; Swirski & Konor-Attias, 2001). In 1996, the average income per person for an Arab household was 44.1% of that for Jewish households (http://www.arabhra.org/). Arab women suffer from a higher proportion of this poverty. In 1997, 80% of Arab women of working age did not work, compared to 45.8% of women nationwide (Central Bureau of Statistics, 1998, Table 12.5). The average income for women in Israel is 57% of the average male income, just as the average income of an Arab man is 68% of that of a Jewish man. In May 2001, a discussion held in the House of the President of the State of Israel (*Poverty in Israel*, 2001) revealed that 42% of the Arab families in Israel are poor compare to 14% in the Jewish sector.

Despite the achievements of Israel's education system, there are great disparities between Arabs and Jews in facilities, funding allocations, number of pupils per class, and academic achievement. In 1997, 42% of Arab students dropped out of school, compared with 12% of Jewish students (Center for Bedouin Studies and Development, 1998). Funding structures for education, as for other municipal and social services, disproportionately hurt the Arab population. For instance, of the 50 localities that receive the lowest government allocations for education, 41 are Arab (Israeli Government, 1997, p. 319).

Though it has declined absolutely over the last few decades, the infant mortality rate for Arabs is still more than twice as high as for Jews: 9.3 per 1,000 live births, as compared to 4.9 per 1,000. The difference is especially striking in the post–neonatal mortality rates (i.e., deaths occurring from 28 to 365 days after birth): 5.8 per 1,000 for Arabs in Israel, and 1.8 per 1,000 for Jews (http://www.arabhra.org/). According to the Israeli Center for Disease Control (1999), "Mortality at this age is primarily related to environmental causes such as infectious diseases and accidents, most of which are preventable" (pp. 39–41).

The Arab social structure emphasizes the collective over the individual, has a slower pace of societal change, and a higher sense of social stability (Al-Krenawi, Graham, & Sehwail, 2002). The family, therefore, is particularly important to the interrelationship between the individual and group, as well as in determining their social and economic status. There are three main Arab family units: the *hamula* (kinship group extending to a wide network of family relations), the extended family (consisting of parents, siblings, their spouses and children), and the nuclear family (the married couple and children) (Al-Haj, 1989). Israeli Arabs tend to have large families. The average Arab nuclear family numbers 5.53, with 3.4 children per family compared with 2.28 children in the average Israeli Jewish family (Dolev et al., 1996).

ARAB WOMEN

Arab society is patriarchal, maintaining men's leadership authority in the household, economy, and polity (Al-Haj, 1987; Al-Krenawi, 1996) and putting women at a structural disadvantage in family and community life (Al-Issa, 1990; Al-Sadawi, 1977; Brhoom, 1987; El-Islam, 1994; Mass & Al-Krenawi, 1994). Women's social status is strongly contingent upon being married and rearing children, especially boys (Al-Sadawi, 1977). Marriages are arranged for girls by parents or parent substitutes; in some cases, even if the girl expresses her objections or desires, a marriage occurs or is forbidden. Marital choice of spouse is based on the family's collective decisions in light of power and status relationships that are intra-familial, intra-extended familial, or intra-*hamula* (Al-Haj, 1987).

Divorced Arab women suffer emotionally and socially (Al-Krenawi & Graham, 1998). Many mothers endure years of marital problems in order to avoid the stigma of divorce or the prospect of losing their children. A divorced woman's marital prospects are poor and usually restricted to becoming the second wife of a married man or the wife of a widower or of an older man (Al-Krenawi & Graham, 1998; Cohen & Savaya, 2000). For both sexes, advanced years and experience are associated with wisdom and knowledge; hence the popular Arab expression "Anyone who is a day older than you in age is a year older than you in understanding." In some communities, postmenopausal women, especially mothers of powerful men, may have considerable power and formal and informal social influence upon virtually all aspects of family life (Al-Krenawi & Graham, 2003).

The stigmatizing nature of mental health issues, to say nothing of expressing problems to those outside of one's community, make it especially difficult for women to access and receive treatment (Al-Krenawi & Graham, 2000). Several scholars have suggested interventions that take into account gender differences. These include, but are not limited to, client–practitioner gender matching where possible (Mass & Al-Krenawi, 1994) and encouraging natural support networks (Al-Krenawi & Graham, 2000) and treatment locations that are accessible to women who often cannot travel outside their community to seek professional help (Al-Krenawi, 1996). Also important is for practitioners to understand the impact—which may be experienced differently between the sexes—of such common psychosocial problems as marital distress, polygamy, or child protection or custody and access (Al-Krenawi & Graham, 2001, 2003).

CLINICAL RESPONSES TO THE CHALLENGES OF WORKING WITH THE MUSLIM ARAB POPULATION IN ISRAEL

The above socioeconomic, cultural, and political contexts of the Muslim Arab population in Israel strongly influence approaches to mental health. This chapter calls for an indigenization of mental health—that it be more consciously adapted, in theory and methods, to the culture in which it is applied (Drower, 2000; Ragab, 1990). Indeed, in many instances, practice may be different from, if not contrary to, assumptions in mainstream mental health.

There are few Arab psychiatrists, Arab clinical psychologists, and *practicing* mental health service social workers in Israel. As a result, practitioners are often outside of the Arab patient's culture. Moreover, the accessibility and availability of these services to the Arab population is poor, occasioning long drives outside the community to access services. Likewise, practice modalities, in the absence of indigenization, are outside the patient's culture. As elaborated at the end of the chapter in Table 4.1, there are several therapeutic requirements in working with Muslim Arab population in Israel. The following paragraphs elucidate several points made in that table, focusing on gender and culture in particular.

Throughout the Arab world, including Arabs in Israel, there is a negative view of psychiatry. As a result, more culturally acceptable somatic symptoms are especially prevalent (Al-Issa, 1995; Racy, 1980), expectations for medicinal treatment are high (Al-Krenawi, 2002), and low utilization of mental health services is widespread (Al-Krenawi, Graham, & Kandah, 2000; Al-Subaie & Al-Hamad, 2000; Okasha, 1999). An Israeli government survey concludes that Arabs in Israel consume mental health services at a rate of 0.5 per 1,000 as compared with 3.3 per 1,000 among Jewish Israelis (Al-Krenawi, 2002). Of those Arabs utilizing services, 62% were men and 38% women—which is consistent with other research confirming the Arab population's underutilization of social services in Israel (Al-Krenawi, 2002) and of mental health and health services throughout the Arab world (Qureshi, Al-Armi, & Abdelgader, 1998; Al-Krenawi & Graham, 1999, 2000; Al-Krenawi et al., 2000). Arab women's use of mental health services is particularly low. It should be noted that such findings are contrary to some other societies. In Canada, as an example, women in one study were substantially higher users of health services for psychiatric problems than were men (D'Arcy & Schmitz, 1979). Rates of termination among Israeli Arabs are likewise higher (Savaya, 1997).

The Arab population tends to feel more stigmatized when seeking mental health services (Al-Krenawi & Graham, 1999, 2000; Al-Subaie & Al-Hamad, 2000; Savaya, 1995; Al-Krenawi et al., 2000). Traditionally, Arab individuals are supposed to deal with their problems by themselves and to seek help only from family members. Therefore, some Arab individuals consider it shameful and inappropriate to acquire help from outsiders—particularly those from outside the patient's culture—to treat psychological and social problems, thus convincing them to delay treatment or seek less-stigmatizing traditional methods to overcome their problems (Al-Krenawi et al., 2000).

Low utilization rates have been attributed to the fact that cultural sensitivity and religious belief have substantial influences on Arab attitudes toward formal mental health services. Many barriers that may influence the individual to avoid seeking formal services were observed within these studies. These include the use of alternative resources for informal healing and treatment (Al-Krenawi & Graham, 1999, 2000), the stigma and shame associated with mental illness (Al-Subaie & Al-Hamad, 2000), the individual's negative attitudes toward formal mental health professionals (Savaya, 1995), and the lack of knowledge of formal mental health services and their availability, importance, and existence (Okasha, 1999). There is political significance to the Arab population in Israel consulting religious leaders or one of several forms of traditional healers during times of psychosocial distress. Healing practices and terminologies vary within Israel's Arab regions. By using the indigenous approach to help, as part of the cultural practices of the Arab in Israel, members of the Arab population are reinforcing part of their culture, collective memory, and identity. Not surprisingly, Koranic healing is an especially noteworthy and growing practice in the Islamic Arab world, including Israel (Al-Krenawi & Graham, 1999).

Al Abdul Jabbar and Al-Issa point out that "publications on psychotherapy in the Arab-Islamic world are rather limited" (2000, p. 278). But there is much potential in enhancing research, theory, and practice with the Arab Muslim population. The psychological values of Islam emphasize particular beliefs, ways of individual behavior, and norms of group involvement in identifying and responding to mental health problems (Al-Krenawi & Graham, 2000). Islam can provide many supporting beliefs to enhance psychotherapeutic process, among them patience (Al-Esawi, 1986), hope, responsibility for individual behavior (Al Abdul Jabbar & Al-Issa, 2000), utilization of group and community support, and use of various religious practices and rituals that enhance group support, catharsis, sense of belonging, and individual well-being (Al-Krenawi & Graham, 1996). (For more on Islam and the helping professions, see Al-Krenawi & Graham, 2000.)

Arab people grow up in a culture that is authoritarian and therefore expect the practitioner to be directive and to advise them like a *hakim* (wise person) (West, 1987). Yet the Arab population's cultural and political experiences may preclude an easy acceptance of this role in a Jewish practitioner. Trust, one of the most basic principles of a helping alliance, may be difficult to achieve for a variety of reasons, including the accumulated impact of political experiences of the patient's population. So, too, might the extensive familial involvement of the Arab patient reinforce such sentiments. Such factors are complicated by gender constructions in Arab society. Cross-gender, social worker–client relations may have complex nuances. Some male clients, for example, may have difficulty accepting a female social worker's directions. Often the difficulty is not necessarily from the male client himself but from a male family member in a position of authority such as a father, uncle, older brother, or any older male family member (Irani, 1999). If the clinician is the opposite sex, then eye contact should be kept to a minimum, and the use of such terms as *sister* and *brother* may be helpful (Mass & Al-Krenawi, 1994).

Members of the Arab population may learn that occurrences in life are determined by external powers—such as family, social leaders, life experiences, or God. This perspective may be reinforced by a community or family context that is collective. Individual responsibility for behavior may not be perceived in isolation of others within the community (Al-Krenawi, 1999, 2000; Bazzoui, 1970; West, 1987). The agency of mental health problems may be seen as a combination of the biomedical, human, supernatural, or political (discrimination, oppression, social exclusion). Arab clients readily understand the socioeconomic and political deprivations they experience in light of their social exclusion in Israel as resulting from the policies of the state. Clinicians should be aware of this worldview in light of the Arab community's political and economic

CASE 4.1

As Al-Krenawi and Graham point out (2001, pp. 674–676):

The case begins with a dispute between a husband and wife, married six years. The wife had a disagreement with the husband's mother over the latter's involvement in her daily life. Because of it, the husband retained his five children and insisted that the wife return home to her parents. The husband's immediate family cared for the children, ages 1 month to 5 years. Theirs had been an exchange marriage: where two men are married to each other's sister. The same day that the wife's brother learned of his sister's plight, he, in turn, retained sole custody of his children and sent his own wife (the first husband's sister) home to her parents. This reciprocal action was seen to have retained power symmetry between the two families, and hence the integrity of his family honour.

These actions immediately precipitated tensions between the two extended families, both of which were within the same tribe and were of comparable social status. Within 20 days of the initial husband sending home his wife, a third husband, in response to increased intra-family tensions, decided to retain custody of his children and send his wife home to her parents. Theirs, too, was an exchange marriage, which led to a fourth husband immediately sending his wife home to her parents, in response to the third husband's actions.

The actions of the third and fourth husband further increased tensions between the two families. There was an increasing likelihood that all communication between the two families would be cut off, and that the four marriages would end in divorce. The first wife visited a general practitioner physician with complaints of anxiety, depression, fatigue, and various stress-related somatic symptoms. The physician, who was not an Arab, in turn referred the woman to one of Rahat's social workers for counselling. The social worker was a Bedouin-Arab from a family of comparable social status to the other two families, and within another of Rahat's tribes. He held bi-weekly sessions with the woman and conducted a visit to the husband's home, where he met the husband, the husband's father, and other male relatives. The social worker explained to the men that he was legally obligated to have the children immediately returned to the mother, according to Israeli law, and that if they did not agree to this plan, the police would have to get involved. (It should be noted that Islam also insists that young children be in custody of a mother, if she is well.) The men were angered by the social worker's intervention, and sent a family delegate to the social worker's family, explaining to the family *sheikh* that further involvement from the social worker would create a dispute between their extended family and the social worker's.

Male elders within his extended family and tribe met with the social worker, and insisted that he not involve himself in the case. The social worker explained that his job legally obligated him to do so. The elders responded that the man should either desist, or quit his job, since the integrity of their family and tribal relations was the greatest priority. The social worker thus had a major dilemma between the cultural and professional canons.

In consultation with his supervisor, the social worker met with four wasits, two from each disputing family and two from other families not involved in the dispute but within the tribe. Together, the social worker and one of the wasits developed three goals. The first and most immediate was to return the children to their mothers. The second was to have the four women return to their husbands, and the third was to restore relations between the two families.

The wasits met separately with powerful representatives from both families. They heard both parties' stories, allowing for the expression of anger and frustration, ate with members of each side, and used cultural stories, such as those that correlated bravery with forgiveness. In discussing the children, the wasits did not appeal to legal explanations. Rather, there were two other arguments. The first was to keep the problem within the tribe, and not to have a member from an outside tribe, or legal apparatuses such as a social worker, the police, or courts, involved. The second was an appeal to the benefits of returning the children to their mother. Both arguments were common ground upon which all parties could agree. On the strength of their reputations, the wasits were able to provide sufficient assurances that the children would be well cared for upon

(continued)

their return to the mothers. The wasits would also act as go-betweens, were any concerns to arise over the children's well being. Also because of their standing, the wasits were able to be directive, and to insist that the children be returned before any further discussions occurred. Within two days of initial contact, the wasits had personally delivered the children to their respective mothers. Over the course of this stage of intervention, the social worker had been apprised of the process.

Turning to the second objective, the wasits had conversations with the first wife, her parents, her mother-in-law, and powerful leaders on both sides. The wasits obtained assurances from the mother-in-law that she would not interfere in the wife's day-to-day affairs as much as she had.

Thereafter, having obtained consensus among these parties, the wife apologized to the mother-in-law, in the presence of the wasits and agreed to respect and obey the mother-in-law, just as she would her own mother. These two compromises led the wife, accompanied by the wasits, to return to her husband. The same day, the other three wives returned to their husbands, accompanied by the wasits.

Stage three, which occurred within 30 days of the initial incident, was a *sulha,* in which powerful male members of each extended family met in the house of the tribe's *sheikh,* one of the wasits. The men shook hands, ate a meal, and agreed that the entire matter would be dropped. With this ritual completed, the social work case was closed.

---

marginalization. But getting at these phenomena may be especially challenging given the commonality of restrained, formal, impersonal communication styles among Arab clients, as well as their use of metaphors and proverbs that may be unfamiliar to the practitioner from an outside culture.

Interventions that are directive and use short-term cognitive or behavioral theoretical assumptions with clear and concrete targets, and those that provide guidance, advice, explanations, and instructions, are helpful among such non-Western societies as the Arab in Israel (Al-Krenawi & Graham, 2000). The practitioner may represent a symbol of authority, going back to the client's relationship with parents (Al-Krenawi & Graham, 2000). This dynamic is likewise political, particularly if the practitioner is Jewish and the client is Arab. As some have observed, "the ongoing Israeli-Arab conflict has its impact on the mental health system" (Fennig, Tevesess, Kashkush, & Zmiro, 1992, p. 228). Here the usual problems of transference–countertransference may be accentuated (Gorkin, 1986), and, according to some observers, "the dialectical process of a psychotherapy is constantly endangered" (Bizi-Nathaniel, Granek, & Golomb, 1991).

All of these aspects may be exacerbated when the clinician is majority background, and the client minority. But even when the practitioner is of Arab background, problems may occur. Al-Krenawi and Graham discuss the challenges of child welfare work in one Arab Bedouin community (2001). The following case highlights the merits of a demonstration project in which various community elders are involved to mediate between social work and the cultural community. The *wasit* are well respected senior men within the collective, who initiate interventions in times of dispute within or between families, extended families, *hamula,* or tribes. In the following case, a wasit is brought in to assist a social work intervention that is rendered problematic because of the interaction between the worker's familial background and that of his client system, which is quite different.

CONCLUSION

Practice with the population of Arab origin in Israel has everything to do with gender, culture, and politics. In the absence of an indigenized approach to practice, an Arab patient might justifiably experience a threat to cultural identity. Some scholars recommend cultural matching to overcome problems inherent in cross-cultural encounters (Ibrahim, 1991). But ethnic similarity does not necessarily imply cultural similarity because of the multiplicity of factors that can influence therapy (Sue, 1988). Without appropriate training, familiarity with the political history of the patient's community, and knowledge of the culture's collective memories, a professional from the same ethnic background as the patient would not provide effective services. Intervention is even more fraught with potential difficulties if the patient is Arab and the clinician is Jewish. It is essential, therefore, that the Jewish clinician is familiar with Arab cultural history and political experiences, for these impact the encounter between Jewish clinician and Arab patient in particular. Therapy is more than skill and knowledge—it involves economic, social, and political values.

It is far better to have a shared worldview and a culturally competent approach to practice that takes into account the worldview of the client. Here issues of recruiting practitioners of Arab background and retaining their services are central. But so, too, is the nature of theory and methods themselves, and the training and upgrading that professionals receive to these ends. Understanding the political experiences that the Israeli Arab population endures is a basic principle for any practice modality in this cultural context.

As they would in other ethnospecific contexts, issues of gender, power, social hierarchy, and cultural differences influence Arab patients and their Jewish practitioners (Gorkin, 1986). Similarly, the limited fluency in Arabic among biomedical practitioners is only one factor—and not the primary one—in defining help-seeking patterns. Language is a point of entry and marker for the more profound distinction between insiders and outsiders. The healers are insiders, who are sought for ailments that are locally construed as being dependent on the social world. The biomedical practitioners are outsiders. They may be considered inept or out of place in the local social world. But they operate in a biomedical system and so possess a technical efficacy that extends both to access to treatments of the body in a highly mechanical sense and to political control (Al-Krenawi & Graham, 1999).

The fundamentally political nature of much of the intervention with the Arab population in Israel and the occupied territories is apparent in three respects. First, it is a result of political issues in the region that give rise to such problems as social dislocation, dispossession of land, and other fundamentally political issues (Al-Krenawi, Graham, & Sehwail, in press). Second, there are psychosocial responses to these problems, including posttraumatic distress and other forms of psychological and physical trauma (Al-Krenawi, Graham, & Sehwail, 2002). Third, any intervention necessarily puts the worker and client into the wider symbolic universe of Middle Eastern politics, particularly if the worker is perceived as an instrument of the state on some level (Al-Krenawi & Graham, 1996).

The Arabs are a minority population in Israel, and by virtue of their political and economic disempowerment are justifiably seen as oppressed. The level of trust between majority Israelis and their Arab counterparts varies according to political circumstance and personal disposition. But cultural competence and self-reflection are not just key components to effective multiple cultural practice (Al-Krenawi, 2002; Weaver, 1998). They are also effective means of attempting, as much as one can, to overcome the real barriers that persist precisely because of the geopolitical contexts in which both communities exist. Jews have biases toward Arab Israelis, and Arab Israelis toward Jews. The imperative in mental health practice is to allow neither to interfere with quality service. To this end, Jewish practitioners could take into account the traumatic political events that the Arab population in Israel has experienced over several generations since 1948. These continue to the present day in discrimination, stereotypes, social exclusion, and lack of services compared to mainstream Israelis. And they must be addressed. To do so is ultimately a political decision, informed by more effective mental health training and practice. This is the essence of culturally competent intervention (Al-Krenawi & Graham, 2003). Practitioners and educators have to adapt the models of intervention to be more culturally appropriate. Policy makers should ensure services that are accessible and delivered with greater cultural competence. Equally desirable are efforts at recruitment and retention of minority Arab students in various helping professional programs at Israeli universities. In the final analysis, all decision makers should reach out to the Arab population to increase its knowledge of mental health practice and to reduce the stigma and poor qualities of service that the Arab population experiences.

PERSONAL REFLECTIONS

Alean Al-Krenawi conveys his own personal and professional experiences as a Bedouin Arab who received undergraduate and advanced social work training in schools of social work in Israel and Canada. After his first university degree, he practiced for 11 years. Early in that career, especially, he noticed apparent dissonances between his home culture, with which he worked and lived on a daily basis, and the assumptions derived from the profession of social work. One of his most decisive career moments was the gradual but resolute discovery that it is essential to bend any social work knowledge, practice, theory, or skill in the direction of the community with which one works. "Walking with the wind, rather than against it" became a metaphor that subsequently guided work with his own community, and in particular his growing comfort in mediating between assumptions that are cultural on the one hand and professional on the other. If there were any one unifying theme for this chapter, walking with the wind would be the most resonant (Al-Krenawi, 1998). He and the second author, a non-Arab born and raised in central Canada, have published extensively on direct social work and mental health practice with Arab populations, especially the Bedouin Arab. Significant portions of this chapter, therefore, are referenced to direct practice.

KEY CONCEPTS

See Table 4.1.

TABLE 4.1

Guidelines	Knowledge	Skills
1. Mental health services can be stigmatizing, particularly for women.	• Knowledge of gender construction in the Arab world. • Knowledge of the psychosocial significance of mental health to both genders.	• Ability to develop programs and deliver services that are less stigmatizing to women. • Ability to work collaboratively with stigmatized populations. • Ability to work collaboratively with key community population to facilitate less-stigmatizing services.
2. Contrary to a Western therapeutic emphasis on the individual, all interventions with Arab patients need to be couched in the context of the family, extended family, community, or tribal background.	• Knowledge of customs and cultural norms of patient, family, extended family, community, and tribal backgrounds of Arab patients.	• Ability to understand and incorporate patient's identity within the family's collective identity into mental health practice in order to be therapeutic. • Ability to understand the importance of the group to individual functioning and behavior.
3. Religion is an important context in which problems are constructed and resolved.	• Knowledge of patient's religion and that of family members. • Knowledge of associated religious practices that may impact patient's behavior. • Knowledge of religious beliefs around mental health issues and associated stigmas.	• Ability to incorporate knowledge about patient's religious beliefs to adapt mental health practice so that it meets the patient's needs (i.e., so that it is not overly intrusive or disruptive of the patient's lifestyle and religious practices).
4. Arab patients' conceptions of their psychiatric or psychosocial problems perceive agency to be based on either–or combinations of the biomedical, human, or supernatural. Particular emphasis is often placed on an external locus of control.	• Knowledge of the patient's and the family's conception of the origin of problems. • Knowledge of recent events in patient's life that may contribute to currently perceived problem.	• Ability to adapt mental health practice to a different paradigm of origin of problems to be effectively therapeutic. • Ability to adapt practice to fit in with family and patient beliefs and norms.

(continued)

TABLE 4.1 | CONTINUED

Guidelines	Knowledge	Skills
5. Arab patients' communication may be restrained, formal, and impersonal. Patients' idioms of distress might rely upon a complex system of metaphors and proverbs.	• Knowledge of past communication styles and patterns of patient and Arab culture. • Knowledge of techniques that may make Arab patients more comfortable in the expression of their distress.	• Ability to assess patient's level of distress based on communication. • Ability to utilize techniques that will not compromise the patient into feeling he or she is betraying the family by divulging information. • Ability to communicate to the patient in a manner the patient is familiar with so that miscommunication and misconceptions do not occur.
6. Treatments are most successful when they are short term and directive. A worker who maintains too rigid a time frame could be perceived as cold or unreasonable.	• Knowledge of Arab cultural norms regarding psychiatric or psychosocial treatment (i.e., familiarity with an instructional-explanatory model). • Understanding of acceptable Arab time frame for psychiatric or psychosocial treatment.	• Ability to instruct patients on the nature of their problem and possibilities for solutions. • Ability to provide treatment within an acceptable time frame and in an acceptable manner.
7. There are several gender and cultural aspects that could assist a worker to sustain a helping alliance.	• Knowledge of Arab beliefs surrounding establishment and termination of relationships.	• Ability to adapt Western paradigms to fit in with patient's needs regarding a less-formal relationship with practitioner.
8. Patients often utilize mental health services and traditional healing concurrently or in succession.	• Knowledge of traditional Arab healing practices and their relevance to mental health issues. • Knowledge of which traditional healing practices are already being utilized by patient.	• Ability to integrate traditional healing with modern mental health practice.
9. Mental health practitioners can learn much from traditional healers, particularly with respect to working with families; they could also effectively collaborate with traditional healers within Arab communities.	• Knowledge of traditional healers' approaches to family practice, engaging family members, etc. • Body–mind–spirituality: a holistic view.	• Ability to effectively work with families and utilize them in mental health therapeutics. • Ability to integrate traditional and modern healing methods to mental health practice.

QUESTIONS FOR REFLECTION

1. Locate a population now in your country that has suffered from discrimination and political oppression (either in its current country or previously in its country of origin). Using the Internet, the library, and various databases, locate vital statistics and important information about this population in your country. For example:

   a. What percentage is this target group of your country's population?
   b. Where do members of this population primarily reside?
   c. What is the population's religious or ethnic composition?
   d. Which of these was the basis for discrimination and oppression against this group?
   e. What indices and evidence can you collect for this discrimination? (Check, for example, income and poverty level, services to their neighborhoods, infant mortality, government support for schools in their neighborhood, children attending school, children dropping out of school, crime level, and violence in the home.)
   f. What is the status of women in this population?
   g. In what ways do women suffer discrimination?
   h. Locate this population's health and mental health needs.
   i. Create a profile of services for this population.

EXERCISE

What are some of the traditional healing or helping methods of your own ethnic cultural group? If you don't know of any, see if you can ask someone from your family. You can also research this issue in the library or on the Internet. Try to obtain a specific story of healing or helping from your own cultural origins. Share these stories and "local knowledge" in groups of four. See what is similar and what is unique to each population. Now take one of the populations you discussed and creatively brainstorm ways in which services in each of your own settings might be modified to better serve this population.

References

Al Abdul Jabbar, J., & Al-Issa, I. (2000). Psychotherapy in Islamic society. In I. Al-Issa (Ed.), *Al-Junun: Mental Illness in the Islamic World* (pp. 277–293). Madison, CT: International Universities Press.

Al-Esawi, A. (1986). *Islam and Psychotherapy* [in Arabic]. Alexandria, Egypt: Dar Alfikr.

Al-Haj, M. (1987). *Social Change and Family Processes: Arab Communities in Shefar-A'm*. London: Westview Press.

Al-Haj, M. (1989). Social research on family lifestyles among Arabs in Israel. *Journal of Comparative Family Studies, 20*(2), 175–195.

Al-Issa, I. (1990). Culture and mental illness in Algeria. *International Journal of Social Psychiatry, 36*(3), 230–240.

Al-Issa, I. (1995). Culture and mental illness in an international perspective. In I. Al-Issa (Ed.), *Handbook of Culture and Mental Illness: An International*

Perspective (pp. 3–49). Madison, CT: International University Press.

Al-Krenawi, A. (1996). Group work with Bedouin widows of the Negev in a medical clinic. *Affilia: Journal of Women and Social Work, 11*(3), 303–318.

Al-Krenawi, A. (1998). Reconciling Western and traditional healing: A social worker walks with the wind. *Reflections: Narrative of Professional Helping, 4*(3), 6–21.

Al-Krenawi, A. (1999). Integrating cultural rituals into family therapy: A case study with a Bedouin-Arab patient in Israel. *Journal of Family Psychotherapy, 10*(1), 61–73.

Al-Krenawi, A. (2000). Bedouin-Arab clients' use of proverbs in the therapeutic setting. *International Journal for the Advancement of Counseling, 22*(2), 91–102.

Al-Krenawi, A. (2002). Mental health service utilization among the Arabs in Israel. *Social Work in Health Care, 35*(1–2), 577–589.

Al-Krenawi, A., & Graham, J. R. (1996). Tackling mental illness: Roles for old and new disciplines. *World Health Forum: An International Journal of Health Development, 17*(3), 246–248.

Al-Krenawi, A., & Graham, J. R. (1998). Divorce among Muslim Arab women in Israel. *Journal of Divorce and Remarriage, 29*(3–4), 103–119.

Al-Krenawi, A., & Graham, J. R. (1999). Gender and biomedical/traditional mental health utilization among the Bedouin-Arabs of the Negev. *Culture, Medicine and Psychiatry, 23*(2), 219–243.

Al-Krenawi, A., & Graham, J. R. (2000). Culturally sensitive social work practice with Arab clients in mental health settings. *Health & Social Work, 25*(1), 9–22.

Al-Krenawi, A., & Graham, J. R. (2001). The cultural mediator: Bridging the gap between a Non-Western community and professional social work practice. *British Journal of Social Work, 31,* 665–685.

Al-Krenawi, A., & Graham, J. R. (2003). Social work with Canadians of Arab background: Insight into direct practice. In A. Al-Krenawi & J. R. Graham (Eds.), *Multicultural social work in Canada: Working with diverse ethno-racial communities* (pp. 174–201). Toronto: Oxford University Press.

Al-Krenawi, A., Graham, J. R., & Kandah, J. (2000). Gendered utilization differences of mental health services in Jordan. *Community Mental Health Journal, 36*(5), 501–511.

Al-Krenawi, A., Graham, J. R., & Sehwail, M. (2002). Bereavement responses among Palestinian widows, daughters, and sons following the Hebron massacre. *Omega: Journal of Death and Dying, 44*(3), 241–255.

Al-Krenawi, A., Graham, J. R., & Sehwail, M. (in press). Mental health and violence/trauma in Palestine: Implications for helping professional practice. *Journal of Comparative Family Studies.*

Al-Sadawi, N. (1977). *Arab women and their psychological struggle* (in Arabic). Beirut: Al-Moassah Al-Arabiah.

Al-Subaie, A., & Al-Hamad, A. (2000). Psychiatry in Saudi Arabia. In I. Al-Issa (Ed.), *Al-Junun: Mental Illness in the Islamic World* (pp. 205–234). Madison, CT: International Universities Press.

Aviram, U. (1996). Mental health services in Israel at a crossroads: Promises and pitfalls of mental health services in the context of the new national health insurance. *International Journal of Law and Psychiatry, 19*(3–4), 327–372.

Bazzoui, W. (1970). Affective disorders in Iraq. *British Journal of Psychiatry, 117*(537), 195–203.

Bizi-Nathaniel, S., Granek, M., & Golomb, M. (1991). Psychotherapy of an Arab patient by a Jewish therapist in Israel during the Intifada. *American Journal of Psychotherapy, 45*(4), 594–603.

Bloch, S. (1991). The political misuse of psychiatry in the Soviet Union. In S. Bloch & P. Chodoff (Eds.), *Psychiatric ethics,* 2nd ed. (pp. 493–515). London: Oxford University Press.

Brhoom, M. (1987). The phenomenon of divorce in Jordan. *Deraast* (in Arabic), *13*(12), 189–205.

Center for Bedouin Studies and Development. (1998). *Facts about Negev Bedouin Arab Education*. Beer Sheva, Israel: Ben-Gurion University of the Negev.

Central Bureau of Statistics. (1998). *Statistical abstract of Israel*, no. 49 (Tables 2.1, 12.5, 12.7). Jerusalem: Author.

Chakraborty, A. (1990). Social stress and mental health: A social-psychiatric field study of Calcutta. Thousand Oaks, CA: Sage.

Cohen, O., & Savaya, R. (2000). Help wanted and help received by Israeli divorced custodial fathers. *Journal of Applied Social Psychology, 30*(7), 1440–1456.

D'Arcy, C., & Schmitz, J. A. (1979). Sex differences in the utilization of health services for psychiatric problems in Saskatchewan. *Canadian Journal of Psychiatry, 24*(1), 19–27.

Dolev, T., Aronin, H., Ben-Rabi, D., Clyman, L., Cohen, L., Trajteberg, S., Levy, J., & Yoal, A. (1996). *An overview of children and youth in Israel: Policies, programs and philanthropy* (in Hebrew). Jerusalem: Center for Children and Youth, JDC-Brookdale Institute.

Drower, S. J. (2000). Globalization: An opportunity for dialogue between South African and Asian social work educators. *Indian Journal of Social Work, 61*(1), 12–31.

El-Islam, M. F. (1994). Cultural applications of social psychiatry in Arabian gulf communities. *Arab Journal of Psychiatry, 5*(2), 77–82.

Fennig, S., Tevesess, I., Kashkush, G., & Zmiro, G. (1992). The Arab nurse and the Jewish psychotic patient in the closed psychiatric ward. *International Journal of Social Psychiatry, 38*(3), 228–234.

Furedi, J., Barcy, M., Kapusi, G., & Novak, J. (1993). Family therapy in transitional society. *Psychiatry, 56*(4), 328–337.

Ghanem, A. (1998). State and minority in Israel: The case of ethnic state and the predicament of its minority. *Ethnic and Racial Studies, 21*(3), 428–447.

Gluzman, S. (2001). Abuse of psychiatry in Ukraine. *Archives of Psychiatry and Psychotherapy, 3*(3), 73–83.

Gorkin, M. (1986). Countertransference in cross-cultural psychotherapy: The example of Jewish therapist and Arab patient psychiatry. *Journal for the Study of Interpersonal Processes, 49*(1), 69–79.

Ibrahim, F. A. (1991). Contribution of cultural worldview to generic counseling and development. *Journal of Counseling and Development, 70*, 13–19.

Ilechukwu, S. T. (1991). Psychiatry in Africa: Special problems and unique features. *Transcultural Psychiatric Research Review, 28*(3), 169–218.

Irani, G. E. (1999). Islamic mediation techniques for Middle East conflicts. *Middle East Review of International Affairs, 3*(2), 1–18.

Israel Center for Disease Control. (1999). *Health status in Israel*. Jerusalem: Author.

Israeli Government. (1997). *State comptroller's report*, No. 48. Jerusalem: Author.

Israeli Government. (2002). *State comptroller's report*, No. 52B. Jerusalem: Author. Available at www.mevaker.gov.il.

Jablensky, A. (1992). Politics and mental health. *International Journal of Social Psychiatry, 38*(1), 24–29.

Kanaana, S. (1992). *Still on vacation* (pp. 67–71). Jerusalem: Center for Palestinian Studies.

Kilonzo, G. P., & Simmons, N. (1998). Development of mental health services in Tanzania: A reappraisal for the future. *Social Science and Medicine, 47*(4), 419–428.

Lee, S. (2002). Who is politicizing psychiatry in China? *British Journal of Psychiatry, 179*, 178–179.

Littlewood, R. (1996). Psychiatry's culture. *International Journal of Social Psychiatry, 42*(4), 245–268.

Lustick, I. (1980). *Arabs in the Jewish state: Israel's control over a national minority.* Austin: University of Texas Press.

Lustick, I. (1993). *Unsettled states, disputed lands.* Ithaca, NY: Cornell University Press.

Madu, N. S. (1998). Psychotherapy in Africa: Past, present, and future. In S. N. Madu & P. K. Baguma (Eds.), *In quest for psychotherapy for modern Africa* (pp. 193–200). Sovenga, South Africa: UNIN Press.

Mass, M., & Al-Krenawi, A. (1994). When a man encounters a woman, Satan is also present: On professional encounters in Bedouin society (in Hebrew). *Society and Welfare, 14*(2), 181–197.

Ng, C. F. (1998). Canada as a new place: The immigrant's experience. *Journal of Environmental Psychology, 18*(1), 55–67.

Okasha, A. (1999). Mental health in the Middle East: An Egyptian perspective. *Clinical Psychology Review, 19*(8), 917–933.

Poverty in Israel: Factors and ways of coping. (2001, May). Report of a discussion in the House of the President of the State of Israel.

Qureshi, N. A., Al-Armi, A. H., & Abdelgader, H. (1998). Traditional catery among psychiatric patients in Saudi Arabia. *Transcultural Psychiatry, 35*(1), 75–83.

Racy, J. (1980). Somatization in Saudi women: A therapeutic challenge. *British Journal of Psychiatry, 137,* 212–216.

Ragab, I. A. (1990). How social work can take root in developing countries. *Social Development Issues, 12*(3), 38–51.

Savaya, R. (1995). Attitudes towards family and marital counseling among Israeli Arab women. *Journal of Social Service Research, 21*(1), 35–51.

Savaya, R. (1997). Political attitudes, economic distress, and the utilization of welfare services by Arab women in Israel. *Journal of Applied Social Sciences, 21*(2), 111–121.

Sue, S. (1988). Psychotherapeutic services for ethnic minorities: Two decades of research findings. *American Psychologist, 43*(4), 301–308.

Swirski, S., Konor-Attias, E. (2001). *Israel: A social report.* Available at www.adva.org/socialreport2001english.pdf.

Wakim, W. (1994, October). *The National Committee for the Defense of the Rights of the Uprooted in Israel.* Presented at the first Conference for Human Rights in Arab Society, Nazareth.

Waldram, J. B. (1997). The aboriginal population of Canada: Colonialism and mental health. In I. Al-Issa & M. Tousignant (Eds.), *Ethnicity, Immigration, and Psychopathology* (pp. 169–187). New York: Plenum.

Weaver, H. N. (1998). Indigenous population in a multicultural society: Unique issues for human services. *Social Work, 43*(3), 203–211.

West, J. (1987). Psychotherapy in the Eastern province of Saudi Arabia. *Psychotherapy: Theory, Research, Practice, Training, 24*(1), 105–107.

Yiftachel, O. (1996). The internal frontier: Territorial control and ethnic relations in Israel. *Regional Studies, 30*(5), 493–508.

Yiftachel, O. (2000). "Ethnocracy" and its discontents: Minorities, protests, and the Israeli policy. *Critical Inquiry, 26*(4), 725–756.

5

CHAPTER

GENDER AND CULTURE ISSUES IN HELPING SURVIVORS OF CHILD SEXUAL ABUSE AND VIOLENCE

SHERI OZ
ISRAEL

OVERVIEW

Although the diverse ethnicity of the Israeli population could provide a unique opportunity to observe the impact of culture on aspects of childhood sexual trauma, no such research has yet been conducted. A survey of the professional literature does unearth a small number of reports for a variety of national and ethnic groups around the world; these will be reviewed here and discussed in light of the author's clinical experience in Israel. It will be shown that for child sexual abuse and sexual violence against children, ethnicity is a less significant factor than gender and that the guidelines for culturally sensitive approaches to the treatment of the victim and his or her family actually cross cultural lines. Moreover, it will be suggested here that the greatest cultural difference is the difference between men and women.

INTRODUCTION

In Israel as elsewhere, there is growing awareness of the problem of sexual violence and abuse against children. Rarely a day goes by without a media report on a new case of abuse and violence. Autobiographies written by Israeli abuse survivors can now be found on the shelves of bookstores. Just a few years ago, the country was reeling in the wake of the trial and conviction of a respected army general and government minister for sexual harassment. His arrest brought the subject of sexual coercion to the attention of every citizen. And the subject remains in the public attention.

More and more adults are coming to therapy openly identified as victims of sexual abuse and sexual violence. Similarly, an increasing number of cases of suspected abuse and violence are now being uncovered in families, neighborhoods, and schools (some of them involving children abusing other children) and brought to the attention of public social service agencies. There is a sense of emergency, and these professionals on the front line are overwhelmed by the magnitude of the problem.

The Israeli Jewish population is highly diverse and multicultural. There are Ashkenazim (northern European origin), Sephardim (Mediterranean origin), and Jews from Arab countries. There are those whose families have been established in the area for five or more generations, those who immigrated or whose parents immigrated, and there are those who are converts to Judaism. Some of the population lives in the cities or villages, whereas a large minority lives on kibbutzim and moshavim (farming communities) that can be characterized as large extended families. I, myself, immigrated to Israel at the age of 26, having been brought up in Toronto, Canada, of Ashkenazi parents. In Israel, I have lived in a small town and a kibbutz, and I currently reside in the city of Haifa, maintaining a private practice and providing supervision for therapists in the public and private domains. For more than 10 years, my work has almost exclusively focused on survivors of childhood abuse and violence. In both the personal and professional realms, I have been in contact with individuals from most sectors of the Jewish population as well as Arabs, Druze, and Bedouin.

CULTURE AND CHILD SEXUAL ABUSE AND VIOLENCE

Definitions of physical and emotional forms of child abuse have been found to be in large part culturally dependent and relative, for example, to the differential emphasis placed upon authoritarianism versus permissiveness in childrearing philosophy (Collier, McClure, Collier, Otto & Polloi, 1999; Elliott, Tong, & Tan, 1997; Segal, 1995). Incest, on the other hand, is regarded as forbidden and detrimental to the healthy development of children in all cultures (Korbin, 1987). Not all sexual abuse is incest, however, and defining the behaviors that constitute child sexual abuse depends partly on defining which acts are and are not sexual. This is not necessarily self-evident. For example, Korbin (1987) writes of the Beach and Ford study that describes the practice in some societies of adult soothing of infants by fondling their genitals and Langness's finding of the nonsexual greeting in a New Guinea tribe that involves touching a man's testicles. However, the paucity of such noteworthy examples perhaps emphasizes the pervasiveness of the fact that touching of genitals implies a sexual act.

In Western society, at least, child sexual abuse has been defined as even including acts in which no touch is involved, such as exposure of minors to the sexual act, masturbation, or nudity of others or preventing them from privacy when undressing or bathing (Courtois, 1988). Finkelhor and Korbin

(1988) defined the criteria of child abuse as being a proscribed behavior that is preventable and which causes direct damage to the child; this would then allow culturally specific variations in the definition of sexual abuse. Clearly, this is a problem that has been receiving more specialized attention both legally and clinically since the 1980s in many parts of the world (Collier et al., 1999; Elliott et al., 1997; Luo, 1998; Marneffe & Broos, 1997; Segal, 1995; Swift, 1997).

Finkelhor (1985), working within the white American culture, developed a four-pronged model of traumatic sexualization, betrayal, stigmatization, and powerlessness. All of these have been found to resonate in other cultures (e.g., Luo, 1998), but given space limitations, we will consider only stigmatization (or shame) and powerlessness. The Chinese sexual abuse victim, for example, is shamed for having lost her virginity and fears that she is thus rendered unmarriageable (Luo, 1998; Tsun, 1999); her Arab counterpart is similarly affected. Interestingly, many calls to the Arab rape crisis center in Israel are for help in finding out where victims can have an operation to "restore their virginity." It is likely that research in other cultural groups would reveal a similar phenomenon of individual shame. In fact, Finkelhor and Korbin claim that sexual abuse and violence thrives on "female sexual shame" (1988, p. 11). In some patriarchal countries, sexual abuse and violence against female children is part of the process of socialization into submissiveness.

Alongside the victim's stigmatization, the shame often is also experienced by the family in which the sexual abuse occurred. Blaming the victim is often socially sanctioned. This is illustrated by the name applied to the killing by a male relative of an Arab girl or woman who has had sexual relations outside of marriage—"family honor killing"—regardless of whether this was adultery on the part of an adult, rape, or child abuse. Family shame has been found to characterize the Chinese family (Elliott et al., 1997), the Palau family (Collier et al., 1999), and the families of Latin American, Asian American, and African American rape victims (Holzman, 1996).

The Israeli kibbutz can be regarded as a kind of extended family, and experience has shown that shame prevents the kibbutz membership from being willing to report abuse of any kind that occurs within its bounds. The family defends itself against shame most easily by denying the veracity of the abuse event. The victim is thus rejected, and anticipation of such an outcome prevents many victims from disclosing their abuse in the first place. The victim's complicity in maintaining the silence increases her sense of shame, betrayal, and isolation. In this way, shame conspires to protect the abuser (Collier et al., 1999).

Racism can also increase the likelihood that abuse will be kept secret by its victims because minority people may not be willing to expose the men of their race to the discriminatory judicial system (McNair & Neville, 1996). Razack (1994) from Canada and Smallwood (1995) from Australia both explain Aboriginal failures to report victimization as related to how the courts, in their attempts to be culturally sensitive, end up being sensitive to the "rights" of the abuser (most often men) while ignoring the harm inflicted upon the abused (most often women). It is possible that the situation is similar for Arabs in Israel and other minority groups who suffer from discrimination within a larger dominant culture. So we have a situation in which women are loyal to their cultural or racial group and find themselves discriminated against by men collectively.

It appears that cultural differences are in degree and not kind. Shame, for example, is a common feature in all cultures, yet the degree to which shame is debilitating and inhibits exposure will differ between cultures. It would seem probable that the more traditional and patriarchal the culture, the more shame would reflect on the entire family. The more traditional the culture, the more there would be protection of the abuser and hiding of the abuse and violence. There might also be more punishment of the victim and less chance for intervention by authorities and the legal system. Within Israel, there are populations with different levels of patriarchy. Women in the Arab Israeli population who have been raped are often in danger of their lives from honor killings by their own kin. Intervention by the authorities has been perceived as racist and insensitive to cultural differences. Yet one universal standard holds for the entire Israeli population: making reporting mandatory.

In my own work with Jews in Israel, I have also found that regardless of socioeconomic level, education, religiosity, or ethnic affiliation, certain aspects of abuse and violence follow similar lines:

1. Perpetrators seem to operate in the same manner regarding the ways in which they select and groom victims or threaten them in order to ensure a bond of secrecy.
2. Victims experience symptoms and outcomes that are almost identical. Wyatt (1990) found a similar result from a study of African American and white American women who were sexually abused in childhood, and Luo (1998) found this to be true when comparing Chinese survivors in Taiwan with findings from U.S. studies.
3. Victims are afraid to talk about the abuse, feeling guilty and ashamed and afraid they will not be believed or supported.
4. The most common initial response to disclosure of CSA is to deny the validity of the claims and to punish or reject the victim. At times, the initial rejection is overcome, and the nonabusing adults do support the child victim or adult survivor.

In contrast to these similarities across cultures, a major difference does appear with respect to gender of the victim: Men and women experience the impact of the abuse and its disclosure somewhat differently. It is this aspect that will be explored in the remainder of this chapter.

GENDER AND CHILD SEXUAL ABUSE

Boys and girls alike suffer from the assault upon their immature minds and bodies both in the short term (e.g., school performance, social skills acquisition, self-image development) and long term (e.g., decision-making skills, career choice, mate selection). And, although boys are abused more often by strangers or extrafamilial perpetrators and girls by members of their own families, other characteristics of the abuse experience such as age at onset and rates of penetration have not been found to differ between the sexes (Gold, Elhai, Lucenko, Swingle, & Hughes, 1998). This finding led these researchers to wonder whether or not there are gender differences of enough significance to warrant different treatment approaches for males than what has been found to work for female survivors.

One difference commonly agreed upon by most of those who study gender effects is that sexually abused boys tend to "act out," becoming aggressive toward others and perhaps criminal, while girls are more apt to "act in," experiencing somatic complaints, nightmares, self-blame, and depression (Darves-Bornoz, Choquet, Ledoux, Gasquet, & Manfredi, 1998; Garnefski & Arends, 1998; Rosen & Martin, 1998). However, there are exceptions to this generalization. Although suicide could be considered the ultimate self-harm behavior (acting in), more boys than girls try to kill themselves (Garnefski & Arends, 1998). A comparison of self-mutilation rates (such as cutting) between male and female survivors has not been reported, and it would be interesting to explore this area.

Recent research literature seems to agree that not only are boys damaged by sexual abuse and violence but also, in fact, they seem to be more disturbed by childhood sexual abuse than are girls (e.g., Garnefski & Diekstra, 1997). It has been suggested that they suffer more developmental delays (Fontanella, Harrington, & Zuravin, 2000), greater anxiety (Gold, Lucenko, Elhai, Swingle, & Sellers, 1999), and sexual identity problems (Rosen & Martin, 1998), and they are more serious substance abusers (Garnefski & Arends, 1998). Could this be related to the observation that in their socialization, men are brought up to believe that men are not victims (e.g., Lisak, 1995)? If men are not victims, then the consequences of male victimization could possibly be more severe than for women who are cognizant of their potential victimization from an early age. In other words, victimization for men contradicts all they learn about what it means to be male. Victimization for women, however, does not contradict what women learn about being female (Brown, 1992). The study by Gold et al. (1999) seems to support this contention: They found that male survivors have more problems than female survivors.

Victimization at a young age, however, is most likely experienced similarly for both boys and girl. Both sexes would be equally aware of their vulnerability and dependent on adults for meeting their needs, as well as equally unaware of the full sexual nature of the abuse.

The difference between the sexes increases toward adolescence as the teenager looks back on the abused child he or she used to be and evaluates the experience. The teenage girl sees the world as an extremely unsafe place (Feiring, Taska, & Lewis, 1999). And, in fact, she has continually been warned from a young age not to let anyone touch her and that boys will try to "take advantage" of her. As part of her basic army training in Israel, she attends lectures about sexual harassment in the armed services. When she has been abused in spite of having been warned, there must be "something very wrong with her that she was not able to prevent it from happening." "She must have wanted it." "She is a slut." The teenage boy, on the other hand, views the world as his arena. He is rarely cautioned about possible sexual harassment. When he has been abused, he feels "not a man." Counter to all expectations, he was not the subject of the sexual desire but the object (Gartner, 1997).

Because the abuser is usually male (Gold et al., 1998), the abuse of girls is heterosexual, and the abuse of boys is homosexual. This may lead the boy to question his sexual orientation and wonder if "his homosexuality" seduced the male perpetrator. (Perhaps the higher rate of suicide attempts on the part of abused males is related to the observation that teenagers who fear they are homosexual have also been found to have high rates of suicidality.) The female victim, also feeling guilty for having caused the abuse, need not call into question her "femaleness" because male power–female subservience is the norm (Gartner, 1997). But the abuse certainly does result in sexual problems for women as well as men.

In spite of the fact that Gold et al. (1998) found that sexual abuse for boys and girls begins at approximately the same age, given the different rates of psychological development for boys and for girls, the sexual abuse, for example, of a 7-year-old girl may be different than that of a 7-year-old boy. The girl's slightly greater maturity and gender socialization, which enhances emotionality, may mean that she has more emotional resources to contend with the assault than does her male age-mate.

Perhaps the greatest impact of the sexual abuse on girls results from the fact that she is more likely than a boy to be exploited by someone in a close relationship with her. This would be experienced as betrayal (Finkelhor, 1985; Freyd, 1996). How does she then look for comfort and emotional support within relationships from that time forward? She probably learns from the abuse that she cannot trust relationships; she will be betrayed. This strikes her in her most vulnerable spot: Girls are socialized to define themselves in terms of their relationships (Gilligan, 1982). She is taught to take care of the needs of others and only afterward concern herself with her own needs. It is hard enough for any woman to define clear boundaries between being empathic and caring and being overly giving to the point of neglecting to take care of herself. The woman who was abused in childhood has learned that her needs are totally inconsequential and that the only way to merit being in a relationship is by providing "services." She tends to either embrace this wholeheartedly or reject it out of hand; there is little ability to find a middle ground here as well as in other aspects of her life (Oz, 2001).

In conclusion, we can see that both boys and girls are hurt by sexual abuse because it attacks them in a way that calls into question their ability to function in what they are socialized to feel is their role in society: Boys to be instrumental, have impact, and be powerful; girls to take care of others and to seek and provide comfort within close relationships. We would expect then, in both cases, that male and female survivors of childhood sexual abuse would find it hard to trust their helpers—men because being needy is not masculine, and women because being needy leads to betrayal.

HELPING SURVIVORS OF CHILDHOOD SEXUAL ABUSE AND VIOLENCE

The helping process for the resolution of sexual abuse can be described as having stages. These stages allow for the gradual unfolding of a victim's own story, coping with the powerful and frightening emotions released, and mourning the loss of innocence. The stages include:

1. the decision to embark upon the healing process;
2. beginning to work on the relationship with the therapist and developing trust;
3. exploring the impact of the abuse on the client's life, the nature of the symptoms experienced, the family background, and the current life situation;
4. experiencing and being able to contain growing emotional intensity along with an increase in symptom intensity and frequency;
5. crossing the wall of fear (Oz, 2001), which involves remembering the abuse or recalling more details of the abuse and connecting with the feelings that were experienced at the time of the abuse before some form of dissociation became active in defending against these overwhelming feelings;
6. mourning the loss of the "ideal" childhood and "ideal" family that children "are supposed to have";
7. reevaluating important decisions taken in the past, such as marital partner, career, and place of residence, and deciding whether or not to change any of these aspects; and
8. establishing a new identity that no longer includes victimization.

PERSONAL REFLECTIONS

For most of my professional life, I have worked with victims and survivors of childhood sexual abuse. I have heard horrific stories of inhumane physical, emotional, and sexual torture of young children by members of their own families. Yet working with these two adolescent victims of acquaintance rape on a kibbutz on the one hand and a violent male rape in a public toilet on the other shook me up in another way. These were not repeat victims, "sitting ducks" as Kluft (1990) called them; they were regular kids who had grown up in regular families with regular problems. And they still were not able to protect themselves or foresee the danger.

Social constructivist methods do not focus on any one version of "the truth," and in hearing narratives the helper is not concerned about what really happened. But in cases of rape and sexual abuse, which arouse anger and possibly denial in those who are involved, the truth is important. Accountability and the appropriate social reactions of adults are crucial in the healing process. Often family, community, and other professionals need to be faced with their own complicity or denial, and trust needs to be restored by concrete changes that make the survivor safer in the future.

CASE 5.1   A FEMALE AND
A MALE
SURVIVOR

I have chosen to present work with two adolescent one-time rape victims. The case material is much simpler and easier to grasp than those that involve ongoing sexual abuse while also being representative of the issues involved in work with teens and adult survivors of abuse that happened during their childhoods.

B. grew up on a kibbutz and was in 11th grade. She had an older brother in the army and a younger sister in elementary school. Her parents were in therapy for marital problems and were highly invested in saving the relationship. At the time of the rape, B. had a boyfriend of several months. The rape occurred after a Purim party on her kibbutz (a holiday celebrating the saving of the Jews of ancient Persia; costume parties mark the holiday, and alcoholic beverages are an accepted part of the fun). The perpetrator was a platonic male friend, also in 11th grade, who lived on the same kibbutz and attended her school but was in a different class. After the party, B. had gone back with him to his room to talk, something that she had done many times before. Her boyfriend was in the army at the time. Shortly after the rape, she told two girlfriends, who encouraged her to turn to her parents.

L. was also the middle child of three, having a brother who had completed his army service and a sister in junior high. The family resided in a small, mainly middle-class town. His parents spoke of having a strained relationship, and no one in the family had sought professional help until then. L. was raped by a stranger who assaulted him in a public toilet at the beach. Shortly before this incident, L. had begun a demanding combat training course in the army, and he was on weekend leave. He had dated several women but had never had a serious relationship.

The similarities in presentation of these two clients were their stable family backgrounds (in spite of conflicted parental marriages), their sibling placement, a lack of traumatic events preceding the rapes, and the fact that the rape constituted their first experiences of sexual penetration. The striking difference concerns the identity of the perpetrator: In B.'s case, he was a familiar player in her day-to-day life; in L.'s case, he was a stranger with whom L. had no further contact. For B., this was a heterosexual event, and for L. it was homosexual. This corresponds to observations noted in the literature referred to above regarding the nature of male and female sexual victimization.

B. was referred for therapy by a social worker at the regional social services office. She was having trouble sleeping, was overeating, was unable to concentrate in her studies, had withdrawn from all but a few close friends, and was spending more time at home with her parents. She was bothered by intrusive images of the rape scene and was not successful at putting it out of her mind. When this happened, she would call a girlfriend, her boyfriend, or her mother.

L. had not told anyone about the rape. He tried to put it out of his mind. When he was bothered by intrusive thoughts, he would try to get busy doing something such as playing the piano or practicing basketball shots at a nearby park in order not to think about the assault. However, his ability to function in combat training went into a downward spiral, and he was visibly upset and angry at everyone. Furthermore, having failed at some crucial tasks, L. was called in to speak with the unit's mental health officer. After the third meeting, L. told him about the rape and was sent home to tell his parents and to have a week's leave. During this time, his parents turned to me for help, and L. agreed to start therapy. The mental health officer arranged for L. to get weekly leave to attend therapy and also worked with L.'s superior officers so that he could remain with his unit and complete training in spite of his difficulties.

In both cases, disclosure of the rape mobilized those around B. and L. to provide support and encourage them to engage in therapy. This also can happen when young boys and girls disclose sexual victimization; however, similar to parents of children traumatized by other forms of trauma (Almqvist & Broberg, 1997), parents often believe that if they do not talk about it too much, then the child will forget that it ever happened, put it out of mind, and no longer be bothered by it. They also may tend not to report the abuse regardless of the identity of the perpetrator. In less favorable instances, the adults in their environment may respond with anger, disbelief, or impotence to child disclosures of abuse.

(continued)

Neither B. nor L. turned to their parents first to disclose the rapes. B. confided in her friends, and L. tried to handle the situation alone. This is representative of gender differences in worldviews: Women define themselves within meaningful relationships, and emotional support is sought within those relationships; men define themselves autonomously in terms of their successes and accomplishments and seek emotional support in activity (alone, in competitive sport, or in sexual performance). Only when threatened with failure in what is a major male rite of passage in Israel did L. tell an authority figure about the rape. It was lucky for him that this particular authority figure was sensitive to the issue of male rape and referred him to his parents for support. The fact that both B. and L. told their parents soon after the initial disclosure indicates that the family relationships included open communication and that the parents were seen as supportive figures. This is not usually the case when there has been prolonged childhood sexual abuse.

Both B. and L. came to their first session with some trepidation regarding the helping process. Both were fearful that I would ask them to tell me the details of what had happened. When I dispelled that fear, both relaxed. What interested me most at the early stage was to understand what life was like before the assault and how it had changed or not changed following the rape. Because this coincided with their own concerns, the helping relationship was "off to a good start."

The tools used most throughout the therapeutic process were cognitive therapy, guided fantasy, and artwork. B. was highly motivated and struggled to make sense of her life after the rape. Discussion of the rape was intermingled with sessions dealing with friendships, the meaning of friendship, and other relationship issues concerning her family and her boyfriend. B. was greatly preoccupied with the conflict between becoming independent of her parents while enjoying the increased emotional closeness that had resulted from their support of her in dealing with the rape. Furthermore, she believed that the need for them to come together to support her at this time contributed to the improvement in their marital relationship.

L., as is typical for males, spoke about being concerned about his ability to function. He found himself to be absentminded, whereas before the rape he had been able to focus well on any task before him. This absentmindedness had even resulted in a broken finger. He was also upset that he felt fearful in places that reminded him of the rape scene, fear being a unique and distressing experience for him.

After some 4 months, L. started to share how much he had been affected by the rape. He hadn't wanted to tell me the extent of his symptoms earlier for fear that I would think he was childish and weak. L. complained of nightmares, a low stress threshold leading to outbursts of anger, periods of uncontrollable crying, and an inability to concentrate. As the therapy progressed, his bouts of crying increased in intensity and duration as did his angry responses to others. Over time, he was able to verbalize the fact that he had been violently raped rather than referring to the incident in oblique terms. He began to consider whether or not to report the rape to the police and have himself tested for possible sexually transmitted diseases. He did the latter only.

He did not want to practice relaxation techniques in spite of the increasing distress he was experiencing. It did not correspond to his image of masculinity, something that he was expressing difficulty with at this point. He was tortured by the thought that if he were "man" enough, he would have fought off his aggressor and prevented the rape from having been completed. And he would not be crying about it now. He would often stand up and demonstrate for me what he should have done.

At this time, we decided to use TIR (traumatic incidence reduction—French & Harris, 1999) to resolve the impact of the rape. Briefly, TIR is a form of exposure therapy in which the exposure session is *time-unlimited*—that is, the session continues until the client has a sense of calm and well-being. This can take from one hour to three hours. Because the thought of using the technique is often frightening for clients, I have found that the timing of the TIR session is important; it is best to wait until the client–therapist relationship is strong and the client feels safe.

L. felt both ready for and apprehensive about the TIR session. However, he quickly became engaged in the process. The entire session took one and one-half hours. He felt the pain of the penetration along with profound humiliation and guilt for not having been able to defend himself. Suddenly, in what was to be the final review of the event, L. became aware of a detail

(continued)

of which he had been incognizant until that moment: One of the toilet stalls was slightly ajar when he entered the bathroom, and it was from behind this door that the rapist watched him and planned his attack. At this awareness, L. opened his eyes and laughed. He said he had had no chance against this man. It was a premeditated, impersonal, and probably well-practiced ambush. He had been pinned to the wall in a split second.

In the following session, L. said he was greatly relieved to discover that no man would have been able to defend himself in a similar situation. However, thinking of the rape still brought about an uncomfortable sensation in his belly. With some exploration, it became clear that this discomfort also arose when he thought of situations in which he had unintentionally hurt someone. One example he gave was having told a joke that the other found insulting and not funny. Another example was when talking with a girl he wanted to date and his arm accidentally brushed against her breast. The look on her face let him know that she was upset by this. L. had become highly sensitive to the impact of his behaviors on others and used the remainder of the therapy to work on some aspects of interpersonal relationships that now concerned him.

Interestingly, both B. and L. were at a stage of life in which there is clear movement out of the family and into the world, and both were sent back to the family as an initial part of their healing process. When B. felt her parents come together in order to help her, she found that her difficulties had a therapeutic effect on her parents' marriage; she wanted them to come see me together at different points of the process in order for

me to help them help her. L. also saw his parents come together in providing support for him; however, beyond the initial session in which I described to them the effects of sexual assault on the victim and the therapeutic process expected, he did not want them to see me again. For him, therapy was an undesirable necessity that was to be kept separate from his daily life.

Some elements of the helping process mirror the issues that also underlie the differential experiences of childhood sexual abuse suffered by boys and girls. For example, B. was concerned throughout her therapy with relationship issues, whereas L. was not so concerned until near the end of therapy. B. sought support within relationships she felt she could still trust; L. did not tell anyone except the army mental health officer and his parents. He preferred to handle things on his own.

As with most girls, B.'s rapist was a familiar figure in her day-to-day life, and therefore the assault constituted a betrayal. Further betrayals were suffered when some of her friends continued to be friends with her rapist. L., having been raped by a stranger, was not disturbed because he had not been betrayed by someone close to him.

At the end of therapy, B. included her brother in those who knew about the rape, and the purpose of this was to enhance their relationship. And we saw that she was reluctant to do so until she was less vulnerable and therefore the news of the rape would be less distressing to him. L. was not prepared to share the experience with anyone. He was proud that he had resolved the negative consequences of the rape and said he would tell his future wife only—and only after they have been married for a long time.

Yet it is in this delicate balance between what is true and what is socially constructed that the helper can uncover biases and stereotyping. It is uncomfortable for me to face the fact that I am not free of the societal stereotyping that gender entails. I was particularly touched by L. Here was a youth, just out of school, facing the tough challenges of the army, which is supposed to "make a man out of a boy." And he was forced to struggle with the questions of masculinity and femininity within a context that included a violent rape. In reflecting about my reactions, I realized that I felt differently toward these two cases. Was I particularly touched by the boy because he seemed so fragile in spite of his attempts to come across as a grown man, thus arousing my "mothering instincts"? Was it because, as a woman I responded to B. more from a place of identification and therefore, perhaps, more judgmentally ("Didn't you know you were supposed to be cautious?")? To L., I perhaps responded more from a position of sympathy ("How awful! Men are not supposed to be raped!"). It would seem particularly important for helpers to pay attention to their gender bias in cases of sexual abuse so as not to replicate societal prejudges within the helping process.

CONCLUSION

This chapter examined cultural and gender aspects of violence and childhood sexual abuse. Although cultural differences can color the impact of sexual abuse on the individual, the family, and the therapeutic process, there are more similarities than differences among peoples of different backgrounds. The helper needs to be attuned to how cultural groups differ with respect to help-seeking behaviors and attitudes toward sexual violence while also recognizing the universal dynamics by which childhood sexual abuse plays itself out both in individual trauma response and family relationships.

More dramatic than cultural differences is the differential impact of childhood sexual abuse on boys in contrast to girls. Victimization is experienced differently by the sexes, and the meaning attached to victimization relates to the meaning attached to masculinity and femininity. Male survivors of childhood sexual abuse and violence experience a threat to their masculine image. They are more likely to keep their experiences to themselves and feel weak. Female survivors are more likely to have known the person and to experience the environment as unsafe. They rely more on their relationships for support and are more concerned with the effects of the childhood experiences on these relationships. As more cross-cultural gender studies are conducted, it may emerge that the greatest cultural divide is the one between male and female.

KEY CONCEPTS

- culturally specific definitions of child abuse
- universality of trauma responses
- patriarchy and family responses of shame
- differential characteristics of sex abuse against boys and girls
- masculinity and femininity determine the impact of sex abuse and violence on male and female survivors

QUESTIONS FOR REFLECTION

1. Explain why it is almost universally true that women are more often shamed by or censured for sexual behaviors than are men.
2. Compare the messages that boys and girls growing up in your family both received about sexuality. Has this changed over the past few generations or

has it stayed the same? Compare this with classmates from different ethnic groups. Do you agree or disagree with the author that gender differences override cultural differences?

3. In the classroom, conduct a debate on whether or not sexual initiation of a minor male by an older woman should be considered sexual abuse.
4. Using the case example in this chapter of the young kibbutz woman, discuss how one would view the situation if the roles were reversed.
5. What challenges does a male helper treating a male sex abuse victim face versus a female sex abuse victim? What are the challenges facing a female helper treating victims of either sex?

EXERCISE

Cut out a newspaper clipping reporting on a child sex abuse case. Rewrite the story twice—once saying the victim was a girl and once saying the victim was a boy. Conduct a survey, showing each person one version, and asking:

1. How long a sentence would they give the perpetrator?
2. How would they describe the victim?
3. What kind of a future would they predict for the victim?

Discuss the results of the survey.

References

Almqvist, K., & Broberg, A. G. (1997). Silence and survival: Working with strategies of denial in families of traumatized pre-school children. *Journal of Child Psychotherapy, 23,* 417–435.

Brown, L. S. (1992). Not outside the range: one feminist perspective on psychic trauma. *American Imago, 48,* 119–133.

Collier, A. F., McClure, F. H., Collier, J., Otto, C., & Polloi, A. (1999). Culture-specific views of child maltreatment and parenting styles in a Pacific-island community. *Child Abuse and Neglect, 23,* 229–244.

Courtois, C. A. (1988). *Healing the incest wound: Adult survivors in therapy.* New York: W. W. Norton.

Darves-Bornoz, J., Choquet, M., Ledoux, S., Gasquet, I., & Manfredi, R. (1998). Gender differences in symptoms of adolescents reporting sexual assault. *Social Psychiatry and Psychiatric Epidemiology, 33,* 111–117.

Elliott, J. M., Tong, C. K., & Tan, P. M. E. H. (1997). Attitudes of the Singapore public to actions suggesting child abuse. *Child Abuse and Neglect, 21,* 445–464.

Feiring, C., Taska, L., & Lewis, M. (1999). Age and gender differences in children's and adolescents' adaptation to sexual abuse. *Child Abuse and Neglect, 23,* 115–128.

Finkelhor, D. (1985). *Child sexual abuse: New theory and research.* New York: Free Press.

Finkelhor, C., & Korbin, J. (1988). Child abuse as an international issues. *Child Abuse and Neglect, 12,* 3–23.

Fontanella, C., Harrington, D., & Zuravin, S. J. (2000). Gender differences in the characteristics and outcomes of sexually abused preschoolers. *Journal of Child Sexual Abuse 9*, 21–40.

French, G. D., & Harris, C. J. (1999). *Traumatic incident reduction (TIR)*. Boca Raton, FL: CRC Press.

Freyd, J. J. (1996). *Beyond betrayal. The logic of forgetting childhood abuse*. Cambridge, MA: Harvard University Press.

Garnefski, N., & Arends, E. (1998). Sexual abuse and adolescent maladjustment: Differences between male and female victims. *Journal of Adolescence 21*, 99–107.

Garnefsky, N., & Diekstra, R. F. W. (1997). Child sexual abuse and emotional and behavioral problems in adolescence: Gender differences. *Journal of the American Academy of Child Adolescent Psychiatry, 36*, 323–329.

Gartner, R. B. (1997). Considerations in the psychoanalytic treatment of men who were sexually abused as children. *Psychoanalytic Psychology, 14*, 13–41.

Gilligan, C. (1982). *In a different voice: Psychological theory and women's development*. Cambridge, MA: Harvard University Press.

Gold, S. M., Elhai, J. D., Lucenko, B. A., Swingle, J. M., & Hughes, D. M. (1998). Abuse characteristics among childhood sexual abuse survivors in therapy: A gender comparison. *Child Abuse and Neglect, 22*, 1005–1012.

Gold, S. N., Lucenko, B. A., Elhai, J. D., Swingle, J. M., & Sellers, A. H. (1999). A comparison of psychological/psychiatric symptomatology of women and men sexually abused as children. *Child Abuse and Neglect, 23*, 683–692.

Holzman, C. G. (1996). Counseling adult women rape survivors: issues of race, ethnicity, and class. *Women and Therapy, 19*, 47–62.

Lisak, D. (1995). Integrating a critique of gender in the treatment of male survivors of childhood abuse. *Psychotherapy, 32*, 258–269.

Luo, T. E. (1998). Sexual abuse trauma among child survivors. *Child Abuse and Neglect, 22*, 1013–1026.

Kluft, R. P. (1990). Incest and subsequent revictimization: The case of therapist–patient sexual exploitation, with a description of the sitting duck syndrome. In R. P. Kluft (Ed.), *Incest-related syndromes of adult psychopathology* (pp. 263–287). Washington, DC: American Psychiatric Press.

Korbin, J. E. (1987). Child sexual abuse: Implication from the cross-cultural record. In N. Scheper-Hughes (Ed.), *Child survival: Anthropological perspectives on the treatment and maltreatment of children* (pp. 247–265). Boston: D. Reidel Publishing.

Marneffe, C., & Broos, P. (1997). Belgium: An alternative approach to child abuse reporting and treatment. In N. Gilbert (Ed.), *Combating child abuse: International perspectives and trends*. New York: Oxford University Press.

McNair, L. D., & Neville, H. A. (1996). African American women survivors of sexual assault: The intersection of race and class. *Women and Therapy, 18*, 107–118.

Oz, S. (2001). When the wife was sexually abused as a child: Marital relations before and during her therapy for abuse. *Sexual and Relationship Therapy, 16*, 287–298.

Razack, S. H. (1994). What is to be gained by looking white people in the eye? *Signs, 19*, 894–915.

Rosen, L. N., & Martin, L. (1998). Long-term effects of childhood maltreatment history on gender-related personality characteristics. *Child Abuse and Neglect, 22*, 197–211.

Segal, U. A. (1995). Child abuse by the middle class? A study of professionals in India. *Child Abuse and Neglect, 19*, 217–231.

Smallwood, G. (1995). Child abuse and neglect from an indigenous Australian's perspective. *Child Abuse and Neglect, 19,* 281–289.

Swift, K. J. (1997). Canada: Trends and issues in child welfare. In N. Gilbert (Ed.), *Combating Child abuse. international perspectives and trends* (pp. 38–71). New York: Oxford University Press.

Tsun, O. K. A. (1999). Sibling incest: A Hong Kong experience. *Child Abuse and Neglect, 23,* 71–79.

Wyatt, G. E. (1990). The aftermath of child sexual abuse of African American and white American women: The victim's experience. *Journal of Family Violence, 5,* 61–81.

6

CHAPTER

SOCIAL AND CULTURAL ISSUES IN MALE SEX PROBLEMS

YVONNE JACOBSON
IRELAND

OVERVIEW

Irish society and culture used to be very much under the influence of the Catholic Church. Schools and hospitals were run by the clergy, and most families were daily churchgoers until the early 1970s. Sex was not discussed and was only meant to exist behind the closed doors of the marital bedroom. Little wonder that children grew up to be adults with sexual problems often traceable to negative family and social attitudes toward sex. Over the last three decades, Ireland has become far more liberal and has not escaped American influence. Today it is common to hear sex talked about freely on radio programs and on television, where many American sitcoms and chat shows are shown. Also, as a result of liberalization of policy makers and academics, sexuality has recently become an acceptable element of education. It might seem that the implication is that sex is no longer a problem and that young people are developing into healthy and uncomplicated sexual adults. This is not the case.

Men and women continue to have sexual difficulties, and where once the negative religious attitudes were obvious contributors to the problem, it now seems that the pendulum has swung so far the other way. People are worried that they do not meet the media's portrayal of sexual liberation. In order not to collude with dominant discourses, helpers need to take into account the social, cultural, and political influences that may be feeding sexual problems. The chapter shows how postmodern narrative approaches conceptualize sexual problems in their cultural and gender context and use reauthoring to empower people to resist oppressive dominant social discourses. A specific case example is given to illustrate what can happen when fear, shame, and guilt dominate an Irish male suffering from "impotence."

CULTURE AND GENDER ISSUES AND SEXUALITY IN IRISH SOCIETY

Sexuality and religion do not usually make good bedfellows. Catholicism in Ireland has had such a strong influence on the cultural, social, educational, and moral contexts of Irish people's lives that it would be no overstatement to say that the Church owned and controlled people's sexuality. Its power over both adults' and children's lives included seeing sex as dirty, sinful, and totally unacceptable outside of marriage. Sex was dealt with by being banned from both speech and the written word as much as possible (Inglis, 1998). Until the 1980s, any contraception other than "natural" methods was unacceptable and unavailable, further influencing the lack of control that individuals and married couples alike had over their sexual needs.

One of the lasting and unwanted consequences of the Church's domination over people's sexual lives is the frequency of sexual problems in couples' relationships. The Church's attitudes and beliefs unquestioningly imposed on its members have contributed hugely to the fear, guilt, and shame that block ordinary desirable sexual behavior. The professional literature consistently cites these negative feelings as resulting in sexual problems (Kaplan, 1974; Cole & Dryden, 1988; Milsten & Slowinski, 1999).

The demise of the Church's authority over the last two decades can be explained by several developments: Politically and economically, Ireland's membership in the European Union has enabled a significant increase in the liberalization of Irish law as well as both affluence and secularization within Irish society. A further significant contributor to the Church's decrease in influence was brought about in the early 1990s when it became known that previously highly respected members of the Church have been involved in a variety of sexual relationships despite their public allegiance to celibacy. Disturbing as this may have been to some faithful churchgoers, even more shocking and likely to cause strong anti-Church feelings is the number of child sexual abuse claims being made against priests.

The decline in the Church's power has provided media with an opportunity to explore and publicly debate the topic of sexuality. At the same time, medical interest and pharmaceutical developments in the area of sexual functioning have provided sexuality with an unexpected and rapidly growing prominence in the public arena. The pharmacological breakthrough of anti-impotence drugs such as Viagra have not only enabled many men to receive help but also provided the media with an opportunity to talk about sex in a socially acceptable way. It is perhaps no small irony that this magic pill is actually manufactured in Ireland! Further oral pharmacological drugs have also been developed in the last five years and are competing in the market.

The development of these drugs has created public and private interest in the subject of sexuality that the media have exploited, enjoying at last a freedom to publish or broadcast both newsworthy and not-so-newsworthy articles and programs. However, although the Church no longer holds its grip on sexuality, commercial interests and the media may have taken over their position of power. As such, sexual problems among young Irish adults have not diminished. The popularity of sex therapy clinics clearly indicates that fear, guilt, and shame are still a significant part of the problem.

Sex therapy as it is known today evolved out of the work of Masters and Johnson, whose work in the United States in the 1960s had evolved from their work on different physiological and psychological stages in sexual response (Masters & Johnson, 1966). This led to their identification of specific sexual dysfunctions and the development of brief behavioral treatment programs to change the problematic sexual response to a more positive one. At the same time, Helen Singer Kaplan was developing hypotheses on the psychological causes of sexual dysfunction (Kaplan, 1974). These works influenced psychiatrists and psychologists in the United Kingdom who adapted and developed sex therapy to meet the needs of British society. Before long, a wide range of medical professionals— among them psychiatrists, urologists, biologists, and psychotherapists—were involved in sex research and development. Their working environments ranged from private hospitals to National Health Service clinics and various centers of the National Marriage Guidance Council (Cole & Dryden, 1988).

By the early 1980s, this knowledge and way of working with sexual problems had arrived in Ireland, where separately a handful of psychiatrists, psychologists, and counselors influenced by colleagues in Britain began to develop their skills. Two couple's counseling organizations operating in Ireland at the time provided an obvious place for sexual problems to present themselves. The Catholic Marriage Advisory Council and the Marriage Counseling Services each operated under their own ethos. The former provided counseling within the organizational framework of the Catholic Church; the latter, which was set up in 1963 with a small amount of government funding, offered nondenominational couple's counseling for people who did not want the limitations of religious views influencing their decisions. The presence of two marriage counseling organizations in a relatively small population is perhaps explained by the fact that marriage, until quite recently, was a lifelong commitment, and all efforts had to be made to try to save troubled marriages. Under the Irish Constitution, divorce was not permitted until public opinion was eventually swayed in its favor and legislation allowing divorce came into place following a referendum in 1997. Although sex therapy became an acceptable part of the service offered by the Catholic Marriage Advisory Council, its availability was restricted to married, heterosexual couples.

Despite the different professional and social contexts within which sex therapists work, sex therapy tends to be uniformly practiced. It involves a detailed assessment of the presenting problem in order to formulate appropriate interventions to bring about the desired change. Sex therapy provides an integration of psychotherapeutic skills to treat a range of sexual problems defined in medical terms as vaginismus, dyspaerunia, premature ejaculation, retarded ejaculation, erectile dysfunction, orgasmic dysfunction, and impaired sexual arousal.

Until recently, this medical model has dominated the textbooks and training manuals. More recently, however, attempts have been made toward demedicalization of the language so that therapists are more likely to refer to "problems" or "difficulties" rather than "dysfunctions." The language of helping professions endeavors to move away from science and medicine wherever possible to emphasize the difference in approach to dealing with problems. Thus, assessment now includes looking at family background influences, educational and psychological factors, and the couple dynamic in the current relationship.

Little attention has been paid to the cultural and political context in which the problem is nurtured. In the last five years, feminist psychology has begun to challenge the medicalization of women's sexuality and highlight the social and political causes of female sexual problems (Tiefer, 2002; Ussher & Baker, 1993). A leading opponent in this area is Dr. Leonore Tiefer, clinical associate professor at the New York University School of Medicine, who runs a Web site to campaign against casting women's sexual problems as medical dysfunctions. Her campaign for a new view of female sexuality calls on us to challenge the cultural assumptions of the research and marketing program of the pharmaceutical industry (Tiefer, 2000). There has been no challenge to the view that male sexual problems are primarily medical or psychological (or both) in nature.

SEXUAL PROBLEMS IN THE CONTEXT OF IRISH SOCIETY

Little research has been done in Ireland on the prevalence of sexual problems, but informal knowledge would suggest that figures conform to statistics in the United Kingdom and United States, with the exception of vaginismus. The frequency of this problem is higher in Ireland, and there is a recognized cultural aspect related to religious attitudes around female sexuality. *Vaginismus* is defined as the involuntary spasm of the muscles surrounding the entrance to the vagina, making penetration of any object, but especially the penis, impossible. Women who have this problem often share certain characteristics. They tend to worry a lot, can be perfectionists, and have close but not necessarily healthy relationships with their mothers. They also are likely to have had strongly negative messages about sex during their childhood, namely, that sex is dirty, sex before marriage is sinful, and—according to the teachings of the Church—sex is only for the purpose of procreation. From our understanding of vaginismus, it seems that these messages may be intellectually rejected but hold strong at an unconscious level. As a result, fear, guilt, and shame can insidiously influence a woman who at one level desires to be sexual and at another level is unable to let go of a deep-seated cultural influence. This religion-based determinant can affect men, too, where "impotence" is often associated with anxiety in general but can also be influenced by the specific anxieties of fear, shame, and guilt.

Of all the categories of sexual problems, impotence is perhaps the most interesting and controversial in terms of how it has been viewed historically. No longer called "impotence," it was medicalized and renamed "erectile dysfunction" or "erectile disorder" by therapists who wished to get away from the negative connotations associated with the word *impotence*. Those who wish to get

CASE 6.1

Ben[1] is 30 years of age and was not in a relationship. He had not experienced a full erection since he was 14 years old. "You're my last hope," he said, proceeding to catalog a long series of experiences with previous professionals he had consulted about his erection problems. Having recently been introduced to narrative therapy, I found myself thinking about dominant discourses relating to gender, culture, religion, patriarchal families, personal oppression, and exploitation (Freedman & Combs, 1996). At the same time, I was questioning the theories that had dominated my training and sex therapy practice for so many years.

Ben described his life, his tormented belief that he could not have a "normal" relationship, and his desperation to rekindle some of his earlier friendships from which he had withdrawn. He was frustrated at the amount of money he had spent trying to "cure" his problem but without success. "Can you help me?" asked the voice of a 14-year-old with beseeching eyes. I told him I hoped I would be able to, but I would like to hear his story in more detail before being sure how I could be of help. He left the room with hope at having been heard in full, and with a sense of relief that at last someone was prepared to listen to him and help him make sense of his life. Previous "treatments" had all focused on his penis. I left the room feeling animated, highly aware of the impact of those powerful discourses and their opposites: impotence versus omnipotence, helplessness versus empowerment, and authority versus self-control.

It struck me that Ben was under the influence of a society that believed medical interventions alone could "cure" impotence, while I subscribed to the belief that sex therapy, with its psychological assessment tools and directive task setting could bring about the desired change in sexual relationships. Because he was not in a relationship, I had only a limited way of helping him if I stayed with the familiar method of primarily focusing on reducing anxiety and rebuilding sexual confidence. I sensed with Ben's story that much could be gained by questioning his beliefs and assumptions

[1]Name and other details have been changed to protect his identity.

and from deconstructing his past rather than concentrating on his current sexual activity or inactivity.

Over the next eight sessions, Ben talked about various influencing factors in his life to date. I was guided by the focus he brought into the room each week, and I did not impose any chronological order on what he wanted to tell me. However, for the sake of clarity here, I am reproducing his story under the themes of family, schooling, work, and the history of the sexual problem, all of which were important subject matters in our work together.

Family Background and Relationships

Ben was the only son and the youngest in a family of four children. In his family, sex was discussed only in terms of how it can get one into trouble, reinforcing the dominant Catholic discourse that sex outside of marriage is sinful. He described his father as a tyrant and a bully, and his mother as a well-meaning, uneducated woman whose faith in Catholicism dominates her everyday life. This would not be unusual among Irish Catholic mothers who have for generations upheld the word of the priest before that of their husbands. Irish women were expected to behave like the Virgin Mary, and their greatest joy was often when their sons chose to enter the priesthood and renounce sexuality. Choosing the Church as a vocation was common for teenage males until the 1960s, after which quite a number of would-be clerics pulled out of the seminaries when they realized the limitations. As far as he knows, his parents have never had a close relationship, and he has the impression that his father needed a wife to provide children to expand the family business rather than a woman with whom he could share an intimate partnership.

Despite the constant arguments and tension in the home, the family is a close one and spends a lot of time together. Ben lived at home with his parents. I asked him what it was like growing up in a family of girls, and he looked at me with fear as he recalled the terror he experienced. As a small boy, he remembered his father threatening him that if Ben didn't behave, his father would "cut his willie off." He described how his mother loved him when he was little, and how she protected him from his father but how disappointed she was when he did not grow physically or become tall and strong. He also recounted, with deep distress, a memory of his mother standing him up on the kitchen table, pulling down his pants in front of his sisters and having his penis smacked with a warning that he was never to let it get him into trouble.

Schooling

Ben attended a private Catholic boys' school that was run by priests and included lay teachers. He was reasonably happy there and had several good friends. He enjoyed studying, and although he was less than average in height, he was confident and sociable until age 16 or so, at which time he saw his sexual problem getting in the way. His increased difficulty in getting erections, even when masturbating, were causing him concern; his way of dealing with this was to appear uninterested in girls and to withdraw from the usual schoolboy conversations about sex whenever they took place in the classroom, during break time, and on the weekends.

There are several discourses that impact on sexuality for teenagers in Ireland. One is the parental influence of religious faith and family morals. Another comes from the educational system's emphasis on teaching only the biological facts of sex and on emphasizing the importance of sexual abstinence until marriage. A third discourse comes from the media and social trends such as discos and nightclubs and their promotion of active sexuality. Peer pressure transmits this discourse, although it contradicts the other discourses (Inglis, 1998). Thus, the average teen is exposed to extremely contradictory messages in an age of transition and confusion about sexual mores.

By the time he was starting in university, Ben was quite convinced that there was something wrong with him but had no idea what to do about it. Despite this, he got through his course and graduated with an arts degree. He described his college years with mixed feelings. There were some good things about it as long as he didn't allow his problem to dominate his thoughts. Because this wasn't always possible, he spent periods feeling isolated and separate from the rest of the students. He was acutely aware that the avoidance of intimate relationships was always his aim, and he made sure that both male and female friends did not get too close to him. When I asked him how his parents might have seen him during this period, he said they would have experienced him as angry and confused but made no attempt to find out why.

Work

After graduating, Ben went straight into his father's business, working in one of the betting offices. He hated this work, having neither interest in nor respect for the service provided, and finding it hard to feel morally positive about making money from other people's gambles, as he put it to me. The "family business" ethic was so strongly enforced by his father that he could see no alternative but to do what his father told him.

After three years of frustration and unhappiness, Ben decided that he had to get away and look for a chance to rebuild his life away from Dublin, away from his family, and away from the terrible sense of inadequacy he carried with him. Despite objections from his parents, he left Ireland and went to Manchester, England, where a college friend was already working. He found a job in a bookstore. They shared an apartment, and at first the newness and excitement of learning to live in a distinctly different environment worked well for him. At 25 years of age, he was at last beginning to feel free, grown up, and out of the clutches of his family. He started partying, going to nightclubs, and generally behaving as his contemporaries had been doing for some time, and he enjoyed it greatly. Still masking his anxiety about his inability to get an erection, he did not let this deter him from falling in love with Nadine, the 19-year-old sister of another friend.

Inevitably, sex became an in issue, and after one particular night of drinking and dancing, they went to bed together. It didn't work. After several attempts to have intercourse, Ben gave up, swamped by feelings of shame, humiliation, and despair. Nadine was understanding and put no pressure on him to perform, but he was so convinced that he was a total failure that she could be of no help. Determined to try and find "a cure," Ben went to a private clinic advertising help for impotent men. There he was assessed psychologically and prescribed some tablets; to this day, he is not sure what they were.

After two weeks of taking the tablets and finding it made no difference to his lack of erections, he went back to the clinic. He was given another supply of the "medication" and shortly after received another large bill. At this stage, he became worried because he did not have the money to pay for them, and in a moment of deep despair told his visiting sister about the mess

(continued)

he was in. She found the £2000 needed to pay the clinic and sorted the financial side out for him, encouraging him to come back to Ireland for further medical tests.

The rise in number of these types of clinics correlates with the rise in publicity and promotion of the availability of pharmacological treatments for impotence. Advertisements for such clinics claim to offer medical checkups, rapid diagnoses, and high rates of success. In reality, they can manipulate people who are feeling vulnerable by charging high prices for a service that may not work if only the physical symptoms of the problem are examined. The commercial side of medicalization thrives where problems are fostered by contradictory messages that also promote the hiding of problems in shame.

The Sexual Problem

The sense of failure led Ben to forgo his independence and return home. Back in Ireland, Ben's unhappiness deepened, aided by the accumulation of shame, guilt, and fear. With no independent means of income and the parental expectation that he must get back into the family business, he moved back in to his parents' house and resumed working for his father. His relationship with Nadine had ended because he could not talk to her about his sexual problem and chose not to see her again rather than admit to his problems. Depression set in, and he isolated himself from the outside world.

The Helping Process

The conventional way for me to work with Ben would have been to take a life history in order to determine the predisposing, precipitating, and maintaining factors for the problem. I would then have decided whether or not to offer him four or five sessions of behavioral work. This would have included giving him relaxation exercises and taking him through a self-help program similar to the ones outlined in the popular and useful self-help manual *The New Male Sexuality* (Zilbergeld, 1992).

Because Ben's arrival on my doorstep coincided with my own new interest in the importance of social dominant discourses in a person's story, I felt compelled to work differently. I wanted Ben to tell his story so that we could understand how and why his problem was the problem rather than himself being the problem. This method is an example of the *externalization* that

is discussed in Chapter 3 as a major form of distancing the self from the social discourse that promotes the problem. In Ben's case, we needed to look at the people, events, feelings, attitudes, and beliefs in his life that contributed to his problem.

By the eighth session, Ben had identified the key characters in his life as Shame, Fear, and Guilt.[2] In our conversations, these had been identified and named on many occasions and in connection with many events and people. By externalizing these feelings as characters, we were able to establish a framework for conversations in which his problems were separated from himself. By locating them outside, he was empowered to stand back from them and consider how they had influenced him; this eventually enabled him to let them go as unhelpful and unnecessary components of his life. While still taking responsibility for our own behavior, externalization allowed Ben to cease to be overpowered by the problem and freed him to look at alternative and preferred ways of thinking and being. In his conversation with me, we discovered that Shame followed Ben around from an early age—as soon as it became evident that he had a soft and gentle nature rather than an aggressive dominating personality like his father's. Shame listened to his mother, who told Ben that by being male he carried the threat of potential harm to women and he must always be aware of this. Shame was able to grow larger during Ben's teenage years when he realized he was not like other boys—he could not get or keep an erection the way they could—or said they did. Shame prevented him from developing relationships with girls until he met Nadine, but even she could not overcome its powerful impact. Shame accompanied him home to Dublin and stayed close to him as he returned to the family work he hated. The final straw adding Humiliation to Shame's achievement was the failure of Viagra when Ben visited a prostitute.

Fear had also pestered Ben from an early age. Fear was fueled by his father's loud and argumentative ways, his horrible threats to cut off Ben's penis, and Ben's mother's contrasting passivity and helplessness except when she was warning him of the dangers of this same part of his body. Even when Ben tried to escape from Fear by going to England, it returned to

---

[2]In keeping with the significance of externalizing the problem, the personification of these feelings will be written as proper nouns.

taunt him when he failed in his work and personal relationship. Most recently, Fear was glaring at Ben in the hospital room, where the doctor was carrying out all kinds of painful tests on his sexual anatomy.

Guilt had established itself firmly in Ben's mind through his childhood when it reminded him that he was a male and must live up to the impossible challenge of never causing harm to a female, and when it reminded him that his sexual feelings and desires would get him into trouble. When he thought about the family business, Guilt surrounded him. He hated working in a job where making profits is so directly dependent on the consumer's losses. When he ran up a huge bill at the sex clinic in Manchester, Guilt followed him; and when he thought about his family's concern for him and his anger at them, Guilt was at its most powerful.

While Ben talked to me about his life, I saw Shame, Fear, and Guilt battling for my attention in the room, but I also saw Courage, Determination, and Charm peeping out from behind Ben's face. By the end of our work together, these alternative strengths emerged. During our conversations, we had been able to bring these out and help them grow. They had always been there, and I had noticed them from the beginning, but for Ben they had been overshadowed. Searching for these alternatives to the problem led to looking for "unique outcomes" (Chapter 3); such occasions and situations that enhanced Courage, Determination, and Charm meant that Ben could be reminded of a side of himself he had lost. His "preferred self," or the person he wanted to be (see Chapter 3) was co-constructed through our conversations once we loosened his relationship with fear, shame, and guilt. In narrative therapy, we do not remove a problem so much as remove a person's focus on the problem by enlisting the person's view of a preferred self who can fight social discourses that fuel the problem.

The first clear sign that Ben was winning the battle against his problem happened 10 weeks into the therapy.

He came bounding up the stairs and bounced into the room like a child who had just been given the best birthday present ever. "Guess what?" he grinned. "The most amazing thing has started to happen." Ben went on to describe how over the week he started to feel physical sensations in the lower part of his body that he hadn't experienced for ages. His feet, his legs, his groin were tingling and alive, and he had woken up several times with a strong erection. In narrative therapy, both the helper and the client enter a space of curiosity about the story unfolding. Together we wondered what had made this possible, and Ben decided that it was his gradual realization that he no longer needed Shame, Fear, or Guilt to accompany him. They were not his anymore, instead he located them in the family and social discourses he was now able to challenge.

Once Ben started viewing himself differently, as not only separate from the problem but also overcoming it, we could utilize other more concrete methods of help. From then on, the work we did was educational, informative, and supportive as he reauthored his life and set about dealing with the issues he wanted to confront. This meant actually confronting his father, telling him he did not want to work for him and that he was planning on changing his career over time. He confronted his mother and told her how she had frightened him by her constant reminders of male dominance and danger and her lack of trust in his development. He made arrangements to start seeing old friends, and within another three months he had moved out of home and was sharing a house with peers. At this point. the helping process focused on those skills he had missed out on learning such as dating. Who would he ask out? What were the social rules that were important to him? How would he know if he was going to be able to have sexual intercourse? Gradually, Ben didn't need to have these conversations with me, and we ended the therapy after 30 sessions over an 18-month period.

---

even further away from the clinical, diagnostic approach will simply refer to "erection difficulties."

Although Leonardo da Vinci noted more than 500 years ago that the penis had a will of its own (Goldstein, 2000), it was not until the 19th century that doctors were able to understand the basic physiological cause of erections. Under Freud's influence, the psychological nature of the problematic penis dominated psychiatric thought up until the 1960s, when it became more readily accepted that both physical and psychological factors were involved in getting and maintaining an erection. Before a drug was invented, there were implants and injections that could be endured by the less squeamish of men but presumably were not popular choices for many (Milsten & Slowinski, 1999). A consistent theme in all ages has been the anxiety and inadequacy many men have felt when their penises refused to respond to their desires. What is changing over time is the social context in which fear, shame, and guilt have been fostered.

To illustrate the importance of recognizing the social, cultural, and political context in which these feelings develop, we present Case 6.1 on pp. 102–105.

PERSONAL REFLECTIONS

I am quite sure that I was able to help Ben more effectively because of my introduction to narrative therapy. Challenging assumptions is something I had learnt to do from an early age, growing up "different" in Irish society. Being different gave me permission to question many dominating discourses, including those about therapy and how best to work with people with problems.

I was brought up in a non-practicing Jewish family, my grandparents having fled with their families from Eastern Europe during the late 19th century. Both first- and second-level schools in Ireland were—and still are to a great extent—owned and controlled by the Church. Nuns and priests ran the Catholic schools, run by a board of management headed by the bishop of the diocese, while lay teachers worked under a similarly structured governing board of management in the Protestant schools. There is one Jewish school. I went to a Protestant girl's school along with a handful of other Jewish girls, where I was made to feel welcome yet different, being exempt from the daily prayers and assembly. As an identity-struggling teenager I loved the opportunity to rebel against societal norms, reading the works of writers such as James Joyce and Edna O'Brien when they were banned from the bookshelves, marveling at their audacity to confront issues of sexuality so openly.

I became a teacher, partly motivated by the hope that I could help to influence people's thoughts and attitudes away from the authoritative, dominating attitudes of Catholicism. Teaching did provide me with such an opportunity, but it also brought me in touch with the area of psychological needs of children and their families, leading me to do a postgraduate diploma in psychology. Like education, the psychological services in Ireland were developed and controlled by the Catholic hierarchy—the religious order of St. John of God being the main supplier of psychological services to the state. Psychological services in schools had not been developed enough to provide job opportunities, and knowing I did not want to work within the confines of mainstream clinical psychology, I joined the Marriage and Relationship Counseling Services and trained in couple's counseling, where the main theoretical influences in my counseling work were the popular psychodynamic concepts, including unconscious processes and defense mechanisms, attachment theory, and loss. I began to think more about the impact of society and of the social and cultural context in the lives of both the therapist and those looking for therapy. My quest for further knowledge was driven not by a need for more psychological understanding but for an ethical, philosophical, and fitting social framework from which to work with the problems I was being presented. Two books inspiring me at this time were *Good Friends, Equal Partners* (Rabin, 1997) and *Face to Face: Therapy as Ethics* (Gordon, 1999). These provided me with a framework within which to take a critical look at and reevaluate my beliefs around what therapy is and does.

It was only when I was introduced to the key concepts of narrative therapy that I was able to put a name to and a structure on what I had struggled to make sense of in the past. The timing of this learning happened to coincide with Ben's decision to confront his problem in sex therapy. It is possible that if I had met him prior to my new understanding I would have found a way of helping him, but I do not think it would have had the same impact or effectiveness. Maintaining a postmodernist stance, I preferred to consider ways in which the work we did aimed at deconstructing his initial assumptions and beliefs and reconstructing a more helpful and empowering way of being. The reauthoring of my own ethical stance as a therapist meant that I could help Ben reauthor his story. Had I worked conventionally with Ben, I might have helped him understand the reasons for his problem, and I might even have helped him to gain some confidence about himself sexually, but I have no doubt that the way we did work together ultimately provided a far deeper and significant change for Ben. At the same time, I was able to experience a deeper and more significant way of working as a sex therapist.

CONCLUSION

This chapter explores the impact of religion, gender, and culture on a person's sexual development and attitudes. If sex is not talked about or is talked about in terms of sin, guilt, and shame, then it can give rise to sexual difficulties that become compounded by increasing the cycle of fear, guilt, and shame. At the other extreme, when sex is highlighted by media, and claims boasting of the power of medical interventions for sexual problems dominate, then sex can still be problematic. An example is given of how one male was influenced by both old and new discourses and how working with him using narrative therapy provided the opportunity for him to deconstruct his old beliefs and replace them with more empowering discourses, enabling him to reauthor his life with hope and courage. At the same time, the therapist's own personal learning and empowerment through narrative therapy is described.

KEY CONCEPTS

- sexual problems as compliance with dominant social discourses
- media portrayals of youthful sexuality
- sex therapy in the world of medicalization of sexual problems
- externalization
- unique outcome

- the preferred self
- combining postmodern and concrete skill training and education
- the mutual impact of helper and client on each other

QUESTIONS FOR REFLECTION

1. What are the dominant discourses that have influenced your sexuality?
2. In what way can these discourses have a negative impact?
3. In what ways might they have a positive impact?
4. In what way might our sexual attitudes impact on our adult relationship?
5. Is sex therapy an outmoded form of therapy?
6. Is sexuality training necessary for health professionals?
7. Does the media's domination of sexuality need to be challenged?

EXERCISE

Each student should bring a popular magazine to class. Twenty minutes can be spent in looking through these magazines and cutting out images that have something to do with sexuality. Students should talk in dyads about what social discourses can be implied by these pictures (e.g., men initiate, women are beautiful but passive, sex is exciting and free between young beautiful bodies, sex is mysterious). Students can share the discourses that influenced them growing up, and whether these discourses fit well or contradicted what the magazine pictures show. A class discussion can then move to how sexuality comes up in the helping process, which of the many discourses the clients seem to be influenced by gender and cultural context issues.

References

Cole, M., & Dryden, W. (Eds.). (1988). *Sex therapy in Britain*. London: Open University Press.

Freedman, J., & Combs, G. (1996). *Narrative therapy: The social construction of preferred realities*. New York: Norton.

Goldstein, I. (2000). August. *Scientific American*, 56–61.

Gordon, P. (1999). *Face to face: Therapy as ethics*. London: Constable.

Inglis, T. (1998). *Lessons in Irish sexuality*. Dublin, Ireland: University College Dublin Press.

Kaplan, H. S. (1974). *The new sex therapy*. New York: Brunner.

Masters, W., & Johnson, V. (1966). *Human sexual response*. Boston: Little, Brown.

Milsten, R., & Slowinski, J. (1999). *The sexual male: Problems and solutions*. New York: Norton.

Rabin, C. (1997). *Good friends, equal partners*. London: Routledge.

Tiefer, L. (2002). A new view of women's sexual problems. *Sexual and Relationship Therapy, 17*(2), 127–131.

Ussher, J., & Baker, C. (Eds.). (1993). *Psychological perspectives on sexual problems*. London: Routledge.

Zilbergeld, B. (1992). *The new male sexuality*. New York: Bantam Books.

CHAPTER 7

PRIDE AND PREJUDICE WITH GAY AND LESBIAN INDIVIDUALS

Combining Narrative and Expressive Practices

ELEANOR PARDESS
ISRAEL

OVERVIEW

This chapter explores many unique issues and challenges in helping gay, lesbian, and bisexual clients develop a positive identity in a society in which prejudice and discrimination are prevalent. A narrative approach within a postmodern framework gives us a new perspective on homophobia and heterosexism and sheds new light on the complexities of identity development and the "coming-out" process as rewriting of one's story and a continuous conversation with oneself and others. Because the definitions and acceptability of same-sex love differ across cultures and are constantly changing, understanding the sociocultural context is imperative. When helpers deny the culture-specific experiences in the lives of lesbian and gay clients, bias is likely to pervade the helping encounter.

Combining the expressive arts with narrative therapy can open new possibilities for practitioners. By rendering the invisible visible, opening lines of communication, and transcending culture barriers, art is a valuable resource. It can be a form of "giving voice" and of protest against dominant oppressive discourses. A detailed case study will illustrate how narrative practices integrated with the expressive arts may provide support and validation as well as strengthen the capacity of the individual to resist the detrimental effects of negative labeling and pathologizing discourses. Finally, based on studies surveyed in this chapter, a table has been prepared that lists guidelines for those affirmative practices that can provide support for identity development and biased practices where helping can harm.

INTRODUCTION

Three decades have passed since the decision to remove homosexuality from the American Psychiatric Association's (APA) list of mental disorders. However, despite the changing social atmosphere in many countries around the world, prejudice continues to be widespread (Haldeman, 1994; Herek, 1995; Perez, DeBord, & Bieschke, 2000). Help providers need to be aware of social stigmatization (i.e., prejudice, discrimination, and even violence) and the risks it poses to the mental health and well-being of lesbian and gay clients. Prejudice and stigmatization have various manifestations, including homophobia, internalized homophobia, and heterosexism.

Homophobia

Merriam-Webster's Collegiate Dictionary (10th ed., 1993), defines *homophobia* as the "irrational fear of, aversion to, or discrimination against homosexuality or homosexuals." Its manifestations range from social avoidance to verbal abuse to civil, military, and religious discrimination, to physical violence (Isay, 1989).

From a postmodern perspective, understanding the social context of homophobia is crucial. Homophobia thrives in societies that are intolerant of diversity. Although the use of the term *phobia* may imply a personal problem of an individual (who, according to psychoanalytic formulations, is threatened by his or her homosexual impulses), homophobia is located in the sociocultural context and supported by dominant social discourses. Antigay attitudes and denigrating messages about homosexuals and bisexuals are socially construed, and discrimination is institutionalized in many aspects of society—legal, military, and so on (DePoy & Noble, 1992).

Numerous and complex social factors contribute to homophobia. Intolerance and prejudice toward the "other" is one factor (Cain, 1991). Another source of homophobia in many cultures seems to be religious traditions that oppose homosexuality (e.g., Christianity, Judaism, and Islam). In recent years, certain "progressive" branches of Protestantism and Judaism have increasingly accepted homosexuality. However, in most religious settings, homosexuality may still be considered a sin. The psychiatric and early psychoanalytic models of homosexuality as a disorder perhaps were meant to "liberate" homosexuality from its status as a sin, yet in doing so they created new pathologizing discourses as an illness or a sign of arrested developmental disorder. These discourses dominated the mental health field for most of the last century (Bieschke, McClanahan, Tozer, Grzegorek, & Park, 2000).

Antigay prejudices are not limited to any specific educational, cultural, or social group. They exist across religions, professions, environments, and ages. However, recent studies have shown that levels of tolerance toward homosexuality are affected by demographics and direct familiarity with people with gay and lesbian sexual orientations as well as by personality traits and interpersonal issues. People with low education levels; traditional, religious, and conservative values; and sexual identity conflicts tend to be more homophobic than their educated, nonreligious, progressive, and sexually confident counterparts (Greene & Herek, 1994).

Internalized Homophobia

Internalized homophobia means the rejection, condemnation, or even hatred of one's own homosexuality (Gonsiorek, 1991). Because of the pervasiveness of homophobia in our culture, we are exposed from the earliest age to a constant stream of messages that denigrate homosexuality and homosexuals. For example, "faggot" or "fairy" are names used by children in elementary school to insult a classmate. There are many myths regarding homosexuality. For many people, these myths and negative messages become internalized as "truths" about "the way things really are." The fact that the messages are culturally constructed becomes invisible as in the case of gender stereotypes—girls are supposed to "be sweet and demure," boys "aggressive and competitive." In many ways, internalized homophobia is similar to the self-hatred based on the internalization of gender stereotypes. Those who do not meet the standards may develop gender-related stress and a lowered self-esteem as a result. Internalizing racism can have similar effects on one's self-esteem. When one lives with rejection day after day, and society discounts one's value constantly, it is difficult to maintain perspective and realize that the problem is *others'* perceptions, not one's own.

Heterosexism

Heterosexism is "a belief system that values heterosexuality as superior to [and] more 'natural' than homosexuality" (Morrin, 1977). In contrast to homophobia, the manifestations of heterosexism are more subtle and difficult to detect (Van Vorris & Wagner, 2002). As Berkman and Zinberg (1997, p. 320) noted, "Heterosexism permeates the culture in which social institutions and social work practice are built." Society sends a clear message: "Be like everyone else!" "One heterosexist assumption is that people assume everyone is heterosexual until proved otherwise" (Berkman & Zinberg, 1997, p. 320).

Different theories exist as to homosexuality and its etiology. Some models stress biology as the primary factor; others stress the role of environment. These models, seen in a postmodern framework as shifting perspectives, can shape one's attitudes and behavior. The evidence from research on etiology is still inconclusive and points to a dynamic interaction between biology and environment. Because each individual develops his or her private theory of the causes of homosexuality, it is important to listen carefully in order to learn about these personal meanings and explore their implications in an open-minded approach.

UNDERSTANDING IDENTITY DEVELOPMENT AND ITS SOCIAL CONTEXT

Identity does not develop in a vacuum but in a specific social context. Developing a strong sense of identity in a heterosexist society means being able to resist negative labeling and stigmatization. Identity development and coming out is a prolonged process in which people rewrite the stories they have about themselves (Cass, 1984; Troiden, 1989).

In general, the development of gay identity involves for the gay world three major stages: (1) coming out to oneself, (2) coming out in the gay world, and (3) coming out in the straight world (*straight*, in this case, being the gay term for heterosexual) (Plummer, 1981). Plummer notes that the first stage of identification is often the hardest because it usually has to be done alone and without support. This step involves confronting insidious messages that homosexuality is rare, a sickness or maladjustment, or just abnormal.

Cass (1979) describes the complexities of coping with prejudice and developing a sense of pride. It is interesting to note that *identity pride,* according to her theoretical model, is the stage in which the individual, having accepted his or her identity, is able to establish connections with the gay community. Living "in the closet" means being cut off from important sources of support (Falco, 1991).

Gaining access to homosexual role models can counterbalance the negative messages and serve to dispel many myths and preconceptions about homosexual people and behavior. Pride in this stage marks the beginning of gay acculturation. The term *pride* seems to express a protest against dominant shame-inducing discourses. Pride can be considered a *counternarrative.* Counternarratives are stories that people tell and live that offer resistance, either explicitly or implicitly, to dominant cultural narratives (Andrews, 2002).

In supporting a developing sense of pride, the gay community can function as a source of support to buffer stress and provide often sorely needed validation. Support networks of close and accepting friends, called "families of choice," are part of this process about which helpers need to be aware.

The coming-out process can be a totally different experience in different cultures, as we shall see in the following parts of the chapter. Choosing to live as a gay man or lesbian can mean, especially for those who live in a culture that is totally unaccepting of homosexuality, a cutoff from one's roots—from one's friends and other support systems—as well as leaving behind an important part of one's identity—values, beliefs, identification, and a sense of belonging (Dworkin, 1996). In many ways, this is like a process of immigration in which multiple losses are inherent as well as a painful transformation of identity. The cutoff from important parts of one's identity may leave the individual with a sense of uprootedness and alienation. The individual may be left "storyless" or with huge gaps and missing pieces in his or her life story.

PREJUDICE IN THE HELPING ENCOUNTER

Many social workers and mental health providers are ignorant of the societal heterosexism and homophobia and of the way it may impact their practices (Ben-Ari, 2001; DeCrescenzo, 1984; O'Dell, 2000; Morrin, 1988; Van Vorris & Wagner, 2002) as well as the impact it has on the way that the client tells (or does not tell) his story. In spite of a trend toward increasing acceptance, homophobic attitudes still exist among social workers, counselors, and psychologists (Berkman & Zingberg, 1997; DeCrescenzo, 1984; Garnets, Hancock, Cochran, Godchilds, & Peplau, 1991; Gelso, Fassinger, Gomez, & Latts, 1995; Morrow, 1996; Wisniewski & Toomey, 1987). For example, clients turn for help for a variety of reasons that may have little to do with their sexual orientation. However, a helper may automatically attribute a client's problems to his or her sexual orientation without evidence that this is so (Garnets et al., 1991). The helper's narrative may be imposed on the client in so many ways. For example, a helper who is trained according to traditional psychoanalytic models may search for evidence to support these models, regarding homosexuality as a sign of arrested development because of unresolved oedipal conflicts. A 26-year-old, talking about his attraction to men, was encouraged to date women in order to get over his fear of women. The helper insisted on working through possible difficulties in his relationship with his mother, assuming that she was dominant and engulfing. This led the client to think that something was deeply wrong with him.

There have been reports of reorientation therapy, although such practices are considered unethical (Haldeman, 1994). "Corrective therapy" that is aimed at changing sexual orientation can be seen as another form of cultural domination in a heterosexist and homophobic society—that is, getting people to return to the mainstream.

Clients who are uncertain about their sexual orientation may seek help to resolve their concerns. A helper may adopt three different approaches. One, called a "must" approach, is to push the client into defining himself or coming out before being ready to do so. The second, a "must not" approach, can entail trying to discourage the client from adopting a gay or lesbian identity. This can be done in many subtle ways. The third approach is a "can" approach that enables the client to find his or her own way (Hanley-Hackenbruck, 1988). The difficulty in achieving the last includes the fact that heterosexism pervades the language, theories, and psychotherapeutic interventions of psychology (Bieschke et al., 2000; Van Vorris & Wagner, 2002). One manifestation of heterosexism is approaching the helping process with a "sexual orientation–blind" perspective. This means ignoring the culturally unique experiences of the lesbian, gay, and bisexual population. Like a colorblind approach, this may be a strategy for avoiding a pathologizing stance by stressing the universal components of human experience. However, when helpers deny the culture-specific experiences in the lives of lesbian, gay, and bisexual people, heterosexist bias is also likely to pervade that work in a manner that is unhelpful to clients (Garnets et al., 1991; Roth, 1989).

A helper may fail to "recognize that a client's psychological symptoms or distress can be influenced by multiple social stresses as well as the client's own negative attitudes or ideas about homosexuality" (Perez et al., 2000).

Talking openly about one's homosexuality can play an important role in changing attitudes. However, it is also important to keep in mind the cultural context and remember that disclosure does not always pave the way to a change of attitudes or a better understanding of what it means to be gay. In some cultural contexts disclosure may actually be too dangerous. A helper, lacking a broader perspective on sociocultural factors or awareness of the discrimination, may push the client into premature disclosure and in some cases even endanger him in doing so. Such an approach conveys an implicitly negative message to those choosing not to disclose—"Something is wrong with you"—and locates once again the problem within the individual rather than recognizing its location in the social context. Actual threats may be implied (losing friends and family members; and, in some cases, losing a job or even facing physical danger). The helper, coming from a different or perhaps more liberal background and lacking social awareness, may be unaware of these possible threats.

PRIDE AND PREJUDICE IN ISRAEL: THE SOCIAL CONTEXT

Having understood how important it is to understand the social context, let us turn to understanding the Israeli sociocultural context: *Ga'avah* (*pride* in Hebrew) is the word associated in Israel with gay community activities, cultural events, and the gay rights movement. The adoption of British mandatory law that banned sodomy was changed in Israel only in 1988. Certain legal changes have been achieved since. For example, an explicit law since 1992 has forbid discrimination because of sexual orientation. The social climate seems indeed to be changing rapidly and is more accepting of homosexuality than it was a decade ago. The visibility of homosexuals and lesbians has greatly increased, as manifested in openly gay parades, numerous publications in the media, regular "pride pages" in the newspaper, gay bars, theater, and other social activities, mainly in urban centers such as Tel Aviv (Sumakei-Fink & Press, 1999).

Well-known artists, authors, actors, and singers have openly come out, talking in public of their personal experiences. A member of the Knesset (the Israeli parliament) gave a famous speech on his own experiences as a homosexual and as a leading officer in the army. Despite the changing climate, many people fear the consequences of coming out and still live behind locked doors in fear of their secret being exposed, paying a heavy price of isolation. Lack of social recognition and legitimacy by Israeli society has also a direct impact on the interaction of couples (Mizrachi, 1990; Rabin, 1991). Religious influences, the coexistence of two legal systems—the one secular and the other religious—and the great value placed on the traditional family have contributed to conflicting trends in the acceptability of same-sex love (Walzer, 2000).

Israel is a multicultural society, a mosaic of people from many diverse backgrounds, bringing with them a wide spectrum of traditions, values, beliefs, and customs. There are great cultural differences in terms of the acceptability of homosexuality in different parts of Israeli society. The "ancient old" in Israel lives side-by-side with the ultramodern in many respects. Coming out is therefore a totally different experience in different populations as well as in different age groups because of the rapid changes in the social atmosphere. The challenge of achieving identity integration and making room for diversity in one's identity as discussed above and the danger of throwing away the baby with the bath water and relinquishing one's roots in order to adopt a gay identity is definitely a problem for those who are trying to reconcile or negotiate conflicting identities. "Keshet Ga'avah" ("The Spectrum of Pride"), the 17th World Conference of GLBT (Gay, Lesbian, Bisexual, and Transgender) Jews held in Israel, chose "Reclaiming Roots, Rites, and Roles" as the central theme of the 2002 conference—focusing on "reclaiming cultural heritage, spirituality, roots and a rightful place within wider Jewish communities around the world" (quotation from conference brochure). This is an interesting example of a community program that promotes the goal of identity synthesis as mentioned above and makes room for diversity.

Stress (and internalized homophobia) may be especially pronounced for those who are living in intolerant environments—for example, the ultraorthodox, Arab Israelis, or, in some cases, those immigrants coming from Arab countries (where homosexuals are actively persecuted and subjects of severe violence). Recent immigrants from the former Soviet Union have also been reported to hold antigay attitudes as reflected in Russian media. Individuals from these communities may face exacerbated stress, stigmatization, and discrimination from multiple sources and at the same time are less able to access and receive appropriate help. The following vignettes illustrate the importance of understanding the social context:

> A Muslim Arab with a steady relationship with a Jew, the two living together for years, could not stand being touched by his partner during the muezzin's' calls to prayer from the mosque nearby.
>
> A 14-year-old boy from an ultraorthodox religious background used to walk around with a bottle of water because he was so afraid that if he had "bad thoughts" being around other guys, "tongues of fire would shoot out of hell" as his rabbi had told him.
>
> A 15-year-old boy from an oriental background, after being discovered with a boyfriend, was taken to many traditional healers, one of whom put a dead dove on his belly. Another told him to pray, and a third told him to drink his own urine. This boy developed severe self-destructive behavior. His parents refused to allow him to consult with a helper.

THE CONTRIBUTION OF THE NARRATIVE APPROACH IN CHALLENGING HOMOPHOBIA

The narrative tradition suggests that the stories we tell ourselves not only speak of the lives we live but also "author" them. Stories are not mirrors of reality; they constitute a map and shape our lives over time. Narrative therapy focuses on the "reauthoring" of one's story, deconstructing the "text" of a problem, and questioning the "taken for granted truths" (Freedman & Combs, 1996; White & Epston, 1990). Questioning the taken-for-granted truths and deconstructing practices can help in identifying and challenging dominant subjugating discourses. This can support the deconstruction of myths about homosexuality as well as assist in combating heterosexism and internalized homophobia. Externalizing practices can provide additional support in combating fear, shame, and guilt as illustrated in the case study. The way people narrate their experiences is influenced by their individual histories and cultural discourses. We can also focus on the way in which clients' stories are constrained by dominant narratives such as patriarchal or oppressive stories.

People's stories are often constrained by finding themselves living out a story into which they have been recruited (Parry & Doan, 1994). For a woman who loves women, being recruited into a cultural story according to which she is expected to marry and raise children with a husband may lead her into hiding her feelings and needs and thus paying a high sense of isolation and alienation from her true self. Narrative therapy can strengthen the individual's capacity to resist negative labeling as well as resist being recruited into stories told by others as to what it means to be a "real man" or "real woman" or what it takes to make a "real family." This means discovering one's own voice and not accepting others' descriptions of one's life.

Narrative therapy can help both helpers and clients shift from seeing problems as internal to seeing them as constructed within the social and cultural context and shaped through use of language. Clients' narratives are influenced by the way in which their cultures view homosexuality (Herdt, 1997). The construction and possible deconstruction of narratives about same-sex love involve complex dynamics that are associated with factors such as cultural values regarding gender roles and religious and procreative beliefs. The degree of individual and family acculturation and the personal and cultural history of discrimination or oppression are also important. All of these factors have been found to have a significant impact on identity integration and psychological and social functioning.

"Dominant culture takes up most of the space and pushes to the edges those experiences that lie outside its normalized standards and values" (Zimmerman & Dickinson, 1996). In order to free oneself from the influence of the problem, one has to "challenge" the dominant meaning that is experienced as oppressive. This challenge is a form of therapeutic protest. Therefore, instead of seeing homosexuality as "the problem," one can realize how myths and misperceptions are "the problems." This is only one example of multiple stories that can be reauthored through the helping encounter. The therapeutic dialogue can promote identity development and synthesis by a flexible use of deconstructive questioning, opening space for exploring one's "landscape of identity" (Bruner, 1989; Freedman & Combs, 1996). This can mean exploring the personal meaning of issues such as the role of gender, sexual orientation, and culture in one's life story. Through the narrative lens it becomes possible to appreciate some of the richness and complexity of human experience.

The "not knowing" stance is particularly important in setting aside preconceptions and truly listening, placing the client as *the expert* on his or her life. Such an approach can be highly effective in combating prejudice. Because narrative therapy stresses multiple viewpoints and alternating perspectives, it is especially helpful in paving the way for the acceptance of diversity within oneself and in society.

COMBINING EXPRESSIVE ARTS WITH NARRATIVE THERAPY

Combining the expressive arts with narrative therapy using visual arts, music, bibliotherapy, and poetry can open new possibilities of telling and retelling one's story and having it authenticated. The use of nonverbal means complements the narrative therapy and its focus on the spoken language. Paintings can also help tell stories. This is true of other forms of art. Art provides rich opportunities to explore the different sides of one's story, making room for diversity (including gender and culture-related issues) and thus promoting identity development and synthesis.

Within a narrative approach, the following practices are supported by creative art:

1. *Externalizing.* Artwork naturally supports externalizing practices in narrative therapy. By getting in touch with one's feelings (such as shame or guilt) and expressing them in a tangible concrete form (through paintings, sculpture, photography, etc.), one can establish some distance and regain a sense of perspective and control.
2. *Thickening the plot.* Art can be utilized to help clients make the stories they are authoring "thicker" and more multistranded. During the creative process, the artwork can be revisited and reworked, thereby adding new dimensions to the reauthoring conversations, promoting identity development, and thickening the plot of preferred emerging stories.
3. *Making room for diversity and multiple viewpoints.* Art can help people recognize the multiple nature of themselves and the world—and to view it as a source of enrichment not to be resisted.
4. *Transcending barriers.* The language of symbols and metaphors creates a universal language that transcends culture and gender barriers, adding new dimensions and depth to one's narrative.
5. *Unique outcomes.* Art as a stimulating and challenging activity helps people connect with the transcendent and growth aspects of their stories, thus promoting a sense of mastery and competence.

Gay culture in general can play an important role in the process of individual identity construction. Art makes visible the invisible (Riley, 2001). Given the invisibility of many facets of the gay experience, this is a valuable resource. Visual arts, films, theater, and literature offer rich opportunities for the expression of voices outside dominating discourses.

Art can serve as a form of "giving voice" as well as a protest against dominant discourses. Through nonverbal means and the elaboration of metaphors within a narrative approach, a client can be helped to find a channel for voicing experiences beyond words. Art can serve as a bridge for communicating with oneself and others, as will be illustrated in the following case study.

"I JUST CAN'T THINK STRAIGHT": REAUTHORING CONVERSATIONS WITH DAPHNE*

Daphne, aged 28, came for help because she was feeling depressed and "on the edge" and was having endless fights with her parents. She was still living at home and working as a waitress, although she had graduated law school with high grades. She felt deeply frustrated and angry, didn't quite know what to do with her future, and had a difficult time with job interviews, being rejected time and again. "I just can't think straight," she said.

During the first session, Daphne, dark-skinned with short hair and sporty clothes on a petite body and looking younger than her age, was edgy and defensive. She was the eldest of three daughters. Her sister, two years younger, was about to get married. Daphne was extremely angry with her parents for praising her sister's fiancé all the time and for spending so much time and money on preparations for the wedding.

Daphne herself had an open and steady relationship with her girlfriend and was considering leaving home but was confined by limited finances. On the surface, it seemed that her parents had accepted her love for women after more than 10 years of struggling with her over the issue. However, on weekends and holidays, her sister's fiancé was welcomed warmly, whereas Daphne's partner of 3 years had never been invited. Daphne expressed her indignation at the deep respect her parents had for every "piece of nonsense" her future brother-in-law said around the table. "It's just because he's a man," she said bitterly. "Well, at last they have found the son they wanted so much," she remarked in another session. The arguments around the table had escalated into shouting, with Daphne leaving the house and slamming the door.

Daphne was most sensitive to every slightest facial response on my part. It was clear that she wanted me to justify her indignation at her parents' conduct. When I hesitated in answering her demands, she was fuming in obvious anger. She was almost about to

*The client's name and identifying information have been changed to protect her confidentiality.

walk out of my room, too, and slam the door behind her. My reflection on how she felt misunderstood only made her angrier. However, she stayed on in silent and sulking protest, totally withdrawn and difficult to reach. Instances such as this of intense anger at my failure to express empathy recurred time after time.

In the second session, when she asked to take off her shoes to feel more comfortable, she threw at me "Next time my shirt!" Each of my reactions was scrutinized and often met with contempt. I often felt stereotyped and accused of being outdated and of not being able to understand. I really was having a difficult time understanding. The chasm between us seemed unbridgeable.

At that time, I was quite exasperated, often embarrassed, and at a loss as to how to reach her. I found myself identifying with her parents and thinking of the difficult time they were going through. As far as I knew, or chose to assume, they had accepted Daphne's love of women, acknowledged the relationship with her girlfriend, and were trying hard to placate her. So why was she making such a fuss and unable to understand their difficulties?

It was much easier then to be empathetic with her parents' distress than with her. It took me time to realize how vulnerable, exposed, and threatened Daphne felt. I had not really understood the impact of the long-standing rejection that Daphne had suffered in her family and social context. She had been talking about being treated unfairly and had spoken of what she called "the dark years" in her adolescence, but I hadn't asked her about those years. I had assumed mistakenly that she was out and in the open and felt comfortable with her identity and life choices. Awareness on my part of the negative labeling seemed to enable the story of those "dark years" to be told. I will focus in the following paragraphs on those related to the complexities of the identity development and coming-out process.

The Pain of Rejection

Daphne had intense love affairs beginning at age 13 but had struggled with defining herself as a lesbian. The derogatory voices and names she heard at school regarding what it meant to be a "homo" contributed to a deep sense of shame. She lived a split life in constant fear of being found out, hiding love letters and other proof of her love. Her world seemed to collapse when, at age 16, her parents discovered the nature of her relationship with her close girl friend and forbade the two to have any further contact. Her mother responded with a deep depression. She refused to speak to her. "How could you do this to us?" Daphne remembers her saying through tears. Her father was outwardly angry and on several occasions even violent. The parents began blaming each other, and it seemed that the whole family was falling apart. Memories about that period were traumatic, and amnesia and dissociation were dominant. All that she could remember is that she wanted to die.

Prior Experience in Obtaining Help

When she was 16, Daphne's parents took her to a helper, hoping that therapy would put her on the right track. The helper did not collaborate with her parents' wish to "convert" Daphne into loving boys. However, as far as Daphne could remember, the helper ignored the deep love and painful longings that Daphne expressed for her girlfriend, whom she deeply missed at the time. Daphne did not feel comfortable enough to admit she was secretly meeting her partner.

When the helper met the deeply worried parents, she told them that Daphne was going through a period of confusion. "This is something she will outgrow," they were told. This is exactly what the parents wanted to hear. They were still waiting 5 years later, urging Daphne to try to date boys.

Feeling a Misfit

Daphne herself, before going into therapy, had been quite sure of her sexual orientation yet convinced that this was a sign of being a "defect," a misfit—indeed, abnormal. She was thoroughly confused. The helper's attitude planted self-doubt and caused her to try dating boys, although she was totally disinterested. She kept meeting her friend in secret, feeling extremely guilty and a disgrace to her family. She tried to compensate by being an excellent student at school and bringing home high grades.

It was only after 3 years of constant struggle with her parents and periods in which her mother didn't talk to her that her parents finally gave up talking about her dating boys. It felt to her that they gave up on her totally. In any case, they stopped talking about her personal life altogether. She was then in the army

and living away from home, which enabled her to gain some distance and restore some self-esteem. She finished the officer's course with excellent results and upon leaving the army registered for law school.

In the years that followed, she continued to experience shame and guilt, living a closeted life. She was successful in her university studies, yet the only real sense of security and of being her true self was achieved when she was with her girlfriend (a new and strong relationship that had developed in university). In therapy she now talked about how she could never fit in. In her words, "I am not a real woman, not a real man, not really anything, not belonging anywhere."

Combating Shame and Guilt

During the period of talking about her parent's rejection and its devastating impact on her life, Daphne shared a recent nightmare. In her dream, she was seated at the end of a long table, being pointed at by blaming fingers and facing the severe faces of her parents, sisters, and brother together with teachers from school, all of them calling her names and shouting accusations of being an unfaithful and ungrateful daughter. She was speechless, trying to but unable to utter a word. She woke up in a deep sweat.

In the session, we were able to explore the multilayered meanings of the dream. Now she became more prepared to face the shame and guilt and identify the internalized homophobia. Externalizing conversations together with deconstructing questioning (Freedman & Combs, 1996) helped her face the shame and guilt that had joined together in silencing her and constricting her steps. Shame coupled with guilt had coerced her into hiding away for so many years.

In one of our sessions, Daphne brought a newspaper clipping with a picture of a woman whose mouth and face are covered with a kind of polythene stifling her (see Figure 7.1). On the image are written quotations from Sefer Hanashim, the Jewish orthodox religious rules. *Sefer Hanashim* is Hebrew for "The Women's Book." "Written of course by men," as Daphne said. "What does this story tell you?" I then asked. She talked about the suppression of the voice of the woman in the picture. While telling the story, she looked closer at the picture and saw actually that the woman herself was stifling her voice with her own hands, holding up the cover. This shed new light and

(continued)

FIGURE 7.1 | Art as "giving voice." Images can evoke powerful feelings that help people tell their own stories. This silenced outcry represented for Daphne the story of oppression of women. It also represents how oppressive rules are adopted and internalized.

Sefer Hanashim ("The Book of Women"), Nechama Golan, 2001. Used with permission.

led Daphne to reauthor her own story. The story now became a story of internalized oppression, with the woman adopting the men's rules and point of view and committing herself to silence. "I have been gagging myself as well," she said. "Gagging herself" became a central metaphor in the therapy.

Exploring Unique Outcomes

In spite of tremendous pressures, Daphne had been able to develop a meaningful and strong bond with the woman she deeply loved. Understanding what had helped her keep up this resistance had an empowering effect, shedding new light on the interactions with significant others and enabling her to draw on resources she was not aware of. She now realized how shame and guilt were interfering with the way she presented herself during job interviews.

FIGURE 7.2 | Identity development is an ongoing dialogue with oneself and others. Gender and culture are interwoven in this dialogue. Through this painting, Daphne was able to talk about the "crippled" and distorted conversations she had been having with others, leaving her with a painful feeling of being labeled and misunderstood.

Dialogue, Hanna Silberstein, 2000. Used with permission.

Soon afterward, she started working as a lawyer for a small law firm. Her success in finding a job appeared to be related to her growing confidence and ability to assert herself. Capitalizing on unique outcomes related to her assertiveness at work helped "thicken the plot" (White & Epston, 1990) of the new story being authored—of her being a survivor and not a victim. Daphne was indeed highly resourceful: The success at work added to her redefining of herself and the restorying of her life.

Harnessing Creative Processes

Reflecting on a painting (*Dialogue*) by Israeli artist Hanna Silberstein (Figure 7.2) Daphne spoke of the "crippled" conversations she had been having in her family. "So much to be said, so much turmoil going on in the mind, and such a little mouth." Speaking of the left figure in the painting, she said, "She looks so miserable. She has been marked like they label cows."

This led to exploring what it meant for her to be labeled as a woman in her upbringing. She had experienced such great difficulty in explaining herself in

FIGURE 7.3 | Challenging dominant discourses. Creative approaches can challenge dominant discourses such as the heterosexism reflected in messages that it is unnatural for a woman to love a woman—"What next? A woman with a goat?"

My Love, Hanna Silberstein, 2002. Used with permission.

the face of ignorance. Responding to another sketch (Figure 7.3) by the same artist, she quoted from Ellen Degeneres's show: "There is this huge debate about same-sex marriage. People say, "Marriage is a union between a man and a woman. A woman marrying a woman! What next? A woman with a goat?" Well, these people scare me—and they think *we* are weird." The gentle tenderness, humor, and playfulness conveyed in the drawing helped Daphne cope with the messages of illegitimacy she had been receiving. Deconstructive questioning and working through these issues enabled her to identify the great difficulty she was having in conversing with others and to see these difficulties as located in the messages she had received instead of resulting from her own "defect." This facilitated the reauthoring of her own story: She had formerly thought of herself as crippled and speechless in the conversations with others. This version gave way to considering herself as being able to speak up for herself even in the most embarrassing situations. In her own words, "My mouth now opens quite easily sometimes to my surprise. I can be called 'a big mouth' but that will not silence me."

With my encouragement, Daphne went back to painting, a hobby she had neglected. This followed the

sessions in which she had discussed the way shame had silenced her. She had talked of her difficulties in expressing herself and articulating her feelings. Using nonverbal means of communication, she was able to explore new territories. She could express experiences for which she had no words.

She brought with her to the sessions some of her paintings such as one sketch of a nude woman sitting before a mirror. She was carefully watching my reactions: Could she speak openly about her sexuality in the room? Would there be enough space in the room? Would she meet rejection? acceptance? empathy?

Reflecting on the meanings of the painting, she was able to explore what it meant for her to be exposed with no clothes on, getting to know herself through looking at the mirror. For years she hadn't dared look at herself. "I just hate myself." Tears poured out as she gave voice to the deep sense of hurt and self-hatred. "My defenses are like this tissue paper," she said through her tears. Expressing these feelings led to exploring what it meant for her to be a woman, feeling she had disappointed her parents and the deep sense of inferiority and shame.

Lesbian community theater in Israel was another source of validating support for Daphne, helping her give voice to what she had not even dared to admit to herself. Daphne's artwork was also a way of helping me understand her and helping her understand herself. In her paintings, she began using a wide spectrum of colors she had never touched before. She felt she could eventually show her true colors and feel good about having such a rich spectrum of shades in her world instead of the black and white monochromatic worldview she held beforehand. The wide spectrum of colors on the pride flag found its way to her artwork. She explored the meaning of tolerating diversity and making room for different colors. The colors were there in her work, and she could see them and take pride in the way they were composed together, side by side, each maintaining its individual identity without mixing with the others.

Daphne resonated deeply with a drawing of a "queer" zebra hidden away within its own body, all closed up in itself. She called the drawing "Feeling So Embarrassed." Daphne, as part of her reflecting and telling her story through the zebra, found great fun in drawing queer zebras in different positions. We talked about striped zebras being so different and set apart from the family of horses. Throughout history,

(continued)

FIGURE 7.4 | Making room for diversity and paving the way to a "shaky sense of pride." Daphne understood the sense of "being different," of feeling awkward, and of "walking on shells" shown in this painting. Still, she was able to show her true colors (which corresponded to the striped colors of the gay pride flag). The painting is multilayered, as are our stories.

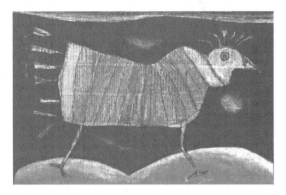

Diversity, Hanna Silberstein, 2000. Used with permission.

attempts to tame zebras to behave like horses have been in vain. A zebra will not be harnessed. "Can this zebra learn to love herself?" Daphne asked.

Celebrating Pride for the First Time

Daphne had never been to a gay party or even to a gay bar. Her girlfriend had tried for years to persuade her to go out together with her. However, she was too apprehensive about whom she could meet there. Going for the first time to a lesbian community party was for her a triumph in overcoming the shame—the paralyzing and overriding force that had been controlling her. It took her four weeks to actually gather the courage to show up at a party. She was able to share her relief and joy: "Such a small step, but a huge leap for me." She had such a good time! It was an enlightening feeling to discover that she was able to feel free to dance with her partner and even kiss her in front of the huge mirror in the room, gradually letting the feelings of stiffness and self-consciousness dissolve and giving way to "just being myself." The shaky sense of pride was also expressed through Silberstein's painting of a sort of "strange creature" as Daphne said, so used to feeling awkward and different, but now showing its true colors for the first time (see Figure 7.4). Telling the

story from the point of view of the figure in the drawing helped her tell her own story.

Exploring Landscapes of Identity and Creating New Roadmaps

Narrative questioning and deconstructing assisted Daphne in exploring her "landscape of identity" (Bruner, 1989). The roadmaps she had received from her parents and society had not helped her find her true self in the landscape of her life. These maps were unsuitable and inapplicable. Same-sex love was not on these maps. She had found paths that did not appear on the roadmaps she was given. Deciphering the keys for those maps was a metaphor elaborated.

The keys to these roadmaps, which had been passed on from former generations, included rigid traditional definitions about masculinity and femininity, definitions of what it means to be a woman, to be a man, as well as the definitions of success. Daphne's mother was from an eastern background. Coming from a highly patriarchal background, she had found it almost impossible to conceive how a woman would give up the idea of getting married. She could not imagine how Daphne could ever possibly be happy or lead a satisfying life as a lesbian. Outright displays of anger by a woman were also unacceptable in her upbringing. Daphne's father had a western European upbringing. Although he was not orthodox himself, he took pride in his grandfather being a well-known rabbi. Same-sex love had definitely not been on his roadmap of life either. He placed great value on career development and achievement. Daphne was proud of him and adopted his high standards and the great value he had placed on perseverance and excellence.

By being a lawyer, Daphne was considered a success and her parents were proud of her. However, being a successful woman meant for both of them, especially for Daphne's mother, getting married and raising children with a husband. Daphne at first had accepted her parents' roadmaps as "essential truths" about life. However, the definitions on the key of these roadmaps were too narrow for her and did not fit into her vision of her reality. According to these, she was indeed a misfit, as well as a troublemaker, causing disgrace to her family. Now she began to consider the possibility that it was not she who did not fit in. The definitions just did not fit her reality. She faced the challenge of creating a new roadmap with a key of her own definitions, finding the freedom to define herself instead of accepting the way others defined her.

Redefining the Meaning of "I Just Cannot Think Straight"

"I just cannot think straight," Daphne had said, referring to her inability to think clearly when overwhelmed with anger. We redefined this to mean that she was still trying to think as a "straight" person. Acknowledging her right to "stop thinking straight" and to think out things her way was an important step in therapy. She could see how she had been able to resist being recruited into the script prescribed to her. She no longer saw herself unquestionably as *the problem*.

We were also able to explore her difficulty with expressing anger—rooted in the messages she had received from early childhood about anger. In her social context, anger was considered unfeminine. Understanding the social context of these messages was important. She had internalized the ideas about anger and had great difficulty in accepting her own anger. Furthermore, being defined as crazy every time she was angry colluded with her deep conviction that something was wrong with her and that she was indeed abnormal. Helping her validate her anger had direct implications on being able to cope with conflict at work and in the family.

Helping Her Parents Understand

Daphne was now able to talk with her parents about the issues they had been avoiding. She was less threatened and prepared to accept that they would not be able to understand without her explaining herself. This replaced her former conviction that her parents, or at least her mother, should have been able to understand her without her having to explain herself.

Her youngest sister helped her bridge the gap between herself and her parents. In one instance, her sister had talked to her father (and later with her grandparents) about the Nazi persecution of homosexuals. The way she put it, in light of the shared plight of Jews and homosexuals, discriminating against Daphne because of her love of women was actually continuing the Nazi persecution. Furthermore, their "conspiracy of silence" was just like the silence about the suffering in the Holocaust. Her father was left speechless after the sister's strong words.

The parents, who in the course of the ongoing conversations between themselves, with Daphne and others, had already gone through many transformations, made it quite clear that her partner was most welcome to come over on Fridays and, indeed, she became an integral part of the family.

Coping with Racism, Sexism, and Heterosexism

Daphne was threatened by certain interactions and "putdowns" both in the office and in court. Coping as the only woman in a predominantly male surrounding stirred a range of feelings. She almost quit the job after an incident in which she felt deeply insulted. Externalizing the shame and reaction of insult helped her gain distance from the strong emotions that took control over her. These had in the past caused her to react in an impulsive and defensive manner instead of asserting herself. In understanding her reactions and overreactions, it was important to work through additional issues, exploring the effects of racism and sexism, among others.

Proud to Be Myself

Together with increasing self-acceptance, Daphne was now able to openly talk with her parents, confront the putdowns at work, and stand her ground. She felt able to take on new challenges and cope assertively. Liberated from the powerful grip of shame and guilt and free of the constraints of labeling, she was now open to explore new horizons, committed to finding and refinding new ways to be herself. In her words, "I am proud to be myself. I am proud of the road I have navigated, of being able to make my choices and be true to myself in spite of tremendous pressures."

PERSONAL REFLECTIONS

The courage and determination demonstrated by Daphne in navigating her own road, her ability to find her own voice, and her resistance to being recruited into someone else's story was and still is a source of inspiration for me. This led me to explore different sides of my own story, to face challenges, and to ask myself questions I had not faced before. Through sharing her pain, as well as the stories of pain and struggles of others, I have become deeply committed to hearing the silenced outcry and closeted stories of those who have been oppressed and forced into hiding their true self.

Through the years of my clinical practice, I have also become more painfully aware of my own biases. I was trained as a clinical psychologist in the early 1980s. Homosexuality, as we were taught then, was conceptualized as a sign of arrested psychosexual development and unresolved conflicts. I had a lot to unlearn. My clients, as well as some dear friends of mine, helped me in this process, showing me how to listen carefully and let each individual find his or her own way. Issues of gender and culture were definitely neglected in my training at the time, which emphasized the universality of human experience and the intrapsychic world of the client (then called *patient*—and yet another example of the language that reflects and shapes our discourses).

The narrative approach of "not knowing" and placing the client as *the* expert on his or her life has, in my experience, an empowering effect and can help bridge differences, whether due to culture, gender, or sexual orientation (or all of them together). By not knowing and by acknowledging the differences as well as the misunderstandings in the therapeutic encounter, we are able to encourage the client to find new ways to translate him- or herself. This, in turn, can be of value in other encounters in his or her life.

The expressive arts are a natural adjunct to this approach of reauthoring conversations. Apart from my private practice as a psychotherapist, I work with groups of traumatized new immigrants to Israel (as a volunteer for Selah, the Israel Crisis Management Center). Incorporating the expressive arts within a narrative framework in a group setting allows the bearing of witness and telling of testimony in new ways. It builds bridges across language and culture barriers. Introducing the expressive arts into my practice has been a challenging, stimulating, and highly rewarding experience.

CONCLUSION

In spite of increasing acceptance and changing definitions of same-sex love, prejudice still pervades the helping encounter in many ways. Table 7.1 lists not only those affirmative practices discussed in this chapter that can provide support for identity development but also those biased practices that can do more harm than good. Some of these points have been covered by the research reported by Garnets et al. (1991). Helpers need to be aware of how their attitudes and knowledge can affect the helping process. This table can be used as a checklist for examining one's own practice.

Combining expressive arts with a narrative approach opens up new possibilities for helping gay and lesbian individuals cope with stigma and negative labeling as well as expanding the reflecting space for exploring one's identity and accepting diversity.

A flexible use of diverse therapeutic strategies can support the deconstruction of oppressive dominant discourses and help the client overcome the debilitating effects of shame, fear, or guilt. Training to become one's own "spokesman" and learning to mobilize internal resources (such as one's creativity) and external

TABLE 7.1 | BIASED VERSUS AFFIRMING PRACTICES

A helper can harm when he or she:	A helper can support when he or she:
believes homosexuality to be a form of psychopathology, developmental arrest, or other psychological disorder	understands that homosexuality, in and of itself, is neither a form of psychopathology nor evidence of developmental arrest
denies or ignores the impact of social prejudice and discrimination on the client's attitudes and self conceptions	acknowledges social prejudice and discrimination and its possible impact on the client's attitudes and identity
focuses on sexual orientation as a therapeutic issue even when that is not relevant to the reason of referral	sees sexual orientation as one facet of the client's identity among others and not in itself as a problem to be adressed in therapy
attempts to discourage a client from having or adopting a lesbian or gay orientation	supports and validates the development of a positive gay male or lesbian identity and provides space for the questioning client to explore issues concerning his or her identity
views gay or lesbian identity merely in terms of sexuality and sexual behavior	has a broad perspective on gay identity, acknowledging the diversity and multifaceted nature of homosexual and lesbian experience
fails to recognize the changing attitudes, definitions, and understanding about same-sex love	is aware of the rapid changes in definitions and understandings about same-sex love
fails to recognize multiple stresses because of the synergistic effects of heterosexism, racism, and sexism	is aware of cultural variations in the acceptability and understanding of homosexuality and keeps in perspective issues concerning culture, ethnicity, gender, and sexual orientation
lacks knowledge of gay and lesbian issues and is unaware of the interplay of issues concerning his or her own gender, culture, and sexual orientation, and their impact on the helping process.	strives to increase knowledge and awareness through continuing education and is prepared to examine the impact of his or her own issues of gender, culture, and sexual orientation on the helping process.

resources (such as siblings, friends, and the gay community) can be of help during the coming-out process.

Gay art and culture is another resource that enables the expression and authentication of voices outside the dominant social discourse.

Narrative practices can also be employed in support groups (Behan, 2002) as well as in training programs for help providers. New ways are yet to be found for increasing the intercultural awareness and sensitivity of helpers of gay male and lesbian issues and of incorporating these in training programs. Narrative approaches combined with creative activity can offer new opportunities for both helpers and clients to reflect on the stories we were told and those we tell ourselves—about being a woman or a man, about being gay, lesbian, bisexual, or heterosexual in our society.

KEY CONCEPTS

- homophobia
- internalized homophobia
- heterosexism
- sexual orientation–blind perspective
- pathologizing discourses
- counternarrative
- gay affirmative practices
- externalizing shame
- coming out and identity

QUESTIONS FOR REFLECTION

1. What experiences have shaped your ideas about same-sex love?
2. What messages were conveyed in your upbringing about being a woman? a man?
3. What messages were conveyed about women loving women? Men loving men?
4. What were the words used for same-sex love?
5. Have the attitudes where you live changed over the years? How? Have *your* ideas changed?
6. How comfortable do you feel talking about men loving men? Women loving women?
7. What does prejudice mean to you? What does pride mean to you? Have you encountered incidents of prejudice, bias, or discrimination?
8. Have you ever felt different? Pressured to be like everyone else? Blamed for not conforming? How did you cope with this? What enabled you to handle the pressure? With whose support?

EXERCISE

This is an exercise that gives a chance to experience some of the expressive work described in this chapter. Look through the illustrations in this chapter. Chose the one that talks to you and look at it for a few more moments. Think about why you chose this illustration—what about your own life attracted you to it? What do you see in it? What associations does it bring up? Now think about one of your own clients. Which picture do you think your client would choose? Why do you think your client might be attracted to that picture? What might that picture say about his or her own life? If you feel comfortable doing this, copy these illustrations and show them to your client. See if your client indeed chooses the one you thought that he or she would and ask why they chose it. If you feel comfortable, share your own choice for them, and both of you can discuss overlap or differences about what you see in the picture.

References

Andrews, M. (2002). Introduction—Counter-narratives and the power to oppose. *Narrative Inquiry, 12*(1), 1–6.

Behan, C. (2002). Linking lives around shared themes: Narrative group therapy with gay men. In D. Denborough (Ed.), *Queer counselling and narrative practice*. Adelaide, Australia: Dulwich Center Publications.

Ben-Ari, A. T. (2001). Homosexuality and heterosexism: Views from academics in the helping professions. *British Journal of Social Work, 31,* 119–131.

Berkman, C. S., & Zinberg, G. (1997). Homophobia and heterosexism in social workers. *Social Work, 42,* 319–332.

Bieschke, K. J., McClanahan, M., Tozer, E., Grzegorek, J. L., & Park, J. (2000). Programmatic research on the treatment of lesbian, gay, and bisexual clients: The past, the present, and the course for the future. In R. M. Perez, K. A. DeBord, & K. J. Bieschke (Eds.), *Handbook of counseling and therapy with lesbian, gay, and bisexual clients* (pp. 309–336). Washington, DC: American Psychological Association.

Bruner, J. (1989). *Actual minds, possible worlds.* Cambridge, MA: Harvard University Press.

Cain, R. (1991). Stigma management and gay identity development. *Social Work, 36,* 67–73.

Cass, V. C. (1979). Homosexual identity formation: A theoretical model. *Journal of Homosexuality, 4,* 219–235.

Cass, V. (1984). Homosexual identity: A concept in need of definition. *Journal of Homosexuality, 9*(2–3), 105–126.

DeCrescenzo, T. (1984). Homophobia: A study of the attitudes of mental health professionals toward homosexuality. *Journal of Social Work and Human Sexuality, 2,* 115–136.

DePoy, E., & Noble, S. (1992). The structure of lesbian relationships in response to oppression. *Affilia, 7,* 49–64.

Dworkin, S. (1996). From personal therapy to professional life: Observations of a Jewish, bisexual lesbian therapist and academic. *Women and Therapy, 18*(2), 37–46.

Falco, K. L. (1991). Psychotherapy with Lesbians. *Journal of Social Issues, 34*(3), 84–100

Freedman, J., & Combs, G. (1996). *Narrative therapy: The social construction of preferred realities.* New York: Norton.

Garnets, L., Hancock, K. A., Cochran, S. D., Godchilds, J., & Peplau, L. A. (1991). Issues in psychotherapy with lesbians and gay men: A survey of psychologists. *American Psychologist, 46,* 964–972.

Gelso, C. J., Fassinger, R., Gomez, M. J., & Latts, M. G. (1995). Countertransference reactions to lesbian clients: The role of homophobia, counselor gender and countertransference management. *Journal of Counseling Psychology, 42,* 356–364.

Gonsiorek, J. C. (1991). The empirical basis for the demise of the illness model of homosexuality. In J. C. Gonsiorek & J. D. Weinrich (Eds.), *Homosexuality: Research implications for public policy* (pp. 115–136). Thousand Oaks, CA: Sage.

Greene, B., & Herek, G. M. (Eds.). (1994). *Lesbian and gay psychology: Theory, research, and clinical applications.* Thousand Oaks, CA: Sage.

Haldeman, D. C. (1994). The practice and ethics of sexual orientation conversion therapy. *Journal of Consulting Clinical Psychology, 62,* 221–227.

Hanley-Hackenbruck, P. (1988). "Coming out" and psychotherapy. *Psychiatric Annals, 18*(1), 29–32.

Herdt, G. (1997). *Same sex different cultures: Exploring gay and lesbian lives.* Boulder, CO: Westview Press.

Herek, G. (1995). Psychological heterosexism in the United States. In A. D'Augelli & C. Patterson (Eds.), *Lesbian, gay, and bisexual identities over the lifespan: Psychological perspectives.* New York: Oxford University Press.

Isay, R. (1989). *Being homosexual: Gay men and their development.* New York: Avon Books.

Logan, B. (2002). Weaving new stories over the phone: A narrative approach to a gay switchboard. In D. Denborough (Ed.), *Queer counselling and narrative practice.* Adelaide, Australia: Dulwich Center Publications.

Mizrachi, S. (1990). *Same sex couples: Coping with stigma.* M.A. thesis, Department of Social Work, Tel Aviv University.

Morrin, S. F. (1977). Heterosexual bias in psychological research on lesbianism and male homosexuality. *American Psychologist, 32,* 629–637.

Morrow, D. (1996). Heterosexism: Hidden discrimination in social work education. *Journal of Gay and Lesbian Social Services, 5*(4), 1–16.

O'Dell, S. (2000). Psychotherapy with gay and lesbian families: Opportunities for cultural inclusion and clinical challenge. *Clinical Social Work Journal, 28*(2), 171–182.

Perez, R. M., DeBord, K. A., & Bieschke, K. J. (Eds.). (2000). *Handbook of counseling and therapy with lesbian, gay, and bisexual clients.* Washington, DC: American Psychological Association.

Parry, A., & Doan, R. E. (1994). *Story revisions: Narrative therapy in the postmodern world.* New York: Guilford Press.

Plummer, K. (1981). Going gay: Identity, life-cycles and life-styles in the male gay world. In J. Hart & D. Richardson (Eds.),

The theory and practice of homosexuality (pp. 93–160). London: Routledge & Kegan Paul.

Rabin, C. (1991). The cultural context in treating a lesbian couple: An Israeli experience. *Journal of Strategic and Systematic Therapies, 11*(4), 42–58.

Riley, S. (2001). *Group process made visible.* Philadelphia: Taylor & Francis.

Roth, S. (1989). Psychotherapy with lesbian couples: Individual issues, female socialization, and the social context. In M. McGoldrick, C. Anderson, & F. Walsh (Eds.), *Women in families: A framework for family therapy.* New York: Norton.

Sumakei-Fink, A., & Press, J. (1999). *Independence park: The lives of gay men in Israel.* Palo Alto, CA: Stanford University Press.

Troiden, R. R. (1989). The formation of homosexual identities. *Journal of Homosexuality, 17,* 43–73.

Van Vorris, R., & Wagner, M. (2002). Among the missing: Content on lesbian and gay people in social work journals. *Social Work, 47*(4), 345–355.

Walzer, L. (2000). *Between Sodom and Eden: A gay journey through today's changing Israel.* New York: Columbia University Press.

White, M., & Epston, D. (1990). *Narrative means to therapeutic ends.* New York: Norton.

Wisniewski, J. J., & Toomey, B. G. (1987). Are social workers homophobic? *Social Work, 32,* 454–455.

Zimmerman, J. L., & Dickerson, V. C. (1996). *If problems talked: Narrative therapy in action.* New York: Guilford Press.

There is no greater sorrow on earth than the loss of one's native land. EURIPIDES (484–406 B.C.)

CHAPTER 8

HELPING IMMIGRANT WOMEN FROM THE FORMER SOVIET UNION

RONI BERGER
UNITED STATES

OVERVIEW

Recent years have seen an exodus from the former Soviet Union (FSU). As political upheaval swept away Communist governments, more than 1.5 million people left the Soviet bloc to relocate mostly in the United States, Canada, and Israel. Since the early 1970s, more than 500,000 Soviet Jews who fled the FSU resettled in the United States (Vinokurov, Birman, & Trickett, 2000). Like other Western countries, the United States selectively granted immigration rights to young, educated professionals and offered them political asylum. This preferred status created animosity among other communities of refugees such as Cambodians, Koreans, and Taiwanese. Emigration to Israel was massive and nonselective, following the law of return that grants every Jew the right to immigrate to Israel and gain citizenship automatically. Approximately 100,000 Soviet Jews immigrated to Israel in the 1970s, and more than 700,000 since 1989, increasing its population approximately by 20% (www.adl.org/Israel/Record/immigration).

In all countries of destination, this flux of immigrants from the FSU presents new challenges for policy makers and service providers (Shen-Ryan, 1992; Schuck, 1999). Immigration is a multifaceted process that creates stresses with potential short- and long-term social, psychological, economic, and legal implications for individuals and families (Garza-Guerrero, 1974; Glassman & Skolnik, 1984; Harper & Lantz, 1996; Berger, in press).

Some groups of immigrants are more vulnerable than others because they are subjected to intersectional effects of immigration status, gender, race, and ethnicity. One such group is immigrant women, who have been identified as particularly vulnerable because they face the same issues that affect all immigrants but are susceptible to additional risk factors related to their gender (Pittaway, 1991; Bernstein & Shuval, 1999). They are often victims of violence, rape, and harassment, and their rights are seriously compromised and threatened (Walsh, 2001). They are the ones who are required to start immediately to function within the new unfamiliar world. They are required to negotiate shops, schools, and medical and social services in unfamiliar language and norms.

In addition to their personal difficulties, women often serve as buffers and containers to the frustrations of husbands and children who are torn between two cultures; they also take care of old relatives. Consequently, immigrant women typically have to perform too many roles and are, therefore, at high risk. However, a lot of the research on the immigration process has lumped together all immigrants, muted gender-related differences, and viewed immigration as gender-neutral. Therefore, we lack clarity about the role of gender in the process of immigration.

To develop services for newcomers and serve them effectively, practitioners in the helping professions need to be knowledgeable about immigrants, their experience and its aftermath, their unique needs, and effective strategies of addressing them. Clients and workers bring with them to the professional encounter different cultural discourses regarding mental health issues and acceptable services. These discourses profoundly influence the helping relationships; therefore, understanding them is crucial for the establishment and operation of culturally appropriate services for immigrants.

Programs to assist people in resettlement are not novel. However, knowledge about particular demands and nuances related to specific immigrations are necessary to equip service providers with tools for effective interventions. The goal of this chapter is to familiarize the reader with characteristics and issues of immigrants from the FSU and principles for servicing them.

The chapter includes three parts. The first part discusses the characteristics, unique needs, and short- and long-term effects of immigration on women and their families from FSU. The second part discusses barriers to service provision and suggests guidelines for servicing women immigrants from FSU. Finally, a case example of a young girl is presented that illustrates typical issues and helpful interventions.

WOMEN IMMIGRANTS FROM FSU: THE NATURE OF THE EXPERIENCE AND ITS AFTERMATH

How do women immigrants from the FSU experience their relocation? What stories do they bring with them? What social discourses affect them and their helpers? How are these experiences and discourses reflected in the process of helping? This section addresses these and related questions.

Unique Characteristics of Immigration From the FSU

Major elements in the social discourse of immigration are marginalization, powerlessness, and oppression. Themes that dominate the life stories of many immigrants include multifaceted processes and multiple losses. Immigration includes losing familiarity with the physical, cultural, and social environment; mastery of the dominant language; significant relationships and support systems; social and professional status; intimate understanding of cultural norms and clues for meaning making; and financial sources and assets (Furnham & Bochner, 1986; Stewart, 1986; Berger, 2004). Many narratives of immigrants show these losses as experiences of losing the sense of who they are, being marginalized and discriminated against, feeling oppressed and powerless, and having limited ability to frame and communicate their ideas.

Because immigrants from the FSU typically move from a totalitarian, socialistic, collectivist, antireligious culture to a Western culture, which offers more freedom for personal decisions, they report facing special challenges in diverse aspects of daily life (Berger, 1996; Slonim-Nevo, Sharaga, & Mirsky, 1999). For example, a preferred way of birth control among many Russian women has been abortion. Women might have as many as 10 abortions. Chapter 14 shows how health care workers in Italy deal with this same phenomenon among immigrant women.

Another example is the common use of corporal discipline, which in the new country would be deemed as illegal and put one at a risk for accusations of child abuse and possibly removal of children to foster care. Immigrants would consider the mere intervention of the state in this matter as an intrusion into the privacy of the family.

Immigrants from the FSU are not a homogenous monolithic entity. They vary in belief system, language, and culture, depending on their origin within the multinational and multicultural FSU. Mutual stigmas are not uncommon. Immigrants from Odessa were deeply involved in Jewish life, immigrants from Asian republics embraced traditional religious practices and are influenced by their Muslim environment, and immigrants from Russia, specifically Moscow, bring with them familiarity with a sophisticated cultural life and a high level of general and professional education.

PHASES IN THE IMMIGRATION PROCESS

Three major phases occur in immigration: departure, transition, and resettlement (Sluzki, 1983; Drachman & Shen-Ryan, 1992). Each phase has special meaning for immigrants from the FSU in addition to universal ones that they share with all immigrants. The *departure phase* starts with the decision to emigrate, which may be driven by diverse motivations such as seeking employment opportunities and better economic conditions; pursuing refuge from political, social, and religious persecution; ideological reasons; and uniting families. Emigrants from the FSU recount a mix of motives. Often, some family members are the driving forces while others join reluctantly—for example, a Jewish spouse may initiate the emigration and the non-Jewish partner join unhappily. These differences in motivation affect the nature of the acculturation. Adolescents are often angry with their parents, who disconnected them from their social environment without an opportunity to participate in the decision process, while the parents feel that they sacrificed their careers to ensure their children better social prospects and save them from anti-Semitism and discrimination.

In the departure phase, the decision of who is to emigrate is made. Given the large percentage of divorced, unmarried, and mixed faith families in the Soviet regime, migration is often a period of crisis because it is not uncommon that one parent decides to emigrate and the other, often a non-Jew, opts to stay, further increasing the already large number of single-mother families. During this premigration period, the prospective emigrants deliberate plans and prepare for their move. Preparations are practical and psychological, and the two are often mixed together. For example, sorting out what to take and what is left behind may lead to revisiting memories of sad and happy moments, thinking about lost relationships, leaving behind people, sometimes with no clear idea of the prospects to meet again. Rational considerations and sentimental reactions mix in the decision making. In many ways, this process involves mourning significant parts of one's old self, feelings of emptiness, sadness, pain, ambivalence, and fear of the unknown.

The departure phase changed significantly before and after *glasnost* and *perestroika.* * Until the mid-1980s, an application to emigrate was treated as a betrayal, often involving prolonged waiting for the paperwork, especially for people who had been involved in pro-Zionist activity. The period also was frequently accompanied by harassment by colleagues and neighbors and punishment by unemployment—or "firing the traitor." People had to make secret preparations and wait with uncertainty about their emigration status; this was often followed by an abrupt departure and the nullification of citizenship with no possibility to return for visits. In the 1990s, a greater degree of openness to Western countries allowed more planned and organized migration.

The nature of the departure phase often contains the seeds for future adjustment. For instance, people who leave life-threatening circumstances but loved ones such as elderly parents and close friends behind may later develop survivor's guilt, posttraumatic stress disorder, or depression associated with the multiple losses.

The *transition phase* consists of actually leaving the country of origin and moving to the new country. Until the early 1990s, many migrants from the FSU had to spend long periods in transition centers in Europe, mostly in Austria or Italy. Although this created a period of uncertainty and prolonged and tense waiting, it also allowed migrants to gradually get used to the change in their life.

Glasnost ("openness") and *perestroika* ("restructuring") refer to the reformed political and economic system as declared by the Soviet Union's leader Mikhail Gorbachev in March 1985. They also involved "lifting the Iron Curtain" and opening to the West with the expectation that the Soviet economy would be invigorated by an increased free flow of goods and information.

In recent years, planes have landed in Israel directly from the FSU. People could leave a frozen Moscow wrapped in fur coats (many emigrants from the FSU brought fur coats and jewelry to cope with the limitations on what they were permitted to take out) and land several hours later in a warm and sunny Tel Aviv. This procedure saves the discomfort of prolonged waiting but at the same time annuls any opportunity of a time-out and creates a sharp, confusing, and disorienting change.

The *resettlement phase* involves a long and complex process of acculturation, at least to some degree, to the new culture's norms and values. Resettlement lasts years; for many immigrants, it lasts a lifetime. Rather than a linear progression from one culture into another, it involves two conceptually interrelated but distinct spheres of separation from the culture of origin and adjustment to the new culture (Birman & Tyler, 1994). Three stages occur in resettlement (Berry, 1986): contact–encounter, conflict, and adaptation.

Contact–Encounter   In *contact–encounter,* the immigrant first meets the dominant new culture, compares it to her or his own original culture, and faces preliminary financial constraints, language and social barriers, prejudice, and discrimination. This coincides with initial efforts to establish a new life and find housing and employment. Being absorbed in the struggle to survive often deprives immigrants at this stage of the opportunity to be in touch with the emotional meaning of the move and mourn their losses.

Many immigrants from the FSU experience a decrease in their professional, social, and financial status because employment may not be available that fits their training or recognizes their credentials. Experienced professionals even may need to pass again exams that they had previously passed and often just to change careers. Even those who manage to achieve work in their field often experience diminished status and income. For many immigrants, the dream of bettering their lives by emigration becomes unrealistic in light of the cost of living and the need to pay for services, such as education and health, that were free for citizens of the FSU.

Conflict   *Conflict* develops when immigrants give up values and patterns from their cultures of origin and substitute them with the values of the new culture. Immigrants vary in their willingness to go through this process, depending on their age, social environment and personality. Typically, younger people, especially adolescents, who wish to be like their peers, are faster to adopt new norms than their parents and other adults. People who live in ethnic enclaves that encourage maintaining the culture of origin change less and more slowly than those who live and work or study in a culturally diverse environment (Landau-Stanton, 1985).

For many immigrants, acculturation does not go smoothly without complaints about the new culture and a great deal of nostalgia for the culture of origin. It is not uncommon for immigrants from the FSU to criticize and reject the Israeli or American culture as superficial, selfish, and materialistic; fashion as tasteless; and manners as barbaric as they gradually adopt some of these norms.

Immigrants from the FSU often comment that in Israel and in the United States, children and adolescents are less respectful to adults and talk back to their parents and teachers, that the academic level is lower, that people are less polite, and that the general atmosphere is less "civilized." Ludmialla, a recent immigrant from Russia, reflects on the differences in a poetic note, "One difference that I noticed very early was the smell of the apples. At home, the fresh and sweet fragrance of the apples displayed on the table would hit you. Here they have a synthetic smell, like everything else." For many immigrants, the culture of origin remains home for various periods of time.

Adaptation   In *adaptation,* immigrants develop a wide array of ways to reduce the conflict between the two cultures. They learn the language of the new culture, its colloquialisms and norms, and how to decode social clues. They mourn the losses that they suffered and experience the loss of their dreams about the new country as they face its reality. They come to grasp the permanence of the change in their life, develop ways of functioning in the new reality, and re-create familiarity with their environment within the context of the new culture.

In this phase, immigrants start the long journey of rehabilitating their sense of self-worth and of mastery over their lives. They struggle to reinvent themselves and develop a new sense of identity. To do so successfully, one needs a social environment that provides support and norms. The search for such an environment drives many immigrants, at least initially, to live in ethnic enclaves and to seek employment, services. and social contacts with compatriots.

A major component in the process of acculturation includes the development of ethnic identity and a new sense of self (Liebkind, 1992). Some immigrants do so by opting for a monocultural solution that entails choosing one cultural identity as one's dominant culture. This can be done either by *assimilation* (i.e., embracing the dominant culture and relinquishing one's original cultural identity) or by *rejection* (i.e., self-imposed withdrawal from the dominant culture). Others choose the bicultural road—that is, living in both cultures either by oscillating between them or by *integrating* components from both of them (Szapocznik, Scopetta, & Kurtines, 1978). Finally, some choose *deculturation,* or striking out against the dominant culture accompanied by stress and alienation and living in a "no-man's land" (Berry, 1986).

Based on working with immigrants from the FSU, Berger (1997) identified and described four modes of coping with identity issues among immigrant adolescents from FSU: *clinging, eradicating, oscillating,* and *integrating. Clingers* adhere to their culture of origin and reject the new culture. They tend to live in ethnic enclaves and develop social and commercial relationships with compatriots. They consume ethnic products such as food, literature, music, movies, and clothes from compatriots and tend to use medical and personal services from fellow countrymen. A recent immigrant from the FSU who lives in Brighton Beach (a neighborhood heavily populated by immigrants from the FSU in southeast Brooklyn, New York, that has been nicknamed "Little Odessa") explains her limited knowledge of English and familiarity with American norms. "It is like we created a replication of our homeland here. Everybody with whom I deal is from the old country. I can get all I need without leaving my neighborhood." The tendency of a fraction of the immigrant community to stick together gives rise to an enclave economy—that is, the development of commerce and industry in which immigrants work for businesses of other immigrants before or instead of finding their place within the general market.

Eradicators reject their culture of origin and fully embrace the new culture. They try to "erase" their culture of origin and maximize their adoption of norms of the new culture. They refrain from speaking their native language; when it is unavoidable, such as when adolescent children must communicate with parents who do not speak the new language, they use English or Hebrew words and idioms in their Russian. Eradicators prefer to dress in the style of the dominant culture of relocation, listen to its music, adopt its behavior code, and maximize their immersion. They change their diet to meet the standards of their new environment and prefer friends of the dominant culture rather than compatriots. Some eradicators, especially children, adolescents, and young adults try to "pass" for being nonimmigrants by changing their names, attempting to eliminate their accents, and distancing themselves from anybody and anything that is related to their culture of origin.

Vacillators oscillate between their culture of origin and the culture of relocation and have a hard time committing to either. They demonstrate inconsistent attitudes toward their "Russian-ness," feeling torn between embracing the relationships, manners, styles, and norms of their original culture and following the norms and styles of their culture of relocation. They "experiment" with various identities and are inconsistent in their affiliation and preferences, fluctuating between the discourse of an immigrant and that of a native.

Integrators combine components of both the culture of origin and the culture of resettlement. They generally demonstrate a "fluid identity," speaking both languages, having friends from both cultures, and consuming the food, goods, and entertainment of both cultures. Although there seems to be a common assumption among many helping professionals that integration is the optimal (i.e., functional and "healthiest") solution, this assumption is yet to be empirically tested.

From a constructivist perspective, these styles can be viewed as life stories with unique outcomes. Such a view is supported by anecdotal data that suggest these modes do not change along the road of adjustment and are rather steady—that is, immigrants tend to adopt and maintain a specific mode of coping. This impressionistic perspective suggests that in planning interventions with immigrants, a differential approach is needed that takes into consideration people's modes of coping.

Historically, the "melting pot" concept prevailed demanding immigrants to totally assimilate within their new culture. Although recognition and respecting diversity is currently advocated, considerable segments of receiving societies still adhere to the expectation that immigrants fully adopt their norms. This is reflected in attacks on bilingual academic programs and public criticism of ethnic-specific cultural activities. The status of the culture of origin in the absorbing society also affects the path that immigrants choose (Lalonde, Taylor,

& Moghaddam, 1992). Immigrants from cultures with high status in the new country tend to assimilate better than immigrants who come from cultures that are looked down upon in the new country.

As immigrants go through the process of settling down, anxieties that have not been previously attended to because of the shock and the urgent demands of everyday life may surface and pose risks to the immigrants' mental health and well-being.

IMMIGRANT WOMEN

Immigrant women often find themselves in a specifically challenging intersection because of their immigration status and gender. The intersection of immigration discourse, ethnic discourse, and gender discourse presents a specific challenge for women. International migration often means a shift in gender relations and gender status when women move from traditional patriarchal cultures with rigid sex roles to cultures with more egalitarian sex roles (Knorr & Meier, 2000). The immigrant woman often finds herself affected simultaneously by racism, sexism, and class inequality.

Immigrant women from the FSU are no exception. A Russian saying describes the allocation of gender-specific roles and power: "Women do everything; men do the rest." In clinical encounters, women who emigrate from the FSU to Western cultures report considerable difference in gender-based and parenting expectations. For example, behaviors that in Western cultures would be viewed as sexual exploitation in the workplace and domestic violence were not uncommon and accepted as a norm. Parenting style in the FSU has been quite authoritarian, and immigrants resent Western liberal parenting styles and consider them inappropriate.

For immigrant women from the FSU, major aspects of adaptation need to occur in their gender-specific roles because of shifts in the role and power structure in the family following immigration, especially as it concerns women. Two processes contribute to and shape these shifts: changes in child care traditions and occupational status.

Traditionally, in the Soviet family both wives and husbands worked and the grandmother played a major role of taking care of the children. Consequently, three-generational families are common (Berger, 1996, 2001; Slonim-Nevo et al., 1999). Immigration often leads to major changes in this arrangement. Because of the different educational and social structures, within the family grandmothers who are not familiar with the new cultures lose power as their role as a major parental figure is discontinued. The mothers are the ones who must take over the role vacated by the grandmothers. Thus, mothers are burdened with additional responsibility.

The multiple and mutually enhancing pressures of immigration, employment, and caregiving in the context of downward socioeconomic mobility and the loss of support networks in immigrant women from the FSU was documented by Remennick (1999). In a qualitative study, she interviewed 30 women who migrated from the FSU to Israel. She found that women often became breadwinners and managers of the family's needs. Immigration-related stresses often exacerbated and complicated stresses related to their multiple roles within and out of the family.

In Israel, just as in the FSU, women are underrepresented in managerial positions, and the feminization of educational and health care professions contributes to their low status and salaries. The aforementioned added responsibilities are often accompanied by women's gaining power out of the family. Because of their flexibility in adaptation to lower status professional positions imposed by immigration, women often achieve employment before men do and gain a central role in providing family income.

The added responsibilities within and out of the family lead to women having more burdens and more power. This challenges the previous balance and allocation of power, leading to a weakening in the husband's status and eventually of the family unit, which was characterized by instability under the Soviet regime—the fruit of years of political, economic, ideological, and historical circumstances. These included oppression, fostering of mutual suspicion even between spouses, and extreme difficulties of daily life because of the unavailability of products to meet basic needs (e.g., food, housing, and clothing).

Theories of stress and trauma have informed our understanding effects of immigration on individuals and families. Immigration is a stressful major disruption in a person's life and a potentially traumatic experience. Like all traumas, it challenges the universal need for continuity (Marris, 1974). Disintegrating familiar patterns of life has negative effects but also offers opportunities for posttraumatic growth. These reactions to immigration have been called *culture shock* (Bock, 1970; Furnham & Bochner, 1986; Stewart, 1986). Negative effects of immigration cited in the literature include an existential crisis that creates feelings of alienation, personal annihilation, emptiness and meaninglessness, marginalization, helplessness, insecurity, lower self-esteem, feeling of inadequacy, confusion, disorientation, frustration, anger, loneliness, anomic depression, and familial instability and discord (Garza-Guerrero, 1974; Glassman & Skolnik, 1984; Stewart, 1986; Drachman & Shen-Ryan, 1992; Baider, Ever-Hadani, & Kaplan-DeNour, 1996; Berger, 1996; Harper & Lantz, 1996; Hulewat, 1996).

Empirical research on the effects of immigration, however, has been mostly conducted from an "external," non–gender-specific, pathologizing viewpoint using linear models. Consequently, much of what is commonly known about immigrants tends to be simplistic and monolithic. Immigrants are portrayed as having homogenous experiences. Only recently have some scholars begun to focus on the subjective experiences of people who have made successful cultural transitions (Bystydienski & Resnik, 1994, p. 2). Thus, the differential effects of immigration for men and women are just recently beginning to be explored; their nature as well as the difference between female and male immigration discourse are yet to be explored. For example, Shepherd (1992) suggests that biological makeup precipitates differences in the way men and women define trauma and some stress reactions that are unique to women, although she does not specify what these differences are. Immigrant women have been identified as particularly vulnerable because of the intersection of gender, ethnicity, and immigration discourse, which expose them simultaneously to racism, sexism, and class inequality (United Nations Department for Economic and Social Information and Policy Analysis Population Division, 1995).

Traumatic events create not only the danger of emotional distress and functional decline but also the opportunity for personal posttraumatic growth (Tedeschi, Park, & Calhoun, 1998), as documented among immigrant children and survivors of natural disasters, war experiences, violent victimization, and breast cancer (Coll & Magnusom, 1997; Calhoun & Tedeschi, 1999; Weiss, 2000). A qualitative study of immigrant women (Berger, in press) shows posttraumatic growth for immigrant women. For example, Ana, left her comfortable life as a piano teacher in Uzbekistan to relocate to Israel, where she was forced to cope with the loss of income, a decline in social status because of a step down the vocational ladder, and eventually the sudden death of her husband. Yet she states, "Had all this not happened to me, I would not have been so strong. I would not have known that I have all these strengths in me."

SERVING WOMEN IMMIGRANTS FROM THE FORMER SOVIET UNION

Attention to immigrants' needs requires application of general practice principles within the context of the characteristics and circumstances of the specific group. Several cultural barriers make the provision of services to immigrants from the FSU challenging. To be effective, services need to be sensitive to these barriers and follow principles that address them.

Barriers to Services Provision

People rely on their previous experience when they face new situations (Marris, 1974). Immigrants from the FSU come with a discourse that considerably differs from that of Westerners and conflicts with many of the assumptions that underlie traditional mental health services. Their tradition discourages discussing personal business with strangers and emphasizes mistrust of establishments and maintaining privacy and secrecy. Consequently, such immigrants often meet unfavorable reactions from personnel who view these behaviors as disrespectful and ingratitude for the provision of services.

In addition, these immigrants are unfamiliar with the helping professions and traditional "talk therapies" and are limited in their language competency. The combination of these factors presents barriers for providing service to immigrants from the FSU.

Mistrust   Trust is the cornerstone in mental health services. Individuals who grew up in the FSU develop from early age a general discourse of suspicion of strangers and a more specific distrust of representatives of the establishment.

They learned that one turns for help mostly to family and a few selected friends among whom mutual favors are expected (Berger, 1996, 2001; Slonim-Nevo et al., 1999). Under the repressive Soviet regime, any stranger was suspected as a potential informer and mental health services were often abused as a punitive instrument of the state for political control and thus were not trustworthy (Ivry, 1992). Therefore, immigrants from the FSU refrain from turning to formal services. They prefer to seek help from their relatives and close friends. Standard intake procedures are perceived as intrusive so that women are reluctant to share personal information with service providers.

However, immigration often cuts such immigrants off from their natural support system. Their family members and friends also may be struggling with their own immigration-related difficulties and therefore be unavailable to help. Going for help from service providers is often the last resort, and then immigrants tend to somatization of emotional problems, seeking concrete help from general physicians rather than framing problems as personal or emotional and seeking mental health services.

Personnel's Reactions to Immigrants' Behavior   A common complaint by professional service providers about immigrants from the FSU is that they do not stand patiently in line, they are "pushy" and aggressive, and they refuse to accept answers and ask several workers the same questions. Personnel who approach the professional encounter with a different discourse of the helping relationship, expecting a trust-based open dialogue, often fail to understand that these behaviors were crucial for survival and receiving services under the Soviet regime. The resulting clash of discourses leads to anger, mutual disappointment and intolerance, underutilization of services, and reluctance to be responsive to immigrants' needs and requests.

Lack of Familiarity with the Helping Professions and with "Talk Therapy"   An additional source for the clash of discourses is the fact that in the FSU psychology and psychiatry were pharmacological in orientation, medical and behavioral models were dominant, and social work was nonexistent. "Just talking" is perceived as a futile waste of time; the expectation is for concrete services and medication rather than counseling.

Consequently, these immigrants prefer to use the help of general physicians and tend not to be receptive to social services (Brodsky, 1982; Ivry, 1992). The negative attitude toward providers of mental health services can start a cycle of mutual misunderstanding, misinterpretation, and mutual blaming. Providers of services to this population often interpret the behaviors of these clients as resistant, uncooperative, manipulative, and overdemanding.

Language Barriers   Language presents an additional barrier. Discussing private and painful experiences is difficult in any language. The need to address such issues in a language that is not the way one thinks further complicates the sharing of feelings, the articulation of problems, and the projection of nuances when one is struggling for the right words and not familiar with subtleties.

Principles for Providing Services to Women Immigrants From FSU

Because immigration creates unique and often intensive needs and because of the barriers to service provision discussed above, women immigrants often require specialized services before they can effectively use mainstream services. Traditionally, services for immigrants include reception services, which are short-term and immediate, and settlement services, which are relatively long-term. Recent years have seen an increasing recognition of the importance of understanding and helping people within their cultural context and developing strategies for culturally competent practice. Services need to be provided in ways that fit the cultural understanding of personal, familial, and mental health issues.

As mentioned before, immigration leads to women's increased burdens and roles in the family. To make services usable for them, services need to take these changes into consideration in setting intervention goals, choosing a focus for work, establishing a context and appropriate model, and recruiting service providers.

Goal   A major initial goal in serving women immigrants is to help them let go of their original story and generate an alternative story that offers a different sense of self within the new life circumstances and their new role expectations as described above. What does it mean for them to have more power and more responsibility? What are the challenges that the new circumstances present to them? How to best cope with these challenges? Exploring these and similar questions within a supportive environment are important intervention goals.

While developing a new story to substitute for the original story, which does not fit the new circumstances, it is crucial to restore some sense of continuity. Immigration interrupts stability and causes insecurity that grows out of unpredictability in one's personal, professional, and social life. Consequently, immigrants experience a sense of breakup and detachment of familiar meaning from the context in which it has been embodied. It is crucial to help women recognize that their credentials, skills, and achievements can be transferred and modified to fit the new environment and thus restore their feeling of continuity and reestablish their identity and sense of self in the new context (Marris, 1974). Services need to be geared toward enabling such reestablishment of a sense of continuity lost in immigration—for instance, by exploring past accomplishments and developing ways of adapting them to life in the new country. This can be done by relating current situations and patterns of coping with them to previous experiences (e.g., with previous crises) and building on past situations that required coping with stress and other changes.

Focus   Understanding universal problems within immigration and culture of origin contexts is of utmost importance (Slonim-Nevo et al., 1999). This may require "walking a fine line" between recognizing and properly addressing issues related to and created by immigration without overpathologizing immigration on one hand or blaming it for nonimmigration-related issues on the other hand. Some mental health issues are created or exacerbated by the stress of immigration such as anomic depression in reaction losses and marital and parental discord. Other problems existed in the culture of origin and would have continued to present themselves irrespective of immigration. Differential assessment and intervention without overblaming immigration for the latter helps in delivering appropriate services.

An especially useful strategy in helping a woman to cope better is exploring unique outcomes, which is the exploring of instances of success in adapting and coping. Such successes might pertain to mastering her situation rather than feeling helpless and dominated by problems ralated to relocation, and then developing strategies to replicate these successes.

Context   To overcome barriers, immigrants need an accessible, affordable, flexible, and immigrant-friendly environment within a nonstigmatized setting. To make the environment feel familiar and nonalienating, it is a good idea to use Russian pictures, magazines, and decoration items and to generate a setting that conveys acceptance and respect for the immigrants' culture of origin. Specific services are needed for women who are struggling with the effects of the interface of gender, immigration status, and ethnicity. Many immigrant women are too discouraged to attend groups that are not gender-specific and underutilize language and training classes. Therefore, offering services for women only is of utmost importance. Traditionally, human services require that clients attend sessions at a prescheduled time to receive services. This commitment to a specific time becomes an additional source of stress rather than help for the immigrant. Therefore, flexibility in scheduling as well as unscheduled walk-in services are necessary.

Models   Clinical experience suggests that in spite of the need of many immigrant women from the FSU for direct guidance from an "expert," the narrative approach is a viable alternative. These models offer women an opportunity to tell their story, an experience that is potentially liberating, validating, and empowering because it conveys the message that their experiences and life stories are important. These models avoid the structure typical of traditional models of a worker in a powerful authority position and a client in a powerless place, reinforcing the experience of dependency that characterizes the experience of immigrant women. Instead, they adopt a more egalitarian approach that promotes women's sense of self-worth.

Brief solution-focused and action-oriented models, cognitive and active interventions, and psychoeducational and family system approaches rather than individual counseling have been found useful with immigrants from the FSU (Slonim et al., 1999; Berger, 2001). In light of the aforementioned lack of trust in strangers, the quest for concrete services, and the heavy emphasis on rational approaches, this population is more receptive to directive and structured strategies for behavioral change than to explorations of feeling and traditional therapies. Because of their familiarity and comfort with groups, group work has also been recommended, even though the evidence for its effectiveness with these clients is inconclusive.

Natasha, 12 years old, has been referred by her English as second language teacher to the school social worker because she seemed to be lonely and sad. Natasha has been reported to be a diligent and hard-working student. In class, she does not raise her hand to answer, and when addressed she looks confused and miserable. During the breaks, she does not participate in games with her classmates, sits alone and away from everyone else, and looks forlorn in her thoughts. She often asks permission to stay in class during breaks and do homework or read a book.

Natasha's family of five emigrated from Russia to New York 2 years before the referral. Her father, who was an engineer in their homeland, speaks little English; except for sporadic unprofessional jobs, he has been unemployed most of the time. He became restless, turned to heavy drinking, and has been reported to be emotionally abusive to his wife and daughter. Natasha's mother is working off the books in home care with the elderly. Natasha's maternal grandparents live with the family in a cramped two-bedroom apartment in Brighton Beach. This neighborhood has been heavily and increasingly populated by immigrants from the FSU for several decades. Gradually, a process of "creaming" has occurred, with those who have rehabilitated quickly moving to suburbs in New Jersey and Long Island and leaving behind the less adjusted population.

In the FSU, Natasha's family and the maternal grandparents lived in adjacent apartments, and her grandmother assumed a major role in raising Natasha while both parents worked long hours. This pattern, which is typical of Soviet Jewish families, reflects the Soviet discourse regarding gender, which situated women in a central and powerful position within the family system. This discourse developed in light of the scarcity of housing and difficult economic conditions that often forced married adults to reside with their parents and depend on them financially—as well as on the high incidence of divorces and remarriages (Drachman & Halberstadt, 1992).

Following the referral, the social worker interviewed Natasha. The worker is herself an immigrant from the FSU who relocated to the United States 6 years ago and went back to school to get an MSW after having

worked as a chemistry teacher in Moscow for more than 20 years. In the meeting, Natasha was extremely shy, avoided eye contact, hardly said anything, and did not even respond to the worker's question as to whether she prefers to speak in Russian or in English. Had the worker not been aware of transient normative reactions to immigration and of the cultural norms regarding the relationships of youth with adults, especially adults in authority positions in the Soviet culture, she could have easily have assessed Natasha's situation as depression or adjustment disorder.

In light of her familiarity with the intersection in which Natasha is located—facing the developmental difficulties of adolescence and the hardships of relocation and pulled between the two incompatible cultures of her home and her social environment—the worker decided to invite Natasha and her parents for a meeting. She understood the reluctance of many immigrants from the FSU to use mental health services because of their discourse of mistrust and care for privacy and thus wanted to recruit the parents' cooperation. Furthermore, involving parents has proven beneficial in working with immigrant children and adolescents from the FSU because of the close nature of the Soviet family, often to the point of *enmeshment*. Such enmeshment, according to Western standards, has been fostered by economic, social, and physical conditions: In families under the Soviet regime, typically both parents worked, and a maternal (sometimes paternal) grandmother—the babushka—raised the children. Because of shortages in housing, the sharing of an apartment by three generations—parents, children, and at least one set of grandparents—was not uncommon. The enmeshment was a natural result of these conditions.

On the designated date, a fuming mother showed up and blamed the school for intruding on the family's private business. She would not listen to the worker's explanation regarding the concerns about the girl, denied that there were any problems with Natasha, and refused to allow future meetings between Natasha and the worker.

The worker was culturally competent and understood that privacy in the Soviet culture was to be protected at all costs. Sharing personal information with strangers, especially those in positions of authority, could cost people their jobs and even their freedom. The worker thus was able to avoid labeling the mother as resistant She decided to wait and advised the teacher to do the same. During the following weeks, the school reported deterioration in Natasha's situation. She withdrew even further and seemed to have lost weight. Her academic performance started to deteriorate. Eventually, the parents were invited for a conference with the teacher, which they attended reluctantly. In the meeting, the parents again declined to see mental health issues in their daughter's situation and required that the teachers find ways to deal with her academic performance. This demand is very much in synch with the Soviet tradition, in which teachers made most educational decisions and were expected to solve issues within the school system with limited involvement of parents. The teacher, following the worker's advice, explained to the parents that Natasha is at academic risk and that her achievements are far below her potential and intellectual ability. The worker was aware of the extreme importance of academic performance for parents from the FSU and was hoping to use the parents' concerns regarding scholastic achievements to serve as a leverage for gaining parental agreement for counseling with the girl.

After the girl's situation worsened even further and more pressure came from the school, the social worker suggested that the family take the girl to be seen by her pediatrician, whom they knew from their city of origin. The physician tried to medicate Natasha for several weeks, but when her situation did not improve, he recommended that the family allow intervention by a mental health professional. At this point, the parents reluctantly agreed to allow the social worker to see Natasha.

The process was difficult and laborious. Natasha sat with her head down, answered only "Yes," "No," and "I don't know," and looked miserable. However, she kept all her appointments promptly. The worker patiently validated the difficulty and did most of the talking. Speaking mostly Russian, she explained that there are children who find it difficult to share private information, are not sure what is and is not okay to share, and feel "like a fish out of water." Teachers reported some improvement in class, but it took several weeks before Natasha started to respond in the sessions.

Approximately 2 months into the meetings, the worker got an urgent phone call from the mother. The grandmother had become quite ill, and the family was facing difficulty negotiating with the health care providers and the insurance company. Natasha's mother was desperate and bitter. She blamed the system, complained that back in her homeland her mother would have gotten the treatment with no delay, "but here they would let you die on the steps of the hospital and not admit you until you proved that you have all the paperwork. They think about money before they think about people." She was devastated by running between different offices, failed to understand their instructions, and was frustrated by her husband's lack of cooperation. "I do not know whom to call," she explained. The social worker decided to seize the opportunity to enhance the family's cooperation. Realizing the importance of proving her usefulness as a means to overcome the family's mistrust, she suggested that she help them sort out and negotiate the difficulties. She accompanied the mother to the hospital, contacted the HMO, and helped resolve the misunderstandings. The grandmother received the desperately needed treatment.

This was a pivotal turning point. Grateful for the social worker's help, the family gradually came to have more trust in her and believe that she indeed cared for them. The worker understood that this required a major change of the family's perception of and attitude toward holders of official positions. The parents became gradually more cooperative and supported her work with Natasha, who slowly started to share some of her concerns, feelings of inadequacy, and social fears. She felt marginalized and rejected "because I do not dress in the right designers clothes, I do not know the right names of bands and actors." Her family did not approve of even the few social contacts that she had with other girls from the FSU. "They think that hanging out is a waste of time and that I should only stay home all day and study."

With the family's permission, the social worker then decided to conduct a home visit. At first, the family was a little suspicious that the worker wished to spy on them and report to the authorities her estimation of their financial situation. They claimed that their place was crowded and not fit to have guests. When the worker reassured them that her intention was to have an opportunity to meet Natasha on her own turf, the mother, who assumed the major negotiation role, developed an elaborate and complicated story about not having bought the computer and TV set but having received them as hand-me-down presents.

(continued)

Eventually, time for the visit was set. The worker spent more than an hour with the family looking at their albums, listening to their story of immigration, and sharing some details about her own immigration. This warmed the atmosphere and helped the family tell their stories of life back home. Self-disclosure by officials refutes the discourse of mistrust and opens the door for sharing. The worker was invited to join the family for tea and Russian dessert.

The following week, Natasha's appearance changed significantly. She seemed less depressed, talked more, and even smiled from time to time. In response to the worker's comment on these positive changes, Natasha explained that she felt relieved to realize that somebody respected how difficult it all has been for them and was genuinely willing to help. She expressed feeling under pressure to perform well in school: "After all, they keep telling me that we immigrated to give me better chances, so I cannot let them down." They then discussed her feelings of emotional burden and enormous responsibility and her conflicted desires to be like everybody else and enjoy friends on the one hand and her sense of family obligations on the other. They discussed possible strategies by which Natasha might handle them.

Four months after the original referral, the work with Natasha was terminated as the school year ended. The worker helped the family enroll the girl in a special subsidized summer program for immigrant adolescents in the local community center.

This case, which is not uncommon, illustrates many of the issues related to the interface of gender and cultural and ethnic backgrounds that are at the heart of this book in general and this chapter in particular. Changes in gender-specific roles for the grandmother, who lost her child care responsibilities; and the mother, whose increased centrality in providing for the family, negotiating external systems (e.g., school and hospital), and being involved in her daughter's education gained her more power and put on her more demands. At the same time, the man was marginalized because of his employment status, his limited language skills, and his alcohol abuse. Furthermore, the power of an additional woman—the social worker—provided the necessary support for the girl to start on the long and bumpy road of adjusting to her new world.

Service Providers   It is important that service providers understand the language and culture of women immigrants and are cognizant of the cultural background for the discourse of privacy, secrecy, and mistrust that immigrants bring with them. The challenge is to develop a cadre of workers who are knowledgeable in the role structure of the family and the place of and expectations for women. These workers should have a knowledge of language, awareness of differences between immigrants from various regions of the FSU, willingness to reserve judgment, and the ability to balance adherence to the norms in the new country with respect for the old ones. This is not a simple task.

Recruiting clinicians from a similar background to serve immigrants is difficult because the absence of social work as a profession in the FSU considerably limits the availability of such personnel. To address the scarcity, special programs have been developed to train psychologists, educators, and physicians from the FSU to become social workers and caseworkers. These professionals are familiar with the immigration experience. They can serve as socialization agents and powerful role models as well as a bridge between immigrants and their new culture. Because of the shared experience of migration, they can also contribute to normalization rather than pathologizing reactions. However, reactions may arise and compromise the effectiveness of interventions, such as the overidentification and overprotection of clients, assessing their situation through the lens of the worker's experience, and expecting them to adhere to the worker's coping patterns.

A combination of nonimmigrant professionals and immigrant interpreters has also been used. This expands the pool of highly trained service providers but may inhibit open discussion of intimate issues and create awkward communication. Furthermore, it potentially causes tension between interpreter and worker by filtering vital information through the perception of the interpreter and strains agency manpower and financial resources (Ivry, 1992).

PERSONAL REFLECTIONS

My experience with immigrants from the FSU includes 5 years of consulting with programs that serve immigrant adolescents and their families and conducting several studies on immigrant stepfamilies and on immigrant women. An immigrant myself (though not from the FSU), I learned firsthand the ordeals of relocation. Immigrant children and adolescents are torn between their two worlds: They are attached to their families and their cultures but want to belong and be like their peers and the world around them. Adult immigrants start from being "somebody" in their homeland to being "nobody" and struggling to become "somebody again." This journey is especially challenging for people who have to cross a cultural ocean, unlearn the ways of functioning within the controlling society in which they grew up, and relearn to function within a totally different mindset. I learned to respect the resilience in struggling with these ordeals and the tremendous potential for posttraumatic growth and the resourcefulness of people.

This learning directed me to adopt a strength perspective in my practice with this population. Building on their resilience, I work with them as partners in a journey toward change, letting go of many of the traditional do's and don'ts and performing in an open dialogue within a mutual context.

CONCLUSIONS

The waves of immigrants from the FSU that engulfed Western countries, particularly the United States and Israel in recent decades, have presented special challenges to service providers. Relocation from a Soviet culture to a significantly different Western culture exposes the immigrant to social, financial, legal, personal, familial, and occupational hardships with potentially devastating effects that social workers should be informed about in order to offer effective culturally competent services. Women immigrants from the former Soviet Union are especially central in their families' adaptation to new cultures.

Services to immigrants from the FSU are most effective when they are short-term, direct, cognitively and actively oriented, family-focused, and provided within nonstigmatized settings. Workers should be familiar with the immigrants' culture of origin and be able to develop culturally contextualized assessments as well as differentiate transient and traumatic stressors in the immigration experience. Because of their mistrust of authorities, immigrants from the FSU should be made active partners in planning and implementing interventions that have been designed to address their issues. Such services have the potential to help immigrants heal the wounds of the multiple losses involved in immigration and enhance posttraumatic growth.

KEY CONCEPTS

- multiple losses in immigration
- posttraumatic growth
- differential effects of immigration on men and women
- cultural barriers to service provision
- somatization of mental health issues
- clients' discourse of privacy and secrecy
- continuity of care
- culture-sensitive assessment
- culture-specific interventions
- culturally competent service providers

QUESTIONS FOR REFLECTION

1. What are my biases or prejudices regarding immigrants, and what are examples of my acting on these biases? (Analyses of examples of specific situations are most desirable.)
2. Reflect on times and events in your life when you felt "like a fish out of the water."
3. What was the experience like?
4. What were the most uncomfortable aspects of the experience?
5. What helped you cope with the situation? What are the potential effects of each phase of the immigration on individuals and families?
6. How would you assess Natasha's situation if the information regarding her immigration status was not available to you? How would knowing her immigration status affect your assessment?
7. Which of the social worker's interventions with Natasha do you evaluate as helpful? Why?

EXERCISE

With one student not present, the class will decide on certain rules of conduct—for example, speaking in a certain way such as avoiding words that start with the letter "A," emphasizing the last syllable of each word, and so on. When the absent student returns, class members must interact in the way they decided and react with criticism to the student who does not obey the norm. Follow this exercise with a discussion of the "alien's" experience.

References

Baider, L., Ever-Hadani, P., & Kaplan-DeNour, A. (1996). Crossing new bridges: The process of adaptation and psychological distress of Russian immigrants in Israel. *Psychiatry: Interpersonal and Biological Processes, 59*(2), 175–183.

Berger, R. (1996). Characteristics of adolescent immigrants from the former Soviet Union. The *Jewish Social Work Forum, 32,* 42–50.

Berger, R. (1997). Adolescent immigrants in search of identity: Clingers, eradicators, vacillators and integrators. *Child & Adolescent Social Work Journal, 14*(4), 263–275.

Berger, R. (2001). Immigration and mental health: Principles for successful social work practice. In R. P. Perez-Koenig & B. D. Rock (Eds.), *Social and economic justice: Devolution and social work practice* (pp. 159–176). New York: Fordham University Press.

Berger, R. (2004). *Immigrant women tell their stories.* New York: Haworth Press.

Bernstein, J. H., & Shuval, J. T. (1999). Gender differences in the process of occupational integration of immigrant physicians in Israel. *Sex Roles: A Journal of Research, 40*(1–2), 1–23.

Berry J. W. (1986). The acculturation process and immigrant behavior. In C. L. Williams & J. Westmeyer (Eds.), *Mental health in resettlement countries.* Washington, DC: Hemisphere.

Birman, D., & Tyler, E. (1994). Acculturation and alienation of Soviet Jewish refugees in the United States. *Genetic Social and General Psychology Monographs, 120*(1), 103–115.

Bock, K. P. (1970). *Culture shock: A reader in modern cultural anthropology.* New York: Alfred A. Knopf.

Brodsky, B. (1982). Social work and the Soviet immigrant. *Migration Today, 10,* 15–20.

Bystydienski, J. M., & Resnik, E. P. (1994). Introduction. In J. M. Bystydienski & E. P. Resnik (Eds.), *Women in cross-cultural transitions* (pp. 1–12). Bloomington, IN: Phi Delta Educational Foundation.

Calhoun, L. G., & Tedeschi, R. G. (1999). *Facilitating posttraumatic growth: A clinician's guide.* Mahwah, New Jersey: Lawrence Erlbaum.

Chiswick, B. R (1993). Soviet Jews in the United States: An analysis of their linguistic and economic adjustment. *International Migration Review, 27*(2), 260–285.

Coll, C. G., & Magnusom, K. (1997). The psychological experience of immigration: A developmental perspective. In A Booth, A. C. Crouter, & N. Landale (Eds.), *Immigration and the family* (pp. 91–131). Mahwah, NJ: Lawrence Erlbaum.

Drachman, D., & Halbertstadt, A. (1992). A stage migration framework as applied to recent Soviet emigrés. In A. Shen-Ryan (Ed.), *Social work with immigrants and refugees* (pp. 63–78). New York: Haworth Press.

Drachman, D., & Shen-Ryan, A. (1991). Immigrants and refugees. In A. Gitterman (Ed.), *Social work practice with vulnerable populations* (pp. 618–646). New York: Columbia University Press.

Furnham, A., & Bochner, S. (1986). *Culture shock: Psychological reactions to unfamiliar environments.* New York: Methuen.

Garza-Guerrero, A. C. (1974). Culture shock: Its mourning and the vicissitudes of identity. *Journal of the American Psychoanalytic Association, 22,* 408–429.

Glassman, U., & Skolnik, L. (1984). The role of social group work in refugee resettlement. *Social Work with Groups, 7*(1), 45–62.

Harper, K. V., & Lantz, J. (1996). *Cross-cultural practice: Social work with diverse populations.* Chicago: Lyceum.

Hulewat, P. (1996). Resettlement: A cultural and psychological crisis. *Social Work, 41*(2), 129–135.

Ivry, J. (1992). Paraprofessionals in refugee resettlement. In A. Shen-Ryan (Ed.), *Social work with immigrants and refugees* (pp. 99–117). New York: Haworth Press.

Knorr, J. S., & Meier, B. (Eds.). (2000). *Women and migration: Anthropological perspectives.* New York: St. Martin's Press.

Lalonde, R. N., Taylor, D. M., & Moghaddam, F. M. (1992). The process of social identification for visible immigrant women in a multicultural context. *Journal of Cross-Cultural Psychology, 23*(1), 25–39.

Landau-Stanton, J. (1985). Adolescents, families and cultural transition: A treatment model. In A. Mirkin & S. Koman (Eds.), *Handbook of adolescents and family therapy* (pp. 363–381). New York: Gardner Press.

Liebkind, K. (1992). Ethnic identity: Challenging the boundaries of social psychology. In G. M. Breakwell (Ed.), *Social psychology of identity and the self-concept* (pp. 147–185). London: Surrey University Press.

Marris, P. (1974). *Loss and change.* New York: Pantheon Press.

Pittaway, I. (1991). *Refugee women: Still at risk in Australia.* Melbourne: Bureau of Immigration Research.

Remennick, L. I. (1999). Gender implications of immigration: The case of Russian speaking women in Israel. In G. A. Kelson & D. L. DeLaet (Eds.), *Gender and immigration* (pp. 163–185). New York: New York University Press.

Schuck, H. P. (1999). *Citizens, strangers and in-betweens: Essays on immigration and citizenship.* Boulder, CO: Westview Press.

Shepherd, J. (1992). Post-traumatic stress disorder in Vietnamese women. In E. Cole, O. M. Espin, & E. D. Rothblum (Eds.), *Refugee women and their mental health: Shattered societies, shattered lives* (pp. 281–296). New York: Haworth Press.

Shen-Ryan, A. (Ed.). (1992). *Social work with immigrants and refugees.* New York: Haworth Press.

Slonim-Nevo, V., Sharaga, Y., & Mirsky, J. (1999). A culturally sensitive approach to therapy with immigrant families: The case of Jewish emigrants from the former Soviet Union. *Family Process, 38*(4), 445–461.

Sluzki, C. E. (1983). Process, structure, and worldview: Towards an integrated view of systemic models in family therapy. *Family Process, 22*, 469–476.

Stewart, E. C. P. (1986). The survival stage of intercultural communication. *International Christian University Bulletin* [Tokyo], *1*(1), 109–121.

Szapocznik, J., Scopetta, M. A., & Kurtines, W. (1978). Theory and measurement of acculturation. *Interamerican Journal of Psychology, 12*, 113–120.

Tedeschi, R. G., Park, C. L., & Calahun, L. G. (1998). *Posttraumatic growth: Positive changes in the aftermath of crisis.* Mahwah, NJ: Lawrence Erlbaum.

United Nations Department for Economic and Social Information and Policy Analysis Population Division. (1995). *International migration policies and the status of female migrants.* Proceedings of the United Nations Expert Group Meeting, Italy.

Vinokurov, A., Birman, D., & Trickett, E. (2000). Psychological and acculturation correlates of work status among Soviet Jewish refugees in the United States. *International Migration Review, 34*(2), 538–559.

Walsh, K. (2001). Personal communication with coordinator of Australian Red Cross Tracing and Refugee Services.

Weiss, Z. (2000). *Post-traumatic growth in husbands of women with breast cancer.* DSW dissertation. New York: Adelphi University.

CHAPTER 9

POSTTRAUMATIC EXPERIENCES OF REFUGEE WOMEN

HURRIYET BABACAN AND NARAYAN GOPALKRISHNAN
AUSTRALIA

OVERVIEW

Migration and the movements of people are complex processes that uproot people and transplant them in a new environment, a transition that is not easy to make in the best of times. People create meaning out of the context in which events occur. Consequently, an experience of migration always involves a strong subjective component of people's lived experiences and their reaction to the new environment. Refugees are people who move involuntarily from their country of residence. A *refugee* has been defined by the U.N. Convention and Protocol for the Status of Refugee Status as a person "owing to a well founded fear of being persecuted for reasons of race, religion, nationality, membership of a particular social group or political opinion, is outside the country of his nationality and is unable or owing to such fear is unwilling to avail himself of the protection of that country." The state is required to give refuge to those who seek asylum on a durable basis, and if it is unable to do so then it is required to at least give them refuge on a temporary basis. States are not allowed to expel or return any refugee to the territory where he or she is likely to face persecution.

Refugees face physical hardships, emotional trauma, torture and deprivation, often witnessing disasters, wars, and the deaths of immediate family members prior to fleeing (Adelman, Borowski, Burstein, & Foster, 1994). In each of these instances, refugees experience situations that provoke strong reactions and emotions. This is often exacerbated by difficult processing systems, detention, and waiting in refugee camps, all of which make migration patterns and settlement processes for refugees quite different from those of other migrants. Refugees carry with them the history of their traumatic experiences that determines how they adjust and settle to a new life in the host country (Axelson, 1993). For many refugees, the trials of settlement are all the more difficult and accentuated as many have passed through harrowing times before arrival in the new country. It is for this reason that the resettlement needs of refugees take on a special importance (Furnham & Bochner, 1986).

This chapter focuses on several different aspects of working with women refugees in Australia. It first covers the cultural context of Australia as the host country, including gaps between the legal structure set up to accept refugees and the actual climate of racism that rejects them. The chapter reviews the stages of settlement and adaptation, and relates how racism impacts on the movement through these stages. The specific problems of women refugees are reviewed, including their particular vulnerability in their role in their families. Trauma is a part of these women's lives but needs to be understood in the context of migration and flight from other countries because normal reactions to this situation often are viewed as signs of mental illness. A case study of a Somalian woman and the way multicultural feminist counseling helped her tell her story is presented.

AUSTRALIA AS A HOST COUNTRY

Australia has always been a country of immigrants, and migration programs have played an important role in nation building (Department of Immigration, Multicultural and Indigenous Affairs, 2002; Papastergiadis, 2000). Since World War II, more than 5.7 million people have migrated to Australia, with nearly 1 million of these being resettled under humanitarian programs (Mares, 2001). Australian immigration policy had little experience with refugee movements before 1945, and the overall philosophy of intake of people related to population and economic concerns. Over the last six decades, Australia's intake of refugees has grown in both size and diversity. Currently, the Commonwealth government annually takes in approximately 80,000 immigrants (whose entry to Australia is based on economic, family, and skill considerations) and 12,000 humanitarian entrants under a range of programs. The "women at risk" program is a subcomponent of the humanitarian program. Women at risk identifies and gives priority to women refugees around the world who are deemed to be at risk. Although the criteria for at risk is not explicit, it generally includes factors such as families with single female heads, older women, and women who are vulnerable to physical harm (e.g., rape in camps). There are only 500 places in this program each year. Upon entry to Australia, these refugees receive the same assistance as other refugees.

With regard to refugees, there are distinct differences between declared legal standards and actual practices. At an international level, Australia is a signatory to several international agreements such as the International Convention on the Elimination of Racial Discrimination. Within Australia, there exists a range of legislation that establish the legal framework against discrimination of immigrants, such as the Human Rights and Equal Opportunity Commission Act of 1986 and a range of legislation at the state levels such as the Queensland Anti-Discrimination Act of 1991. These are accompanied by a series of national policies and programs that assist refugees and immigrants in settlement and in managing the cultural diversity of Australia's population.

However, in Australia, attitudes toward immigrants reflect confusion, anxiety, skepticism, ambivalence, lack of knowledge, and racism (Lukomskyj, 1994). Australian nation building has been based on an obsession with the invasion by the "yellow peril." The White Australia policy, until its demise in 1973, excluded Asians and other "non-whites" from migrating to Australia. Although the Australian government has adopted a so-called nondiscriminatory immigration and humanitarian program, the legacy of the White Australia policies remain. Jupp (1994) argues that in the selection process of humanitarian entrants, emphasis is placed on those with "settlement potential" and filters out others. He points out that "Australian resettlement policy has never recognized any special obligations to the more destitute refugees, most of whom are women and children" (Jupp, 1994, p. 55).

In recent times, the federal government has embarked upon a campaign to detain asylum seekers and label them as "illegal immigrants." Often these people are ethnic minorities from Afghanistan, Kurds from Iraq and Turkey, Tamils from Sri Lanka, and people from different strife-torn parts of Africa such as Sudan. However, there has been little recognition of the situations from which these people have come. In fact, there has been a public demonization of asylum seekers that has increased the negative attitudes of the general population toward refugees. Many authors have pointed to the inhumane treatment of the so-called boat people, and there have been calls for Australia to observe the international agreements to which the nation is a signatory (Mares, 2001; McMaster, 2001).

SETTLEMENT AND ADJUSTMENT

Negative attitudes on the part of the general public toward immigrants, especially racial minorities, has impeded the settlement process of many refugees. The term *settlement* refers to the period following an immigrant's arrival in a new country. It is about making a new start, finding one's place in society, playing a role, and feeling as much at home in the new place as in the country of origin (Cox 1987, 1996). Babacan (1998) confirmed that there was a significant correlation between "success" in settlement and racism. This study found that people were unsettled, irritable, and anxious and did not have a sense of belonging in an environment of racism and hostility. The study further found that the political rise of the anti-immigrant One Nation and silence by the prime minister against such views reinforced insecurity and community fragmentation among newly arrived immigrants and refugees

Jupp, McRobbie, and York (1991) point out another factor that plays a role in determining settlement. The voluntary nature of immigration is an important contributor of successful settlement because this provides psychological stability and a congruency of expectations about life in Australia. This is less likely for refugees because of the traumatic situations they experience and the likelihood of receiving little or no information about Australia before their arrival. The nature of migration and the decision-making process involved can have positive or negative consequences for successful settlement into Australian society.

What constitutes successful settlement is a matter that is often debated and varies with individual, social, and cultural factors. In the cultural context of Australia, Jupp has developed a range of settlement indicators that are useful in monitoring progress of individuals. These indicators are based on degree of equity and social justice experienced by the person attempting to settle.

- A migrant or refugee who is employed at the same level of qualifications and experience as before departure is settled.
- A migrant or refugee whose lifestyle is better than in the previous homeland by the migrant's own judgment is settled.
- A migrant or refugee who has full command of the majority language is settled.
- A migrant or refugee who has full access to public services that are available to all is settled.
- A migrant or refugee who has taken out citizenship and intends to remain in the country is settled.
- A migrant or refugee who does not feel discriminated against is settled.

Refugees are particularly vulnerable to a hostile environment when the prospect of being sent back to their country of origin has dire consequences for them and their families. It is useful for a counselor to identify what stage a client is in. Chapter 8 reviews these stages. These stages are a valuable guide to the counselor in several ways: First, they can assist with the initial assessment of the issues and problems that a refugee is facing; second, they can assist in understanding the manifest behavior and expressed feelings of the client; and third, they can assist in the types of intervention that a counselor may put in place. Some interventions may be just simple settlement support provisions rather than issues related to trauma.

REFUGEE WOMEN

The United Nations High Commission for Refugees (UNCHR) estimates that there are 28 million displaced people in the world with more than 50% of them being women. Women are recognized by both international agencies and national governments as being at risk. The United Nations' Decade for Women in Beijing (1995) and Nairobi (1985) determined that refugee women and children would be given priority. The director of the United Nations' Division for the Advancement of Women, Ms. Sellami-Meslem (1990), urged that

> we must be careful to avoid the trap of dealing with the issue of refugees as being the same as the issue of refugee women. Indeed, refugee women experience most of the same problems as refugee men, and these can be very serious. But what we are examining . . . are problems for which the situation of refugee women is different than for refugee men. We have to apply the gender test to the questions raised. (p. 1)

In Australia, women have a harder time with the settlement process than men. Women have been more vulnerable to settlement and adjustment problems. Female immigrants and refugees generally have poorer English proficiency than men and are more likely to immigrate as dependents than in their own right. Compared with men, women are more likely to have limited economic means and be subjected to traditional family constraints on behavior. Separation from family and kin-based social support systems is a particularly important factor for women. Unfavorable employment and housing circumstances, prejudice, and discrimination in the labor market and in the community also have disproportionate impacts on women (Alexander, Kohn, Clarke, & Feeney, 2000; Jupp, 1994; Pittaway, 1991; Wooden, Holton, & Sloan, 1994).

A reluctance to use social services has especially disadvantaged migrant women and children, leading to a process of social marginalization. Social marginalization occurs when individuals find themselves on the borders of two cultures without being fully members of either. This is often what happens to refugees who come into uncertain environments; do not trust people of their own community because of political, racial or religious tension; and cannot integrate with the mainstream society. This leaves many to face isolation and a lack of support that impedes their adjustment (Babacan, 1992).

Social marginalization interacts to exacerbate the vulnerable situation of the traumatized refugee. Refugees arrive already traumatized and separated from family. These two factors are considered by many refugees as much more serious than any of the practical obstacles to resettlement. Refugee women were particularly affected severely by separation from families because of the loss of children or husbands, missing immediate family members, and breakdowns in family structures, particularly extended family support networks. Some of the separation problems were created by the selection processes of Australia, which define family in terms of the Western nuclear unit and hence raise questions about the role of the state as a sexist and racist entity (Bottomley, De Lepervanche, & Martin, 1991). The separation of families prolongs the adjustment process as refugees devote their resources and efforts to trying to reunite with or find family members.

The history of Australia is the history of displacement, disruption, journeys, and resettlement. Australia was founded through invasion, conquest, and dispossession of the Aboriginal people. Representations of the Australian nation identity are masculine and have rendered women invisible (Yuval-Davis & Anthias, 1989). Aboriginal and ethnic women are depicted as the "other." Racism, like sexism, is a social construct that embraces both discourse and practice. In some ways, racism is even more arbitrary than sexism because sex is a biological reality while race is not (Essed, 1991). Racism always implies the power to impose a definition of the other as the subordinate group. Minority women are frequently subject to "normalized absence" or "pathological presence" treatment in which their problems are not seen or the women are viewed as victims (Pettman, 1992).

It is clear that racism and sexism intersect, and this is the reality of many refugee women in the Australian context who face exclusion at the institutional and interpersonal level. Thus, in Essed's words, "everyday racism is the integration of racism into everyday situations through practices (both cognitive and behavioral) that activate underlying power relations" (Essed, 1991, p. 50). Thus, everyday racist practices become unquestionable and seen as normal. This leads to many outcomes for refugee women such as sensitivity to their environments, insecurity, anticipation of racism when it does not exist, paranoia about simple questions, and being defensive. Though not all refugee women experience racism at the same level, the questions of racism and being excluded are well documented in several studies (Babacan, 1998; Jupp, 1991; Pittaway, 1991).

Refugee women face many of the problems faced by other ethnic women in Australia in addition to the ones stemming from their refugee experiences. Elladis, Colanero, and Roussos (1989) conclude that migrant women who are not present in decision-making structures are not empowered to make decisions for themselves. For example, refugee women often do not have a say in the way health services are run because they are often not aware of the ways in which health systems are run, do not speak English, and are rendered powerless by the medical hierarchy and medical jargon. Furthermore, the processes of consultation are inappropriate linguistically and culturally. Information on programs is usually inaccessible to ethnic women. For example, informational brochures were produced for refugee women from Sudan in the state of Queensland. Apart from problems of dissemination, it was later found that many Sudanese refugee women who arrived in Australia at that time were illiterate, so they could not read the information. Services are usually monocultural and monolingual in orientation, and service providers are not sensitive to cultural and linguistic differences. Resources for programs for ethnic women are often ad hoc and of short-term duration. All these factors act as barriers to participation by ethnic women in Australian society. The same study identified many priority areas in need of urgent attention for migrant women: improved health, safety, and working conditions; improved access to language instruction, education, and training; improved services for elder care; and improved access to child care. Migrant women are portrayed in the media as occupying the lowest social category: as cleaners, domestic help, or sex objects (Jakubowicz, Goodall, Martin, Mitchell, Randall, & Seneviratne, 1994). In developing a model of the Australian labor market, Collins (1991) states that migrant women are at the bottom of the occupational and employment ladder in Australian society, often encountering discrimination by employers, having poor access to training, and facing nonrecognition of their overseas qualifications (Babacan, 1996; Collins, 1991). These areas are equally relevant for refugee women and will influence their adaptation process.

The family is the nexus of support, growth, and identity for many women. The process of migration and resettlement negatively affects the family and particularly disadvantages women. The traditional sources of support from extended family and social networks are broken through uprooting. The new settlement process brings about new pressures such as financial struggles, conflict, and illness. Guarnaccia and Lopez (1998) state that women and girls are more vulnerable to this kind of family stress than are men and boys. Their explanation is based on the emphasis placed on the social development of women that relates self-development with that of nurturing and caring roles across many ethnic communities. Males are protected because of their greater social freedom, lesser responsibilities for domestic duties, and lesser exposure to family dysfunction.

EFFECTS AND SYMPTOMS OF TRAUMA

Although many refugees exhibit classical symptoms of posttraumatic stress disorder (PTSD), Lin (1986) cautions us neither to equate symptomatic behavior of refugees with those of major mental illness nor necessarily offer a psychiatric diagnosis. He argues that there are common psychological reactions to stress such as depression, anxiety, somatic complaints, and sociopathic behavior. Moore (2000) gives examples of misdiagnoses and overdiagnoses of disorders such as schizophrenia and paranoia among certain ethnic groups. Some relive the distressing moments, have recurrent dreams, or exhibit physical symptoms that were part of the traumatic moment. The sequel to traumatic experience seems to be deep personality change, a mental disability that affects every side of psychic life, the intellectual functions, emotional life and the will to live, all involving difficulties in adjustment and consequent complications. In an environment that involves risk-taking behavior, many refugees are reluctant to engage because of fear, a lack of trust, insecurity, and emotional instability (Herman, 1997; McDonald & Steel, 1997).

The research on refugee and immigrant mental illness in Australia is ad hoc, contradictory, and inconsistent. Several studies over the years, however, have demonstrated that when refugees experience premigration stress, there are serious consequences. A study conducted by Stoller and Krupinski (1973) found that Eastern Europeans who lived through severe wartime experiences showed the highest rates of schizophrenic states and also scored highly in disorders. They found that the Jews had the highest rate of severe neurotic symptoms. The complexities of trauma and settlement reoccur particularly when the person is getting older. The complexities of assessment and diagnoses are a major problem for psychogeriatrics when refugees regress to their former state, lose English language skills, and relive their traumas (Paoletti, 1988). Minas, Szmukler, Demirsar, and Eisenbruch (1988) found that Turkish women, refugees from military regimes, had high rates of depression and anxiety because of social marginalization, cultural maladjustment, and isolation. The most common symptoms were anxiety, depressed mood, insomnia, somatic symptoms, irritability, and suicidal ideas. Mestrovic (1988) outlines the trauma caused in the former Yugoslav communities and identifies many conditions, including schizophrenia, paranoid states, alcohol- and drug-induced psychosis, affective psychosis, neurotic disorder, acute stress, and depressive disorder. A major study of the Indochinese refugees in Australia—that is, refugees from Vietnam, Cambodia, and Laos—concluded that approximately 35% of those who took part in their study showed psychiatric symptoms such as anxiety and depression as a result of their journey to Australia. Their stories included incidents of robbery, rape, and loss of family members (Tan, Krupinski, & Chiu, 1985). Hosking (1990) points out the high levels of torture survivors among refugees from Latin America.

As refugees often move from one location to another before their arrival and have experienced a continuum of movement, their traumatic experiences intersect with the experience of translocation (Burdekin, 1993). Sometimes they have to leap across highly distinct settings—and a leap across centuries from traditional to modern lifestyles. Each change brings with it added ambiguities, new requirements for psychological adjustment, uncertain expectations, and minimal control over one's own destiny. Many refugees have learned survival skills that may be viewed as aversive or even sociopathic.

Looking at the larger context of violence against women, Brautigam (1996) refers to the extraordinarily vulnerable position of women refugees as "disproportionately affected by the consequences of their status as refugees or displaced persons." Women and girls are vulnerable to gender-based discrimination, exploitation, and violence and are at risk in the communities from which they are fleeing, during flight, as well as in refugee camps, or other places where they seek protection. Yet while women are at risk for and under assault, they continue to remain responsible for the survival of their children and other members of their families.

Fry (2000) points to the way in which women, particularly young women, are differentially and negatively affected by migration and dislocation. A study involving women from diverse cultural backgrounds in Australia concluded that many salient factors contribute to women's vulnerability to suicide attempts, including cultural conflicts embedded in gender roles such as male dominance in families, double standards for men and women in the family or culture, intergenerational conflicts, marriage customs, restriction of freedom, lack of awareness of legal rights, and acceptance of cultural inequality as a norm that cannot be changed.

The risk factors of mental health disorders in refugees vary according to gender. High rates of mental disorders in refugees occur early after migration. There are differences between men and women in the occurrence of mental illness and length of stay in the country. The incidence of mental illness for males is highest 1 to 2 years after arrival; in contrast, the highest incidence in females occurs 7 to 15 years after migration. The difference is attributed in part to the fact that men experienced increased levels of stress early when trying to interact with the outside world such as in learning the language and in finding employment. Women tend to remain protected from these early pressures but experience stress later when they remain the only people in the families unable to relate to their environment (Westermeyer, Williams, & Nguyen, 1991). A common theme identified with refugee women is that many cannot retell their stories either for fear of doing harm to others or because of feelings of loss of control, rage, and shame over their vulnerability and helplessness at the violation of their rights, failure to save others, and loss of innocence (Bashir, 2000). Therefore, the act of telling one's story is a key healing strategy that should not be overlooked in counseling refugee women.

In the early stages of arrival of a refugee community, questions of meaning of symptoms and diversity of emotional expression can lead to major diagnostic mistakes. This is particularly so in the absence of early screening

CASE 9.1 | MS. M.

The civil war that broke out Somalia in the 1990s led to the exodus of many people. Ms. M., a 28-year-old Muslim woman, escaped the country with her 8-year-old son after witnessing the death of her husband by armed gangs of a particular clan. After days on foot with little food and water, they got to a refugee camp. At the camp, she realized that her sister had been killed and that her sister's four children had been brought to the camp in a destitute state. The father of the children was missing. Ms. M. now took care of all five children. The conditions in the camp were extremely difficult and included the constant threat of rape by men in the camp. She started to have nightmares. After 2 years in the camp. she was resettled in Australia with the five children. However, she was placed in a semirural area with few support services. The area was also not accustomed to seeing people with visible differences, and she received many hostile comments from people in the community. Her support network comprised church-based charity groups. Ms. M.'s nightmares intensified in this environment. She often suffered from panic attacks and found herself bursting into tears. She lost the motivation to do things around the house, clean up, feed the children, and take them to school. She also stopped going to English language classes herself.

She was referred to a counselor in the area, as there was the threat that her children could be taken away from her because of neglect. The counselor tried to find an interpreter to communicate with Ms. M., but Ms. M. became extremely agitated, covered her face, and would not speak at all with the interpreter. The counselor assumed that she was covering her face because the interpreter was a man from her community and, as a Muslim woman, Ms. M. was covering up. This later proved to be an incorrect cultural assumption. The initial interview ended without any progress. The counselor contacted several multicultural organizations and tried to gather background information about the client's culture. He came up with a set of key issues. The first was that the unrest in Somalia was caused by clan fighting of kinship and religious nature. The issue of trust in the context assumed great significance. The interpreter, who had

been called for the first meeting, was of the clan that killed Ms. M.'s husband. Her extreme reaction came from an association of this person with what happened in the past and a fear of what might happen to her in the future. The issue of physical and personal safety for refugees was reinforced once again in this case. Having understood this, an appropriate interpreter was arranged. In the preinterview stage, it became clear that her Muslim upbringing had prevented Ms. M. from opening up to a strange male counselor.

A female counselor took over Ms. M.'s case. Having taken care of two important points, Ms. M. was able to tell her story in her own words and express the nature of her problems. The counselor recognized that the act of telling one's story is a healing process because it:

1. unburdens the client of the issues she is carrying,
2. is a way to work through issues that trouble the person,
3. validates the experiences of the person by sharing them with a second person,
4. enables the building of a trusting relationship with the counselor and the development of empathy by the counselor,
5. empowers and builds the confidence of the person as having something worthy to say, and
6. develops pathways to address the issues raised.

Therefore, storytelling is a powerful tool that was used successfully in the case of Ms. M.

In telling her story, Ms. M. revealed that she had been raped in the camp by a person in charge and could not disclose it to anyone as he had threatened to stop her resettlement if she were to tell anyone. She had not had the opportunity to debrief with anyone and felt extremely "dirty and unclean." This related to her cultural understanding of morality and sex out of wedlock. She also felt that she was somehow to blame for this. Her belief that she was "dirty" was reinforced by arriving in a hostile environment where she was confronted with overt racism as a black woman in a predominantly white environment. Further, the support group was constantly forcing Ms. M. to learn English, to assimilate, and to convert to Christianity. This was a source of tension and further fear for Ms. M. She felt unsafe and responded through withdrawal, retreat, and a diminished will to live.

(continued)

Many challenges faced this counselor. First, she had to overcome her own biases against refugees and black people and understand a specific set of cultural differences. This is a key aspect of multicultural counseling as assumptions regarding normal behavior are often based on the counselor's cultural context. Behavior that is quite normal in a different culture can be misunderstood and mislabeled in the process. For example, clients can believe that they can become sick or die or have some harm come to them because a bone has been pointed at them or a curse put on them by people with the knowledge to do so (e.g., elders or shamans). Often counselors who are based in Western knowledge systems can negate these beliefs as mental illness rather than cultural phenomena. Some of the key areas in which mistakes are likely to be made include family relationships, greetings, dress codes, communication (e.g., avoiding eye contact), gender relations, approaches to the body (e.g., in some cultures the head is sacred and should not be touched), and ways of address (e.g., a certain status may be needed to talk to elders).

The counselor also needed to understand the connections between gender and culture—in this case, understanding the context of being both a Somali and a woman. The counselor had to understand the role of history and its impact on the client. This counselor adopted the view that human development and the origin of psychological problems are seen as a result of the interaction between the individual and their environment. From this position, assessment and therapeutic solutions would need to incorporate the impact of sociocultural factors. This was aided by gathering factual and historical background information on Somalia. Establishing rapport was difficult at first because it is not permissible in the Somali culture to express emotions publicly. It thus took an unusual amount of time to create an emotional connection. Over a 12-month period, Ms. M. was able to stop the panic attacks and resume caring for people in her family and take a more active interest in the environment.

Anthropologists spend months or years studying cultures to gain a true appreciation of them. Counselors do not have the opportunity to observe their clients interacting within their cultural environments because the work takes place in the world of the counselor. For this reason, multicultural counseling is not about exhaustive training in the culture and norms of different groups, which is possibly an enviable but

not realistic objective. Instead, it is about being able to apply several models to different cultural situations with sensitivity and developing cultural competencies. Multicultural counseling challenges both the client and the counselor by bringing together different sets of norms, values, and beliefs that need to be negotiated. To show cultural empathy and to negotiate the differences, the counselor needs to be flexible and open to key ideas, values, and frameworks. Cultural empathy was used to overcome the impossibility of having prior in-depth knowledge of the client's cultural context. In this case, some of the questions the counselor needed to ask within the context of multicultural counseling included:

1. How is reality understood in this particular culture? Is it viewed as dualistic or as holistic?

2. What is the concept of self? Is it perceived as autonomous or as bounded?

3. What is the sense of morality, including issues around values and choices?

4. What is the concept of time—that is, is it viewed as linear, circular, segmented, or future-oriented?

5. What is the concept of relationships, including issues around face and respect for elders and the role of women versus men?

6. What is the sense of land, environment, and place?

Through recognition and acceptance of different answers to these questions, multicultural counseling can yield successful outcomes. The counselor was able to engage with Ms. M. and work with her through establishing trust by drawing on culturally appropriate issues of responsibility and care for children. By adopting a multicultural counseling method, she was able to empathize with Ms. M. and to understand the nature of her problems. Through a feminist counseling strategy, Ms. M. was empowered to talk about her own problems and understand that the rape was not her fault and that she was not dirty. Interventions in feminist counseling deal with helping people understand the impact of gender roles and power differences in society and helping them make changes in situations that hurt them.

The counselor also became skilled in understanding the stages of settlement. It was clear that Ms. M. was in the frustration phase. Her ability to interact with the society around her was minimal, and she was frustrated, angry, and resistant to people around her. Her ability to cope was tested. Establishing trust for the environment became a major counseling goal. This was achieved by connecting Ms. M. with support networks other than the church-based charity. However, this could only happen by the recognition of the stages of settlement and what stage Ms. M. was in. Within 2 years, Ms. M. was able to have English proficiency and enrolled in university to complete her studies in engineering.

For most refugees, holding onto cultural norms is both comforting and reinforcing, as it was for Ms. M. The counselor was able to recognize this. However, she was also able to recognize that the refugee experience is filled with changing cues and permeable boundaries—and that the protective mechanism that facilitates survival of both the individual and the culture may also militate against adjustment at times. By understanding that cultural adaptation presents an external threat to the person, the counselor was able to provide the cultural support through appropriate cultural resources (e.g., an interpreter) and thus minimize the risk taking required by the client. The counselor was able to display specific multicultural standards and competencies that define a culturally competent counselor. The three basic characteristics are awareness, understanding, and skills (Sue, Arrendondon, & McDavis, 1995, p. 625).

programs for refugee entrants. The role of culture, the assessment tools utilized, and the temporary or permanent phases of manifested conditions become quite tricky for the helping professional. In some instances, this is further impeded by language barriers and considerations of gender and religion. Because many refugees do not use the community mental health support services out of fear of stigma, their needs are not represented in psychiatric hospital statistics.

There are numerous levels of intervention beginning with generic issues of loss, grieving, difficulty in adjustment, impaired self-concept, familial and generational conflict, and disparity between inflated expectations and disappointing realities. Many issues arise for counselors: Which types of interventions do they adopt? How appropriate are the types of interventions for that culture? Does the counselor understand all aspects of the person's life history? Does the counselor have the cultural competence? Does the counselor go beyond the clinical role and become an advocate? These questions are complex and cannot be resolved easily. The case study that begins on p. 157 illustrates some of the complexities involved in counseling across cultures.

CONCLUSION

Refugee women are a major proportion of people who are displaced in the world today. Their experiences are quite different from those of male refugees. Women often have to care for their own children as well as be responsible for the children of extended family members. The premigration experiences of refugee women vary but include destruction of their homes, threat of rape, war, witnessing the deaths of family members, and torture. Although all refugees display symptoms of posttraumatic stress disorders, there are significant differences between those of men and women.

Refugee women often display courage, strength, and skill in their quest to survive the most bleak of human conditions. They support and give hope to their families and children, often at a personal cost. The settlement process for refugee women is fraught with obstacles and barriers. The contextual factors that cause added hardship include local negative attitudes toward refugees and dealing with differences. Australia, like other Western countries, has had an increased level of overt racism against its ethnic and indigenous people, often aggravated by structural problems created by the state and political parties. Furthermore, being a woman in a predominantly patriarchal society brings about complexities in relation to gender bias in the labor market, the role of the state in what is public and what is private, and responsibilities for caring for aged members of their families, children, and others. In many instances, refugee women are single heads of households. Therefore, refugee women face a triple burden as immigrants, refugees, and women.

We have argued that, in the context of Australia, caring professionals have largely operated from Western frameworks and in ways that have not addressed the needs of refugee women (Vasta & Castles, 1996). Of particular concern has been lack of understanding of cultural and gender issues in therapy. This problem, of course, has roots in both the conventional theoretical frameworks of therapy and counseling and in the personal attitudes of individual practitioners. The role of the counselor is critical in working with refugee women. Counselors must be familiar with specific stressors that are the products of cultural, demographic, and experiential differences among refugee women. Having examined the alternative frameworks, we argue that the form of therapy that is best suited to working with refugee women draws from the feminist and multicultural frameworks. Feminist therapy is concerned with influences on the individual that stem from the impact of gender roles and the belief that the "personal is political." Interventions in feminist therapy deal with helping people understand the impact of gender roles and power differences in society and helping them make changes in situations that hurt them.

Multicultural counseling adopts a set of strategies that make it distinctive from other frameworks. It involves cultural flexibility on the part of both counselor and client to enable the client to develop skills in working across cultures (Ridley, 1989). Linkages also need to be established between personal problems and political or social realities. Unlike dominant forms of therapy, multicultural counseling also looks at the broader picture and the need for social action to remedy situations that extend beyond the individual. Racism and its impact on the individual is a prime example for this approach. Cultural empathy is used to overcome the impossibility of having prior in-depth knowledge of the client's cultural context. It entails maintaining an attitude of cultural naiveté and respectful curiosity to work collaboratively with each client in a mutual exploration of their cultural contexts.

Both the multicultural and feminist approaches endeavor to empower the client. It entails supporting refugee women with resources, other forms of support, and empathy. It is also about changing dominant discourses that disempower women and immigrants and inhibit them from reaching their full potential, accessing inner and outer resources, and their voices being heard. Validating a person's feelings and experiences and supporting inner healing is achieved through several means. Storytelling emerges as a key way to empower the refugee. Sharing stories of trauma and change are healing and empowering not just for the sake of the person but also for the sake of all those who are privileged to hear them.

PERSONAL REFLECTIONS

We started working with refugees in different stages of our lives. Hurriyet migrated to Australia from Turkey as an adolescent in the 1970s just before a military takeover; her family would have been persecuted had it stayed. At an early stage in her life, she heard many accounts of torture and saw fear and anxiety in Turkish refugees. It was not until she started working with Kurdish refugees that she developed professional and personal insight and empathy about the challenges of working with refugees. Being of Turkish background, she had to understand her own biases (although unconscious) about Kurds. Although the majority of Kurds live in Turkey, Hurriyet had not heard of them before migrating to Australia. This led to much soul searching and pain as to why. On the one hand, there were many personal challenges in overcoming these biases; on the other hand, being accepted by Kurdish refugees as an empathic person was a difficult task. She was, by association, deemed part of the oppressors because she was Turkish and sometimes seen as an enemy of the Kurds. This raised many issues about cultural assumptions, the power of the counselor, stereotyping, developing empathy, and creating trust.

Also, there were broader challenges from one's own community—that is, the Turkish community in this case—and being ostracized and criticized for supporting and working with Kurdish people. The working relationship provided Hurriyet with strong personal and professional growth. It has been a richly rewarding experience, and Hurriyet has come away with great respect for the Kurds and the humanity and humility they have retained under great repression. Hurriyet has subsequently worked with many other refugee communities of diverse backgrounds and has been inspired by their spirit, determination, and resilience.

Narayan gained insight into marginalization in society in a first hand manner when he started working with the indigenous peoples in Orissa, a state in eastern India. Having come from working in the private sector, this experience was life-transforming for Narayan. He had made the switch from the private to the community development work following an extensive and in-depth search about the nature of life, meanings associated with power and society, and inhumane treatment of humans by other humans. In the context of multicultural, multilingual, and multifaith India, Narayan was able to draw from the rich traditions of Hindu philosophy in his thinking.

Narayan found that the indigenous Orriyas he worked with had different values and approaches to their lives and their environment, and he witnessed the destruction of the livelihoods of indigenous people by modern development and the market system. Consequently, his work with the indigenous people was aimed at empowerment so they might have some control over their lives. This led him to learn their language and live among them for 6 years. Narayan found that the people were genuine and had much to give of their compassion, trust, and selves. Their expectations from life were simple, and they were not caught up with the traps of consumerism. They witnessed the destruction of their forests and land and the environment with which they held a special relationship. Their simple way of living inspired Narayan to commit himself to values of humanity, sharing, and justice wherever he was in life.

After migrating to Australia, Narayan worked for the Australian Red Cross and in nongovernment refugee services. He was moved by the resilience, strength, and contribution of refugees. His work involved helping refugees in tracing their lost families. He saw that their hope for finding loved ones did not disappear even after 40 or 50 years. He witnessed their grief and trauma of resettlement to Australia and the pain associated with guilt, exile, and survival. Narayan saw many refugees fulfill their potential as successful and innovative human beings when the conditions of nurturing, trust, and security were provided.

KEY CONCEPTS

- settlement
- stages of adaptation
- trauma in cultural context
- telling a personal story in one's own words
- racism
- gender
- sexism
- refugees
- multicultural counseling
- cultural empathy, naiveté, and empowerment
- awareness of differences between cultures
- use of interpreters
- research about personal history
- marginalization

QUESTIONS FOR REFLECTION

1. What is similar and different between immigrants and refugees? Which would you find harder to work with and why?
2. What does the host country owe the refugee? Do you agree or think that the state should do more or less?
3. What specific traumas are refugees exposed to? How might these express themselves?
4. What is the special problems of women refugees in a male-oriented society?
5. How do racism and sexism intertwine in these situations?
6. What social discourses that exist in the host country affect the plight of refugee women?

EXERCISES

Exercise 1

The following is a case involving a refugee woman. Read this material and answer the questions below.

Case Study

Ms. Z. is a single woman refugee from Iran who belongs to the Baha'i faith. While in Iran, Ms. Z. was training to be a medical doctor. After Ayatollah Khomeini took over Iran, the rights and treatment of women changed. Ms. Z.'s family was persecuted because of its different faith, and she could not complete her studies. She was physically and mentally tortured in the initial years of the new regime. She was accused of being immoral and a representative of the "Devil." She was publicly humiliated, her head was shaved, and she was put in a bag full of rats. She received other forms of torture to her body, including her genitalia. She developed a range of posttraumatic conditions including sensitivity to any form of noise, flashbacks, nightmares, insomnia, disassociation, and paranoia of being followed. She also exhibited physical symptoms such as a rash on her skin.

In Australia, Ms. Z. was placed in a psychiatric unit in a public hospital. She was aware that her behavior was not "normal," and she wanted help. She was dissatisfied with the hospital assistance but had no other choice. She contacted a community-based agency where one of the authors of this chapter worked as a counselor. Because of structural reasons, it was difficult to change Ms. Z.'s therapist or assist in the intervention. With Ms. Z.'s permission, several welfare workers from her community and of the Baha'i faith and other refugees were contacted. However, there were problems of trust as the people contacted had left Iran earlier and were not persecuted in the same way as Ms. Z. This led to a cultural and political difference within the same culture, which many outside of it did not understand. So Ms. Z. remained in hospital with just a 1-hour counseling session, once a week, with one of the authors.

The hospital was an environment of noise, total insecurity, and cultural and gender insensitivity. Her condition was made worse by the constant drilling noises that were taking place as part of a hospital wing reconstruction. Ms. Z. spoke English fluently and therefore did not need an interpreter. However, the therapist at the hospital did not know about the Baha'i faith or the conditions in Iran that forced Ms. Z. to flee. He was trying to attend to her immediate needs such as insomnia and physical symptoms.

One day, the construction noise was especially loud and Ms. Z. could not bear it. She begged the nurse in charge to be moved elsewhere but her request was ignored. In an effort to escape the noise, Ms. Z. left the hospital premises and was further disoriented by the traffic noise on the busy roads near the hospital. In this disoriented and fearful state, she tried to cross the street and was hit by a truck, sustaining severe injuries and a disability to her legs.

Questions

1. What facts of this case would you consider as relevant when working with this client?
2. Which stories would you want to hear about?
3. What information do you have about Iran? How would you acquire this information? In what ways would this information be relevant to the case study?
4. What issues does the case raise about cross cultural counseling?
5. What issues does the case raise about gender?
6. What impact does the counseling environment have on the client?
7. What stage of settlement and adaptation is the client in?
8. What problems do you see in the way this client was treated?
9. If you were to see the client from her initial arrival in Australia, what counseling interventions would you adopt?

Exercise 2

In order to increase your awareness of cultural values that vary between different societies, it would be helpful to reflect on your own culture and answer the following questions. This exercise can help you compare and contrast your own culture to those of your clients, and it will help you learn to think of these variables in your work.

1. How is reality understood in your particular culture? Is it viewed as dualistic or as holistic?
2. What is the concept of self such as whether it is perceived as autonomous or bounded?
3. What is the sense of morality, including issues around values and choices?
4. What is the concept of time—that is, is it viewed as linear, circular, segmented, or future-oriented?
5. What is the concept of relationships, including issues of face and respect for elders and the roles of women versus men?
6. What is the sense of land, environment, and place?

References

Adelman, H., Borowski, A., Burstein, M., & Foster, L. (1994). *Immigration and refugee policy: Australia and Canada compared*. Melbourne, Australia: Melbourne University Press.

Alexander, N., Kohn, M., Clarke, S., & Feeney, K. (2000). The changing face of anorexia nervosa. In M. Bashir & D. Bennett (Eds.), *Deeper dimensions: Culture, youth and mental health* (pp. 119–122). Sydney, Australia: Transcultural Mental Health Centre.

Axelson, J. A. (1993). *Counseling and development in a multicultural society*. Pacific Grove, CA: Brooks/Cole.

Babacan, H. (1992). Experiences of Kurdish refugee women. In *Refugee women should not have to settle for less* (Proceedings of Women At Risk Forum) (pp. 9–16). Melbourne, Australia: Office of Ethnic Affairs.

Babacan, H. (1996). What do I have to do to get a job? An exploration of issues facing women from non-English speaking backgrounds in the labour market. In R. Hicks, P. Creed, W. Patton, & J. Tomlinson, *Unemployment developments and transitions* (pp. 221–232). Brisbane: Australian Academic Press.

Babacan, H. (1998). *I still call Australia Home: Exploration of racism and settlement*. Brisbane, Australia: Centre for Multicultural Pastoral Care.

Bashir, M. (2000). Immigration and refugee young people: Challenges in mental health. In M. Bashir & D. Bennett (Eds.), *Deeper dimensions: Culture, youth and mental health* (pp. 64–74). Sydney, Australia: Transcultural Mental Health Centre.

Bottomley, G., De Lepervanche, M., & Martin, J. (1991). *Intersexions: Gender, class, culture and ethnicity*. Sydney, Australia: Allen & Unwin.

Brautigam, C. A. (1996). Traumatized women. In Y. Danieli, N. S. Rodley, & L. Weisaeth (Eds.), *International responses to traumatic stress*. New York: Baywood.

Burdekin, B. (1993). *Human rights and mental illness*. Canberra: Australian Government Publishing Service.

Collins, J. (1991). *Migrant hands in a distant land: Australia's post-war immigration*. Leichhardt, Australia: Pluto Press.

Cox, D. (1987). *Migration and welfare: An Australian perspective*. Sydney, Australia: Prentice-Hall.

Cox, D. (1996). *Understanding Australian settlement services*. Canberra: Australian Government Publishing Service.

Department of Immigration, Multicultural and Indigenous Affairs. (2002). *2002–2003 migration and humanitarian programs: A discussion paper*. Canberra, Australia: Author.

Elladis, M., Colanero, R., & Roussos, P. (1989). *Public policy and non-English speaking background women*. Canberra: Australian Government Publishing Service, Office of Multicultural Affairs.

Essed, P. (1991). *Understanding everyday racism*. London: Sage.

Fry, A. (2000). Suicidal behaviour in young migrant women. In M. Bashir & D. Bennett (Eds.), *Deeper dimensions: Culture, youth and mental health* (pp. 146–163). Sydney, Australia: Transcultural Mental Health Centre.

Furnham, A., & Bochner, S. (1986). *Culture shock: Psychological reactions to unfamiliar environments*. London: Methuen.

Guarnaccia, P. J., & Lopez, S. (1998). The mental health and adjustment of immigrant and refugee children. *Child and Adolescent Clinics of North America, 7*(3), 537–553.

Herman, J. H. (1997). *Trauma and recovery*. New York: Basic Books.

Hosking P. (1990). *Hope after horror: Helping survivors of torture and trauma*. Sydney, Australia: Uniya.

Jakubowicz, A., Goodall, H., Martin, J., Mitchell, T., Randall, L., & Seneviratne, K. (Eds.). (1994). *Racism, ethnicity and the media*. St. Leonards, Australia: Allen & Unwin.

Jupp, J. (1994). *Exile or refuge? The settlement of refugee, humanitarian and displaced immigrants*. Canberra: Australian Government Publishing Service.

Jupp, J., McRobbie, A., & York, B. (1991). *Settlement needs of small, newly arrived ethnic groups*. Canberra: Australian Government Publishing Service.

Lin, K. M. (1986). Psychopathology and social disruption in refugees. In C. L. Williams & J. Westermeyer (Eds.), *Refugee mental health in resettlement countries* (pp. 61–73). Washington, DC: Hemisphere.

Lukomskyj, O. (1994). *An overview of Australian government settlement policy 1945–1992*. Canberra: Australian Government Publishing Service.

Mares, P. (2001). *Borderline: Australia's treatment of refugees and asylum seekers*. Sydney, Australia: University of New South Wales Press.

McDonald, B., & Steel, Z. (1997). *Immigrants and mental health: An epidemiological analysis*. Sydney, Australia: Transcultural Mental Health Centre.

McMaster, D. (2001). *Asylum seekers: Australia's response to refugees.* Melbourne, Australia: Melbourne University Press.

Mestrovic, R. (1988). Mental health of Yugoslav community. In E. Chiu & I. H. Minas (Eds.), *Mental health of ethnic communities: Proceedings of symposium* (pp. 13–21). Melbourne, Australia: St. Vincent's Hospital and Department of Psychiatry, University of Melbourne.

Minas, I. H., Szmukler, G. I., Demirsar, A., & Eisenbruch, M. (1988). Turkish patients presenting to the Royal Park Hospital Ethnic Psychiatry Service. In E. Chiu & I. H. Minas (Eds.), *Mental health of ethnic communities: Proceedings of symposium* (pp. 22–31). Melbourne, Australia: St. Vincent's Hospital and Department of Psychiatry, University of Melbourne.

Moore, L. J. (2000). Psychiatric contributions to understanding racism. *Transcultural Psychiatry, 37*(2), 147–182.

Paoletti, N. (1988). Mental health of the Italian community. In E. Chiu & I. H. Minas (Eds.), *Mental health of ethnic communities: Proceedings of symposium* (pp. 41–51). Melbourne, Australia: St. Vincent's Hospital and Department of Psychiatry, University of Melbourne.

Papastergiadis, N. (2000). *The turbulence of migration.* Cambridge, England: Polity Press.

Pettman, J. (1992). *Living in the margins: Racism, sexism and feminism in Australia.* St. Leonards, Australia: Allen & Unwin.

Pittaway E., (1991). *Refugee Women Still at Risk in Australia.* Bureau of Immigration Research, Canberra: Australian Government Publishing Service.

Ridley, C. R. (1989). Racism in counseling as an adversive behavioral process. In P. B.

Pedersen, J. G. Draguns, W. J. Lonner, & J. E. Trimble (Eds.), *Counseling across cultures* (pp. 55–78). Honolulu: University of Hawaii Press.

Sellami-Meslem, C. (1990). *Statement to the expert group meeting on refugee and displaced women and their children.* United Nations meeting notes, Vienna.

Stoller, A., & Krupinski, J. (1973). *Immigration to Australia: Mental health aspects.* In C. Zwingmann & M. Pfister-Ammende (Eds.), *Uprooting and after.* New York: Springer-Verlag.

Sue, D. W., Arrendondon, P., & McDavis, J. (1995). Multicultural counseling competencies and standards: A call to the profession. In J. G. Ponterotto, J. M. Casas, L. A. Suzuki, & C. M. Alexander (Eds.), *Handbook of multicultural counseling.* Thousand Oaks, CA: Sage.

Tan, E. S., Krupinski, J., & Chiu, E. (1985). Stresses experienced prior to arrival in Australia. In J. Krupinski & G. D. Burrows (Eds.), *In the price of freedom.* Sydney, Australia: Pergamon Press.

Vasta, E., & Castles, S. (1996). *The teeth are smiling: The persistence of racism in multicultural Australia.* St. Leonards, Australia: Allen & Unwin.

Westermeyer, J., Williams, C. L., & Nguyen, A. N. (1991). *Mental health services for refugees.* Washington, DC: Department of Health and Human Services.

Wooden, M., Holton, R., & Sloan, J. (1994). *Australian immigration: A survey of the issues.* Canberra: Australian Government Publishing Service.

Yuval-Davis, N., & Anthias, F. (1989). *Woman, nation, state.* London: Macmillan.

TRIPLE OPPRESSION

CHAPTER 10

Mexican and Mexican American
Women Living in the United States

JEANNE M. HINKELMAN
UNITED STATES

OVERVIEW

The purpose of this chapter is to describe Mexican culture and issues faced by Mexican women living in the United States. In 1988, the United States had the sixth largest Spanish-speaking population in the world (Texidor del Portillo, 1987), and numbers are growing rapidly. Also called Hispanic, this population was predicted to constitute the largest ethnic minority group in the United States by the year 2000 (Texidor del Portillo, 1987; Padilla, Cervantes, Maldonado, & Garcia, 1998). The United States' Hispanic population will roughly triple in size by midcentury, mainly because of explosive growth in immigration (Armas, 2004; Spencer, 2004). By 2050, Hispanics will increase their ranks by 188% to 102.6 million, or roughly one-quarter of the United States population (Armas, 2004). No single chapter could address the myriad of problems facing Mexican American females (Organista & Muñoz, 1998). Many terms have been used in the literature describing ethnic and racial groups. It is important to understand this terminology in order to be clear about what particular groups are being described or referred to and because usage is inconsistent across resources. Terms that denote ethnicity or race (or both) at times indicate not only the ethnic descent of the person but also where a person was born as well as where they reside.

Following is a brief list of terms in the research literature (see Marger, 1991; Organista & Muñoz, 1998; Segura, 1984; Taylor, 1984; Texidor del Portillo, 1987). *Hispanic* is a generic term that describes immigrants to the

United States and descendants from more than 30 North, Central, and South American as well as African and European countries in which the Spanish language is spoken (Texidor del Portillo, 1987). *Latinos* and *Latinas* are individuals with personal and family roots in Latin America who may belong to any racial group, including those with roots in Europe, Africa, Asia, and the Middle East (Organista & Muñoz, 1998). *Latinas* are therefore women of Spanish ancestry who are likely to have other roots as well. In 1987, Mexican Americans (men and women combined) made up approximately 60% of Hispanics in the United States (Texidor del Portillo, 1987). Specifically, Mexican Americans constituted the majority (62%) of Latinos and Latinas in the United States in 1991 (Marger, 1991). *Chicanas* are women of Mexican descent who are living in the United States (Segura, 1984) and can be either immigrants or Mexican Americans. *Mexican immigrants* are Mexico-born persons who have left Mexico to go to other countries, including the United States. Hispanic immigration, particularly by Mexicans, will likely continue as political unrest and economic conditions worsen in Mexico. *Mexican Americans* are U.S.-born persons of Mexican descent.

This chapter will look at the way women of Mexican descent are perceived in the United States, the way they perceive themselves, and issues that helpers need to know about to help them. In addition, it will look at gender roles of this culture that underlie family structures and need to be recognized in work with this population. Questions related to the use of language, especially the degree to which people are free to express themselves in a foreign language in therapy, are raised. The kinds of interventions that are useful with this population are described, and a case example is presented. This chapter should sensitize the reader to both universal issues related to immigration and acculturation of women, as well as the unique aspects of the particular culture of these women as they attempt to integrate into another society.

THE PROBLEM OF TRIPLE OPPRESSION: EXTERNAL ISSUES OF POWER AND OPPRESSION RELATED TO CULTURE, GENDER, AND CLASS

Triple oppression describes the unique class, culture, and gender subordination of women of color. These factors also interact with the stress created by immigration. For Chicanas to get help, they first need to understand the nature of their situation and learn how to exercise their rights. Many problems that Mexican women face are potentially related to triple oppression resulting in external stressors including poverty, poor nutrition, and exposure to pathogens (Phinney & Rotheram, 1987). Mexican women often face situations such as inadequate food and shelter, unemployment, and stressful interactions within the sociopolitical system. Stressors in the lives of Chicanas also include culture conflict, language barriers, and minority group status. These issues all need to be kept in mind in the helping process.

RACE, DISCRIMINATION, AND STEREOTYPING

Stereotypes for Latinas include "passive, submissive, male-dominated, and all-suffering" (Rivers, 1995). Latinas are thought of as having low self-concepts (Texidor del Portillo, 1987) and have been commonly seen as "unclean, alcoholic, criminal, deceitful, and unintelligent" (Levine & Padilla, 1980). Attempts to overcome such stereotypes can lead to stress because Latinas must deal not only with the images applied to them by larger society but also images held by their own people.

SOCIOECONOMIC STATUS AND CLASS ISSUES

Segura (1993) attempts to explain the lack of labor opportunities for Mexican women living in the United States in that they have fewer economic resources and employment opportunities than Mexican men do in Mexico. This trend continues after Mexican women come to the United States because they may arrive lacking money or marketable skills. Thirty percent of Mexican Americans (versus 10% of non-Latino whites) live below the poverty level (Healey, 1995). This is important considering the stable inverse relation between socioeconomic status (SES) and psychopathology (Kessler et al., 1994). Few Chicanas who have financial problems as a primary source of psychosocial stress indicate that returning to Mexico would be a viable solution (Padilla et al., 1998).

Hispanics have been at the lowest rung of the economic ladder (Texidor del Portillo, 1987). Employment attained immediately after migration often is a step down from jobs left in the country of origin (Rogler et al., 1983). Hispanics have been mostly unaffected by affirmative action, and economic movement is slow because of discrimination, which has kept many second-generation Latinas from achieving independence (Texidor del Portillo, 1987). The interaction of race and gender has resulted in consistently lower income and status of Chicanas relative to other groups (Segura, 1984). Chicanas are frequently underemployed or unemployed and are overrepresented among the poor. There persists an income differential unfavorable to women despite their progress in climbing white-collar professional ladders.

Stress may be experienced directly as the result of frustration about racism and discrimination in employment. Because Latinas are likely to have earnings that fall below the poverty level, trying to raise and maintain a family can be a challenge (Rivers, 1995). Consequences of poverty may also include lowered social status, inadequate or no health care, substandard housing, inadequate nutrition, and reduced quality of life (Kerner, Dusenbury, & Mandelblatt, 1993).

Forty-five percent of Mexican Americans (versus 83% of non-Latino whites) complete high school (Healey, 1995). Hispanics have had the highest dropout, illiteracy, and school enrollment below grade-level rates. Hispanic teachers are generally underrepresented, which contributes to school dropout (Texidor del Portillo, 1987). Those who remain in school are less likely to earn top grades, and almost two-thirds were enrolled in vocational education programs that make college improbable if not impossible (Texidor del Portillo, 1987).

Those in higher education are often enrolled in two-year community colleges, with relatively few transferring to four-year colleges. Hispanics experience poor educational achievement, including low numbers enrolled in graduate schools, though recent efforts have significantly increased minority student recruitment. Inner turmoil may be common for high-achieving Chicanas who complete advanced degrees because their success contradicts ethnic, gender, and class traditions (Gandara, 1982). Chicano men tend to credit themselves with their achievements, whereas Chicanas tend to connect success with family support, especially encouragement by the mother to do well in school (Vasquez, 1982). When there is a consensus between family and school regarding career possibilities for individual Chicanas, educational achievement can be enhanced (Segura, 1984).

GENDER ISSUES

Traditional gender roles are the norm for Chicanas, who have historically been ascribed an inferior status to men (Rivers, 1995). With the arrival of the Spanish in Mexico, women were viewed as property, and each came to belong to the man who married or raped her. The Church sanctioned this, which helped maintain sexual abuse and dominance of women by men. The trend began with Spaniard men marrying or raping Mexican women when the Spanish arrived in Mexico. The trend continued in the United States, where Chicana women have been dominated by men, partly as a result of the Church sanctioning the earlier practice.

Some of the cultural issues and beliefs that Mexican women contend with may include *machismo* ("Submissive women are best; men are more intelligent than women."), affiliative obedience ("One should never question the word of a mother."), value of virginity ("To be a virgin is of much importance for a single woman."), abnegation ("Women suffer more during their life than men."), fear of authority ("Many children fear their parents."), family status quo ("A good wife should always be faithful and loyal to her husband."), respect over love ("It is more important to respect than to love a parent."), family honor ("A woman who dishonors her family should be punished severely."), and cultural rigidity ("Young women should not go out alone at night with men.") (adapted from Diaz-Guerrero, 1987).

Marianisma is the value of the idealized woman, having spiritual superiority. This notion teaches that women are semidivine and morally superior to men, and it is directly connected to the veneration of the Virgin Mary in Mexican Catholicism (Arredondo, 1991). *Marianisma* creates a double bind for Mexican women who are expected to accept *marianisma*, to identify with the emotional suffering of the "pure, passive bystander"—that is, the Virgin Mary, the ultimate role model (Nieto-Gomez, 1976). From the concept of *marianisma* grew the notion that the woman was to blame for her husband's problems, and *marianisma* convinced women to endure injustices committed against them. This concept encouraged the submission and passivity of women while facilitating *machismo* in men. The patriarchal structure of Mexican culture has instilled anxiety in women (Levine & Padilla, 1980) because Chicanas are often torn between that structure and more liberal Anglo norms (Rivers, 1995). Women are taught to be selfless and self-sacrificial. Although women are seen as perpetuators of the culture, they are trapped in the interface of family structure that reinforces dependence and subordination (Julia, 1995).

ISSUES RELATED TO IMMIGRATION

Padilla et al. (1998) found that major stressors reported by immigrants include not being able to communicate in English, difficulties finding employment (e.g., not knowing anyone who could help them find a job), and being in the United States illegally. These stressors are associated with others such as lacking money to pay bills, difficulty in finding adequate housing, having to take whatever job is available at whatever wage the employer offers, adaptation problems, discrimination, and lack of child care.

Latino families have to adapt to different food, transportation, lifestyles, English, a new educational system, differences in morality, and high divorce rates. Some Latinos do not want their wives to work outside of the home lest they become influenced by their surroundings. Other concerns and worries include ensuring that children receive a good education; that children not develop drug, alcohol, or tobacco addictions; hope that children will develop healthy friendships with "good" children; a need to improve living conditions; and general health and well-being (Padilla et al., 1998).

The problem of language is a major stressor in association with other problems in adapting and carving out a market niche in the United States (Padilla et al., 1998). Most Hispanic immigrants have little formal education and are intimidated by formal methods for learning English such as adult education. Few Chicanas indicate that studying English independently is their chosen solution. The most common method is listening to others speak English (30%), followed by depending on others to interpret, speaking with only those who are fluent in Spanish, and looking for work in places where there are other Spanish speakers (Padilla et al., 1998). Because they have few financial resources to sustain themselves, they have no alternative but to find employment quickly, leaving no time to acquire survival English skills. Higher levels of English proficiency are associated with greater self-esteem scores (Padilla et al., 1998). Language proficiency obviously is key in achieving success in the United States.

In dealing with stressors related to leaving their countries, the most difficult thing for Latinas is leaving behind family members and friends, their neighborhood, and the customs of their country. Coping with the absence of loved ones is dealt with by writing letters, telephoning, helping economically by sending money, visiting family by returning home for a period of time, and bringing (or intending to bring) their children to live with them. For some, there is nothing to do but resign themselves to the fact that they are separated from their families (Padilla et al., 1998). This may be one cause of depression in this group. However, a woman may not necessarily present this issue in therapy although it may be manifested via somatic complaints.

Rivers (1995) argues that values conflicts may result from trying to accommodate two different cultures, particularly as U.S. and Mexican values are often incongruent. Culture conflict can cause a great deal of stress as Chicanas are expected to acculturate and accommodate to U.S. society, which in turn may cause depressed economic conditions (Canino, 1982), sex-role conflict, an identity crisis, or feelings of isolation, alienation, language, loss, loneliness, or depression, which are frequently presented in therapy (Espin, 1987). These issues are reflective of the stresses created by the migratory process rather than as issues of individual psychopathology and interact with roles imposed by the culture in which they live. Latinas are disproportionately affected by prevailing conditions of the society at large and personal conditions brought about by poor education, lack of quality health care, and poor self-concept (Texidor del Portillo, 1987). Mexican women also face the conflict of the U.S. female standard of beauty, which may be unattainable, producing stress and leading to lowered self-concept. Hispanic women may use various strategies to minimize role strain such as establishing successful compromises in their roles and values. Others reject traditional Hispanic culture outright or never fully resolve the conflict, and they may exhibit psychological or psychosomatic symptoms as a result (Levine & Padilla, 1980).

Fatalism has been linked to a high prevalence of depression in Mexicans in general. The Catholic Church continues to play an important role in the family life of Chicanas, and some life events may be attributed to luck, supernatural forces, or acts of God. These attributions might be manifested in terms of clinical issues such as what may appear to be passivity, external locus of control, and irrational beliefs. When in need of assistance, it is likely that a Chicana would first turn to family or a Church member rather than a psychological clinician because the former take a more prominent role in many Chicanas' lives.

Problems related to acculturation to a society that is prejudiced, hostile, and rejecting put Chicanas at risk for personality disintegration and subsequent need for mental health services (Olmedo & Parron, 1981). Most research has found a strong relationship between mental disorders and degree of acculturation of ethnic minorities (Escobar, 1993). Women experience high levels of depression and anxiety as a result of acculturation stress (Salgado de Snyder, 1987). Spousal or intergenerational conflicts may result from faster acculturation of some family members. Younger members generally acculturate more rapidly than older individuals (Chamorro, 1997).

Padilla et al. (1998) found that, despite all barriers, immigrants express satisfaction with their decision to immigrate, and few express an interest in returning to their native countries mainly because they believe ultimately that their life circumstances will improve. Immigrant Hispanics express hope for the education of their children, though they worry about an abundance of drugs and a lack of values and respect for the family. In response, they try to instill a sense of respect in their children and instruct them about the harmful consequences of drug use. Illegal immigrants, including Chicanas, may experience more stressors than legal immigrants and may have a different experience than legal immigrants, including additional fear and anxiety related to the possibility of being caught and deported and problems with obtaining work at all or work with reasonable pay.

TREATMENT ISSUES

Economic status and physical health affect mental health. The mentally healthy enjoy benefits of their capabilities and avoid preventable harm to self and others. Conditions of well-being include economic stability, adequacy of income, good health, and a positive self-concept. People living in poverty do not enjoy the material and psychological aspects of well-being. Hispanics, including Chicanas, are therefore at high risk and are likely to experience poor mental health (Texidor del Portillo, 1987). Symptoms of external stresses are often similar to those displayed in personal conflicts. Other issues are intrapsychic and may include common psychiatric conditions such as psychological conflict, depression, anxiety, problems of self-concept and identity, low self-esteem, eating disorders, and psychosomatic symptoms. Hispanic women in the United States are at high risk of developing mental illness (Becerra, Karno, & Escobar, 1982), being frequently diagnosed with depression and psychosomatic disorders, with depression being the most common condition (Newton, Olmedo, & Padilla, 1982). Some mental health problems that may be associated with stressors include low self-esteem, depression, anxiety, alcohol and substance abuse, anger and hostility, psychosomatic symptoms, and psychosis (LaFromboise, Heyle, & Ozer, 1990). Other problems may include domestic violence and child abuse. Organista and Muñoz (1998) have reported that Latinos and Latinas have significantly higher prevalence of diagnosable affective disorders and active comorbidity, meaning three or more concurrent mental disorders.

Helpers may see unhealthy attitudes toward eating among Chicanas (Chamorro, 1997). This is of particular concern among young women who are aspiring to meet the standards of beauty in United States because their own cultural standards and their own eating habits do not match those of the dominant culture. Low self-esteem, isolation, and marginalization may result from issues related to body image and social stereotyping.

Chicanas, particularly those of lower SES, tend to have limited access to medical and mental health care, including information about clinical issues and their treatment. Treatment approaches that may be appropriate with this population vary depending upon the nature of the problem (e.g., biological versus intrapsychic versus external). Biological concerns originate from aspects of bodily structures or functions. Intrapsychic issues are those that emanate from the individual; external challenges are those faced by the individual but which originate from social, political, and economic forces or structures. For example, a woman might feel depressed because of hormonal changes occurring in her body (e.g., biologically based postpartum depression), or she may feel depressed because she tends to catastrophize in her way of thinking, or she may become depressed because of what she perceives to be a sexually discriminating workplace environment. It is difficult to discriminate between internal and external factors that may be affecting an individual and that may also interact with each other.

COPING AND LANGUAGE

Language differences can hinder effectiveness of therapy with Latinas (Russell, 1988). Bilingual clients sometimes "maintain independence between two language systems which can serve to compartmentalize feelings" (Espin, 1987, p. 497). Some bilinguals, when making the translation to English, may exhibit flat affect or appear withdrawn (Espin, 1987; Russell, 1988). The therapist may also have difficulty understanding the English translation from another language (Yamamoto & Acosta, 1982), and it may take the client some time to make the translation in a way that the therapist understands clearly. Latinas may also encode experiences with affective meaning in Spanish so that accurate understanding when translated to English can be problematic (Espin, 1987; Russell, 1988). In all helping settings, there are realistic time constraints based on how much time a helper can give. Language barriers can accentuate these constraints and pacing therefore needs to be adjusted.

Research on linguistic issues in clinical practice indicates that early language learning is related to the expression of feelings (Spielberger & Diaz-Guerrero, 1976; Sundberg & Sue, 1989). Language differences may be the most important stumbling block to effective multicultural counseling and assessment. For example, language barriers may lead to misdiagnosis and inappropriate treatment (Romero, 1985) and may impede the counseling process when clients cannot express the complexity of their thoughts and feelings or resist discussing affectively charged issues. Counselors, too, may become frustrated by their lack of bilingual ability (Bolton-Brownlee, 1987). It is not uncommon for acculturation to be situation-specific in the sense that one may act Anglo and speak English at work but maintain a traditional Hispanic lifestyle and speak Spanish at home (Malagady, Rogler, & Constantino, 1987). However, language and lifestyle choices vary from individual to individual.

Helpers should remember that experiences are stored in the language of the environment in which the experience occurred. The helper needs to facilitate bicultural development and assist the client in learning behaviors that are adaptive in both the minority and majority cultures. Therapists should be sensitive to language differences and not assume understanding. Because some experiences will be interpreted differently in Spanish than in English, the helper needs to go slowly and ask questions that allow misunderstanding to emerge. When determining the language to use in clinical practice, one needs to decide on which language to use when both client and therapist speak more than one.

Martinez (2000) has offered several suggestions for the helper in these situations. The language that the client speaks best or feels more comfortable with is one important criterion. The helper should ask the client about preference or comfort level. In general, the native language is more likely preferred if the client is elderly or a recent immigrant. Many Hispanics are equally fluent in English and Spanish but usually have a preference. Some clients insist on using English even if it is not the dominant language, perhaps to deny or avoid painful experiences or to control the session. This point highlights how even the question of which language to use in the helping process is relevant and should be considered thoughtfully.

USEFUL METHODS FOR HELPING CHICANAS

Chicana clients often do not respond to traditional, psychodynamic, insight-oriented psychotherapies (Torres-Matrullo, 1982). It is important to remember that Hispanics often expect help with their immediate symptoms, guidance and counseling, and a concrete problem-centered focus. The interpersonal aspects of the process are especially relevant because of the high regard this population has for relationships. To be accepted, the helper has to show responsiveness, cultural sensitivity, and reliability (Miranda, 1976).

These women seek help for problems that reflect a combination of both intra- and extrapsychic issues. An important part of counseling Mexican women is considering their psychosocial, economic, and political needs (Ponterotto, 1987). It is important to understand how cultural conflict, poverty, educational and occupational levels, sex bias, racial discrimination, and stereotyping contribute to the stress and psychological functioning of Latinas. Assisting Latinas with increasing their education, training, and employment status can improve their standard of living and quality of life and enhance their rapport (Rivers, 1995). Helpers need to become aware of community programs, opportunities, and advocate for their clients using a multiservice approach with appropriate social service and government agencies as well as private-sector businesses. In addition to this overarching need for meeting concrete problem-solving needs, the helper can utilize other methods. The most useful have been found to be cognitive–behavioral therapy, family therapy, narrative therapy, prevention-oriented community education, and feminist therapy.

Cognitive–Behavioral Therapy

Cognitive–behavioral therapy (CBT) is advocated for tradition-oriented Latinos of low SES (Organista & Muñoz, 1998). Short-term, directive, problem-solving therapies are consistent with Latino life circumstances that frequently demand immediate attention and interfere with long-term treatment. A didactic style helps quickly orient Latino clients to treatment, an educational approach demystifies therapy, and role preparation prevents dropout and enhances treatment (Orlinsky & Howard, 1986). Latino clients may think of therapy as a classroom if there is homework, didactic instruction, and experience that alleviates stigma. Stigma is strong where scarce mental health services are reserved for psychotic patients in mental hospitals. The strengths of CBT are its emphasis on individual differences, focus on empowerment (also consistent with feminist therapy), attention to conscious processes and specific behaviors, and assessment of the client's progress from her or his perspective throughout the process of intervention.

Unfortunately, cognitive–behavioral treatments tend to include core values that emphasize self-control, lack of attention to history, and rational thinking that may devalue other cognitive styles, worldviews, and ways of interacting (Hays, 1995). Organista, Muñoz, and González (1994) found significant reductions in depression in ethnic minority clients using CBT (e.g., CBT was later moderately successful in treating a severe case of major depression and panic disorder; Organista, 1995) but not to the same extent as reported in prototypical outcome studies of non-Hispanic white, middle-class individuals. Helpers have to adapt behavioral interventions to make them culturally sensitive. For example, one aspect of behavioral work includes increasing reinforcements in one's life. Because of the economic hardships that many Latinos endure, lists of local pleasant activities that cost little or no money should be discussed as "taking time out for oneself"—a concept that is less emphasized in Latino culture, especially for women (Organista & Muñoz, 1998). Latinos are usually willing to increase pleasurable activities for the purpose of *distraerse*, or distracting themselves from worry and problems. Framing these activities as ways of making a person a better family member may be culturally acceptable.

Family Therapy

Family therapy matches the values of this culture and is often recommended in working with Chicanas. It is important to understand extended family issues, to involve the family in treatment where appropriate, and to formulate interventions with the family's support and within their cultural framework (Rivers, 1995). Working with the family allows issues of culture, sex-role conflict, and boundaries to be addressed. Parents frequently blame family problems on their children's over-Americanization, and children, in turn, blame their parents for being too old-fashioned (Szapocznik, Santisteban, Kurtines, Perez-Vidal, & Hervis, 1984). Family members can be taught to locate their problems in the acculturation process rather than see them as caused by other family members, which thus challenges them to assist each other in adapting to U.S. society. *Cuento* (folklore) therapy may be appropriate for the children of Mexican women. It should also be remembered that helping women means thinking about the effects of that help on her family. Women play an important role as mothers and wives, and in these often traditional families, change is perceived as threatening to the traditional family structure. The case example that follows highlights some of the issues that emerge that have to do with sex roles and gender.

Narrative Therapy

Narrative therapy emphasizes understanding the personal stories and experiences of Chicanas and can provide vital information in the evaluation, diagnosis, and treatment of all individuals, especially for those clients who are different from us.

In her book *Women Crossing Boundaries,* Espin (1999) tells some of the stories and narrative themes that arose in her interviews with women who migrated to the United States. She noted how important language is in determining how a person can tell her story. For example, women from traditional cultures use the new language to discuss issues related to their advancing status, such as freedom of sexuality. She also demonstrates how immigrant women successfully renegotiated their traditional gender roles within the context of loyalty to family, with each story showing how women can become more egalitarian by developing individual strategies for change. Narrative therapy opens up the possibility for women who are in the process of negotiating new roles to tell their personal stories of change. This process allows helpers to support and strengthen such stories, helping each woman find her own unique solution to universal problems. The process also allows better understanding of how change occurs within the contexts of conflicting cultural demands.

Prevention-Oriented Community Education

Prevention-oriented community education can be developed to address the employment, health, and mental health needs of Latinas and other Hispanic groups. In addition, national health campaigns are needed for parents and children on preventative physical and mental health care issues, including substance abuse (Texidor del Portillo, 1987). Appropriate community education and screening procedures for depression are also needed for treating Latinas (Van Hook, 1999).

Feminist Therapy

Feminist therapy goals with Latinas should include empowering them to handle the stress of everyday life (Zavala-Martinez, 1987). Therapy should focus on Latinas' strengths and assisting in examining options and choices (Texidor del Portillo, 1987). Empowerment may lead to positive identity and increased self-esteem. Empowerment and social support may be enhanced, as has been suggested for African American women (Mays, 1986), through participation in organized and self-help groups around issues of racism, social or civic activity, civil rights, and sexism. Traditional Latino values and role prescriptions, as well as characteristic social circumstances, may precipitate or exacerbate mental health problems (Organista & Muñoz, 1998). Although *marianisma* prescribes attention to family well-being and high respect for husbands, negative aspects may manifest themselves in excessive self-sacrifice, lack of individuation (Young, 1994), low assertiveness with husbands, and deference to authority (Organista & Muñoz, 1998).

One way to balance women's empowerment versus their role in the family is to focus on spirituality. In Mexico, Catholicism has had a major influence on the role of women and sex-role attitudes that likely affect non-Catholics as well. The Church is typically seen as a major source of support, and spirituality

CASE 10.1

My current work takes place within a university counseling center. María was a 21-year-old Mexican and European American single female graduate student from the Southwest who was born in Mexico to a Mexican mother and a European American father. She later moved to the United States. She was having problems with getting to sleep because, while in bed, she was fearful and worried about what she had to do the next day, and she was eating more than usual. María spoke English in session but with a Spanish accent. Her mother's family spoke only Spanish, but her parents had spoken English at home. She had performed successfully as a staff trainer at a Mexican restaurant in her hometown and was having difficulty adjusting to her new surroundings since moving to the mid-South to attend professional school.

María's school program was highly competitive, and she was in classes with a lot of upper-class colleagues. She was one of the youngest students in her class and said she was more mature than her age but that older classmates treated her as if she were young. María was disappointed to find that the Hispanic professional student organization affiliated with her program was inactive and that her classmates seemed "cliquish." María and her boyfriend of four years (who had a high school education and worked full-time as a waiter at a restaurant in the Southwestern town where her mother lives) were "on a break" and had been having problems because of the long-distance nature of their relationship. María's boyfriend was Mexican and "a bit controlling, dependent, and jealous" as evidenced by his repeated phone calls asking her what she was doing, with whom, and what time she would return home if she was to go out.

María's parents divorced when she was 5 years old, and both parents had remarried. María had two half-sisters and one half-brother and grew up with her mother's large family, including many cousins, who were originally from Mexico. María had little contact with her father, who spent half of the year in Asia and half in the United States because of his work. He had one child, a son, with his European American second wife. María stated that her mother's sister overate and was overweight, depressed, and on medication but denied that there was any problem. This same aunt was supporting her own child as a single mother as well as her own brother and his three children.

María was having "bad days" on Tuesdays, Thursdays, and Saturdays when she usually cried, possibly because of a heavy course load and a lack of sleep on those days. María came to counseling because she did not want to tell her mother what was happening and cause her to worry about her. She had been exercising regularly with aerobic videos and also walked or ran with her dog, Rex. María appeared motivated to get help, and her therapist asked her to complete a sleep log, depression and anxiety inventories, and a stress management questionnaire for the next session's discussion. The therapist recommended interpersonal treatment including discussion of relationship and family issues (in-person consultation with the family was not possible because they lived out of state), adjustment and acculturation to school, cognitive–behavioral therapy for her school fears, and coping strategies including stress management.

During the second session, María reported that she was having difficulty relating to classmates who came from a different background than hers. María was from a working-class family, and many of her peers were of upper middle class. She was the first person in her family to attend college, much less professional school. María noted cultural differences such as classmates' assertive to near-aggressive nature and said she would like to become more assertive so that she could perform more successfully in her classes and profession. She and her therapist discussed the pros and cons of developing assertiveness as it related to both her school and home cultures. María said that her boyfriend had unexpectedly come to visit over the weekend and that "it was nice, but a bit of a distraction" and that she felt worse after he left.

María returned the completed stress management, anxiety, and depression inventories, which were discussed along with stress management strategies (e.g., exercising, socializing, and pleasurable activities). The therapist normalized María's difficulty with adjusting to a new environment. María reported that she ate in order to comfort herself. María and the therapist agreed to goals of completing a food log and increasing exercise and additional stress management strategies, and they considered possible relaxation training and attempting to increase María's social support.

María reported that she had a good weekend with a cousin who had visited, but she felt worse after her cousin left (much like she had when her boyfriend left). She felt good about having been able to complete some school assignments while her cousin was visiting. María was excited that she had received an "A" on her first paper, and she wanted to continue doing well in school. However, she said she was still having difficulty getting to sleep. María also said that she was concerned about her boyfriend visiting because he "tended to create more work than fun." The therapist discussed with María how she could continue having more successes, as well as boundary-setting issues regarding her boyfriend. The therapist also requested that María bring in a blank audiotape for relaxation training and planned to continue discussion of relationship issues.

María returned with her completed sleep log and discussed it. María reported increased social support and exercise, and her choice to reduce contact with her boyfriend. Developmental changes María was experiencing were discussed, as well as adaptation to professional school. A relaxation exercise was recorded on an audiotape for home practice. The therapist gave María an article on local activities and events, including some in the Hispanic community, to help enhance her involvement in pleasant activities and social support. María was to continue regular exercise, use the relaxation tape, and complete a relaxation practice log.

María had a good weekend visiting friends and family at home, and she changed her phone number so that her boyfriend would not call her because she had broken off her relationship with him. María had been spending more time with friends and watching TV while at her apartment at school. Coping strategies and plans for upcoming holidays were discussed. María said that next week would be the last session she could have because she needed time to study for final exams.

María reported that she cut all contacts with her ex-boyfriend after having an argument with him about his possessive behavior, which he did not see as problematic. María requested another relaxation exercise, to learn cognitive strategies to cope with worries,

and to complete possible personality assessment during the coming semester. María said she would call at the beginning of the New Year to schedule an appointment.

Culture and Gender Issues in the Case

Although Maria identified herself as Mexican, her culture would probably be identified by others in the United States as Mexican American because she had lived in Mexico only until early childhood and had parents of both backgrounds. María experienced a conflict between differing cultural norms. She had to be assertive in her school culture, which clashed with the behavior expected in her culture at home. María realized that she would have to develop assertiveness skills to be able to compete for jobs. It is possible that her depression was related to unexpressed anger about this choice. She was caught in a bind between her own role as an achiever and her role as the girlfriend of a traditional man and the traditional gender role for women. This kind of cultural conflict is especially common for women who migrate from traditional cultures to those that promote the advancement of women. It means that in certain situations one may be forced to choose between cultures because it may be impossible to adapt to or respond in a way that is consistent with both simultaneously.

María's Mexican boyfriend challenged her desire to become more acculturated because he wanted her to conform to traditional Mexican gender roles by being passive. He may have held her back from her relationship and her career goals. It appeared that Maria's educational and occupational goals may have been less important to him than her relationship with him and his caring for her. She experienced inner turmoil because of the conflicting messages she was receiving between achievement from her family, which supported her career goal, and the oppression of her boyfriend, who may have been afraid of the influence of U.S. majority culture on María. However, she was decidedly neither submissive nor wanting to obey him. It was evident that there were many differences in the educational and professional achievements that both María and her boyfriend sought. It appears that he was not able to support her in her goals and was at times an impediment to her success. As a result, she made the decision to end the relationship rather than

(continued)

stay in the relationship and possibly drop out of school and return to her hometown to be with him. She clearly did not live up to the Latina stereotype, rejected the idea of *marianismo*, and was not selfless or passive at school. She did, however, care a great deal about what her family would say (an example of familialism, or the level of importance of family in decision making) and may have wanted to avoid conflict with family and friends at home.

How does one make the choice between sticking with your own culture or changing to be more like the dominant culture? The helper does not make these choices for the client. Rather, by helping the client reduce the stress engendered by the conflict and alleviating the emotional suffering, the client becomes able to make her own choices. Being bilingual, the therapist was able to understand words that María had used in Spanish that she was unable to come up with in English when she was discussing her childhood. This helped in building a good relationship that facilitated Maria in making her own choices while being supported and understood.

---

tends to play an important role in the lives of ethnic minority women (Boyd-Franklin, 1991). Religion is a cognitive-related domain in which therapists need to work with traditional or religious Latino clients (Organista & Muñoz, 1998). Religion can be supported through reinforcing churchgoing and prayer, as well as exploring and challenging forms of prayer that seem to lessen the probability of active problem solving. For example, "Ayudate, que Dios te ayudará" is the Spanish equivalent of "God helps those who help themselves." This phrase emphasizes empowerment and can be used to bridge the gap between autonomy and community. Spirituality offers values that are compatible both with self-enhancement and family and community loyalty.

All helping interventions must be given within the culturally acceptable attitudes that would make them useful for this culture. Attitudes that can underline all helping modes include:

1. engaging Latino patients in treatment;
2. formally addressing clients with *respeto* (respect);
3. adapting a *para servirle* ("to serve you") attitude;
4. taking time to engage in self-disclosure (*personalismo*); and
5. engaging in *plática* (small talk) by which the therapist and client share background information about where they are from, their families, work they have done, and so on (e.g., a non-Latino therapist could share the experience of being different or moving from one city to another).

PERSONAL REFLECTIONS

For many years I have had an interest in bilingual and Hispanic issues, partly as a result of having had a Chilean exchange student live with my family while I was in high school during the same year in which my sister was on exchange in Würzberg, Germany. It was not until after Mónica left us to return to her homeland that I began my study of Spanish and Hispanic culture. I studied three years of Spanish in high school and minored in Spanish to complement my bachelor of arts degree in psychology. As a graduate student, I began traveling internationally, and since that time I have traveled frequently to Spanish-speaking countries including Spain, Mexico, Costa Rica, Venezuela, Chile, Guatemala, and Peru. After completing my Ph.D., I moved to Tulsa, Oklahoma, from Kansas City, Missouri, to work in my current position as staff psychologist in counseling and psychological services at the University of Tulsa, where I also hold a faculty appointment in the Department of Psychology.

I became aware early on that there was a large Hispanic student population at the university and was informed by a colleague that there are more than 30,000 Hispanics living in Tulsa, the majority of whom are of Mexican descent and many of them recent immigrants. After conducting some of my own research, I discovered that there were extremely limited bilingual resources available in Tulsa, and I realized that my contribution to the Hispanic community could be immense. As a way of preparing for my position working with Hispanic students at the university and also for pro bono work in the Hispanic community, I became a member of the Hispanic American Foundation of Tulsa and a (bilingual) volunteer for the Tulsa Chapter of the American Red Cross in Disaster Mental Health Services where I co-taught the first Introduction to Disaster Services course offered in Spanish. I also attended seminars on Latino and Latina issues, and I began investigating issues that affect Mexican and Mexican American women. As a result of my work with Mexican women, I have become more aware of own biases and prejudices related to this and other groups. I have also become more sensitive to multiple socioeconomic, political, and historical factors that influence oppression, and I have an increased awareness and understanding of how these factors might impact a person's life.

Over the years, I have learned more about my own ethnic background as a German American through travel to Germany, visiting with relatives who still live there, and learning more about German history and our family's genealogy. Obviously, when working with Mexican women, there are many cross-cultural issues that I need to take into account. For example, although I was raised Roman Catholic, the form of Catholicism that I practiced as a German American is very different in many ways from Catholicism as it is experienced and practiced in Mexico. Linguistic issues are also critically important in cross-cultural work. Although I am fluent in Spanish, I am not as fluent as a native speaker. However, I pursue professional development opportunities to enhance my language capabilities, including auditing Spanish courses at the university where I work, maintaining collegial and friendship relationships with members of the Hispanic community, traveling regularly to Spanish-speaking countries, attending and presenting at international conferences where presentations are made in Spanish, and consulting as needed with bilingual Spanish-speaking mental health professionals in Tulsa. I am also currently the National Representative (U.S.) to the Society for Interamerican Psychology, Inc., a professional organization that was formed to connect North American psychologists with those from Latin America, a role that requires knowledge of Spanish and Latin American cultures.

CONCLUSION

Mental health issues of Latinas are tied to the interaction of social issues including acculturation, stereotyping, poverty, sexism, and discrimination (educational, economic, and racial). These are experienced differently from individual to individual. Some Mexican women continue to hold low-wage jobs while attempting to raise families. Stress results from poverty, fighting stereotypes, role strain, and cultural conflict. However, most Mexican women manage to cope. Further understanding of the issues faced by Mexican women and resources available to them will help serve this population more effectively.

KEY CONCEPTS

- triple oppression
- acculturation level
- cuento therapy
- cultural identification
- familialism
- language and coping
- *marianisma*
- *para servirle*
- *personalismo*
- *plática*
- *respeto*

QUESTIONS FOR REFLECTION

1. What are the first things you think of when you hear the phrase "Mexican woman"?
2. How would you describe a Mexican woman to someone else?
3. What are some of the assumptions you make about Mexican women?
4. Do you know any Mexican women? If so, what have you learned from them about their experience as Mexican women?
5. Should clients receive help in their native language or in the language of their new home?
6. What is the relationship between a person's experiences and language and culture?

EXERCISE

Write three sentences about your life in your native language. Make those three sentences express something valuable to you (e.g., "I love my family very much" or "My work is extremely important to me"). After each sentence, write down how it feels to acknowledge these aspects of your life. Now find someone who speaks another language and have him or her teach you how to say those three sentences in another language. Try speaking those three sentences in this new and unfamiliar language. Now, in your own language, write about how it feels to you to express important aspects of your life in an unfamiliar language. Talk to a partner about what you have learned from this experience. How might this be relevant to helping people who are talking to you in an unfamiliar and new language? How would you want someone to help you if you had to speak an unfamiliar language with him or her?

References

Armas, G. C. (2004). U.S. to be nearly half minority by 2050. [Associated Press]. Available at www.herald-sun.com/firstnews/37-459790.html.

Arredondo, P. (1991). Counseling Latinas. In C. C. Lee, B. L. Richardson, & L. Bernard (Eds.), *Multicultural issues in counseling: New approaches to diversity* (pp. 143–156). Alexandria, VA: American Association for Counseling and Development.

Becerra, R. M., Karno, M., & Escobar, J. I. (Eds.). (1982). *Mental health and Hispanic Americans.* New York: Grune & Stratton.

Bolton-Brownlee, A. (1987). Issues in multicultural counseling. *Highlights: An ERIC/CAPS Digest.* ERIC accession number: ED279995.

Boyd-Franklin, N. K. (1991). Recurrent themes in the treatment of African-American women in group psychotherapy. *Women and Therapy, 11,* 25–40.

Canino, G. (1982). The Hispanic woman: Sociocultural influences on diagnoses and treatment. In R. M. Becerra, M. Karno, & J. I. Escobar (Eds.), *Mental health and Hispanic Americans: Clinical Perspectives* (pp. 117–138). New York: Grune & Stratton.

Chamorro, R. (1997, November). Acculturation and disordered eating patterns among Mexican-American women. *Dissertation Abstracts International: Section B: The Sciences & Engineering, 58*(5-B), 2666.

Diaz-Guerrero, R. (1987, January–June). El problema de la definicion operante de la identidad nacional mexicana. 2a parte. The issue of the operational definition of Mexican national identity: II. *Revista Mexicana de Psicologia, 4*(1), 25–28.

Escobar, J. I. (1993). Psychiatric epidemiology. In A. C. Gaw (Ed.), *Culture, ethnicity, and mental illness* (pp. 43–73). Washington, DC: American Psychiatric Press.

Espin, O. M. (1987). Psychological impact of migration on Latinas: Implications for psychotherapeutic practice. *Psychology of Women Quarterly Special Issue: Hispanic Women and Mental Health, 11*(4), 489–503.

Espin, O. (1999). *Women crossing boundaries: A psychology of immigration and transformation of sexuality.* New York: Routledge.

Gandara, P. (1982). Passing through the eye of the needle: High achieving Chicanas. *Hispanic Journal of Behavioral Sciences, 4*(2), 167–179.

Hays, P. A. (1995). Multicultural applications of cognitive-behavior therapy. *Professional Psychology: Research and Practice, 26,* 309–315.

Healey, J. F. (1995). Hispanic Americans: Colonization, immigration, and ethnic enclaves. In J. F. Healey (Ed.), *Race, ethnicity, gender, and class: The sociology of group conflict and change* (pp. 341–401). Thousand Oaks, CA: Pine Forge Press.

Julia, M. (1995). Revisiting a repopulated village: A step backwards in the changing status of women. *International Social Work, 38*(3), 229–242.

Kerner, J. F., Dusenbury, L., & Mandelblatt, J. S. (1993). Poverty and cultural diversity: Challenges for health promotion among medically underserved. *Annual Review of Public Health, 14,* 355–377.

Kessler, R. C., McGonagle, K. A., Zhao, S., Nelson, C. B., Hughes, M., Eshleman, S., Wittchen, H., & Kendler, K. S. (1994). Lifetime and 12-month prevalence of DSM-III-R psychiatric disorders in the United States. *Archives of General Psychiatry, 51,* 8–19.

LaFromboise, T. D., Heyle, A. M., & Ozer, E. J. (1990). Changing and diverse roles of women in American Indian cultures. *Sex Roles, 22,* 455–476.

Levine, E. S., & Padilla, A. M. (1980*). Crossing cultures in therapy: Pluralistic counseling for the Hispanic.* Monterey, CA: Brooks-Cole.

Malgady, R. G., Rogler, L. H., & Constantino, G. (1987). Ethnocultural and linguistic bias in mental health evaluation of Hispanics. *American Psychologist, 42*(3), 228–234.

Marger, M. N. (1991). Hispanic Americans. In M. N. Marger (Ed.), *Race and ethnic relations: American and global perspectives* (2nd ed., pp. 279–320). Belmont, CA: Wadsworth.

Martinez, C. (2000). Conducting the cross-cultural clinical interview. In I. Cuellar & F. A. Paniagua (Eds.), *Handbook of multicultural mental health* (pp. 311–323). San Diego: Academic Press.

Mays, V. M. (1986). Black women and stress: Utilization of self-help groups for stress reduction. *Women and Therapy, 4,* 67–79.

Miranda, M. R. (1976). *Psychotherapy with the Spanish-speaking: Issues in research and services delivery* (Monograph No. 3). Los Angeles: University of California, Spanish-Speaking Mental Health Research Center.

Newton, F. C., Olmedo, E. L., & Padilla, A. M. (1982). Hispanic mental health research. Berkeley: University of California Press.

Nieto-Gomez, A. (1976). A heritage of LaHembra. In S. Cox (Ed.), *Female psychology: The emerging self* (pp. 226–235). Chicago: Science Research Associates.

Olmedo, E. L., & Parron, D. L. (1981). Mental health of minority women: Some special issues. *Professional Psychology, 12,* 103–111.

Organista, K. C. (1995). Cognitive-behavioral treatment of depression and panic disorder in a Latina client: Culturally sensitive case formulation. *In Session: Psychotherapy in Practice, 1*(2), 53–64.

Organista, K. C., & Muñoz, R. F. (1998). Cognitive behavioral therapy with Latinos. In P. B. Organista, K. M. Chun, & G. Marin (Eds.), *Ethnic psychology* (pp. 353–366). New York: Routledge.

Organista, K. C., Muñoz, R. F., and González, G. (1994). Cognitive behavioral therapy for depression in low-income and minority medical outpatients: Description of a program and exploratory analyses. *Cognitive Therapy and Research, 18,* 241–259.

Orlinsky, D. E., & Howard, K. I. (1986). Process and outcome in psychotherapy. In S. L. Garfield & A. E. Bergin (Eds.), *Handbook of psychotherapy and behavior change* (3rd ed., pp. 311–381). New York: Wiley & Sons.

Padilla, A. M., Cervantes, R. C., Maldonado, M., & Garcia, R. E. (1998). Coping responses to psychosocial stressors among Mexican and Central American immigrants. In P. B. Organista, K. M. Chun, & G. Marin (Eds.), *Ethnic psychology* (pp. 249–259). New York: Routledge.

Phinney, J. S., & Rotheram, M. J. (Eds.). (1987). *Children's ethnic socialization: Pluralism and development.* Newbury Park, CA: Sage.

Ponterotto, J. G. (1987). Counseling Mexican Americans: A multimodal approach. *Journal of Counseling and Development, 65*(6), 308–312.

Rivers, R. Y. (1995). Clinical issues and intervention with ethnic minority women. In

J. F. Aponte (Ed.), *Psychological interventions and cultural diversity* (pp. 181–198). Needham Heights, MA: Allyn & Bacon.

Rogler, L. H., Cooney, R. S., Constantino, G., Earley, B. F., Grossman, B., Gurak, D. T., Malgady, R., & Rodriguez, O. (1983). *A conceptual framework for mental health research on Hispanic populations* (Monograph No. 10). New York: Fordham University, Hispanic Research Center.

Romero, D. (1985). Cross-cultural counseling: Brief reactions for the practitioner. *The Counseling Psychologist Special Issue: Cross-cultural counseling, 13*(4), 665–671.

Russell, D. M. (1988). Language and psychotherapy: The influence of nonstandard English in clinical practice. In L. Comaz-Diaz and E. E. H. Griffith (Eds.), *Clinical guidelines in cross-cultural mental health* (pp. 33–68). Oxford, England: Wiley & Sons.

Salgado de Snyder, V. N. (1987). Factors associated with acculturative stress and depressive symptomatology among married Mexican immigrant women. *Psychology of Women Quarterly Special Issue: Hispanic women and mental health, 11*(4), 475–488.

Segura, D. (1984). Labor market stratification: The Chicana experience. *Berkeley Journal of Sociology, 29,* 57–91.

Segura, D. (1993). Chicanas and triple oppression in the labor force. In T. Córdova, N. Cantú, G. Cardenas, J. Garcia, & C. M. Sierra (Eds.), *Chicana voices: Intersections of class, race, and gender* (pp. 47–65). Albuquerque: University of New Mexico Press.

Spencer, G. (2004). Cited in G. C. Armas, U.S. to be nearly half minority by 2050. [Associated Press]. Available at www.herald-sun.com/firstnews/37-459790.html.

Spielberger, C. D., & Diaz-Guerrero, R. (Eds.) (1976). *Cross-cultural anxiety.* New York: Wiley & Sons.

Sundberg N. D., & Sue, D. (1989). Research and research hypotheses about effectiveness in intercultural counseling. In P. B. Pederson, J. G. Draguns, W. J. Lonner, & J. E. Trimble (Eds.), *Counseling across cultures* (3rd ed., pp. 335–370). Honolulu: University of Hawaii Press.

Szapocznik, J., Santisteban, D., Kurtines, W., Perez-Vidal, A., & Hervis, O. (1984, December). Bicultural effectiveness training: A treatment intervention for enhancing intercultural adjustment in Cuban American families. *Hispanic Journal of Behavioral Sciences, 6*(4), 317–344.

Taylor, P. (1984, May 28). Hispanic Americans haven't found their pot of gold. *Washington Post* (national weekly edition).

Texidor del Portillo, C. (1987). Poverty, self-concept, and health: Experience of Latinas. *Women and Health Special Issue: Women, Health, and Poverty, 12*(3–4), 229–242.

Torres-Matrullo, C. (1982). Cognitive therapy of depressive disorders in the Puerto Rican female. In R. M. Becerra, M. Karno, & J. I. Escobar (Eds.), *Mental health and Hispanic Americans* (pp. 101–113). New York: Grune & Stratton.

Van Hook, M. P. (1999). Women's help-seeking patterns for depression. *Social Work in Health Care, 29*(1), 15–34.

Vasquez, M. (1982). Confronting barriers to participation of Mexican American women in higher education. *Hispanic Journal of Behavioral Sciences, 4*(2), 147–165.

Yamamoto, J., & Acosta, F. X. (1982). Treatment of Asian Americans and Hispanic Americans: Similarities and differences. *Journal of the American Academy of Psychoanalysis, 10*(4), 585–607.

Young, J. (1994). *Cognitive therapy for personality disorders: A schema focused approach* (2nd ed.). Sarasota, FL: Professional Resource Press.

Zavala-Martinez, I. (1987). En la lucha: The economic and socioeconomic struggles of Puerto Rican women. *Women and Therapy, 6,* 3–24.

EMOTIONAL ISOLATION, DEPRESSION, AND SUICIDE AMONG AFRICAN AMERICAN MEN

**DERYL F. BAILEY AND
JAMES L. MOORE, III
UNITED STATES**

OVERVIEW

Racial oppression and discrimination have inflicted devastating effects on the masculinity of African American males (Lazur & Majors, 1995; Lee & Bailey, 1997; Poussaint, 1983; White & Cones, 1999) as well as their social, physical, psychological, and emotional well-being (Lee, 1990; Madison-Colmore & Moore, 2002; Majors & Billson, 1992; Moore, Flowers, Guion, Zhang, & Staten, in press; Moore, Madison-Colmore, & Smith, 2003; White & Parham, 1990). Data from popular, social science, and scientific literature indicate that African American men represent a population at risk (Lee, 1990; Moore, 2000; Parham & McDavis, 1987). Many social scientists, psychologists, and counselors (Lee, 1990; Majors & Billson, 1992; Moore, 2000; Parham & McDavis, 1987; Poussaint & Alexander, 2000) believe that national statistics on unemployment, mental and physical health, incarceration, and education illustrate the apparent disadvantages of being *black* and *male* in the United States. Today's data reflect the historical and cultural experiences (e.g., slavery and discrimination) of African American men in the United States (U.S. Department of Health and Human Services [DHHS], 2001). In juxtaposition with this notion, African American men are confronted with the arduous challenge of overcoming the statistical odds even when circumstances (as supported by data) are stacked against them (Cose, 2002; Lee, 1990; Moore, 2000).

In the United States, race and gender are significant demographic variables in psychological and social science research. They are not only consistently used for research conceptualizations but also employed to understand and interpret patterns of behaviors. For both white and African American men, role expectations are governed by rigid codes of masculine behavior (Franklin, 1999; Lazur & Majors, 1995; Pollack & Levant, 1998; White & Cones, 1999). However, African American men tend to struggle more with actualizing their masculinity because of the apparent roadblocks (e.g., racism and discrimination) in American society. In succinct with this notion, Grier and Cobbs (1968) write:

> For the Black man in this country, it is not so much a matter of acquiring manhood as it is a struggle to feel it his own. Whereas the White man regards his manhood as an ordained right, the Black man is engaged in a never-ending battle for its possession. For the Black man, attaining any portion of manhood is an active process. He must penetrate barriers and overcome opposition in order to assume a masculine posture. For the inner psychological obstacles to manhood are never so formidable as the impediments woven into American society. (p. 59)

It is worth noting that many African American men are at risk of emotional isolation, depression, and suicide because of the daily stressors that they experience in different domains of American society (Franklin, 1993; Gary & Berry, 1985; Jones & Gray, 1983; Parham & McDavis, 1987; Poussaint & Alexander, 2000; Washington, 1987). The purpose of this chapter is not to further intensify or exacerbate the problems of African American men but to frame their experience in such a way that counselors, psychologists, and other helping professionals in the United States and other parts of the world can better understand how historical and sociocultural factors impact the social, physical, psychological, and emotional well-being of African American men. First, the authors provide an overview of African American males' historical and sociocultural experiences in the United States. Second, we highlight some of the reasons why African American men are reluctant to use and thus underutilize counseling services. Third, we describe different counseling interventions and strategies that have been shown to be effective with this specific population. Fourth, we explain how to integrate and use two of the counseling models in a therapeutic session. Last, but not least, we conclude the chapter with a case study, personal reflections, important concepts, and discussion questions.

HISTORICAL AND SOCIOCULTURAL EXPERIENCES

> The Negro's color and the unique conditions under which it forces him to live have telling effects on him. His Blackness and the dominant group's reaction to it cause to swell up in him deep feelings of self-rejection, cultural alienation, and social estrangement. . . . (Essien-Udom, 1964; cited by Vontress, 1969, p. 271).

The extent to which African American men are accepted and embraced in the United States is a function of internalized beliefs and perceptions of white Americans. Historically, *blackness* and *maleness* in the United States have represented derogative connotations and have stirred negative feelings and attitudes upon the dominate culture. Although the United States has made great strides in the area of race relations, stereotypical notions and perceptions of African American men still linger in the minds and hearts of American society. These attitudes tend to have pervasive effects on the experiences and interactions of white Americans as well as African Americans (Grier & Cobbs, 1968; Vontress, 1966). Thus, it is no surprise that these attitudes represent a perpetual cycle that is socially learned from preceding generations and passed down from cohort to cohort.

From the moment that African American men are born, it is apparent that their racial and gender status represents, ostensibly, a spoiled identity through the lenses of American society (Vontress, 1966, 1969). In effect, the social status of African American men, regardless of their socioeconomic backgrounds, political connections, or social reputations, is replete with obstacles and "road blocks" in different social domains of the United States (Madison-Colmore & Moore, 1999, 2002; Moore, 2000; Moore et al., 2003). It is quite likely that these challenges contribute to African American men's reluctance to forge intimate and meaningful relationships with their white counterparts (Grier & Cobbs, 1968; Washington, 1987) as well as their African American culture (Franklin, 1992; Smith, 2000; Wilson, 1990). The extent of these relationships is easily assessed in both personal and professional contexts where African American men consistently interact and dwell. It appears, according to Vontress (1969), that African American male's "relationships not only to society at large, but to his parents, grandparents, and siblings, are in some measure affected by the color of his skin" (p. 272). This sociocultural phenomenon is a function of race and the attitudes it espouses in American society. Not surprisingly, racial oppression has contributed to many of the psychological scars, emotional stresses, and economic strains of African American men in the United States (Cose, 2002; Johnson, 1998; Madison-Colmore & Moore, 1999, 2002; Moore, 2000; Poussaint & Alexander, 2000).

Numerous African American men find themselves in a constant quandary—forced to negotiate the constructs of their racial and masculine attributes as well as other converging aspects of identity (e.g., social class and age). To some extent, they are coerced to find a "happy" medium between what is and is not expected of them from both the African American and dominant cultures (Lazur & Majors, 1995). W. E. B. Dubois (1970), a highly regarded African American social scientist, refers to this psychological dilemma as "double consciousness." Inherent in the psyche of African American men is to "take into account the obstacles that interfere with [their] acceptance" (Lazur & Majors, 1995, p. 340) and to employ survival tactics that create the least estrangement between the two cultures (Majors & Billson, 1992; Madison-Colmore & Moore, 2002; Moore, 2000; Moore et al., 2003). In these situations, some African American men choose to suppress their individual needs to achieve social acceptance from both cultures, and some go as far as to fabricate their true "selves" in order to gain approval. The double consciousness often calls for in-depth pragmatism and a clear understanding of the situation. In many cases, the nature of the problem and its psychological consequences dictate the overall rationale.

As a group, it is clear that African American men share a collection of distinct psychological and social realities that differ from both their African

American female and white male counterparts (Hilliard, 1985; Moore, 2000). In the United States, there are various sociocultural contexts in which African American men experience attacks on their sense of humanity; however, there are some domains that seem to be more pervasive than others as it relates to African Americans' intellect, behavior, emotion, and spirit (Moore et al., in press; Moore et al., 2003; Parham & Brown, 2003). This is especially true in environments where intellectual abilities and performances are being evaluated (Moore et al., in press; Moore et al., 2003; Steele, 1992, 1997; Steele & Aronson, 1995). African American men frequently disengage psychologically (Steele, 1992, 1997) or develop aloof personas in order to maintain their sense of self in these kinds of environments (Grier & Cobbs, 1968). It is conceivable that disengagement serves as a psychological mediator for channeling mistreatment, prejudice, and bias (Franklin, 1993).

The dynamics of neglect and rejection may partly contribute to African American men's distrust of white Americans (Grier & Cobbs, 1968) and discontent for different social institutions (e.g., schools, social services, mental agencies) in American society (Franklin, 1992; Moore, 2000). Poussaint and Alexander (2000) assert that centuries of dehumanization and racial oppression have taken their toll on African American men. As a result of years and years of mistreatment and neglect, many African American men have developed a sense of *cultural paranoia* to successfully interact with the American social system. Grier and Cobbs (1968) conceptualized the term *cultural paranoia* as being the degree of reluctance to reveal oneself and trust in a social system that imposes psychological pain and injustices. It is quite likely that *cultural paranoia* can be associated with protective mechanisms used by African American men in day-to-day interactions with white Americans as well as other social groups.

Through much research, Pleck (1981) has found that prescribed norms such as emotional detachment and male aggression produce potential short- and long-term, harmful psychological outcomes for men in Western societies. This is especially true for African American men. Similar to their white male counterparts, African American men are expected to adapt to social norms as well as the capitalistic demands of American society (Madison-Colmore & Moore, 2002; Vontress, 1962). However, from their first days in the New World, they have had more difficulty accessing traditional gender values and behaviors such as "power, control, status, and achievement" (Lee, 1990, p. 126); this difficulty can be traced to the effect of overt and covert racism on the mental health of African American men. Racism has the power to limit the African American males in their attainment of financial security for their families. This factor alone with its connection to the image of the male as the "breadwinner" adds an incredible amount of stress for the African American male. In addition, dealing with the day-to-day interactions in the dominant culture that are a constant reminder of the stigma and negativity associated with being black and male further compound this problem (Gary & Berry, 1985; Lee & Bailey, 1997; Majors & Billson, 1992). If this is an accurate description of the experience of African American men, then this would seemingly explain the negative psychological effects of emasculation (e.g., rage, frustration, and hostility).

The "powerlessness" associated with these negative effects can manifest itself through several damaging behaviors, including "problems with aggression and control, cultural alienation/disconnection, self-esteem issues, and dependency issues" (Lee & Bailey, 1997, p. 138). With regard to aggression and control, African American men exhibit either too much control or not enough control over feelings of anger, resentment, and frustration. For some African American men, distancing themselves from meaningful relationships and positive roles within the community or overcompensating for low self-esteem through antisocial behaviors becomes a way of avoiding the true issues connected to racism. Dependency on drugs or alcohol also represents an adaptive response to the mental health issues that face the African American male (Lee & Bailey, 1997).

As early as 1970, Vontress suggested that these defensive mechanisms can truly represent to some extent a mask to hide the pain and hurts experienced as a result of racial oppression. This can help explain why African Americans are apt to conceal their frustrations from white Americans and are more likely to project or even displace their aggravations onto individuals closest to them such as other African Americans (Vontress, 1966, 1970, 1995). Parham, White, and Ajamu (2000) suggest that these cultural patterns of behaviors are both functional and seemingly self-destructive to African American men. In some ways, they are "black norms" (Grier & Cobbs, 1968) that must be factored in when assessing both the inner and outer world of African American men (Moore, 2000).

UNDERSTANDING THE ADOLESCENT CONNECTION

We propose that many adult mental health problems begin long before adolescents reach adulthood. That being said, other scholars suggest that if adolescent African American males are prevented from mastering both the crucial universal and race-specific developmental tasks during adolescence, then their academic, career, and social success may be impeded (Lee, 1996; Lee & Bailey, 1997), thus affecting their mental health. The suicide rate for adolescent African American males is both frightening and alarming: "Between 1980 and 1996, the rate of suicide among African American males aged 15–19 years increased 105% and almost 100% of the increase in this group is attributable to the use of firearms" (U.S. Department of Health and Human Services, 1999, p. 3). Because of the stigma attached to suicide for this particular population, researchers believe that many cases listed as homicides may actually have been suicides, thus pushing the percentage even higher (Poussaint & Alexander, 2000).

Not being able to master critical adolescent developmental tasks may also explain some of the negative statistics associated with African American adolescent males in comparison with their white peers. For example, African American adolescents represent only 17% of the total school population, yet they account for 32% of school suspensions and 30% of school expulsions (Bailey, 1999; Lee, 1996; Trescott, 1990). Anger, frustration, and depression could be underlying reasons for this defiant behavior. Socially, the number of adolescent African Americans males involved at one level or another in the juvenile justice system remains at a critical level. Data from the 1995 FBI report *Crime in the United States* (Sickmund, Snyder, & Poe-Yamagata, 1997) indicate that "black adolescents represented 15% of the juvenile population in 1995 yet were involved in 28% of all juvenile arrests." While they represent only 15% of the juvenile population, African American adolescents constituted 43% of the juvenile populations in public facilities and 34% in private custody facilities (Bailey, 1999; Sickmund, Snyder, & Poe-Yamagata, 1997). The risky behaviors that resulted in their association with the juvenile justice system could have resulted from underlying mental health issues. Furthermore, members of this population rarely seek professional help, and when they do it is not by choice; therefore, many mental health issues remain unresolved. Moreover, this population's disproportionate association with the juvenile justice system could have an ongoing negative impact on its members' mental health as a result of the inappropriate or ineffective mental health services. This is not meant to be critical of the mental health services within the juvenile justice system; however, the ratio of adolescents needing services compared to the number of available service providers makes it next to impossible to render or receive quality care when needed. When we factor in the traumatic experiences that some adolescents experience while in detention and in correctional facilities, their already fragile emotional and mental state becomes even more endangered.

In addition, it is not uncommon to find environmental forces converging to impact negatively on the psychosocial development for adolescents of color (Lee, 1996; Madhubuti, 1990; Majors & Billson, 1992). They are often confronted with extreme environmental stressors during the crucial early years of life (Hilliard, 1985; Lee & Bailey, 1997; Myers & King, 1980). The resulting stress may manifest itself in home, community, or school experiences and directly impact the mental health of this particular population.

For example, it is not unusual for African American males to reach adolescence with a basic mistrust of their environment, doubts about their abilities, and confusion about their place in the social structure. This makes developing an identity during the crucial boyhood-to-manhood transition of the adolescent years extremely problematic. Compounding this problem is the social reality that many African American male youth may have to engage in the process of identity formation with minimal or no positive adult male role modeling. Significantly, identity formation during adolescence is a process in which youth develop aspects of their personal and social identities by selecting and identifying with various role models. Given the historical, social, and economic limitations placed on black manhood in the United States, the range of adult African American role models available to adolescent males is often severely restricted. The developmental passage to adulthood becomes a confusing experience for many African American male youths because the evolution of gender appropriate roles and behaviors for African American males has often been stifled by historical and social powerlessness.

By age 18, the sum total of these impediments to psychosocial development in adolescence can often manifest itself in negative and self-destructive attitudes, behaviors, and values among young African American males. The impact of such factors has resulted in negative consequences related to educational under-achievement, unemployment, delinquency, substance abuse, homicide, and incarceration (Cordes, 1985; Gibbs, 1988). All of these represent indicators for problems associated with mental health issues.

In addition to negative environmental stressors and additional developmental tasks, many minority adolescents come from families with limited financial resources. Poverty has a direct impact on minority women and their children. This is important to understand because a lower socioeconomic status has long been associated with mental health issues. Although the exact nature of the relationship is not understood, researchers believe that increased stress levels and having to deal with more frequent uncontrollable life events may be part of the problem (U.S. Public Health, 2002). Research indicates that the rate of mental disorders for African Americans is higher than their white counterparts until socioeconomic differences are factored out—and then the rates are similar (Regier et al., 1993; Vontress & Epp, 1997). The burden of trying to pay bills and handle the unexpected financial responsibilities can cause such stress and worry that it can have an impact on every aspect of one's life, especially a person's mental state. Although adolescents in this environment have no direct financial stake in their predicament, they still feel the effects experienced by the adults surrounding them.

UNDERUTILIZATION OF COUNSELING

In the research literature, there is considerable discussion about the underutilization of counseling services in the United States by men in general (Lazur & Majors, 1995; Lynch & Kilmartin, 1999) and African American men in particular (Franklin, 1992; Madison-Colmore & Moore, 1999, 2002; Moore, 2000). There are several explanations for this occurrence as it relates to both populations. However, cultural beliefs tend to be one of the most significant reasons why African American men are reluctant to utilize counseling services. They are socialized at an early age to live by a set of explicit and implicit rules that have been determined by preceding generations (Vontress, 1995). These traditional rules embrace a specific gender role identity. More specifically, they represent the internalized manifestations of what "being a man" or "being a woman" means (Pleck, 1981; Pollack, 1995). These unconscious and conscious psychic notions are widely accepted norms in the United States across demographic groups (Lazur & Majors, 1995; Lynch & Kilmartin, 1999). Men often tussle with aspects of their emotional life when gender roles are contradictory to the sociocultural norms of American society (Pleck, 1981).

African Americans in general are reluctant to obtain counseling services for many historical, political, and social reasons, and they are typically underserved by mental health services (Parham, White, & Ajamu, 2000; Poussaint & Alexander, 2000; U.S. Public Health Service, 2002). Cost, mistrust, and stigma are a few of the reasons cited by researchers for the lack of appropriate services (U.S. Public Health Service, 2002). Cost represents the most obvious barrier to receiving mental health care or participating in preventative measures because too many African American males are employed in jobs that have poor to nonexistent health benefits.

Issues surrounding mistrust further compound the problem of African American males seeking help from mental health services. Because most mental health professionals are white, African American males would not be receptive to establishing a relationship that depends so much on trust and understanding. This mistrust of mental health professionals by African American males may seem unfounded, but it stems from their actual experiences with racism. Therefore, it is important that clinicians do not ignore or minimize the effects of racism in African American males' lives. If institutional racism exists in other agencies, then the possibility that it exists in mental health agencies can be assumed. Clinician bias has already been cited as a possible explanation for both the overdiagnosis of schizophrenia and the underdiagnosis of depression for African Americans (Primm, Lima, & Rowe, 1996; Lawson, Hepler, Holladay, & Cuffel, 1994).

Finally, the stigma associated with mental illness can also act as a barrier for prevention and treatment. Too often, African American males try to deny the existence of any problems associated with mental health and instead depend on their own self-reliance as a possible cure (Snowden, 1998). In addition, for some African American males, to seek help is to admit to a weakness—which can be construed as committing "social suicide."

This information is crucial for developing relationships and rapport when counseling adolescent African American males. Mental health professionals need to be aware of the differences that exist for African American males and how those differences impact the clinician's view of the client as well as the client's view of the clinician.

COUNSELING METHODS AND STRATEGIES

Researchers who are interested in developing effective strategies for counseling African American men and adolescent males cite several key components that need to be incorporated into counseling sessions: group work, dealing openly with racism, establishing rapport, and understanding the influence of personal biases.

Group Work

The counselor should consider forming groups with commonalities for discussion. Groups will probably be more effective because they represent a zone of comfort for the African American male. "Street therapy" naturally occurs in local barber shops and gyms, so group discussion may not seem so threatening (Franklin, 1997; Lee & Bailey, 1997). Later, one-on-one sessions might be a possibility, depending on the rapport that exists between the counselor and the client. Counselors must be extremely mindful of the mistrust that already exists and be careful to nurture any advances toward intimacy and disclosure.

Dealing Openly With Racism

Counselors must be sensitive to the effects of racism on their clients and avoid discounting their experiences. This is especially critical for white counselors; too often, even the most sensitive counselors are quick to assure an African American client that a racial incident should not be taken seriously and should just be ignored. To deny that reality for the African American male is to deny part of his experience as a human being.

Establishing Rapport

The counselor will need to be willing to try different approaches in order to establish a rapport. Establishing a connection may take time (Franklin, 1992) and requires patience and empathy. Counselors should also consider exploring spirituality because that may be a critical component in the African American client's life. For many African American men, "solving problems" usually has a spiritual connection, so that avenue should not be avoided as part of the discussion (Lee & Bailey, 1997; Moore & Madison-Colmore, 1999, 2002).

Understanding the Influence of Personal Biases

Counselors must understand their own biases and stereotypes regarding African American men. To do so, counselors are encouraged to respond to the following questions:

1. What stereotypes, biases, and other negative attitudes do I have regarding African American men?
2. What are the sources of these stereotypes, biases, and other negative attitudes?
3. Given the nature of my work, are these appropriate?
4. If so, how?
5. If not, why not—and how can I address them?

Lee and Bailey (1997) suggest five guidelines that provide the framework for culturally specific counseling with African American male youth in educational or community mental health settings:

1. **Be developmental in nature.** Far too often, the only counseling that young African American males receive comes after they have committed an offense against the social order. Generally, the goal of such an intervention is not development but punishment. Counseling should focus on helping African American male youth to meet challenges that often lead to problems in school and beyond in a proactive manner.
2. **Be comprehensive.** When working with adolescent African American males, counselors should utilize counseling strategies that are comprehensive in nature. All areas of the young men's lives—school, family, community, religion or spirituality, work, and so on—should be considered before a treatment plan is implemented (Bailey, 2001).

3. **Provide for competent adult African American male resources as appropriate.** Only African American men can teach African American male youth how to be men. By virtue of attaining adult status as African Americans and males, they alone have the gender and cultural perspective to address accurately the developmental challenges that African American male youths face. Although African American women and individuals of both sexes from other ethnic backgrounds can play a significant role in helping to empower young African American males, it is only an adult African American man who can model the attitudes and behaviors of successful African American manhood. As necessary, therefore, efforts should be made actively to recruit, train, and support competent African American men to serve as facilitators or consultants in counseling interventions.

4. **Incorporate the strengths of black families.** Counseling initiatives for African American male youth must be based on an appreciation of the historical strength of the African American family. Such an appreciation is critical because much of the social science literature presents a generally pathological view of African American family life rather than the long-standing alternative view that disputes pathological notions of black family life. This alternative view reveals a legacy of continuity, hard work, kinship, love, pride, respect, and stability in the evolution of African American families—despite the history of discrimination, racism, oppression, and poverty that has characterized much of the African American experience. In the face of extreme environmental hardship, scores of African American families have found the inner resources to cope effectively, promote the positive development of children, and prevail ultimately across generations. Promoting family involvement in counseling with African American male youth, therefore, should be approached with the understanding that this institution is a strong and viable force for enhancing psychosocial development.

5. **Incorporate African and African American culture.** Counselors should find ways to incorporate African and African American cultural dimensions into interventions for male youth. Culturally specific approaches to counseling take basic aspects of African American life that are generally ignored or perceived as negative in a traditional psychoeducational framework and transform them into positive developmental experiences. For example, African and African American art forms (e.g., music, poetry, and graphic expression) and culturally specific curriculum materials can be incorporated into counseling.

Case 11.1 represents the complexity and magnitude of issues faced by some African American men. Although many of the presenting issues are not exclusive to African American men, many are intensified by the overwhelming external or environmental influences (i.e., historical, societal and political influences) (Lee & Bailey, 1997) in the life experiences of African American men. Crawley and Freeman (1993) suggest that racism and prejudice are omnipresent for African American men as they try to negotiate life as both African Americans and males.

The case study presented here highlights some of the possible issues and challenges associated with counseling African American men. Derek is a 45-year-old male. He is currently an assistant professor at a prestigious university in the South. He is divorced from his wife of 6 months and has no children. Derek lives in a middle-class suburb of a small college town.

Derek grew up in a public housing development in a large city. His mother and father were divorced when he was an infant, and his mother died when he was 6 years of age. He and his younger brother were then adopted by his mother's parents, who were both retired. It is important to note that his grandmother worked as a domestic and his grandfather as a truck driver for a local furniture store. His grandparents instilled in Derek and his brother a strong work ethic and often relayed the message that if you worked hard you would earn the respect and love of your fellow man. Growing up, his idols besides his grandparents, were his "uncle Johnny," who had a Ph.D. in urban planning; and his uncle (by marriage) Charles, who was the first African American to play basketball at one of the major state institutions and later became an NBA legend.

Derek often spoke of his Uncle Johnny as being the "smartest black man" that he's ever known. Derek was taught that education was a "black man's freedom," and that to be truly free, "a man had to be educated." As a teenager, Derek was an average student, but the family saw him as the next "Uncle Johnny" who had earned a B.S., an M.A., a Ph.D., and a postdoctoral degree without ever having to pay tuition because of scholarships and fellowships.

When he graduated from high school, Derek attended a predominately white, private four-year college in a small Southern town and later continued there for his M.Ed. As a student at this institution, he was often the target of racist comments, jokes, and other actions. As an undergraduate, he was accused of cheating on a British literature exam. The professor commented, "In all my years of teaching, no black student has ever earned a perfect score on my exam, so you must have cheated." After taking a different version of the exam and achieving a similar score, he was told by the dean of students that he would have to retake the course the following semester or be expelled for cheating. He never told his family about this situation for fear that they would be disappointed in him.

As a master's student, Derek was the youngest student ever accepted in the master's program and the first African American. During his second semester, the department chair announced to the class that Derek did not belong in their program because he was the "wrong kind of student." During his final semester, Derek registered with the on-campus career center and was scheduled for several on-campus interviews. After intense research and preparation, the day of the first interview arrived. Upon entering the interview room, the interviewer introduced himself and stated "Our company's not ready for people like you," closed his briefcase, and quickly exited the interview room. Unable to deal with the anger and frustration, Derek went through a period of depression. His roommate, a white male, suggested that Derek seek help from the university's counseling center, but Derek refused to go.

After graduating and getting his first job as a teacher, Derek experienced several good years of teaching. He was recognized as the Land-of-the-Sky Outstanding Teacher of the Year for a four-region area. After the recognition, he had several run-ins with the building administrator and received low performance evaluations. Again, he began to experience periods of depression. His friend, a white female, encouraged Derek to seek help and gave him the name of a therapist in the area. When Derek told her that he could not go to a counselor, she asked, "Why not?" He replied, "Because black people don't go to counseling unless they're forced to. And besides everyone will think I'm crazy, and he [the principal] will use it to get rid of me then. Anyway, I'm supposed to be able to handle my own problems." The following year, Derek decided to quit his job and return to school to get his Ph.D.

After entering the doctoral program at a prestigious Southeastern university, Derek continued to face covert and overt forms of prejudice and racism, although it could not often be proven. He recalls one incident in which a white female graduate assistant who was coteaching a class with a white female professor, refused to acknowledge him during a class discussion. According to Derek, out of a class of 40 graduate students, only three were African American and he was the only African American male. The graduate assistant posed a question to the class regarding working with nontraditional families. Derek, seated on the front row in front of the graduate assistant, raised his hand. To his surprise, she acknowledged people seated all around him. At first, he thought she was trying to make sure certain students participated in the discussion, but after continuous efforts on his part to participate, other students seated around him started making comments. To this he stated, "I've had enough of this to last me a lifetime." He gathered his stuff and headed for the door. After leaving the room, the professor, who was sitting in the back of the room the entire time, followed him and apologized for the incident.

Upon graduation, Derek was approached by several institutions regarding employment; after several months of interviewing, he experienced another period of depression. He recalled feeling isolated, confused, and depressed. He reported that "this was one of the most important decisions of my life and there was no one to process with, no one to seek advice from. There was no father or even father figure who could understand my dilemma." With few African American students in the program and even fewer African American professors, Derek began to seek advice from African American male faculty members from other institutions. After doing so, he chose his current place of employment.

The first couple of years were filled with ups and downs. There were good semesters, and there were bad semesters. Although there were semesters when student evaluations were good, other times they were bad, especially when he taught courses that were emotionally charged. He made several attempts to discuss his evaluations with other faculty members but felt his concerns were downplayed. After his third year, he simply stopped reading his evaluations because they

made him feel inadequate. Unfortunately, his passion for his work began to dissipate, and he began to feel detached from his colleagues with the exception of Dick. Dick was a tenured full professor, and Derek considered him to be "the smartest white person I've ever met." Sensing that Derek was experiencing an unhealthy level of stress, Dick convinced Derek to make an appointment with a therapist he knew and trusted.

Derek was extremely reluctant to talk with the therapist. He initially attended the counseling sessions because he trusted Dick and valued their friendship. Derek gradually revealed to the therapist that he had been under a great deal of stress. His grandmother had passed away several months earlier, and he felt guilty for not being around to help his brother take care of her during her final years. In addition to feeling the pressures of being a young professor at a prestigious Southern institution, his guilt and his past and current experiences had begun to affect his work. Derek stated that his colleagues neither valued nor understood the nature of his work or the level of stress that he was experiencing. However, he was most upset about the level of support that graduate students were receiving, especially white males. He claimed that he had watched graduate students and other beginning professors (all white) receive offers to be included in major projects when he was left to fend for himself. Knowing that success in his field and at his level partly depends on being apart of "the network," he felt he did not have access to that network. Derek reluctantly confided to the therapist that to deal with the stress, fears, anger, frustration, and depression, he had begun to drink heavily and take pain pills: "It is the only way I can get through the day."

Crawley and Freeman (1993) also suggest that during early adolescence young African American men are faced with challenges that require them to learn how to negotiate situations in which race and/or culture is an issue. Failure to master this task could prove problematic later in life. Because this is Derek's first counseling experience, the counselor should explain to Derek what counseling is and what it is not. We also suggest allowing Derek to ask questions regarding the counseling process to help alleviate any fears or misconceptions he may have.

Derek reports a series of negative experiences that may or may not have resulted from his being African American and male. However, If he believes that his ethnicity and gender are the cause of these experiences, then it will be important for the counselor to explore these possibilities with him. With that said, we recommend using basic counseling or helping skills first. For example, it will be extremely important to develop rapport with Derek by allowing him to tell his story, listening carefully to his experience, and summarizing his experiences as you've heard them. This will allow him to hear his own experiences as someone else does. This will also provide him with an opportunity to clarify for you and himself how he has made sense of these experiences and their impact on his life experience.

As we suggested earlier, counselors must be sensitive to the effects of racism and be willing to explore openly with the client—in this case, Derek. For white counselors, it will be extremely important to be aware of your reactions to the clients' experiences. It is imperative that the counselor be careful not to discount Derek's experiences as being normal or assume that they never really happened. For white counselors, we highly recommend exploring your own biases and attitudes regarding men—and African American men, in particular—before entering a therapeutic relationship with them. Failure to do so could result in appearing less than genuine and create a sense of mistrust or exacerbate the clients' current level of mistrust.

Derek has encountered many incidences in which he has experienced unfair treatment. His grandparents' belief that "if you work hard you will earn the respect and love of your fellow man" does not seem to describe his experience; in fact, it appears that it has been just the opposite. It will be important to have Derek recount experiences in which he has felt "respect and love." This should not be done to discount a negative experience but to bring to the forefront the other side of it.

We acknowledge that there is not one approach to working with African American men. However, we do believe that patience and empathy on the part of the counselor are critical to the success of the counseling experience. Once a working alliance has been established, it will be helpful for both parties to become clear as to which issue they will address first. Once this decision is made, a discussion regarding Derek's coping strategies will assist in identifying what has and has not worked for him in the past—with a major focus on what *has* worked. What we know is that no one can guarantee Derek that he will not have similar experiences in the future but helping him gain control over how he responds should prove helpful to him. It will also be good to help Derek understand the dangers of mixing alcohol and pain pills and how both substances only mask his depression and enhance his isolation. If the counselor has limited knowledge of substance use and abuse, then we highly recommend arranging consultation with a colleague who is more knowledgeable in the area of substance abuse.

If you realize at the onset of the counseling intervention that you are not prepared to address the issues of racism head on, then we advise you to refer to someone who is more equipped to do so. This being Derek's first experience with counseling, a good first encounter will be critical if he is to continue with counseling. It is most important that counselors from all backgrounds understand the power of both racism (overt and covert) and prejudice. Coupled with depression and substance use or abuse, these collective experiences can lead to serious bouts of depression and prove fatal in the end.

PERSONAL REFLECTIONS

For the past 19 years, I (Bailey) have had the opportunity to work with adolescent males and men in varying roles, as students, athletes, fathers, grandfathers, brothers, uncles, cousins, spouses, partners, friends, and combinations of all of these. In retrospect, I wonder if in some small way my presence in their lives at a particular moment made a difference. Did I make the lives of these men better? Years ago, after a hurtful altercation with my brother, my grandmother sat us down and, in the cool and collected way that only a grandmother can, she said, "Boys, no matter what, always try to leave people better than you find them." By no means was she suggesting that in some way everyone we would come across in life would need to be "fixed"—and, to be honest, at the time I'm not sure I fully understood what she meant. It was not until years later as a high school counselor that I began to truly understand what this frail old lady meant by "Leave people better than you find them." In my role as a high school counselor, I often found myself spending a lot of time and energy trying to help young men mend. Oftentimes, the one thing that prevented this from happening was the way in which males in general were socialized to be men. To show emotions other than anger or frustration was considered a weakness. To cry when you were hurt, scared, or just confused was considered feminine. In addition, if you were an African American male who exhibited academic promise, you were said to be "acting white." The notion that "real men" don't cry or show compassion for someone else has always disturbed me almost as much as the notion that only women and white men were supposed to be smart. I find myself struggling with this "ability to cry." I was shocked when my wife informed me that she has only seen me cry three times in the 15 years that we have known each other. Yell, I can do, but crying is another story. Trying to convince young African American males that crying was a healthy and normal way to cleanse your soul and gather strength was and continues to be a major challenge. These notions of what it means to be a "real man" have caused many men to self-destruct and destroyed others in the process. However, I believe that, deep down inside, all men want a place to cry, care, and be nurtured without the fear of being considered gay or weak. Unfortunately, many men are not able to find this "safe place" to be human.

In March 2002, during her last days, my grandmother would once again remind me "to leave people better than you find them." However, she added something or maybe I just did not hear it before or just ignored it; she said, "Leaving them better will give them reason to do the same for someone else someday. Who knows, it may be you." My grandmother was no scholar; she actually only completed the third grade. However, my grandmother knew people, and she knew how to read your soul. She also knew how to make the pain and confusion disappear. She truly knew how to leave people better than she found them. Her lessons were many, but this one has had a lasting effect on me. This one lesson has shaped not only my work but also my life. As I've worked with the aforementioned groups of men, my goal has always been to leave them better than I found them.

My work with African American men, especially young men, has been both rewarding and challenging: challenging in that the traditional ways of bringing boys to manhood continue to be problematic. Young men still view sex, drugs, and other risky behaviors as markers for achieving manhood. The sad part is that society does, too. Many young men are lacking positive male role models in their lives. They make every attempt to appear tough and noncaring. However, my work has been extremely rewarding, because there are some young men who believe that to be a man is to be caring, nurturing, sensitive, responsible, giving, trusting, and academic. They are willing to develop strong bonds with other males without fear of being labeled gay, weak, or white. They understand the power in letting others know when and how they hurt, thereby acknowledging and expressing their emotional needs. Some fathers and father figures have even been willing to express their love for their sons. Many have even been willing to challenge the old taboo of "Men don't cry." By doing so, I believe they have modeled for their sons how to be "real men." Acknowledging mistakes, experiencing emotions other than anger and frustration, and realizing the importance of developing healthy bonds with other males (outside of sports), has given these young men a gift that will serve them well. The phenomenon we have identified as emotional isolation finally has a potential remedy. We truly believe that communities that produce emotionally and spiritually healthy young men will produce emotionally and spiritually healthy men. This end in and of itself will reduce the overrepresentation of African American males in the justice system, reduce the ever-increasing homicide rate (both as perpetrators and victims), suicides, single-parent households, and African American men who die from heart attacks, strokes, and other stress-related illness. Instead, the number of healthy African American men who are scholars, professionals, family men, and men who contribute to their communities and society as a whole will increase.

With both the challenges and every rewarding encounter, I've learned more about myself as an African American and as a man. There were times in my life when I wanted to crawl under a rock or just run and hide—and, yes, there were even times as a young man when taking my own life crossed my mind. Fortunately for me, I found someone, oftentimes my grandmother, who would listen, process, and help me make sense of the crisis that seemed to consume my every waking moment. However, there were times when even she had the right words but not the understanding because—no matter how wise, loving, strong, and courageous she was—there was a part of my experience she just could not understand. For you see, while she was African American, she was not male. No matter how hard she tried, she could not understand my experience. The lessons I learned from my grandmother continue to serve me well, and some lessons have come through the grace of God. One of the most important lessons was that sometimes help does not seek you—you have to seek it. For some men, the old way of male socialization continues to haunt them, and the "new way" to manhood is foreign to them. But there is some good news: Many men have found the "road less traveled," the new road to manhood as we have described it. The result is men who are caring, nurturing, strong, courageous, and both spiritually and emotionally well. These men are looking to be role models, mentors, and friends. They, too, have learned how to "leave people better than they found them."

CONCLUSION

In closing, we want to encourage you as counselors and counselors in training to remember that it is not so much what we do when men, young and old, are in crisis that makes the difference but what we do or say before they enter a state of crisis that is most important. Let us explain.

Once an African American man has entered a state of crisis (e.g., depression, suicidal thinking, or some other life-threatening behavior), it is quite difficult to get him into therapy. As counselors, we believe our most important work takes place when there is no crisis. It is during this time that rapport and a working alliance should be developed, an alliance that will be there in crisis. This means going out of the way to create opportunities for African American boys and men to engage in conversations that would be preventive and challenging but rewarding.

KEY CONCEPTS

- black norms
- double consciousness
- cultural paranoia
- emasculation
- street therapy
- working alliance

QUESTIONS FOR DISCUSSION

1. What are the presenting issues in the case?
2. In what order should they be addressed?
3. If Derek is reluctant to discuss his problems with the counselor, then what action should the counselor take?
4. How might the counselor's ethnicity and gender affect the outcome of counseling for Derek?
5. Where might the counselor look for assistance should he or she need it?

EXERCISE

Circles of My Multicultural Self (by Paul Gorski)

This activity requires 20–30 minutes.

Purpose   The Circles activity engages participants in a process of identifying what they consider to be the most important dimensions of their own identity. Stereotypes are examined as participants share stories about when they were proud to be part of a particular group and when it was especially hurtful to be associated with a particular group.

Preparation   Distribute copies of the "Circles of My Multicultural Self" handout.

This activity highlights the multiple dimensions of our identities. It addresses the importance of individuals self-defining their identities and challenging stereotypes.

Place your name in the center circle of the structure in Figure 11.1. Write an important aspect of your identity in each of the satellite circles—an identifier or descriptor that you feel is important in defining you. This can include anything: Asian American, female, mother, athlete, educator, Taoist, scientist, or any descriptor with which you identify.

1. Share a story about a time when you were especially proud to identify yourself with one of the descriptors you used above.
2. Share a story about a time when it was especially painful to be identified with one of your identifiers or descriptors.
3. Name a stereotype associated with one of the groups with which you identify that is not consistent with who you are. Fill in the following sentence: I am (a/an) _____ but I am *not* (a/an)_____.
   (So if one of my identifiers was "Christian," and I thought a stereotype was that all Christians are radical right Republicans, my sentence would be: "I am a Christian, but I am *not* a radical right Republican."

Instructions   Ask participants to pair up with somebody they do not know well. Invite them to introduce themselves to one another and then follow these steps:

1. Ask participants to write their names in the center circle. They should then fill in each satellite circle with a dimension of their identity they consider to be among the most important in defining themselves. Give them several examples of dimensions that might fit into the satellite circles: female, athlete, Jewish, brother, educator, Asian American, middle class, and so on.
2. In pairs, have participants share two stories with each other. First, they should share stories about when they felt especially proud to be associated with one of the identifiers they selected. Next, they should share a story about a time it was particularly painful to be associated with one of the identity dimensions they chose.

FIGURE 11.1

Circles of My
Multicultural Self
Handout

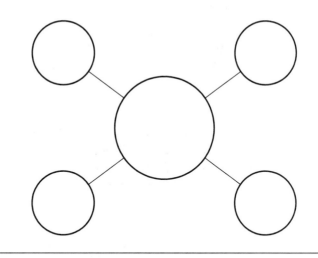

3. The third step will be for participants to share a stereotype they have heard about one dimension of their identity that fails to describe them accurately. Ask them to complete the sentence at the bottom of the handout by filling in the blanks: "I am (a/an) _____ but I am *not* (a/an) _____." Provide your own example such as, "I am a Christian, but I am *not* a radical right Republican." Instructions for steps 1, 2, and 3 should be given at once. Allow 8–10 minutes for participants to complete all three steps, but remind them with 2 minutes remaining that they must fill in the stereotype sentence.

4. Probe the group for reactions to each other's stories. Ask whether anyone heard a story she or he would like to share with the group. (Make sure the person who originally told the story has granted permission for it to be shared with the entire group.)

5. Advise participants that the next step will involve individuals standing up and reading their stereotype statements. You can simply go around the room in some order or have people randomly stand up and read their statements. Make sure that participants are respectful and listening actively for this step because each individual is making him- or herself vulnerable by participating. Start by reading your own statement. This part of the activity can be extremely powerful if you introduce it energetically. It may take a few moments to start the flow of sharing, so allow for silent moments.

6. Several questions can be used to process this activity:
    a. How do the dimensions of your identity that you chose as important differ from the dimensions that other people use to make judgments about you?
    b. Did anybody hear somebody challenge a stereotype that you once accepted? If so, what?

    c. How did it feel to be able to stand up and challenge your stereotype?

    d. (There is usually some laughter when somebody shares common stereotype such as "I may be Arab, but I am not a terrorist" or "I may be a teacher, but I do have a social life.") I heard laughter several times. What was it about?

    e. Where do stereotypes come from?

    f. How can we eliminate them?

Facilitator Notes   The key to this activity is the process of examining one's own identity and the stereotypes associated with that identity, then having one's own stereotypes challenged through others' stories and stereotype challenges. Encourage participants to think about the stereotypes they apply to people and to make a conscious effort to think more deeply about them, eventually eliminating them.

As with most activities, it can be especially effective if you participate while you facilitate. If you are willing to share your own experiences, then participants are more likely to feel open to sharing theirs.

It is crucial to allow for silences, especially for the final part of the activity when participants are sharing their stereotypes. People will be hesitant to share initially, but once the ball starts rolling, the activity carries a lot of energy. Allow time at the end for participants to talk more about whatever stereotype they shared.

After everyone has shared their stereotype challenge, announce that anyone who would like to share another one can do so. Model by sharing another one about yourself.

References

Bailey, D. F. (1999). *The relationship of family environment dimensions and components of hope among adolescent African American and white males in the juvenile justice system.* Unpublished doctoral dissertation, University of Virginia.

Bailey, D. F. (2001). Empowering and transforming African American adolescent males. *Georgia School Counselors Association Journal, 2*(2), 42–47.

Cordes, C. (1985, January). At risk in America: Black males face high odds in a hostile society. *APA Monitor,* 9–11, 27.

Cose, E. (2002). *The envy of the world: On being a black man in America.* New York: Washington Square Press.

Crawley, B., & Freeman, E. (1993). Themes in the life views of older and younger African American males. *Journal of African American Men Studies, 1*(1), 15–29.

Dubois, W. E. B. (1970). *The souls of black folk.* Greenwich, CT: Fawcett. (Original work published 1903.)

Essien-Udom, E. U. (1964). *Black nationalism.* New York: Dell.

Franklin, A. J. (1992). Therapy with African American men. *Families in Society: The Journal of Contemporary Human Services, 73*(3), 350–355.

Franklin, A. J. (1993). The invisibility syndrome. *Networker,* 33–39.

Franklin, A. J. (1999). Therapeutic support groups for African American men. In L. E. Davis (Ed.), *Working with African American males: A guide to practice* (pp. 5–14). Thousand Oaks, CA: Sage.

Gary, L. E., & Berry, G. L. (1985). Depressive symptomatology among black men. *Journal of Multicultural Counseling and Development, 13,* 121–129.

Gibbs, J. T. (Ed.). (1988). *Young, black, and male in America: An endangered species.* New York: Auburn House.

Grier, W. H., & Cobbs, P. M. (1968). *Black rage.* New York: Basic Books.

Hilliard, A. G. (1985). A framework for focused counseling on the African American man. *Journal of Non-White Concerns, 13*(2), 72–77.

Johnson, E. H. (1998). *Brothers on the mend: Understanding and healing anger for African American men and women.* New York: Simon & Schuster.

Jones, B. E., & Gray, B. A. (1983). Black males and psychotherapy: Theoretical issues. *American Journal of Psychotherapy, 37*(1), 77–85.

Lawson, W. B., Hepler, N., Holladay, J., & Cuffel, B. (1994). Race as a factor in inpatient and outpatient admissions and diagnosis. *Hospital and Community Psychiatry, 45,* 72–74.

Lazur, R. F., & Majors, R. (1995). Men of color: Ethnocultural variations of male gender role strain. In R. F. Levant and W. S. Pollack (Eds.), *A new psychology of men* (pp. 337–358). New York: Basic Books.

Lee, C. C. (1990). Black male development: Counseling the "native son." In D. Moore & F. Leafgren (Eds.), *Problem solving strategies and interventions for men in conflict* (pp. 125–137). Alexandria, VA: American Association for Counseling and Development.

Lee, C. C. (1996). *Saving the native son: Empowerment strategies for black males.* Greensboro, NC: ERIC/CASS Publications.

Lee, C. C., & Bailey, D. F. (1997). Counseling African American men and youth. In C. C. Lee (Ed.), *Multicultural issues in counseling: New approaches to diversity* (2nd ed., pp. 123–154). Alexander, VA: American Counseling Association.

Lynch, J., & Kilmartin, C. (1999). *The pain behind the mask: Overcoming masculine depression.* Binghamton, NY: Haworth Press.

Madhubuti, H. (1990). *Black men: Obsolete, single, dangerous? Afrikan American families in transition: Essays in discovery, solution, and hope.* Chicago: Third World Press.

Madison-Colmore, O., & Moore, J. L. (1999, February). *Working with the oppressed and depressed African American males: A counseling model for therapists.* Paper presentation at the meeting of National Association of African American Studies, Houston, Texas.

Madison-Colmore, O., & Moore, J. L. (2002). Using the H.I.S. model in counseling African-American men. *Journal of Men's Studies, 10*(2), 197–208.

Majors, R., & Billson, J. M. (1992). *Cool pose: The dilemmas of black manhood in America.* New York: Touchstone.

Moore, J. L. (2000). Counseling African American men back to health. In L. Jones (Ed.), *Brothers of the academy: Up and coming black scholars earning our way in higher education* (pp. 249–261). Sterling, VA: Stylus.

Moore, J. L., III, Flowers, L. A., Guion, L. A., Zhang, Y., & Staten, D. L. (in press). Non-Persistent African American males' experiences in engineering: Implications for improving academic and social integration, academic preparation, negative stereotypes, and mentoring. *National Association of Student Affairs Professionals Journal.*

Moore, J. L, III., Madison-Colmore, O., Smith, D. M. (2003). The Prove-Them-Wrong Syndrome: Voices from unheard African-American males in engineering disciplines. *Journal of Men's Studies, 12*(1), 61–73.

Myers, H. F., & King, L. M. (1980). Youth of the black underclass: Urban stress and mental health. *Fanon Center Journal, 1,* 1–27.

Parham, T. A., & Brown, S. (2003). Therapeutic approaches with African American populations. In F. D. Harper & J. McFadden (Eds.), *Culture and counseling: New approaches* (pp. 81–98). Boston: Allyn & Bacon.

Parham, T. A., & McDavis, R. J. (1987). Black men, an endangered species: Who's really pulling the trigger? *Journal of Counseling and Development, 66,* 24–27.

Parham, T. A., White, J. L., & Ajamu, A. (2000). *The psychology of blacks* (3rd ed.). Upper Saddle River, NJ: Prentice-Hall.

Pleck, J. (1981). *The myth of masculinity.* Cambridge: MIT Press.

Pollack, W. S. (1995). No man is an island: Toward a new psychoanalytic psychology of men. In R. F. Levant & W. S. Pollack (Eds.), *A new psychology of men* (pp. 33–67). New York: Basic Books.

Pollack, W. S., & Levant, R. F. (1998). Introduction: Treating men in the 21st century. In W. S. Pollack & R. F. Levant (Eds.), *New psychotherapy for men* (pp. 1–10). New York: Wiley & Sons.

Poussaint, A. F. (1983). Black-on-black homicide: A psychological-political perspective. *Victimology, 8*(3–4), 161–169.

Poussaint, A. F., & Alexander, A. (2000). *Lay my burden down: Unraveling suicide and the mental health crisis among African-Americans.* Boston: Beacon Press.

Primm, A. B., Lima, B. R., & Rowe, C. L. (1996). *Integrated mental health services: Modern community psychiatry.* New York: Oxford University Press.

Regier, D. A., Farmer, M. E., Rae, D. S., Myers, J. K., Kramer, M., Robins, L. N., George, L. K., Karno, M., & Locke, B. Z. (1993). One month prevalence of mental disorders in the United States and sociodemographic characteristics: The epidemiologic catchment area study. *Acta Psychiatrica Scandinavica, 88,* 35–47.

Sickmund, M., Snyder, H. N., & Poe-Yamagata, E. (1997). Juvenile offenders and victims: 1997 update on violence. Washington, DC: Office of Juvenile Justice and Delinquency Prevention, U.S. Department of Justice.

Smith, G. E. (2000). *More than sex: Reinventing the black male image.* New York: Kensington.

Snowden, L. R. (1998). Barriers to Effective Mental Health Services for African Americans. Manuscript submitted for publication.

Steele, C. M. (1992, April). Race and the schooling of black Americans. *Atlantic Monthly,* 68–78.

Steele, C. M. (1997). A threat in the air: How stereotypes shape the intellectual identity and performance. *American Psychologist, 52,* 613–629.

Steele, C. M., & Aronson, J. (1995). Stereotype threat and the intellectual test performance of African-Americans. *Journal of Personality and Social Psychology, 69,* 797–811.

Trescott, J. (1990). Fate, hope, and the black child. *Emerge,* 22–26.

U.S. Department of Health and Human Services (1999). *Mental health: A report of the Surgeon General—Executive summary.* Rockville, MD: Author.

U. S. Department of Health and Human Services. (2001). *Mental health: Culture, race, and ethnicity—A supplement to mental health: A report of the Surgeon General.* Rockville, MD: Author.

U.S. Public Health Service (2002). Fundamentals of mental health and mental illnesses. In Mental health: A report of the Surgeon General (Chapter 2). Available at www.surgeongeneral.gov/library/mentalhealth/chapter2/sec5.html.

Vontress, C. E. (1962). Patterns of segregation and discrimination: Contributing factors to crime among negroes. *Journal of Negro Education, 31,* 108–116.

Vontress, C. E. (1966). The negro personality reconsidered. *Journal of Negro Education, 35,* 210–217.

Vontress, C. E. (1969). Cultural differences: Implications for counseling. *Journal of Negro Education, 38,* 266–275.

Vontress, C. E. (1970). Counseling blacks. *Personnel and Guidance Journal, 48*(2), 713–719.

Vontress, C. E. (1995). The breakdown of authority: Implications for counseling young African American males. In J. G. Ponterotto, J. Manual Casas, L. A. Suzuki, & C. M. Alexander (Eds.), *Handbook of multicultural counseling* (pp. 457–473). Thousand Oaks, CA: Sage.

Vontress, C. E., & Epp, L. R. (1997). Historical hostility in the African American client: Implications for counseling. *Journal of Multicultural Counseling and Development, 25*(3), 170–184.

Washington, C. S. (1987). Counseling black men. In M. Scher, M. Stevens, G. Good, & G. A. Eichenfield (Eds.), *Handbook of counseling and psychotherapy with men* (pp. 192–202). Newbury Park, CA: Sage.

White, J. L., & Parham, T. (1990). *The psychology of blacks* (2nd ed.). Englewood Cliffs, NJ: Prentice-Hall.

White, J. L., & Cones, J. H. (1999). *Black man emerging: Facing the past and seizing a future in America.* New York: W. H. Freeman & Co.

Wilson, J. T. (1990). *Implications for effective psychotherapy with African-American families and individuals.* Matteson, IL: Genesis.

12 RESTRUCTURING SOCIAL IDENTITY THROUGH SELF-CATEGORIZING GROUPS

The Interface of Group Dynamics, Gender, and Culture

TAMAH NAKAMURA AND CATHY COLLINS
JAPAN AND THE UNITED STATES

OVERVIEW

We are connected daily to groups, whether in our professional life, family life, or social life. These groups help construct our social identity. For those of us—particularly women, people of color, gays and lesbians, the elderly, the physically challenged, and ethnic minorities—who participate in groups in which we feel oppressed or are considered low-power members, the construction of social identity becomes more complicated. We often find our identities marginalized when the norms of the dominant group are imposed on us. In our search to reconnect more authentically with the aspects of our social identity shaped by gender, race, and ethnicity, we often find ourselves in self-categorizing groups in which the process of reconstruction of social identity can occur.

This chapter explores this process and its value in coping with the effects of oppression. Specifically, the chapter establishes a theoretical base for social identity, outlines a model for reconstructing social identity, and shows the relevance of the model in two case studies that demonstrate both a formal and informal application of the model. The chapter concludes with the authors' own experience with the model.

INTRODUCTION

The idea for this joint chapter emerged when Tamah Nakamura and Cathy Collins shared home and workplace settings. We both had experienced leadership positions in male-dominated organizations in cross-racial and cross-cultural settings. In May 2000, Collins visited Nakamura in Japan. Shared conversations about similarities in group interaction at each of our workplaces led to a curiosity about why, on two different continents, we had experienced oppressive interactions at our respective institutions of employment.

We took the opportunity to apply our experience in a scholarly manner through the lens of social psychology. Anthony Giddens (Giddens & Pierson, 1998) says that a sociologist—or, in both our cases, a scholar-practitioner—is first and foremost an ordinary member of the world she investigates whose explanations help transform the very world she seeks to explain and analyze. Nakamura's visit to Collins' home and workplace in Little Rock, Arkansas, in August 2001 brought further reflection and clarification to this joint investigation.

Our prereflection expectation was that, because of cultural differences, there would be few similarities in the patterns of oppression and marginalization in our work settings. However, from our individual reflections on our work contexts and follow-up dialogue reflections, commonalties surfaced immediately and unexpected patterns emerged. We noticed that the dominant group functioned in modes in which salient oppressive features such as gender and race bias surfaced frequently in patterns of communication. Women's opinions were neither elicited nor offered by women who had lost voice and were silenced. When the voices of women and people of color were present, they were often overlooked or restated by those in the dominant group. Thus, the dominant interaction patterns were mainstream male, in one case Western male, in the other case Asian male, and both included race bias.

Our discussion about our reflections moved us to consider how we functioned in the dominant group. In the process of being silenced, we recognized that we both shared a feeling of cognitive dissonance with the dominant interaction patterns—and, rather than conform to those patterns, we cognitively, psychologically, and emotionally distanced ourselves or withdrew from the dominant group. We further discovered that both of us had taken our energy to the outer community where we joined, formed, or facilitated groups of self-categorizing members of like interests and identities. In hindsight, we realized this action was a coping strategy. The interaction in these self-categorizing groups provided validation and reconfirmation of our values and abilities as women. The following excerpt from our dialogue reflects our realizations.

NAKAMURA: You're right when you say that my voice isn't strong. I noted in my Tavistock Group interaction in July 2000 that I did not stay with the group's agenda if it was not progressing in my estimation.

COLLINS: Withdrawal or distancing is a coping strategy. When we did a group simulation of oppression within the curriculum of the Healing Racism Institute, several types of groups emerged, and one of them always was the withdrawal group.

NAKAMURA: I moved my energy out into the community. From about 8 years ago, I slowly became involved in facilitating the gender issues discussion class, the cross-cultural discussion group, and I'm on the academic advisory board of a local city's gender equality commission. I have gotten reconfirmation of my ability and was able to create meaningful community in my life.

COLLINS: That's what happened to me, too. The work I did with the community and in the schools sustained me in the craziness of city hall. I shifted out of cognitive dissonance through doing community work. I still am working in the community.

NAKAMURA: There's no other way to reconcile the dissonance. If the institutional support for change is not in place, one person cannot do it alone.

COLLINS: You're right. The situation will not change unilaterally. We choose not to buy into the existing structures. We are not willing to conform to the structure, so we go out into the community to gather the strength and the strategies to become change agents.

The further we explored what was actually happening, the more we saw similar patterns emerge in our doctoral program experiences, and our community and social interaction patterns, in addition to our work settings. Energized by these reflections, we analyzed our process to define underlying patterns of meaning. The model explicated below and represented visually reflects the analysis that we developed.

THE SHAPING OF IDENTITY

The composition of our identity is complex, fluid, and often elusive. Until the work of Tajfel and his colleagues (Tajfel, 1970; Tajfel, Billig, Bundy, & Flament, 1971), the foundation of our identity construction lay primarily in the realm of the psychological, the individual. With the advent of social identity theory, Tajfel introduced the role of the social structure and social context into the mix of identity creation. Specifically, Tajfel (1982) and Tajfel and Turner (1979) integrated "people's need for self-esteem and positive intergroup distinctiveness with macrosocial analysis of social belief structures," providing an account of the connection between the social group and social identity (Hogg & Abrams, 1988, p. 10).

Kay Deaux (2000) explains that Henri Tajfel developed social identity theory as a way to "explain the relationship between categorization and intergroup discrimination" (p. 1). Social identity theory is often interpreted as a way in which people enhance their self-esteem through social identities constructed through the groups in which they belong. The desire to increase one's self-esteem often results in establishing in-groups and out-groups to set up a system of favoritism or privilege. This differentiation usually results along social categories.

In the years following Tajfel's initial work, social identity has been one of the most studied and expanded-upon theories within social psychology (Hogg & Abrams, 1988; Abrams & Hogg, 1999). Many models have emerged proposing different categories for social identity. Deaux (2000) identifies five types of social identity categories: "relationships, vocation/avocation, political affiliation, stigma, and ethnicity/religion" (p. 3). Brewer and Gardner (1996) suggest that the individual, the interpersonal, and the group serve as the categories. Klink, Mummendey, Mielk, and Blanz (1997) identify cognition and emotion as two ways in which elements within the social identity category can differ. The dimensions of individualism versus collectivism are emphasized by Brown et al. (1992). Prentice, Miller, and Lightdale (1994) make the distinction between social identities that are created as a result of common bonds and common identity. Ellemers, Kortekaas, and Ouwerkerk (1999) posit that self-categorization, group self-esteem, and commitment to the group are areas of division. Deaux concludes that this discussion demonstrates the complexity and nuance with which social identity can be explored.

A recent development within social identity theory is self-categorization theory (Hogg & Terry, 2000; Abrams & Hogg, 1999). Terry, Hogg, and White (2000) explore the role of the collective self in terms of social identity and social categorization theories. Self-categorization groups use salient characteristics, or representations of defining features, to create identity through participation in the group. "When social identity is salient, people construct a context-specific group norm from available, and usually, shared, social comparative information" (Terry et al., 2000, p. 72). Gender, race, and ethnicity are common salient characteristics that bring people together in a self-categorizing group. The process of self-categorization differs from other group membership because of its contextualized nature around a salient social identity characteristic and the self-identity with the group's constructed norms, which are context-specific. Specifically, norms arise out of beliefs, feelings, behaviors constructed from experiences, and information that individual members bring with them to the group concerning the salient feature that connected them to the group initially. The individual then often defines him- or herself in terms of the group's constructed norms, thus changing her personal sphere and her behavior and actions when she functions in her life outside the self-categorizing group as well. The feminist consciousness-raising groups of the 1970s followed a similar process of linking salient feelings and experiences of oppression with others. In particular, they examined, criticized, found similarities, and gained empowerment through shared salient features in women's lives (Butler & Wintram, 1995; Mezirow & Associates, 1990; Hart, 1990).

We can understand the need for self-categorizing groups by examining high-power and low-power group dynamics. Understanding the characteristics of high-power members and low-power members establishes a foundation from which to discern better the dynamics experienced in the groups in which both high-power and low-power members are present. Participation in self-categorizing groups is a way for low-power members to restructure social identity outside their high-power group experience. Table 12.1 highlights the list of characteristics offered by Johnson and Johnson (2000, pp. 250–253), based on the work of several people, most notably Murninghan and Pillutla (1995), Gilbert (1992), Oubuchi and Saito (1986), Lindskold and Arnoff (1980), and Tjosvold and Sagaria (1978).

TABLE 12.1 | MODEL OF RECONSTRUCTING SOCIAL IDENTITY FOR LOW-POWER MEMBERS BELONGING TO HIGH-POWER MEMBER DOMINANT GROUP

High-Power Characteristics	Low-Power Characteristics
Establish norms or rules in the group as well as severe penalties for attempting to change status quo.	Even with attempts to understand high-power behavior, often feel frustrated and uncertain because of its unpredictability.
Devalue the performance of low-power persons and often claim a role in the success of low-power persons.	Perceive relationship to be competitive. Stifle criticism of and direct attention and communication to the high-power member.
Make fewer concessions in conflict situations. Tend to avoid efforts involving cooperation, conciliation, and compromise and reject demands for change.	More compliant to threats when negotiating, make more concessions, and tend to be more cooperative and less aggressive.
Uninterested in learning about the intentions and plans of low-power members and underestimate the degree to which the intentions are positive.	Distort perceptions of the positive intent of high-power members toward them. Unwilling to clarify position to high-power member.
Offer rewards to low-power members when they refrain from rebelliousness. Believe that low-power persons do not "know their place" and "rock the boat" out of ignorance and spite.	Ingratiation, conformity, flattery, and effacing self-presentation to induce high-power members to like them and keep on good terms with them. Some resist attempts to be controlled.
Feel more secure than low-power members and tend to keep a psychological distance from them.	Experience psychological reactance or attempts to regain one's freedom and control. Attraction, mixed with fear and sometimes dislike toward high-power member.
React more strongly to a low-power person's harm. As Aristotle noted, people think it "right that they should be revered by those inferior to them."	Experience feelings of abuse and mistreatment.
View low-power persons as objects to be manipulated.	Expect exploitation.

Source: Cathy Collins and Tamah Nakamura © 2001

In general, life is good for high-power members. Things tend to go well for them, and they are typically oblivious to the role that power is playing in their relationships. Low-power members usually know the role that power plays in their relationships intimately because it often prevents them from meeting their own goals. There are several strategies, however, that low-power members use to influence high-power members. Some of these strategies include building their own organizations and developing their own resources, allying themselves with a third party, using existing legal procedures, changing attitudes through education or moral persuasion, or using harassment techniques. Nonetheless, the power differential is still challenging and difficult to shift.

More detailed understanding of the specific aspects of social identity with regards to racial, cultural, and gender identity has also emerged. The contributions of Cross (1991), Helms (1990), Sue and Sue (1999), Tatum (1992), Gilligan (1982), Miller (1986), and Fletcher (1999) are particularly noteworthy. Table 12.2 depicts three racial identity models. Briefly, William E. Cross, Jr. (1991) developed a model of black identity that involves a black person moving through five stages in the development of her or his racial identity. Helms (1990, 1999; Helms & Piper, 1994) developed a model that proposed a process whereby whites became increasingly more conscious of their role in perpetuating racism and more active in their responsibility to do something about its existence. Her model proposes two phases of white identity development. The first phase is the abandonment of racism, which involves the first three statuses. The second phase involves defining a positive white identity and includes the final three statuses. The racial/cultural identity model (R/CID) developed by Sue and Sue (1999, 1990) attempts to identify common features of population-specific models. This model defines five stages of development that oppressed people experience as they try to understand themselves in terms of their own culture, the dominant culture, and the oppressive relationship between the two.

The dominant–subordinate relationship, then, between the two different cultural bases of the participants (mainstream dominant group and subordinate group) is the key issue of power dynamics in racial and cultural identity creation. When members of the low-power cultural group try to adjust to the high-power group that possesses greater power, confusion often occurs in the person with low-power status. The pressures for assimilation and acculturation are strong, allowing the power of the dominant group to impose its standards onto the less powerful group or person.

Gender identity development models suggest that many of the same dominant–subordinate power differentials are in place with regard to gender identity. Theories of gender identity development show that women develop in relationship with each other based on equality and mutuality, not as independent social agents (Fletcher, 1999; Miller, 1986). Miller and Fletcher (1999) describe this as "participating in growth fostering relationships" (p. 1). Gilligan (1982) says that a woman's place in man's life cycle has been one of nurturer and caretaker, as well as creator and maintainer of relationships. In men's theories of psychological development, however, maturity is equated with individual achievement and personal autonomy. Relational work, therefore, appears as a weakness of women, rather than the sustaining function it serves in women's lives. Miller and Stiver (1998) show that listening and responding in relationships creates connections that lead to psychological growth. Set within a gender social identity and power model, relational theory (Fletcher, 1999), explicates that women are expected to engage in a host of relational activities without calling attention to them or expecting recognition for them. This invisibility results in much of women's relational and often stereotyped work getting devalued and overlooked. Furthermore, women's engagement in relational work intimates that

TABLE 12.2 | A COMPARISON OF IDENTITY MODELS

Black Identity Model	White Identity Model	Racial/Cultural Identity Model (R/CID)
Stage 1 Pre-Encounter	Status 1 Contact	Stage 1 Conformity
A black person will have a low salience, neutral, or antiblack perspective about her or his membership in the black race.	Involves literal contact with black people.	Identifies and conforms to the values and beliefs of dominant group. Attitude toward self and others of the same minority are deprecating and discriminatory.
Stage 2 Encounter	Status 2 Disintegration	Stage 2 Dissonance
A time of transition in which one or more events call into question her or his identity as a black person. Many people in this stage may at first feel confused, depressed, or alarmed.	A white person becomes more conscious of and recognizes the advantages that come with being white and the role that whites play in perpetuating a racist system. Guilt, shame, depression, helplessness, and anger often accompany this recognition.	A dissonance occurs based on personal discrimination or a distrust of certain dominant group members.

A conflict arises between the self-deprecating belief and appreciation of and beliefs about the dominant group. |
Stage 3 Immersion–Emersion	Status 3 Reintegration	Stage 3 Resistance–Immersion
A person immerses her- or himself into the black culture. This immersion is often reflected in dress, hairstyles, actions, or organizational memberships that depict an idealistic standard and authenticity of blackness (Cross, 1991; Helms, 1990).	An acknowledgment of a white identity and an understanding of the belief in white superiority (Helms, 1990; Tatum, 1992). The guilt and anxiety felt in the previous status may be redirected toward people of color passively (avoiding situations with people of color) or actively (exhibitions of overt fear and anger, including acts of discrimination, violence, and exclusion).	Feelings of cultural centrism and anger at the oppression of the mainstream group may be present during this stage. Empathy for other minority experiences and a sense of connectedness with other members of the same racial or cultural group begin the strengthening of new identity.
Stage 4 Internalization	Status 4 Pseudo-Independence	Stage 4 Introspection
A high salience for blackness is achieved and expresses itself through a nationalistic perspective at one end of the spectrum and a multicultural perspective at the other end.	White people abandon their cognitive thinking of superiority and inferiority yet may continue to behave in ways that unintentionally perpetuate the system of white privilege (Helms, 1990; Tatum, 1992). The process of redefining a positive white identity begins.	Introspection and self-definition occur in a proactive nature regarding social identity. Persons in this stage reach out to others and discover what types of oppression they have experienced as well as the coping mechanisms they have employed.

TABLE 12.2 | A COMPARISON OF IDENTITY MODELS (CONTINUED)

Black Identity Model	White Identity Model	Racial/Cultural Identity Model (R/CID)
Stage 5 Internalization–Commitment	Status 5 Immersion–Emersion	Stage 5 Integration–Awareness
Expands the fourth stage through a commitment to and execution of a plan of action in black affairs over a long period of time.	Replacement of white and black myths and stereotypes with accurate information about what it means to be black and white in the United States. No longer focuses on changing black people but instead seeks to change white people (Helms, 1990).	In the final stage, there is an integrated awareness and support for all oppressed people. There is an openness to members of the dominant group who seek to eliminate oppressive activities as well as an identification and acceptance of constructive elements within the dominant culture.
	Status 6 Autonomy	
	The internalization and nurturing of the newly defined white identity. There is openness to other standards and criteria besides white ones and a willingness to learn from other cultural groups.	

women may find social identity created and sustained by relationships within a group (Gilligan, 1982) rather than by the intergroup competition that is more characteristic of men (Kelly & Breinlinger, 1996).

While all of these models of racial, cultural, and gender identity have slight variations among them, they all share some commonalities. They all involve a process of transformation, which includes a deconstruction of the stereotypes and myths placed upon their group from the dominant group. A good example of this process can be seen in the experience of a female student who faced the judgment of a white male professor that the only valid method of study was a rigorous, written scientific mode of scholarship. In confronting her professor, she became overwhelmed with a sense of academic inadequacy even though every indication she received from other professors was of superior academic work. Working with a group of women and a male ally, they helped her see how the dominant culture placed that value upon the definition of scholarship. In naming that myth and stereotype of scholarship, she was able to deconstruct her own reaction to the situation and gain strength in following a different type of scholarship production. In the end, she did not succumb to the myths and stereotypes, but protested and deconstructed their significance for her.

Furthermore, even though these models focus on individual experience, the definition that a group is "a collection of individuals whose interactions are structured by a set of norms and goals" (Johnson & Johnson, 2000, p. 17) is particularly useful in understanding how the dominant group constructs identity. The ability of the large group to function effectively tends to depend upon the majority of the members adhering to these norms and goals. It is important to note that not only do such norms—which translate into acceptable behaviors, beliefs, and values—delineate high-power and low-power group members, but also their regulation and structure is largely controlled by the high-power group. The result is a socialization process in which the identity of all members is constructed to conform to the characteristics of the dominant group.

Looking at gender and cultural identity from high-power and low-power group dynamics, groups that are self-categorizing tend to demonstrate less differentiation in the power status of group members. The group is created to share similar experiences around the salient social identity characteristics. Within the self-categorizing group, it is usually this characteristic that brings people together as a group. Occasionally, people will have come together for some other reason (for example, a charity event) and discover an opportunity for the emergence of a self-categorizing group around being professional women in a male-dominated profession.

Through dialogue and shared experiences, members reconstruct social identity. They accomplish this reaffirmation process through the support and reconfirmation of self they find in the self-categorizing groups that embody similar norms and beliefs that are congruent with their social identity. In many ways, the dominant group does not construct social identity for the low-power member as much as it oppresses the authentic social identity by deeming characteristics of one's social identity as being low-status. This process of having one's social identity pushed to the margins is often witnessed in lost voice, lack of self-esteem, and internalized oppression. "Authentic" self-identity occurs when an individual is aware that her experience is connected to her own inner history and is not imposed by external groups or individuals (Boyd & Myers, 1988).

It is here that our work departs from the typical path of the social identity literature. We show how a marginalized group member can be empowered by first joining a self-categorizing group around the salient issue that caused marginalization. For example, a woman in a male-dominated group may feel marginalized and as an outsider. In a self-categorizing group of women, she can become more central, which then changes her sense of self and ability to return to the original group from a different place. Our model is not a replacement for the other social identity models but a further delineation of the process. Our model provides the deliberate opportunity for consciousness raising that may allow one to understand more deeply how aspects of one's social identity have been socially constructed by the dominant group. This process of consciousness raising is often what is needed to move from one stage or status to the next in the racial, cultural, and gender identity models.

A MODEL OF RECONSTRUCTING ASPECTS OF SOCIAL IDENTITY THROUGH SELF-CATEGORIZING GROUPS

Although our model of reconstructing aspects of social identity is applicable to anyone who finds her- or himself experiencing dissonance or marginalization within a group context, it is particularly relevant to women, people of color, and people participating in a multicultural or cross-cultural realm because of their heightened exposure to oppression and subsequent encounters with internalized oppression. The model is presented as Figure 12.1 and represents a process of reconstructing identity when the norms and values of the dominant group oppress one's social identity.

Essentially, the dominant group imposes group values and norms on the individuals of the group, thus constructing the social identity of the individual members. Because "a group cannot exist, cannot survive, cannot function, and cannot be productive unless most members conform to its norms most of the time" (Johnson & Johnson, 2000, p. 263), conformity to the group norms and values is expected. If the dominant group is inclusive of differences, then the individual will be able to function as a whole person. However, if there are patterns of oppression, through high- and low-power structures (Johnson & Johnson, 2000), and the individual does not feel she belongs to the group in terms of value and significance, then the individual's social identity (Haslam, 2001) often will not be interpreted in a positive or authentic way. In addition, a sense of low status may be internalized as a result of this group membership.

When this happens, individuals often experience a dissonance (Aronson, 1999; Johnson & Johnson, 2000) with their own perception of their social identity and the social identity being imposed upon them by the dominant group. An individual may begin to question his or her value and ability to function, lowering his or her self-concept as a member of the group. When dissonance occurs, a common coping strategy for the individual is to distance or withdraw cognitively, psychologically and, when possible, physically from the dominant group. Kondo (1990) calls this distancing a deconstructing of imposed identity.

Reconstruction of identity can occur when the individual interacts in a self-categorizing group in which similar salient identity characteristics such as gender, race, and ethnicity are present. People in a group share patterns that enable them to see the same thing, which holds them together (Hall, 1973). The interaction in the self-categorizing groups helps restore a positive social identity around the salient characteristic. Through support for one's beliefs and reaffirmation of one's authentic identity, the individual gains strength in one's ability to become a change agent. With renewed hope, the individual can participate in the dominant group to bring about change to the norms and values of the dominant group.

Utilizing the strength gained from the self-categorizing group, the individual often works creatively to change the treatment and status of the marginalized within the dominant group. In this process, the marginalized members move from a dominant group experience in which a social identity is forced to a self-categorized group experience in which the social identity imposed by the dominant group around the salient characteristic is deconstructed and an authentic

FIGURE 12.1

Model of
reconstructing
social identity for
low-power
members belonging
to high-power
member dominant
groups

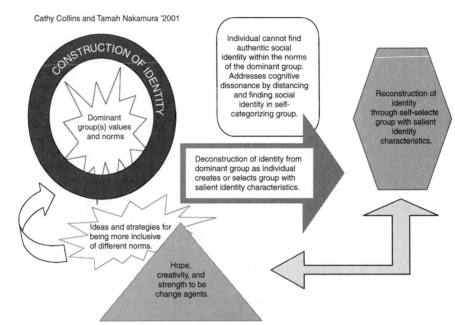

Cathy Collins and Tamah Nakamura '2001

CONSTRUCTION OF IDENTITY

Dominant group(s) values and norms

Individual cannot find authentic social identity within the norms of the dominant group. Addresses cognitive dissonance by distancing and finding social identity in self-categorizing group.

Reconstruction of identity through self-selecte group with salient identity characteristics.

Deconstruction of identity from dominant group as individual creates or selects group with salient identity characteristics.

Ideas and strategies for being more inclusive of different norms.

Hope, creativity, and strength to be change agents.

social identity is reconstructed. This reconstructed social identity then often
provides courage for the individual to return to the dominant group with voice
restored.

APPLICATION

As described in the introduction of this chapter, the development of the model itself
emerged from our actual life experiences. Highlighted below are some of the experiences and subsequent reactions that inspired the development of the model, as
well as other experiences analyzed with the model.

For several years, Nakamura had been experiencing loss of voice in Japanese
faculty meetings in which she participated as a full faculty member. On an interpersonal basis, she experienced individual interactions with the same faculty members as amicable and cooperative. Group dynamics was the apparent variable in
communication differences. The minimal group paradigm identified by Tajfel
(Abrams & Hogg, 1999) accounts for the discontinuity behavior she experienced
among her colleagues. This paradigm depends on a social categorization generat-
ing intergroup discrimination.

A specific incident that occurred in which the full faculty of approximately 30 members was meeting (6 women, among which she was the only non-Japanese woman, and 24 men, of whom one was non-Japanese) is described in her own voice:

> The chair of the meeting, a woman, in soliciting opinions from faculty members on a specific committee, omitted asking the opinion of one of the committee members, who also happened to be a woman. None of the other female faculty spoke in her defense. I watched and waited for them to ask her to speak or for her to initiate speech, and even though I wanted to say something when she was passed over, I did not. I, too, was silenced by the awareness of the underlying pressures of gender-biased social norms which would surface in the following days in attitudinal sanctions to encourage conformation. (The low-power characteristic manifested in this reaction is compliance to a perceived threat, and a stifling of my criticism to direct attention toward communication with the high-power members.) The anger I felt at the loss of not only my own voice but of all the women's voices was an indescribable dissonance. There was no outlet for that emotion in the moment. As I think back on this incident, and others like it, I realized that I internalized the oppression that I not only was not expected to or allowed to speak, but that if I did I would be perceived as having nothing significant to say.

Collins shares a similar experience when she describes a situation with restructuring process of a city commission for which she was the executive director.

> I vividly remember sitting in the Mayor's office with the Assistant to the Mayor and the City Manager and being asked how I thought the Commission should be restructured. While I had my own ideas, I knew that there were not enough perspectives in the room to make that decision, which is what I said. In hindsight, I realize that they interpreted that statement to mean that I did not have any ideas. Nonetheless, I was able to promote a participatory process involving several different voices for the restructuring process. Within the process, though, my own voice got lost. We had had several meetings culminating in a big meeting in November of 1997 in which all current and former Commissioners as well as the Restructuring Committee attended to make final recommendations. I still am shocked when I think back to this meeting. After years of asking for a job shocked evaluation from the Commission, I finally received one, from some of the Commissioners—it came in the form of a press release handed out at the meeting. To say the least it was not very flattering. My anger had nowhere to go. I remained silent, which I knew for the process was best. Unfortunately that silence lingered. During the next few months, I noticed how often I was asked to speak up because people could not hear me. And I silenced my feelings by gaining weight. The silencing of my voice had literally silenced me and hidden my identity.

Looking at these two examples in terms of power dynamics, concepts of social identity are linked to the dominant group's maintenance of its power through exclusion and hierarchy. High-power characteristics are evident in the actions outlined above in devaluing the performance of low-power persons and viewing low-power persons as objects to be manipulated.

Cases 12.1 and 12.2 illustrate how self-categorizing groups can help restore a positive sense of social identity.

CASE 12.1

A WOMEN'S GENDER ISSUES DISCUSSION GROUP

The Women's Gender Issues Discussion Group in Japan demonstrates a formal implementation of the process entailed, while the university women's group offers a more informal perspective. In response to the 1975 "International Year of Women," the Japanese government instituted new policies that were aimed at improving the status of women. Women's centers appeared as a visible result of these policies.

The Fourth World Conference on Women in Beijing, China, in 1995 brought the emergence of English discussion courses on women's issues at these women's centers.

The women enroll in the classes for a 10-week period in the spring and in the fall. The class itself, facilitated by Nakamura, introduces the 12 points of the Beijing Platform for Action, followed by small group discussions of topics selected by the participants. It is in the small group discussions that the consciousness raising begins to occur, the process of identity restructuring. The reports to the larger group during the course demonstrate that the women begin to question and transform their perspectives of what it means to be women in Japan and the world.

The expression and examination of people's lives through their stories helps them create a larger framework, often allowing them to connect to community and global action. The sequence of identity restructure begins in the small group discussions, which are organized by self-categorization of topic of interest. At this stage, the participants reflect on individual psychological experiences of oppression that they report back to the large group.

One of the group members, Junko, exemplifies the predictable process of change. On the first day of class, during the self-introduction period, she responded to my question of what gender means to her by describing her husband as being an unsupportive partner because he did not help her with any of the housework. During the small group discussions of four to five participants in which women often share more detailed stories of their experiences and current life situations, Junko chose the topic concerning women and employment. These groups are highly animated. Participants lean forward to catch what others are saying. Bursts of laughter from one group punctuate the air, while another group listens attentively to one of its participant's intense explanation. When it comes time to regroup into the large group, the participants reluctantly leave the small groups with unfinished conversations left hanging. They return to the more formal setting of the large group with quieter demeanor. After gathering back in the large group, Junko shares that the participants in her group found that not only did practically none of the husbands do any household chores or child-rearing responsibilities, but also they all expected the wife to be responsible for those duties. Furthermore, she explains their premarriage employment lifestyle and marriage expectations were that both partners would share home and child-rearing duties. Junko expresses to the group that she has been frustrated by this aspect of her marriage for several years and thought she was not a "good wife" for having such negative thoughts about her husband. She describes her relief at finding other women who feel the same frustrations, and she realizes she is not alone and that what she is experiencing is a common factor in the marriages of at least the people in her group.

At this point, Junko's experience becomes more than just a personal one and a symptom of gender oppression. This collective recognition starts the chain of transformational learning toward connection to larger social structures. In the weeks that follow, Junko and other women in the group initiate the outward connection through self-directed activities such as attending lectures on feminism, gender-related legal and social issues, reading books available in the women's center library, observing and making note of gender-stereotyped conversations in their daily lives, and gender bias in the media. Many prepare mini-presentations and report back to the class. Through this process, they restructure their identity as women and socially aware human beings utilizing the collective knowledge created in the group presentations and discussions. They connect their personal experiences through their own voice to larger self-identified social issues. Poignantly, Junko made this point while sharing several newspaper articles she had clipped and brought to class pertaining to topics discussed during the previous weeks, "The topics just jump out at me from the pages of the newspaper now. I find 'me' on those pages."

In a retrospective cumulative participant survey (Nakamura, Ostu, Taniyama, & Drake, 2001), outcomes reflect that many of the women after the 10-week formal group remained connected with each other through extended informal self-categorizing groups. Out of these informal self-categorizing groups, discussion groups and presentations have been created. One such group is Mint no Kai which was organized by participants to continue discussion of women's social issues in English. Members rotate responsibility for researching and presenting social issues for discussion. Another group prepared a proposal and was granted funding to interview

Korean women and men in Korea about their family and social roles. The team presented its research results at a women's center symposium and in Korea. Other participants work as volunteers in nonprofit work in the community. Thus, the women have become aware of the construction of their social identity as women by the dominant group, have begun to deconstruct that social identity, and are replacing it with one that encompasses the full range of their identity as women. Some have even begun to raise their voices to encourage the dominant group structure to include this more comprehensive range of social identity.

AN ONLINE
SUPPORT
GROUP FOR
WOMEN
DOCTORAL
STUDENTS

Both Collins and Nakamura share a group experience with women in their doctoral program outside the context of the official curriculum that serves a similar function as outlined by the model. Initially, a group of seven women, which has now grown to 10, connected through collegial friendships and forged a deeper connection to each other around their experience as intelligent and strong women in a university context. While geographically dispersed, the group remains connected via e-mail and instant messenger as well as biannual face-to-face visits of approximately 1 week as a group, supplemented by other separate one-on-one visits at each other's homes.

This group of women openly discusses the challenges of being women in a setting that still overwhelmingly privileges white men, supports the processes of surviving a doctoral program, and provides a safe place to share and react to the emotions, insights, and transformations that occur. Long and short e-mails to the group often appear and are responded to, creating an atmosphere of deep sharing that contribute to positive decision making. Many members comment that without this forum and group

support they might be forced to drop out of the doctoral program, stay in an unhealthy relationship, quit work, or give up on yet to be realized potential. This process is not one of just "feel good" emotion but a constant push for transformation.

Recently, one of our members was ready to quit her doctoral program after receiving faculty feedback about a paper. Recognizing her state of exhaustion and the fact that the paper she had written was deeply connected to her personal passion, the group offered her both loving support and pressed her to see where she was falling victim to internalized oppression in her reaction. Instead of quitting the program, she emerged a stronger, more confident person and student. She describes her experience in her own words:

> The professor's feedback indicated that my paper did not have a logical conclusion but "just ended with some stories." I felt emotionally crushed and I cried because the "ending with just some stories" were the stories of my workshop participants' experiences and my own transformation using theory and practice I had learned at the graduate school. I had put my whole heart and experience into a creative presentation of the content of the paper but the faculty response was a request for a traditional format with little comment on the content. The paper could not receive a passing grade without the revision. As my shock turned to anger, I spilled out the entire story framed in the emotions of my unfulfilled expectations to the women's group online. E-mail responses from group members ranged from

(continued)

understanding and supportive ("The feedback is quite good. The faculty is only asking you to write a conclusion.") to one member's challenge to take another look at my reaction ("What is your reaction saying about YOU?"). Because our group of women has built trust around the salient identity feature of our experiences as women in a doctoral program, the following comment helped me to recognize that my original perspective was from an internalized dominant voice telling me that my creative, "feeling" approach to the paper was not sufficient, and not acceptable. "The feedback you received from the faculty in no way diminishes you. It is not even about you. The responses are based on a historical process that has been used and abused." Now I realized that the faculty did not know how to respond to me because my approach was not part of their traditional way of knowing in the world, so they had responded from the historically learned bias. I began to feel a strong belief and confidence in my own way of knowing. This belief centered my thinking, allowing me to prepare a non-emotional reply to the faculty feedback. I revised the paper in the traditional format

the faculty would appreciate, submitted it a week later, and it was immediately passed. The process of support and challenge allowed me to work through the process at a much deeper level and brought me to a more appropriate response for my own growth.

Together, this group of women is also poised to begin to make changes in the larger institutional setting through their modeling of support for each other and the strength of their collective voices, as well as their individual voices strengthened by their collective one. As the depth of their connection continues to grow, so does the potential for their own individual transformations, a transformational process that is unlikely to have occurred to the same depth and breadth without the experience of this group of women. This transformation process becomes visible in their social identity by the enhanced confidence in their intellectual abilities, their ability to recognize when systems of oppression are at work, in access to information and feedback to their work and methods of research, and their reduced susceptibility to the norms and values often enacted by the dominant group.

SELF-CATEGORIZING GROUPS AND INDIVIDUAL TRANSFORMATION

Individuals who have used self-categorizing groups as a vehicle for reestablishing authentic social identity can serve a valuable function by recursively bringing strategies for transformation of the dominant group to become more inclusive of different norms and beliefs. This happens only through individual transformation and regaining one's authentic social identity. Transformation occurs through contemplative insight coupled with dialogue resulting in the participant becoming aware that her experience is authentic because it is "vitally connected to her own inner history, and only incidentally triggered by an outside facilitator" (Boyd & Myers, 1988, p. 277). When this authentic self emerges, it allows one the strength to potentially return to the larger group as a change agent. The implications for social change are that the redefinition described outside of the original group will lead one to be in a conflict situation when one reenters and engages in efforts to change the social context in ways that will support that new identity. The other alternatives are to leave the group or go back to the former way of being. The reality, then, may be that to return to the oppressive group as a social change agent is the ideal situation. One alternative way of acting after returning to the main group is to create self-categorizing groups from within the larger group in hopes of changing the dynamics of the group. The other reality is that one may not always be able to return. Either way, the self-categorizing group often allows one the ability to make that choice more effectively.

INTERVENTION OPPORTUNITIES

The helping practitioner's role is to help the client recognize the need for a self-categorizing group and to help find or create such a group as well as for the helping practitioner to recognize the self-categorizing group's value in general. The practitioner may also help the client become aware of any current group activities in which she may already be functioning in a reconstruction of social identity. The intervention will be both at the therapist level to help the client raise her awareness of the need for a self-categorizing group and for the client "to be heard" by participating in the self-categorizing group.

Membership in self-categorizing groups does not have to be a permanent proposition to have affect and benefit in reconstructing identity. For example, large group training sessions may be well served by breaking into such self-categorizing groups within the training. This type of breakout is often called *caucuses*. The National Coalition Training Institute uses them as opportunities for a variety of social categories such as black women, blacks, white men, Asians, and professional people to share with the larger group what they never want said, thought, or done to their group again. This process gives voice to the pain, unexpressed anger, and the courage to speak out to the larger group. Most participants agree about the empowering nature this experience has for them. Mindell (1995) observes that resolutions sometimes occur after a break in large group work because smaller group interaction has occurred. He surmises that, in the small group, people experience a safe place to know themselves and how the problems being discussed at the center of the large group are related to themselves.

Self-categorizing groups may be found or developed within the community, workplace, or online. They may be formal, such as professional associations, or informal, such as a group of women or people of color from the same workplace or school. Self-categorizing groups may have only a few members or hundreds. There are no specific parameters for makeup; it is more the process of reconstructing one's social identity that distinguishes them. The advancement in technology has made the formation of these groups easier. For example, online groups are a major method for discussion of salient issues for dispersed members living in isolated cross-cultural settings. Whether groups develop from face-to-face interactions or from online initiatives, they are fluid in terms of length, number of meetings, and joining or leaving the group. The core members may have strongly bonded over time and shared awareness-raising activities. This atmosphere extends to newcomers who are rapidly gathered into the group. Newcomers generally learn about the group through word-of-mouth networks.

CONCLUSION

Although there are a variety of arrangements that a self-categorizing group may take, there are some underlying guidelines that help ensure that, regardless of their design, the self-categorizing groups create an atmosphere that is conducive for the reconstruction of social identity to occur. Based on methodologies outlined by Mertus, Flowers, and Dutt (1999) for consciousness-raising and action groups, the following guidelines are not ranked in order but must be taken as a whole approach. They are not rules and should be revised or changed depending on the group and design. There may be a formal facilitation process, or some of these aspects will be coordinated by the group informally.

1. *Affirm each individual's experiences:* Provide a receptive situation to describe their own experiences and personal histories that can be used a basis for understanding and learning about one's individual and social identity.
2. *Reduce hierarchical approaches:* Activities and discussion should be inclusive. The group, including facilitators and guest speakers, should sit in a circle.
3. *Create an atmosphere of trust and respect and of language awareness:* Avoid overgeneralizations and stereotypes that distort facts or limit ideas about effecting change. Discourage judgment and correct answer solutions. Encourage everyone to speak (the option to pass should be respected) and listen to others with one person speaking at a time.
4. *Workshop or content development from subjective to objective:* Engage participants personally, then increase the focus to specific issues, moving toward behavioral change, commitment, and action.
5. *Promote participant ownership of the group:* Give the group a voice in discussions about the directions of the workshop—for example, the purpose or goal of the workshop, choice of agenda topics, membership boundaries (fluid or closed), and feedback survey design.
6. *Consider participant diversity:* Consider the experiences and needs of the participants.
7. *Provide an action component:* Encourage motivation toward behavioral change by seeking to connect the workshop to activities in the community. Keep consciousness raising and action separate by reporting action activities before or after the group discussion.

Understanding the value of self-categorizing groups can also be taken to the community and organizational level. Often it is not so much the need to create such groups as it is to help clients not feel threatened by their existence. Often we hear the rhetorical questions about why is there a need for the Black Police Officers Association or Women Architects Association or the Latina beauty pageant. The challenge and the intervention then becomes being an advocate for such opportunities with the understanding of how their existence improves the health of one's identity and self-esteem. Paradoxically, instead of hurting the progress being made with the dismantling of oppression, they actually serve as an opportunity for progress to be made.

Regardless of the value a self-categorizing group can offer to an individual or a community, it is important to note that a self-categorizing group does not end the reality of oppression for people; it only serves to mitigate the internalization of it. Self-categorizing groups need to be viewed as one possible vehicle to help a client cope with and heal from the affects of oppression.

PERSONAL REFLECTIONS

As our reflections on our experiences began to emerge into the reality of our model, we ourselves were empowered to discover how we had power at the margins through our ability to seek out self-categorizing groups. Naming the pattern has given us tremendous strength to cope more effectively with our internalization of oppression. We suspect that the strength of our network within our doctoral program is attributable to our increased understanding of the power of such a self-categorizing group. We also have become more thoughtful and strategic about building in these types of opportunities for self-categorizing groups to emerge or to be sustained within our work both professionally and socially.

Over the past 8 years, Nakamura, in reaction to her experience in her workplace group dynamics, has found shared social identity with community members on gender-related issues through facilitation of a gender-issues discussion group for Japanese women and a cross-cultural discussion group for long-term non-Japanese women residents. She has developed research interests in feminist pedagogy and gender studies, and she has found validation for her beliefs and values as a human being in society. More important, she has found voice and is recognized in the community as a person of value. Nakamura's experience with outside self-categorizing groups, through the reconstruction of her social identity, gave her courage and strategies to return to the university setting and expand the discussion of gender issues. Specifically, she has given a public lecture on gender issues in Japanese as a faculty representative of the university, published articles on gender issues in her university's academic journal, has been instrumental in forming a self-categorizing discussion group of like-minded women faculty, and teaches gender issues in her seminar classes.

Nakamura is also one of the original members of a group of non-Japanese women with Japanese spouses who started a political discussion forum online for the purpose of discussing social and global issues. General rules for discussion include respect for all opinions. Candid discussion of common experiences that relate to gender and cultural bias in the workplace quickly became a common discussion issue. This highly active online discussion has continued into the second year. This is clearly an example of how technology can support the creation of a self-categorizing online group of geographically dispersed participants.

Collins has sought and found similar validation in the community through her work with the Healing Racism Institute and her service on Vision Little Rock's racial and cultural diversity community planning work group. Collins's work with the community Healing Racism Institutes provided her with the courage and voice to initiate the Institute for City Government Employees. This organization questions the structures within city government that perpetuate racism as well as promotes behaviors to break the cycle of racial conditioning.

Collins continues to work in the community with people who are interested in dismantling racism. She is particularly interested in the work that can happen among white people trying to reconstruct their identities to ones that are antiracist, and the value of coming together to support each other in this process. European Dissent is a group that formed in New Orleans as a response to the undoing racism work done by the People's Institute for Survival and Beyond. It is a group of white people who come together to talk about the role they play as white people in the perpetuation of the system of racism and the shifts they can make in their own identities to begin to change that reality. Their process of coming together has raised their voice in speaking out as white people against city policies and procedures that are racist.

KEY CONCEPTS

- social identity
- personal self and collective self
- salience
- self-categorization
- power dynamics
- in-group and out-group
- high-power and low-power group status
- racial, cultural, and gender-identity models
- reconstruction of identity model

QUESTIONS FOR REFLECTION

1. What group experiences have shaped and continue to shape your social identity? In answering this question, you may wish to do a timeline, a collage, or some other pictorial description to augment your written answer.
2. What aspects of your social self have salience for you?
3. Where do you think you would fit within the racial and cultural identity models? Why? What experiences suggest your status to you?
4. Can you think of times when you were a member of a self-categorizing group? Describe that experience. What led you to join or form the group? How does your experience relate to the process outlined by the model of reconstructing identity?
5. What situations currently do you see where the creation or promotion of a self-categorizing group would be valuable? What steps would you need to take to move that potential forward?

EXERCISE

Think of two clients you are currently helping, one male and one female. What salient social characteristics (gender, ethnic, culture, class) are impinging on the problem they need help with? With what groups is each person involved that might be negatively influencing their social identities through their low-status positions? You do not need to think only in terms of small groups but also community, social, and societal groups. Are either or both of these people already using a self-categorizing groups to bolster her or his identity? If so, can you elicit a story from them about the experience so as to highlight and extend the effects of this positive identity-enhancing factor in their lives? If not, can you think of a self-categorizing group that would help this person? Whether or not you can help in starting such a group with your clients, think with your clients what the effects of having such a group would be like. This process can be used to create images of empowering group situations that could support your client in the subsequent initiation of such a group.

References

Abrams, D., & Hogg, M. (1999). *Social identity and social cognition*. London: Blackwell.

Aronson, E. (1999). *The social animal* (8th ed.). New York: Worth.

Boyd, R., & Myers, J. G. (1988). Transformative education. *International Journal of Lifelong Education, 7*(4), 261–284.

Brewer, M. B., & Gardner, W. L. (1996). Who is this "we"? Levels of collective identity and self representations. *Journal of Personality and Social Psychology, 71*, 83–93.

Brown, R., Hinkle, S., Ely, P. G., Fox-Cardamone, L., Maras, P., & Taylor, L. A. (1992). Recognizing group diversity: Individualist-collectivist and autonomous-relational social orientation and their implications for intergroup processes. *British Journal of Social Psychology, 31*, 327–342.

Butler, S., & Wintram, C. (1995). *Feminist groupwork*. London: Sage.

Cross, W. E., Jr. (1991). *Shades of black: Diversity in African-American identity*. Philadelphia: Temple University Press.

Deaux, K. (2000). Models, meanings and motivations. In D. Capozz & R. Brown (Eds.), *Social identity processes* (pp. 1–14). Thousand Oaks, CA: Sage.

Ellemers, N., Kortekaas, P., & Ouwekerk, J. W. (1999). Self-categorization, commitment to the group and group self-esteem as related but distinct aspects of social identity. *European Journal of Social Psychology, 29*, 371–389.

Fletcher, J. (1999). *Disappearing acts: Gender, power, and relational practice at work*. Cambridge: MIT Press.

Giddens, A., & Pierson, P. (1998). *Conversations with Anthony Giddens*. Palo Alto, CA: Stanford University Press.

Gilbert, P. (1992). *Depression: The evolution of powerlessness*. New York: Guilford Press.

Gilligan, C. (1982). *In a different voice*. Cambridge, MA: Harvard University Press.

Hall, E. T. (1973). *The silent language*. Garden City, NY: Anchor Books.

Hart, M. (1990). Liberation through consciousness raising. In J. Mezirow (Ed.), *Fostering critical reflection in adulthood* (pp. 47–73). San Francisco: Jossey-Bass.

Haslam, S. (2001). *Psychology in organizations: The social identity approach*. London: Sage.

Helms, J. E. (1990). *Black and white racial identity: Theory, research, and practice.* Westport: Praeger.

Helms, J. E. (1999). Another meta-analysis of the white racial identity attitude scale's Cronbach alphas: Implications for validity. *Measurement and Evaluation in Counseling and Development, 32,* 122–137.

Helms, J. E., & Piper, R. E. (1994). Implications of racial identity theory for vocational psychology. *Journal of Vocational Behavior, 44*(2), 124–138.

Hogg, M., & Abrams, D. (1988). *Social identifications: A social psychology of intergroup relations and group processes.* New York: Routledge.

Hogg, M., & Terry, D. (2000). Social contextual influences on attitude-behavior correspondence, attitude change, and persuasion. In D. Terry & M. Hogg (Eds.), *Attitudes, behavior, and social context: The role of norms and group membership* (pp. 1–30). London: Lawrence Erlbaum Associates.

Johnson, D., & Johnson, F. (2000). *Joining together: Group theory and group skills.* Boston: Allyn & Bacon.

Kelly, C., & Breinlinger, S. (1996). *The social psychology of collective action: Identity, injustice and gender.* London: Taylor & Francis.

Klink, A., Mummendey, A., Mielke, R., & Blanz, M. (1997). *A multicomponent approach to group identification: Results from a field student in East Germany.* Unpublished manuscript.

Kondo, D. (1990). *Crafting selves: Power, gender and discourses of identity in a Japanese workplace.* Chicago: University of Chicago Press.

Lindskold, S., & Arnoff, J. (1980). Conciliatory strategies and relative power. *Journal of Experimental Social Psychology, 57,* 165–188.

Mertus, J., Flowers, N., & Dutt, M. (1999). *Local action, global action: Learning about the rights of women and girls.* New York: UNIFEM and the Center for Women's Global Leadership.

Mezirow, J., & Associates. (1990). *Fostering critical reflection in adulthood.* San Francisco: Jossey-Bass.

Miller, J. (1986). *Toward a new psychology of women.* Boston: Beacon Press.

Miller, J., & Stiver, I. (1997). *The healing connection: How women form relationships in therapy and life.* Boston: Beacon Press.

Mindell, A. (1995). *Sitting in the fire: Large group transformation using conflict and diversity.* Portland, OR: Lao Tse Press.

Murninghan, J., & Pillutla, M. (1995). Fairness versus self-interest: Asymmetric moral imperatives in ultimatum bargaining. In R. Kramer & D. Messick (Eds.), *Negotiation as a social process* (pp. 240–267). Thousand Oaks, CA: Sage.

Nakamura, T., Ostu, Y., Taniyama, Y., & Drake, D. (2001). Engendering self-development through women's discussion of gender issues. *Journal of Intercultural Communication, 4,* 147–160.

Oubuchi, K., & Saito, M. (1986). Power imbalance, its legitimacy, and aggression. *Aggressive Behavior, 12,* 33–40.

Prentice, D. A., Miller, D. T., and Lightdale, J. R. (1994). Asymmetries in attachments to groups and to their members: Distinguishing between common-identity and common-bond groups. *Personality and Social Psychology Bulletin, 20,* 484–493.

Sue, D. W., & Sue, D. (1999). *Counseling the culturally different* (3rd ed.). New York: Wiley & Sons.

Tajfel, H. (1970). Experiments in intergroup discrimination. *Scientific American, 223,* 96–102.

Tajfel, H. (1982). *Social identity and intergroup relations.* Cambridge, England: Cambridge University Press.

Tajfel, H., Billig, M., Bundy, R. P., and Flament, C. (1971). Social categorization and intergroup behavior. *European Journal of Social Psychology, 1,* 149–177.

Tajfel, H., & Turner, J. C. (1979). An integrative theory of intergroup conflict. In W. G. Austin & S. Worchel (Eds.), *The social psychology of intergroup relations* (pp. 33–47). Monterey, CA: Brooks/Cole.

Tatum, B. D. (1992). Talking about race, learning about racism: The application of racial identity development theory in the classroom. *Harvard Educational Review,* 62(1), 1–24.

Terry, D., Hogg, M., & White, K. (2000). Attitude-behavior relations: Social identity and group membership. In D. Terry & M. Hogg (Eds.), *Attitudes, behavior, and social context: The role of norms and group membership* (pp. 67–93). London: Lawrence Erlbaum Associates.

Tjosvold, D., & Sagaria, D. (1978). Effects of relative power of cognitive perspective-taking. *Personality and Social Psychology Bulletin, 4,* 256–259.

CHAPTER 13

FACILITATING TELLING OF STORIES THROUGH PSYCHODYNAMIC GROUPS

Traumatized Women in the Former Yugoslavia

DORIS GÖDL
AUSTRIA

OVERVIEW

This chapter describes group work with traumatized women in the former Yugoslavia. The chapter highlights how processes of social transformation, political transition, and disintegration in the former Yugoslavia can be interpreted as collectively experienced historical trauma. This chapter shows the interconnection between a psychodynamic approach to trauma and sociopolitical processes. Psychodynamic theory has much to offer in understanding the development of ethnic identity. It also has much to offer in the elaboration of narratives in situations of emotional crisis leading to increased ability to function and overcome trauma. The chapter will show how the use of psychodynamic theory linked to social processes can be helpful in working with women in situations of trauma caused by war. As an example, the chapter will provide insight into the political and social disintegration processes in the countries of the former Yugoslavia and describe and discuss some of the significant sequences of the group process with an emphasis on dream analysis to facilitate the telling of traumatic stories. The chapter discusses problems of the therapeutic setting that arise in this kind of work, such as changing places during wartime from one meeting to the next, and the results of differences in language and cultural background between the group therapist and members.

SOCIOPOLITICAL CONTEXT AND ETHNIC IDENTITY

The last century was often described as an age of extremes, as a time of violence and barbarism (Hobsbawm, 1995). Political and social instability characterized conflicts in all parts of the world. After 1945, there was a period of relative stability until 1989, when political and socioeconomic changes and upheavals started in the former socialist countries. Some countries such as Hungary, the Czech Republic, and Romania achieved transition in more or less peaceful ways, whereas other countries such as the former Yugoslavia went through a period of war. To understand the political and social context, I will describe the background leading to the disintegration of the Federal Republic of Yugoslavia and its consequent ethnic group identity.

The death of President Josip Broz Tito in 1980 meant the disappearance of the last figure who symbolized the unity of Yugoslavia and started the process of nationalism that replaced the vanishing power of Marxist ideology. A concrete expression of this nationalization is to be found in a memorandum circulated in 1986 by the Belgrade Academy of Sciences in which intellectuals and scholars call for the Serbian people to play the leading role in the economy, politics, and culture. Veteran party cadres—such as Slobodan Milosevic in Serbia and Franjo Tudjman in Croatia—attempted to secure political power with a turn toward ethnic nationalism. This became manifest in 1987 as Milosevic, who had in the meantime risen to the position of secretary of the Communist Party, paid a visit to the Serbian minority in the province of Kosovo and expressed support for the minority's nationalistically tinged demands. When he was elected president of Yugoslavia, the spokespersons of several foreign governments (such as the United States, England, and France) were talking of "a new Tito" who would preserve the unity of Yugoslavia (Ramiz, 2000). Despite all pledges of unity, the secession efforts of certain individual regions such as Slovenia and Kosovo began in 1989. In the meantime, in Croatia, Tudjman and his Nationalist Croatian Party had assumed power. And so the socialist and multiethnic Federal Republic of Yugoslavia began to disintegrate into separate ethnically based individual states through a series of wars in the early 1990s—in 1991 in Slovenia and Croatia, in 1992–1995 in Bosnia and Herzegovina, and in the Federal Republic of Yugoslavia (Serbia and Montenegro) with the still unresolved status of Kosovo.

These ethnically based states that emerged actually had a long-shared but denied mutual history. Dissimilarity and diversity were emphasized, and shared memories of the past—particularly those from the two world wars—were systematically repressed, reconceptualized, and enlisted in the service of politics.[1]

Why did the construction of an individual ethnic identity become so important? Psychodynamic theory has much to offer in understanding the processes involved in the emergence of ethnic identity. The "narcissism of small differences" described by Sigmund Freud makes possible a better understanding of the principles of maintaining one's "non-sameness" and the associated gulf between the

---

[1]Compare this with the "policy of dealing with the past" practiced after World War II in Germany and Austria.

individual groups. In his 1917 essay "The Taboo of Virginity," Freud wrote, "[E]very individual sets himself off from others by means of a 'taboo of personal isolation,' and that it is precisely the small differences among what is otherwise similarity that serve as the basis of feelings of alienation and enmity" (Freud, 1917, p. 169). In his essay "The Uneasiness in Culture," Freud expands on this approach by going into the so-called small differences in politics:

> Once, I investigated the phenomenon whereby it is precisely neighboring and otherwise closely related communities that carry on feuds and mock one another I named this "narcissism of the small difference," which did not contribute much to an explanation. One can now recognize in this a convenient and relatively harmless way to satisfy the tendency towards aggression, by which coexistence is made easier for members of society. (Freud, 1948, p. 473)

With this, attention is turned to the relation between the "narcissism of the small difference" and aggression: Precisely because the differences are too small, they must often be expressed in an aggressive way.[2] In other words, "The nationalist chooses the 'small differences'—that are, as such, neutral—and transforms them into big differences" (Ignatieff, 2000, p. 67). In times of peace, these fine distinctions or borders can become greatly blurred because people construe their identity more in connection with their individuality and less with respect to their membership in an ethnic group. However, if this condition described as "peaceful" changes, then the feeling of "being different" wins out over that of "recognizing similarities in others." "It is not the feeling of radical difference that leads to conflicts with others, but rather the refusal to acknowledge others. Even before violence is done to others, violence must be done to oneself by destroying the living fabric of connectedness and mutual recognition" (Ignatieff, 2000).

Yugoslavia after Tito's death was characterized by two overlapping developments. While, in the early 1980s, the Communist system got into increasingly dire straits because of social, economic, and political factors and feelings of uncertainty and a lack of orientation became widespread, nationalistic ideologues exploited the vacuum that emerged, thereby offering their ideologies as a "safe port in the storm." This did not essentially mean a radical change; rather, one totalitarian ideology was exchanged for another. The population, which had adjusted to this sort of political maneuvering, was a mere plaything in the conflict between those in positions of political and ideological power whereby nationalistic concepts and programs to establish national truths occupied the spotlight. Thus, the political catastrophe was already looming on the horizon—instead of democratic forces joining together in solidarity, there was a breakdown of solidarity along national lines.

---

[2]For example, the subtle differences between the Croatian and Serbian languages took on added significance during times of political crisis. Thus, T. Butler (1993) quoted a Croatian woman who insisted in an interview that the Croatian language was superior to Serbian because of its greater musicality. In other words, identity questions are associated with minute differences (see Butler, 1993, pp. 120ff).

TRAUMA IN POLITICAL CONTEXT

In recent years, the terms *trauma* and *traumatization* have been often used in connection with domestic violence against women and children. When the war in the former Yugoslavia broke out, we were confronted with politically induced violence against women and children. "Armed conflicts often mean loss of livelihood, abuse, and rape. Rape and sexual abuse is frequently used as a tool of military strategy" (Schott, 1997, p. 53). Rape is used to destroy individual people who belong to a national, political, or cultural groups to destroy their group identity and to decimate cultural and social bonds (Card, 1997, p. 33). When women are forced for political reasons of terror and war to undergo traumatic events such as rape and violence, these occur in especially aversive conditions. In many cases, there are no preparations, and these circumstances are experienced as catastrophic. There are feelings of overpowering helplessness. In this context, some women survivors experienced rape by people who had previously been neighbors. The psychic consequences of the disruption of social bonds go along with a loss of confidence and trust in other people. Some therapists use the term *extreme traumatization* for this kind of destruction of personal and social connectedness. In this context, the experiences of war and terror could be seen as central assault on the dignity of men and women leading to a loss of confidence in the world.

Politically induced violence has rarely entered into the clinical debates on trauma and traumatization. In the use of the term *posttraumatic stress disorder* (PTSD), there is increasing lack of differentiation of the term within the professional discourse. The professional literature on PTSD deals mainly with the consequences of traumatic events and less with the causes of the trauma. As Becker noted, in such cases "either the fates of the individuals became the focus of attention, which will lead to a neglect of the political context, or we will focus on the political circumstances and will lose the suffering individuals out of our sight" (Becker, 2000, p. 29). Psychodynamic theory about trauma and traumatization can help us bridge the gap between the personal and the political with regard to trauma.

Laplanche and Pontalis (1980) are French psychoanalysts who describe trauma as

> an event in the life of an individual that is defined through its intensity, the inability of the individual to react in a adequate way to it, and the shock and the long-term pathogenic effects to which it gives rise in the psychic organization. In relation to the tolerance of the psyche if the stimulus is excessive, whether this is a matter of a single intense event or an accumulation of stimuli, trauma will have occurred. (p. 513)

This approach will be augmented with the term *extreme situation* developed by Bruno Bettelheim, who himself experienced political traumatization during imprisonment in a concentration camp. With this term, Bettelheim describes a situation in which "nothing about it was predictable, the lives of those affected were in constant jeopardy, and they couldn't do anything about it. This experience was so extraordinary that I needed a new term to describe it. I selected the term 'extreme situation'" (Bettelheim, 1977, p. 613).

Masud Khan (1977) also proposed the idea of *cumulative trauma* in which

a trauma can therefore develop from a sequence of experiences that are in and of themselves not traumatic but which develop and intensify in an interactional framework, and finally lead to a breakdown. These considerations are especially important because they very clearly shift the focal point from the trauma to the traumatic situation. Thus, the view is turned from the event to the process without failing to acknowledge the significance of external influences. (Cited in Becker, 1992, p. 130)

Keilson (1979) shows that

a cumulative traumatization can lead to a chronic trauma in every case in which social-political processes of persecution and oppression constitute the content of the traumatic situation. He shows clearly that the traumatization can go on even when the persecution has already finished. (Cited in Becker, 1992, p. 132)

Extreme traumatization is a term used by some Latin American therapists (e.g., Becker) who worked mainly with victims of torture and political violence. "This type of traumatization is marked by a certain way of carrying out power in a society, meaning that the sociopolitical structure of society is based on the destruction and wiping out of some members of this society through other members of the same society" (Becker, 2000, p. 37). Inventing the term *Situationsdiagnostik* ("diagnosis of the situation"), Becker connected the individual traumatic experience with the political circumstances that give rise to traumatic events. Doing so, Becker avoided giving attention not only to the individual (giving the diagnosis PTSD) but also to the political context. When the team of David Becker was working with victims of torture in Chile (through Centro de Investigación y Tratamiento del Stress, or CINTRAS), the therapists tried to make their clients understand that the traumatic event wasn't a personal failure but had to do with the violated political circumstances. Taking this approach seriously, it was necessary to bring the connection between the individual and the political into the therapeutic treatment.

CASE MATERIAL: GROUPWORK WITH TRAUMATIZED WOMEN

Between 1994 and 1997, I worked with a group of women who were highly diverse with respect to profession, social background, ethnic origins, and nationality. All were actively involved in establishing and running women's projects for the advancement of democracy in Zagreb, Croatia, and its vicinity. At this time, the group consisted of eight women who were reading psychodynamic literature about "working with traumatized women" to help themselves in their practical work. Some of the members had already some experiences with "helping teams" from other countries (with different therapeutic approaches) but weren't content with this kind of work because these teams came only for a few days. The group came to the conclusion that they needed someone who would work continuously with them. Because there was no "psychodynamic culture" in Croatia, they looked for some psychodynamic trained therapists from Germany and Austria.

When I met the group for the first time in Zagreb, we discussed the members' expectations on the groupwork and also what I could give them.

I started with the work in spring 1995 and traveled to Zagreb every 2 months for 2 days. Each summer, we met for a week—mostly outside of Zagreb—to improve the therapeutic and educational process. I saw my work as connected to the democratic movement all over the country and declared my solidarity with the antiwar movement that had been started mainly by women. This movement traversed strong nationalistic and ethnic boundaries and therefore saw itself as a basic democratic movement (e.g., Women's Solidarity Network Against War, Women in Black). Out of this movement, some women's groups started to establish different women's projects focusing on war and traumatization in different parts of the former Yugoslavia (Croatia, Bosnia, and also Serbia). The work in these projects was financed by Western countries and therefore gained a great deal of freedom and independence, which provided much help and positive input to the political as well as the social and psychological rehabilitation of women and children.

From the start, I faced the problem of "naming," which demanded that, through language, I take a political position I was not willing to take. With the processes of disintegration from the heterogeneity of the Federal Republic of Yugoslavia to the newborn nations, the use of the name *Yugoslavia* (this was the usual term for the whole country before the war) became problematized. In a period of such insecurity I couldn't call the newborn nations by their names because that meant an acceptance of their ethnic goals. On the other hand, I could not use the term *Yugoslavia* because that was a rejection of the ethnic identity of the new states. I decided to use the term "former Yugoslavia." Using this term, I describe an area that still exists but whose territories no longer belong to one state.

Other issues came up that I needed to address, such as: How do I enter a country that seems strange to me? Benz (1997) lists questions that relate to what he calls the "cultural dramaturgy" of the country: Who was fighting for what reasons against whom? Who was following the nationalist propaganda and who was not? Who wanted to bring ethnicity to the public's awareness and to whose benefit? In realizing that I did not have answers, my feelings of insecurity and strangeness only increased.

As psychodynamic theory teaches, I tried not to avoid or suppress these feelings as I looked for clarification in the field of ethnopsychoanalysis. Dealing with the understanding of foreign cultures, psychoanalysts such as Goldy Parin-Matthey, Paul Parin-Matthey, Fritz Morgenthaler, and Tobias Nathan focused the relationship between culture and psychotherapy through the lens of the therapeutic relationship. Focusing on this kind of relationship, they showed that it is possible to adapt the therapeutic setting to the cultural circumstances.[3] I was concerned not to become one of the many "invasive helpers" from all over the world. "First they invade us with troops and military and afterwards they

---

[3]From their experiences in Africa, the authors showed how to conduct psychodynamic talking in public (such as under the village tree). Passersby or other curious people will, along the needs of the patient, be included in the talking. See Parin, Parin-Matthey, & Morgenthaler, 1981.

invade us with the helping teams," stated one member of the group. Therefore it was necessary to be aware that I was working with two different cultures and that there was no superior one. Getting in touch with the work of the ethnopsychoanalysts helped me to understand my work.

A women's association in Germany was willing to pay for my travel costs as well as the costs of translation. I saw my going there as an act of solidarity with the democratic movement and as a support for these women. As for language, I was not fluent in Serbo-Croatian, so I was working with translators. This became a problem over time because, after working continuously with one translator for a year, the subsequent translators frequently changed. The first translator, besides possessing good language skills, was also well trained in psychoanalysis, which helped a lot in the work. The translators who followed did not have basic psychodynamic knowledge and therefore had to have the basic psychodynamical method explained to them. In psychodynamic practices, every word and sentence said in the group is of importance. In this, psychodynamic work shared much with narrative practices, which focus on the language of the client and the way they express their feelings, ideas, and needs. Translators often give summaries of the spoken material and judge what they heard. This made the work more difficult and strenuous. It was necessary to repeat the working instructions again and again so that often I almost lost my temper. I needed to focus all of my energy to keep myself calm.

Another problem was of the ever-changing places for working. The first meetings were held under the circumstances of war, and it was not always clear where they could find a safe working place. So we moved from one place to another. Under these circumstances, I realized that I needed to adapt the therapeutic setting to the existing possibilities. Before going to work in the former Yugoslavia I was used to the setting in my private practice at home, which means fixed appointments, working with the patient who is laying on the "couch" or in a sitting position on the chair. For this I was trained in "psychodynamical abstinence," which means that the therapist should not bring him- or herself into the therapeutic relationship so that the patient could use him or her as a mirror. With "psychoanalysis in my suitcase," I had to leave some main points and issues of the traditional work setting and develop standards that went with the new situation.

I had mixed feelings when I considered the journey on which I was about to embark and the ensuing work with women. Fear, curiosity, and a certain sense of being about to experience something extraordinary accompanied me before and during the train trip to Zagreb. Looking out at the landscape rushing by triggered feelings of irritation; everything seemed so normal—a line full of laundry fluttering in the wind, people sitting in front of houses, kids playing on fields. The thought that a war was going on clashed with my observations.

I arrived in Zagreb. The downtown train station gave me the feeling of having traveled back in time to the days of the Habsburg monarchy. The marble slabs on the platform and the design of the colossal terminal lobby more closely resembled the décor of an aristocratic ballroom than that of a train station. Mira, a woman from the group who speaks German and English, was there to meet me, and her accounts of everyday political life quickly brought me back to reality. We went for a walk in downtown Zagreb, and I was astounded by the people I saw drinking, laughing, and dancing on the squares of the old city. It was absolutely bustling with activity, even beyond what I was used to in busy Salzburg. Mira described this existential feeling as "very lively" and explained to me that it was connected to the war. Because great uncertainty prevailed about how the war would turn out, many people were trying to "live life to the max" while there was still time. I was amazed by this "agitated liveliness," but I was unable to reconcile it with my images of war. This high-spirited, almost hysterical activity seemed forced or put on to me. Becker (1992) believes that, in such situations, the superimposed liveliness serves to keep depression at bay. This was a phenomenon that I would encounter again later in my group work.

THE USE OF PSYCHODYNAMIC GROUP METHODS FOR TRAUMA AS A RESULT OF POLITICAL UPHEAVAL

In the situation of war, people are not prepared for the experiences of violence and destruction. Therefore, they experienced this overwhelming violence with helplessness and without mechanisms of defense. Concerning the group, most women were confronted with experiences of personal loss, escape, and hiding. Furthermore, in their work they had to deal with the results of war crimes such as rape and other atrocities. All the women in the group were working in different nongovernmental organization projects or in various antiwar collectives.

Working in collectives that are in opposition to nationalistic politics means an alleviation of individual isolation in favor of the group collective. This is profoundly against the aims of a totalitarian system, which wants people in social and political isolation.[4] Establishing a group brought the women a certain awareness of being connected to each other, even though they were different (from age, their status of life, their profession, and their origins from different parts of the country). It is possible to think about an unconscious wish to be with other people on whom one could rely and trust. Seeing my work as a long process to bring these unconscious wishes and feelings to consciousness, I will use the following narratives to show the process from the individual to the collective.

From the beginning, I stated that they had to keep themselves to our arranged time schedule. This last point is considered crucial in psychodynamic work. Keeping the setting steady and consistent is viewed in this approach as necessary to create enough safety and stability for accessing traumatic feelings and memories. However, cultural differences between my professional beliefs and their own attitude to time created big differences between us in the handling of time schedules. The women were not really aware of time: They came late or tried to rearrange our fixed schedules along their needs (for cigarettes, coffee, etc.).

---

[4]This isolation can be seen in the concentration on one's own family and avoiding other contacts during times of totalitarian politics.

Even though I was a little bit experienced with this behavior from previous journeys to Nicaragua, I couldn't avoid feelings of impatience and anger. Although I did not impose my own professional discourse about setting, I was aware of the tension between us and attempted to understand their use of time and setting as a function of their own turbulent feelings. This idea will be explored further in the case studies.

METHODS

Free Association

One major tool for group work in this model is to allow the women to *free associate*—that is, to talk about everything that comes into their minds while listening to each other's narratives and following the process. The method of free association needs time to develop, and this depends on the group process. Increasing feelings of confidence and trust in each other and in me as their therapist led to an extended ability to generate free associations. It is possible to gain access to the unconscious mind when this level of trust is achieved.

Transference and Countertransference

Transference describes a process in which the unconscious wishes, fantasies, and thoughts from the (recent) past come up to the surface of consciousness. Talking about the suppressed emotional side of the past allows an actual experiencing of these feelings. Strongly connected with transference is *countertransference,* or the emotional response of the therapist to the transference. I started to use my countertransference reactions as a sort of "navigator" through the working process. As a following step, it is necessary to connect transference and countertransference. This will be done in the interpretation.

Dream Interpretation

In this chapter, I focus on dream interpretation as one example of the use of interpretation. In my work with the group, we used many other types of interpretation at different points in the process. The meaning of dreams helps us understand transference and countertransference. Sigmund Freud wrote that the dream is the "Via regia to the unconsciousness" (1942, p. 613), and I think it is important to focus on this point because he shows the character of the process and therefore different meanings and aspects of dreams. With this knowledge in the back of my mind, I was telling the group members to associate as freely as possible with their different dream narratives. Doing so, I wanted to get near the unconscious material in the group such as suppressed fantasies and wishes. In the background of the working process, I was interpreting the dream material in connection with the upcoming free associations, which lead to understanding the unconscious backgrounds of the dreams. In the work with this group, an attempt was consistently made to locate interpretations of their

| CASE 13.1 | E S M A |

At the outset of my work with the group, Esma, a frail-looking woman who had fled with her two daughters from Bosnia to Zagreb, related the following dream to me. She and her daughters were sitting in a bus full of passengers, riding from her hometown (where her parents lived) to the town where she had lived for the last 20 years. Suddenly, the bus halted before a frozen ravine and the passengers had to walk across the ice to continue on their journey. Despite her fear, she tried to walk across the ice. Then she came to a tunnel, which she could get through only by crawling. The further she got inside the tunnel, the greater her fear became and the torrent of water that accompanied her progress became stronger. Then she realized that she had lost her children. With a cry of terror, she awoke.

The women's associations with this dream initially concentrated on the bus trip, which was seen as a way of fleeing. Esma agreed with this interpretation but did not want to go into it any further. Then the images of the frozen ravine and traversing the tunnel were shifted to the center of attention. Over time, I was able to interpret the image of the ice as "frozen grief," which I regarded at this point as mourning for that which had been lost—the place where she had spent her childhood. The women's associations began to revolve around what they themselves had lost—

family, friends, homeland, and a sense of belonging. Feelings that Esma was unable to speak about were taken up by the group, so I interpreted these feelings as showing grief and fear. This act of calling these feelings by name provoked a degree of uneasiness among the women—after all, what would happen when the rejected feelings were openly acknowledged?

According to the entirely justified sense of anxiety in the group, couldn't this lead to an impairment of these women's ability to cope with everyday life? In light of the war and the daily violence that goes with it, these women's fear is not to be regarded as a neurotic process of dealing with conflict but rather as an appropriate reaction to a daily threat. In my interpretation, I tried to show that the upcoming feelings of anxiety and fear were not personal problems but had to do with daily threats in times of war. Therefore, it was important to show that their feelings were "normal" emotional reactions in a not normal time and that they were not crazy to have these feelings. Speaking loudly about this emotional status meant also to work against the political propaganda that legitimated only positive feelings such as power, strength, and victory, while disallowing feelings of fear, mistrust, and doubt. Giving a respectful place to these suppressed emotions and meanings is a form of protest to the ruling ideology of war. In this way, we can link individual psychological work being done through the release of suppressed feelings. They can be linked as well to an oppressive sociopolitical situation.

---

dreams in their own traumatic recent past experiences in the war. In this way, a bridge was created between the individual's unconscious and the external social and political unrest in their countries.

The "Containing Function" of the Group

In my description of trauma and the consequences of traumatization, I tried to show that traumatic experience disrupts personal and social connectedness and confidence. The consequences of these disruption processes are seen in a loss of meaning in the world. This means that the traumatic experience cannot be "contained" in personal and social life. With different mechanisms of defense (such as *disavowal* or *repression*[5]), the individuals try to avoid coming into touch

---

[5]Here *disavowal* means the refusal to recognize the reality of a traumatic experience or traumatic event. With *repression,* the individual tries to keep the feelings and emotions that come along with the traumatic experience in the unconsciousness.

CASE 13.2 | BOJANA

Bojana, a slim woman with highly expressive facial features, also presented herself through a dream. She told of how the cottage in which she lived with her boyfriend was destroyed, and she had to move away. On the way, she encountered a girlfriend from intermediate school who had since married and had two children. This girlfriend complained about her marriage and seemed to be unhappy. Bojana then went back to her house, but the owner told her that she wasn't allowed to return there anymore. After that, she drove off in a red car but left her boyfriend behind.

The theme of this dream also deals with that which was lost (a girlfriend from school) and the destruction associated with it. Whereas prevailing circumstances forced Esma to leave her homeland and the act of fleeing is the crucial experience, Bojana wishes to escape the destruction by climbing into a red auto—that is, one with an eye-catching color—driving away and thus turning her back on what was destroyed.

This narrative caused great unrest among the women. They no longer wanted to remain seated and work; instead, they needed to take a break. "It's time for a smoke," one woman said; another, cigarette already in hand, agreed. I, however, came out adamantly in favor maintaining the setting and attempted to articulate the feelings of uneasiness that had arisen. Doing so, I tried to bridge the dream narrative and the upcoming unrest in the group, which was shown in the wish to break the given time schedule of our sessions. I thought about the unconscious feelings below this acting, and I asked the group, what was so dangerous that they wanted to leave the session?

I got the impression that telling the dream created an emotionally intensified group process to the theme of loss, which had obviously provoked tension and fear on the part of the women. Unable to speak about this, they attempted to do what Bojana had done in her dream—to counter the tension that had arisen and the feelings of anxiety associated with it by fleeing from the group setting. When I indicated—that is, verbalized—my perceptions of the group's feelings, the unrest and tension indeed subsided a bit, but a

certain gloominess, which I would characterize as a sort of melancholy, still remained and was even more palpable.

The next morning, there was tension in the air. The women seemed concerned and uneasy. The morning coffee ritual dissipated this nervousness to some extent, but when Bojana had still not shown up a half hour past the agreed-upon starting time, the unrest within the group increased. The women in the group waited rather anxiously for the arrival of their missing member. I had the fleeting fear that she had driven off in that "red car" and abandoned the group and her work in the Center for War Victims! Still waiting for her, I found Bojana's behavior quite aggressive. I was asking myself if my anger could be connected with the different cultural handling of time or could her delay also be seen as an unconscious aggressive act against the group and me as the therapist? Still thinking about the latter and just as the mood became touch and go, she appeared without any apology for showing up late, and we could finally get started. I wanted to address Bojana's late arrival right at the outset of this session and vent my anger about her conduct, but then I sensed a certain diffuse anxiety that my aggression could possibly have some destructive consequences. Following my countertransference feelings, I asked myself what kept me back from addressing the Bojana's behavior. In addition to anger, I also felt some fear. Using my imagination and fantasies, I realized that I had connected my feeling of anger to a fear of destroying the group. At this point, I felt myself insecure about this, and I couldn't frame my feelings. Therefore I kept them in mind and was looking forward to bringing them up whenever appropriate in connection with the group process. I attempted to sound out the feelings of the group rather than relate to my own countertransference feelings. In psychodynamic theory, the assumption is that my feelings might well reflect the group's concerns in a "parallel process" that could be of use to them. As a psychodynamically oriented therapist, I had learned to allow my fantasies to come up in my mind, to pay attention to them, and to use them at a point when they might help the group members reflect on themselves.

According to the theory, it is not surprising that there indeed was a connection between what I was feeling and what they were feeling. It was not anger but rather fear that predominated among individual women. As we began to work on this fear, we first succeeded in uncovering its "source": The women feared that, as a result of Bojana's "dreamed departure," the existence of the entire group could be placed in jeopardy, which would be tantamount to the group's destruction. I was able to recognize in this the fear of destroying something that I myself had experienced earlier that morning.

I still wondered about why I had experienced such intense countertransference feelings. I had obviously gotten into a situation that David Becker (1996) described as the "trap of trauma therapists." The essential aspect of this trap is that the work with traumatized individuals "does not succeed in attaining clarity either in a direct therapeutic sense or within the context of a broader political analysis, to say nothing of linking the two with each other" (Becker, 1996). But why did I allow myself to be "seduced" or led into ignoring the external reality of war? Why did the traumatic components of this behavior—the union of the external real dangers with the internally fantasized aggressiveness and destructiveness—not become obvious to me right from the start? I became aware that I had entered into the "defensive" organization of the group. I, too, had become *afraid of destruction,* something that was foreign to my own experience but familiar to them. Recognizing countertransference is especially important when working with a group whose members are quite different from the therapist, either in culture or in the experiences they have undergone. When recognized as the group's feelings and not those of the therapist, they can be used to help the group move forward. If not recognized as such, the helper is in danger of replicating unhelpful defenses such as the anesthetizing of feelings.

The usual ritual was repeated the next morning, but the mood was different than that of the previous day—somehow merrier and more sociable. When I arrived, the women were already seated around the table, and there was a great deal of laughing and whispering. The impression they made on me was of pubescent girls trying to keep a secret from their mother. When I inquired into their behavior, they revealed the object of their laughter—Slavenka had received as a birthday present from her girlfriend a lipstick in the shape of a penis. She had demonstrated it to the group just before my arrival, which is what had led to the merriment. When I joined the group, the lipstick was hidden away but the giggling continued. But having had my curiosity whetted in this way, I wanted to see the lipstick, too, whereupon it was produced with a degree of embarrassment and then placed in the middle of the table around which we were seated. And that's where it stood the whole day—the table was set with coffee cups and then cleared, the ashtray was emptied, but the lipstick-penis remained "erect." This scene amused me, and I really enjoyed the women's girlish playfulness. At that moment, such a heavy weight seemed to have been removed from the group, and this made room for a certain lightness. With this, the defensive mechanism of insensateness—also described as the "anesthesia of the feelings"—was broken through, and "laughing about it" could be interpreted as the reaction that materialized in response to it.

This sequence of events ended the weekend's work. The group then invited me to join in a visit to a café on one of the most charming of the narrow little streets in Zagreb's old city. This was the first time that the group members didn't go their separate ways after the session, and they also asked me to come along. Because the language barrier made further substantive encounters impossible, I simply enjoyed the setting, listened to their voices, and let the events of the last 2 days pass in review.

---

with the feelings that come along with the process of experiencing the trauma. In lifting these defense mechanisms, it is also necessary to contain the resultant feelings that are released. Establishing satisfying and trusting relationships during the working process, the group became a "container," holding not only all of the hidden and suppressed stories, feelings, and emotions but also allowing the women to reconnect with each other. Therefore, the therapeutic process

| LEPA

Lepa, a young woman with an open face and warm eyes, dreamt she was in Zagreb. The sky above the city was dark and tinged with red, and an air raid siren was howling. She wanted to pick up her son, who was staying with her parents, even though it seemed dangerous to her. She hesitated because of the air raid warning, but in spite of it she boarded the bus. Inside of it, there was a great commotion. The siren sounded over and over again, which made the mood even more hectic. Then she saw her sister standing at a bus stop, and she wanted to get out to warn her sister to go to an air raid shelter. Even though the bus driver didn't stop, she tried to force her way out of the bus. At this point, she was seized by panic because she couldn't warn or save her sister. Thereafter, she was filled with self-reproach and felt like a bad person. These thoughts released such tremendous energy within her that she demanded that the bus driver stop the bus and open the doors. When he refused to comply, she summoned all her strength, forced the doors open, and jumped from the bus. At this point, the bus driver stopped the bus and began to run after her. She ran into a park in the vicinity of the school she had previously attended; she ran faster and faster. Finally, she reached the high-rise in which her parents lived and went to the doorman in order to alert her parents that she was already in the building and would be up in the apartment in a matter of minutes. But the telephone's rotary dialer spun crazily. She tried it over and over again but couldn't get connected to her parents' apartment. The telephone rotary dialer's repeated malfunctioning is what caused her to wake up. Then she said that she didn't know now whether her parents and her son were still alive.

Both the group and I were completely electrified by this account. The women seemed for a moment to have shaken off their depressive feelings of hopelessness, impotence, and grief, and the underlying feeling of being alive emerged. This temporary alleviation of the oppressive insensateness (anesthesia of the feelings) triggered the release of a veritable flood of narration accompanied by much laughter from the group. In this mood, the women began for the first time to tell their stories from the time of the air raid warnings. For instance, they were driving around in the city in their cars—the headlights turned off—which they claimed

was a pretty weird experience because, as a result of the curfew, they were practically the only ones on the streets. It gave them the feeling that the streets—and even the whole city—belonged to them alone. They also held parties in their blacked-out apartments in an attempt "to get a little bit crazy" in a world that had gone mad, and in this way to feel alive. Whereas the accounts of this "crazy life" covered a wide spectrum, all of the group participants agreed that they had never entered an air raid shelter.

At this point, I remained fixated on the image of the malfunctioning rotary dialer and began to interpret it as a metaphor of the war. In reliance on the work of Hannah Arendt, for whom the worst thing about war was the fact that "one no longer knew who one's friends were" (Arendt 1963), the war could be construed, among this group, as a break in the political, social, and private lines of communication, which could be interpreted as the structural side of the violence of war.

Moreover, the dichotomy of "friend and foe" as described by Hannah Arendt was further underpinned in this conflict by the "ethnification of politics" (Parin, 1998). Whole families were divided along ethnic lines into friends and foes, torn asunder and murdered. In light of the description of the highly complex, multifaceted nature of the violence of warfare—which has only been suggested here—the group became cognizant of how important social contacts are to survive in times of extraordinary peril and destruction. In their everyday lives both at home and in the workplace, these women were confronted with the dreadfulness of war and had to spend a great deal of energy fending off this horror in order to somehow maintain their capacity to work and to experience love.

The group itself can be regarded as a symbol of collective and individual social "survival" in the face of the violence of warfare. As a result of their self-organization, the women in the group alleviated this "crazy malfunctioning" to some extent; through their encounter with themselves and through their work, they created a network of relationships that became—with outside support—ever more tightly interwoven over the course of several years. "The triumph of survival . . . formed the keystone of the defensive arch." This was designed "to prove that [they] had succeeded in not being overwhelmed by the horror and in getting on with life" (Benz, 1997, p. 30).

should enable the individuals to integrate the trauma into their lives and create a renewed connection to the world. This should free them from the role of victims of war and violence.

CONCLUSION

Psychodynamic theory discovers social phenomena in the innermost reaches of the individual psyche and thus always deals with the tension and interplay between internal and external reality. It thus becomes clear that the antagonism between individual and social circumstances, something completely ignored by the conventional discourse concerning trauma and traumatization, is an inherent part of psychodynamic approaches. Unfortunately, psychodynamic theory has not been recognized enough for its contribution to contextual and societal problems. In this chapter, I show that, along with narrative and other therapies, psychodynamic ideas have something to contribute to linking the personal to the political. Psychodynamic thinking has always given a prominent place to the individual's own story. Here I have shown how this thinking links the stories of the people seeking help to the therapists' own experiences and to external world events.

On the basis of my own experience, I would pose the question of what can be said in this connection about the ethnological use of psychodynamic principles. How does one factor in social background in order to be able to understand the unconscious? The truth brought to light in therapeutic work is not only on the individual personal truth of the person seeking help but also contains the cultural experiences involved in individual experience.

This discussion has been revived of late in German-language psychoanalysis, especially in the process of dealing with the victims of Nazi persecution, and augmented by the understanding that in certain sociopolitical contexts reality can be crueler and more violent than fantasies of individual human beings. "Reality can be extreme and more horrible than the worst unconscious fantasies; faced with such a reality, in which the psychotic world suddenly become real, primitive early defense mechanisms can be healthy in that they make survival possible" (Becker & Becker, 1987, p. 290).

Another issue that arose from my work deals with the outsider who comes into an unstable and even chaotic situation. This means that the analysis of countertransference phenomena as I have described them on the basis of case studies assumes special significance. My foreignness as an Austrian has to be transformed into an instrument of understanding and insight. The "intercultural meta-transference" described in the literature (Luc, 1999, p. 36) thus assumes great significance. Both the therapist and the members of the group bring their cultural baggage with them into the therapeutic dialogue. In order for our diversity not to be overshadowed by an emphasis on unconsciously assumed similarities during the working process, I was under supervision throughout the work. This helped me maintain my objectivity and understand how different these women's experiences were than anything I had ever experienced in my own life.

I am fully aware that many questions remain unanswered; nevertheless, it was important to me to fix my attention on the reciprocities between individual suffering and extreme political events and activities. I have attempted to accomplish this by placing the stories of these women and their dreams in their social and political context. The group also constitutes the attempt to alleviate the destructive elements of the traumatic experiences and to transform them into individual and collective autonomy—that is, to reverse somewhat the mentally unbalancing results of war.

Finally, I would like to go briefly into the connection between remembrance and forgetting as consequences of traumatization. The discourse focusing on the past and on the cultural memory connected with it ought to concentrate on a central dilemma: Is the price for establishing political and social stability forgetting and repressing? Or should we go ahead with a process of coming to terms with the past through bringing up repressed memories? The importance of this dilemma is evidenced by the variety of scholarly discussions about "Vergangen-heitspolitik" and "Vergangenheitsbewältigung" after National Socialism in Europe.

From this perspective, we can at least begin to see that the confrontation with the past takes on tremendous significance for the formation of the collective memory and the identity of a society. On the political level, the question that arises in this connection is what consequences the lifting of the ban on reality (for example, the prohibition on mentioning realities such as rape) has on political, social, and cultural concepts and symbols. If a society is making an effort to deal sensitively with remembrance, then it becomes possible to place the consequences of an "unhealable time" into a political context as well as to advance the democratization of political relationships and structures. Facilitating narratives from women about violence and war, I wanted to show the possible effects of trauma and traumatization and ways of coming to terms with them, both with respect to the individual as well as the collective.

KEY CONCEPTS

- ethnological use of psychodynamic principles
- transforming small differences into big differences: political manipulation of ethnic identities
- violence against women (e.g., rape) as a tool for the destruction of ethnic identity
- cumulative trauma in extreme situations
- dialectic between internal and external events
- insensateness and the anesthesia of feelings
- release of feelings and remembering as a form of social protest
- free association

- transference and countertransference
- dream interpretation
- group as a container

QUESTIONS FOR REFLECTION

1. How does a sociopolitical situation develop that emphasizes differences instead of similarities among people?
2. What is the psychodynamic explanation for how individuals continue this situation and oppress others?
3. What are some of the ways that this chapter combined and integrated external sociopolitical factors into individual psychological factors?
4. How did the helper combine these two in her work?
5. How did the helper combine psychodynamic and narrative helping methods in her work?
6. In what situations that you work with would a group experience be a real contribution to your client and why?

EXERCISE

1. Think of a situation in which you experienced some form of oppression. It might be a situation at work, at home, or at school. Tell a story that describes your feelings in this situation.
   a. What contextual factors could counter your freedom to tell this story? In what situations would you be free to tell this story? What situation would not allow the ventilation and expression of feelings attached to this story?
   b. What do you think is a price you might pay for not expressing these feelings?
   c. What might be a hypothetical group context in which these feelings could be expressed?
   d. Hypothetically, what could be the result of expressing these feelings?
2. Now think about a particular client you are working with or have worked with who has suffered from some form of trauma that resulted from an oppressive sociopolitical situation. This can include trauma resulting from being a woman or a particular ethnic group, from class status, or from any other personal characteristic that is targeted as different and that invites discrimination. Tell a story that describes your client's experience.
   a. What contextual factors have countered your client's freedom to tell his or her story?
   b. What price has your client paid for not expressing these feelings?
   c. How has your work facilitated your client's freedom to tell their story and access their feelings about oppression? Is there any way in which the helping situation was a "container" for this client? If so, in what ways?

    d. What countertransference feelings did your client's situation evoke in you and how did you react to these? How might you have used your own countertransference feelings to better help this client?

    e. How could you have used free association and dream interpretation in your work with your client? What might these methods have contributed to your work?

References

Arendt, H. (1963). Talk with Günter Gauss [Videotape]. ARD.

Becker, D. (1992). *There is no reconciliation without hate: The trauma of the victims of political persecution*. Freiburg, Germany: Kore.

Becker, D. (1996). Report about a journey to Zagreb. Unpublished working paper.

Becker, D. (2000). Prüfstempel PTSD—Einwände gegen das herrschende, Trauma-Konzept. In Medico International (Ed.), *Schnelle Eingreiftruppe* (pp. 25–49). Frankfurt: Seele.

Becker, H., & Becker, S. (1987). The psychoanalyst in tension between internal and external reality. *Psyche, XLI*(4), 289–306.

Benz, Andreas (1997). *The survivor*. Hamburg: Europäische Verlagsanstalt.

Bettelheim, B. (1977). *The birth of the self*. Frankfurt: Suhrkamp.

Butler, T. (1993). Yugoslavia mon amour. *Mind and Human Interactions, 4*.

Card, C. (1997). Martial rape. In Wiener Philosophinnen (Ed.), *War: A philosophical analysis on a feminist perspective* (pp. 31–41). Munich: Wilhelm Fink Verlag.

Freud, S. (1917). *The taboo of virginity*. Collected works, Vol. XII (1947). London: Imago.

Freud, S. (1942). *The interpretation of dreams*. Collected Works, Vol. II. London: Imago.

Freud, S. (1948). *The uneasiness in culture*. Collected works, Vol. XIV. London: Imago.

Hobsbawm, E. (1995). *The age of extreme*. Munich: Hanser.

Ignatieff, M. (2000). *The civilization of war*. Hamburg: Rotbuch.

Keilson, T. K. (1979). Cited in D. Becker (1992), *There is no reconciliation without hate: The trauma of the victims of political persecution*. Freiburg, Germany: Kore.

Khan, M. (1977). *Self experience in therapy*. Munich.

Laplanche, J., & Pontalis, J.-B. (1980). *The vocabulary of psychoanalysis*, Vol. 2. Frankfurt: Suhrkamp.

Parin, P. (1998). Ethnification of politics. In E. Modena (Ed.), *Das Faschismus Syndrom* (pp. 100–119). Giessen, Germany: Psychosozial Verlag.

Parin, G., Morgenthaler, F., Parin-Matthey, P. (1981). *White people think too much*. Munich: Kindler.

Ramiz, P. (2000). *Mask for a massacre. Tracing the war in the Balkans*. Munich: Kunstmann.

Rüsen, J., & Straub, J. (1998). *The dark trace of the past*. Frankfurt: Suhrkamp.

Schott, R. M. (1997). Gender and "postmodern war." In Wiener Philosophinnen Club (Ed.), *War: A philosophical analysis on a feminist perspective* (pp. 51–59). Munich: Wilhelm Fink Verlag.

IMMIGRANT WOMEN, ABORTION, AND PREVENTIVE INTERVENTION IN ITALY

MAURO GONZO
VICENZA, ITALY

OVERVIEW

This chapter deals with the relationships between the health worker and the immigrant woman in the context of an interview aimed to assess her request of voluntary abortion. The high frequency of abortion among immigrant women in this region of Italy is examined. The context and attitudes toward abortion are not unique to Italy only. As in other countries health workers are faced with contradictions: On the one hand, culture suggests that abortion should be avoided and prevented; on the other hand, the law also protects the rights of women to free choice on this matter. Despite this particular context, in all countries the health and human service worker often needs to deal with issues related to abortion. This chapter hopefully is an example that will stimulate a discussion about how to find the best paths to face issues around abortion in a culturally sensitive way.

This chapter describes an intervention tool that comes in the form of an assessment interview about abortion. The interview is often a first contact between the health services and the female immigrant population and offers an opportunity for culturally sensitive preventive intervention. The interview is conceptualized as an instrument to collect and introduce information with regard to a system, which is a central idea in systemic family therapy. This interview is conducted using systemic concepts in conjunction with specific attention to intercultural communication, gender difference, and the wider social aspects involved. Thus, the interview—besides being a useful collection of information, becomes also a significant occasion of change for the woman with regard to her couple and family relationships and awareness about her own health.

SYSTEMIC FAMILY THERAPY

From its inception, family therapy, or systemic therapy, has selected public health and social services as particularly suitable spheres of action in which to apply its social and egalitarian values. The systemic approach—with its sharp attention for the social context and relationships—found a fertile soil particularly in Italy, where the laws of the late 1970s established a new welfare system that integrates health and social services and consists of many centers located throughout the country. The public health and social service sector came to represent a context that was especially sensitive to issues concerning the general public and the social changes that took place during that period and later.

In the 1990s, a new social phenomenon occurred in Italy, the rest of Europe, and other developed countries. A wave of immigrants from poor countries in Eastern Europe, Africa, and Asia had the effect of transforming the last culturally homogeneous Western countries—such as Italy—into multiethnic and, in perspective, multicultural societies. This social demographic shift has also led to new issues for the public health and social service system.

The approach modalities of systemic therapists operating within the public-service sector had to be adapted to the new context. From its inception, family therapy in Italy has focused on those relational aspects of family dynamics that had an influence upon the symptomatic individuals and their relative pathogenic effects. From the 1990s, Italian family therapy has placed increasing focus on family problems as they relate to social inequality and power imbalance between the sexes. Currently, the field is concerned with including aspects relative to cultural differences, including ethnic diversity, class differences, race, and sexual orientation.

MIGRATION IN ITALY AND HEALTH SERVICES: THE PROBLEM OF ABORTION

Italy has always been characterized by a significant historical and cultural diversity among its regions, where different dialects or even different languages have been maintained in many areas, as in the cases of German and French in northern Italy or Greek and Sardinian in the south. The presence of these different cultures has nevertheless favored a certain degree of open-mindedness at the intellectual level on the part of family therapists. The attention given to "culture," has always been "inscribed" in the "genetic code" of Italian systemic family therapy, itself born out of the anthropological positions of Gregory Bateson (1972) through the reinterpretation given by Mara Selvini Palazzoli's group in Milan (Boscolo, Cecchin, Hoffman, & Penn, 1987).

Although generally motivated in their approach to their clients by a keen social understanding, public service health workers are not completely ready to deal with the social complexities and difficulties encountered by the patients and their families as a result of their immigration experience. Italy has been influenced as well by the reemergence of ethnic conflicts and new and violent forms of fundamentalism. This has resulted in an unwillingness to accept the diversity also present in other parts of the world as shown by many of the contributions to the present volume.

The West Vicenza district where I work for the local family planning center[1] attracts a large number of immigrants thanks to the job opportunities offered by its thriving tanning industry. Statistical data for Italy and the Veneto region—which makes up the West Vicenza district—indicate that abortion has been decreasing among Italian women (thanks to a highly developed awareness of the problem and an extensive use of contraception) but increasing among immigrant women (Giorio, 1992; Bondi, Neri, & Bonfirraro, 1997; Puzzi, 1998; "Relazione ministero sanità," 2000; Bollettino Ufficiale Regione Veneto, 2002).

The problem caught my attention while working as a psychologist in the public-service sector and giving daily assistance, through counseling and assessment interviews, to a large number of foreign women who came to the center asking for abortions.

Interviews with male and female psychologists are aimed at helping the gynecologist decide whether abortions should be granted. In compliance with current Italian legislative norms, it is the gynecologist who, at the end of the assessment process, must prescribe (or refuse) the hospital operation on the basis of the patient's motivations and also on the basis of the psychologist's evaluation of her psychological state of mind and her situation within the relationship.

In Italy, abortion is allowed within the third month of pregnancy when the woman's psychological and physical health is at risk. The woman has to request and give her consent freely, and she is entitled to have the final decision on the matter. In any case, this decision has to be confirmed and validated by a gynecologist. Italian law further states that it is the specific responsibility of the health worker to try to convince the woman to change her mind and to consider other solutions, but the woman must be allowed to make the final decision. Similarly, Italian law specifies that health workers are to take action to prevent abortion by promoting the use of contraceptives. Italian law, therefore, takes the position that abortion is an option with largely negative ethical, medical, and psychological implications, but it is a legally recognized possibility.[2]

Abortion is, in any case, a painful and dramatic choice that pits the woman's (or the couple's) vital interest and psychological well-being against those of the unborn child—even though these interests are not or should not, in

---

[1] Within the center, a team of health, social workers, and psychologists assists those clients, mainly women, who access the service for issues such as pregnancy, minor gynecological problems, contraception, and general counseling about relationships with partners, adolescent children, family crises, and the like.

[2] This position, which incidentally underlies most Western legislation regarding abortion, is the result of a compromise between two differing factions of society, one favoring the rights and emancipation of women and the other maintaining consistency with ethical and religious values. In Italy, in any event, public opinion is still on the side of defending current legislation, which guarantees a woman's right to free choice, despite attacks on this viewpoint by traditionalists.

normal circumstances, be seen as antagonistic to each other. At any rate, this is the perception of those who, like the author, have a Catholic background that cannot be easily discarded from within the profession. It is nearly universally accepted by the medical profession—and is a position which I, as a health worker, share—that abortion, regardless of any ethical issues that may be raised regarding the unborn child, is a situation to be avoided and prevented, given that it is an improper form of contraception and harmful to the woman—but that the woman must be guaranteed full freedom of choice.

Abortion in immigrant populations is a good example of the clash between traditional values of the specific immigrant cultural group and the wider host society. It is this writer's opinion that even though cultural differences are important and to be respected, health workers have the responsibility to promote the options that modern medicine has to offer. In my opinion, we should make exceptions out of respect for cultural differences when faced with cases such as infibulations or other practices that interfere with the human rights of women. The same could be said for antiquated, invasive medical practices that are pointlessly destructive to a woman's body.

The required goal of the health worker—as a public health care figure with precise, legally defined professional tasks and responsibilities—is to lower the tendency for immigrant women to look to abortion as a form of contraceptive through efforts of prevention and information, as well as to avoid relapses by providing psychological guidance to those who come to the center asking for this service. In fact, relapses often involve women who are unaware of or unable to overcome certain psychological or social issues that can be resolved through counseling with a health worker.

To ensure free choice, the woman has to be helped to become aware of her situation and the personal and relational implications of her choice. This is why the interview with the psychologist may represent a useful occurrence, provided it is not treated as a bureaucratic situation in which all responsibility is delegated to the patient or the couple.

Unfortunately, this happens when the health workers do not have sufficient instruments to suggest to the client a new and significant reading of her experience and her relationships. This complete relocation of responsibility to the woman or the couple happens particularly often in the case of abortion, a subject that because of its ethical implications arouses strong emotional reactions in health workers and causes them to close the discussion. This happens even more frequently with immigrant women, in relation to whom the health or social workers do not seem to strive sufficiently to overcome the linguistic and cultural barriers.

In our region (the area to the west of the Vicenza province) are a very large number of immigrants from outside the European community, known in Italian as *extracomunitari*. Most of the latter come from former Yugoslavia and Ghana. Sizable numbers of them began to settle in the area before any other group in the 1990s. In the last few years, there has been more diversification; in particular, there has been an increase in immigrants from India. According to the statistics, the women belonging to the two major ethnic groups present in the area—the Serbian and the Ghanaian—show one of the highest abortion rates relative to all other ethnicities in the whole Veneto region. In fact, until recently, they were those with the highest percentages[3] (Giorio, 1992; Bollettino Ufficiale Regione Veneto, 2002).

This is why I decided to examine these issues more closely. Furthermore, the reasons most frequently given to justify the abortion request seemed not to be clear, and—most disconcertingly of all for the Italian health workers, having practiced several abortions throughout their lifetime[4]—these women's behavior often provoked moral disapproval, thus fostering the emergence of prejudices toward all immigrants both inside and outside the service.

My hypothesis was that, far from being innately "immoral" or "guilty of negligence," women from these countries had their own reasons for behaving the way they did in relation to birth control. Given that their psychological and socioeconomic conditions were not much different from those of other ethnic groups in the area and that their level of information about contraception did not vary in any substantial way, these reasons had to be found in their respective cultural differences. In fact, in the case of the women from the former Yugoslavia, and given the secular political tradition of this government in the socialist period, it was justifiable to presume that their level of information was fairly high. The hypothesis, though, that later proved to be most useful came to me while leafing through a book of African art when I came across the image of a small statue representing a pronouncedly pregnant goddess. The caption to the illustration explained the importance of the *fertility cult* in West African societies.

From an anthropological investigation of the population in question, the Ashanti, to whom most of the Ghanaian immigrants in the West Vicenza district belong, it emerged that fertility is particularly important in their religious and social context. Furthermore, according to the traditions and mythology of this society, the well-being of the community depends on a positive and harmonious relationship with the surrounding environment, which may be endangered by the presence of an infertile woman. Thus, infertility was seriously punished in this society (Sarpong, 1977; McLeod, 1981).[5]

While, on the one hand, these findings corroborated my initial idea, on the other, my attention was drawn to the investigation by a Yugoslavian researcher who had come to similar conclusions. Serbian women who had emigrated to countries such as Sweden or France, where the social services were efficient (and in those days, at least) free of charge, made regular use of the abortion provisions

---

[3] For years, these two ethnic groups occupied the first positions in the regional statistics, but quite recently Serbian women have been overtaken by Nigerian women, who are present in large numbers in the area but whose high incidence of abortion is connected to their wide-scale prostitution. Next come Eastern European countries geographically close to former Yugoslavia, and then Morocco, which presents a much higher percentage of immigration than Ghana (the sixth largest ethnicity in Italy today).

[4] In the interviews I conducted, I met Serbian and Ghanaian women who had as many as 15 to 20 abortions.

[5] The barren woman could be repudiated, as often happens in many African societies. Sometimes, at her death, briar and curses were put on her grave to exorcise the curse of barren women.

available to them, showing a marked unwillingness to adopt any form of contraception. According to the author, these women were influenced by the particular idea of fertility that prevailed within their society and often treated pregnancy as an instrument of power regulation within the couple. In fact, in a social context in which the woman's role was traditionally subordinate and the concept of fertility of prime importance, pregnancy and maternity conferred a higher status upon the woman (Morokvasic, 1981).

Faced with the loss of all traditional family ties and consequently with a loss of identity definition and seeing her own sense of security so drastically undermined by the phenomena of emigration and cultural adaptation to an alien social setting (Tognetti Bordogna, 1991), it is possible that the woman tries to find assurance in her traditional maternal function. Within this context, a temporary, soon-to-be interrupted maternity is for her preferable to contraception practices that deny her reproductive potential and cause anxiety in her.

Culturally based hypotheses may help in understanding the complexity of the psychological factors that influence immigrant women in their decision to abort. This complexity must be considered if we want to avoid letting our prejudices undermine the appropriateness of our intervention or if we wish to overcome the difficulties caused partly by our ignorance of a specific culture.

METHODOLOGY OF THE INTERVENTION

The methodology followed in the interviews regarding cases of voluntary abortion is rather complex and, from the point of view of communication, comprises many different levels. First of all, we have to make a distinction between, on the one hand, the *assessment* level, relative to the institutional requirements, and, on the other hand, what could be called the *assistance* or *therapeutic* level of the procedure. In the former case, the psychologist assesses the reasons that motivate the request for an abortion and the appropriateness of such a decision and then informs the physician who gives or refuses permission, even though, in the final instance, it is the woman who takes the final decision. The *assessment* level introduces a certain element of control and authority in the procedure: It frequently remains implicit; as such, it represents an aspect of the interview about which the health worker appears mostly unaware.

Equally, the level of *assistance* is not as straightforward as it would seem. Generally, there is no specific request for "help" or "therapeutic intervention" on the woman's part. It is the psychologist who suggests the need for such "help." Often unaware of the psychological consequences of an interrupted pregnancy, women make simple requests for an operation so as to solve the problem in the shortest possible time on the medical level.

In carrying out the interview, the health care worker (i.e., psychologist, social worker, nurse, or physician) needs to consider the above factors so as to avoid lack of clarity surrounding the different levels of communication. Furthermore, in assessing the complexity of the situation, we must bear in mind that there are different possible lines of development within the interview. There is an initial stage in which the woman must be helped to decide whether to continue with her pregnancy. Then, if the woman opts for an abortion, the following stage entails that support must be provided to help her face the operation and deal with related emotional aspects such as fear, sense of loss, guilt, and shame. If the woman decides to bring her pregnancy to completion, then the health worker is expected to organize a plan of assistance and support so that she can keep her baby and cope with a variety of difficulties such as being underage, economic and housing problems, disagreement within the couple, or simply her refusal to undergo the required medical checkups.

The *systemic analysis of the context* of the communication described so far helps the health worker define more clearly his or her objectives and establish a more productive relationship with the patient. The attention given to the specific *cultural differences* that exist between the woman (or the couple) and the health worker is a critical factor. In fact, to intervene effectively, the health worker must examine the client's cultural framework and be aware of the norms and cultural assumptions in force within the social context of her or their country of origin. This understanding will determine the correct hypotheses for the reasons why the woman must resort to (or, in the case of repeated abortions, continue resorting to) such a problematic procedure and why she so often fails to protect herself from an unwanted pregnancy. The Family Advisory Center has developed an instrument and interview that is designed to introduce new information about various hypotheses that might change attitudes and open options for new thinking and different behaviors at a later stage.

THE ASSESSMENT INTERVIEW

Our major tool for assessment is a semistructured interview. The interview aims at helping the therapist and the woman describe her ethnic, social, and family situation. This is achieved by collecting useful data that are later added to a pool of information taken from other women, thus increasing the quantity of information which is circulating within the communication system of the service (i.e., between operators and clients).

The increase of information and viewpoints within the system has a positive effect. It opens different perspectives and facilitates the communication between clients and health worker, which are often closed because of prejudice and stereotyping (Boscolo et al., 1987). There is, in fact, a tendency in women who resort to abortion to stay fixed in a limited, static mindset in which avoidance of abortion prevention, and the difficulties related to it, is the only thought or behavior pattern used: They are unable to see, or are not interested in seeing, the consequences of their immediate behavior, and they are unable to connect their behavior with their own cognitive and cultural assumptions.

Health workers, in turn, also get stuck in a limited and unfruitful mind set. They often tend to passively accept their lack of knowledge of these women's psychological and cultural mechanisms and their resistance to change, while not questioning their own cognitive and cultural patterns.

However, the introduction of new information on the culture of origin and the assumptions of the client and health worker make it possible to see other ways of thinking and more options for action. An example of this can be seen in what happened initially in our region regarding the hypotheses that health workers accepted when they considered the reasons for the high number of abortions by immigrant women. By accepting the prejudice that these women turn readily to abortion because they are "less evolved morally," the health workers became close-minded and looked down on these clients, which led to reduced dialogue with them. This only served to perpetuate the situation (lack of contraception and high rates of abortion).

By bringing into the system new information about the concept of fertility was a decisive factor (as described above), a cultural assumption that health workers had not previously considered. Communication with clients improved because the negative assumption no longer limited dialogue. This increased the ability of health workers to introduce the practice of contraception, thereby reducing the number of abortions. The new information (the new "anthropological" hypothesis regarding abortion factors) increases the number of options and makes the system more functional.

This is what we have seen in the center in which I work. By challenging health workers' prejudices with the introduction of the new hypothesis, we improved cooperation with the clients and increased acceptance of contraception, with the resulting decline in abortion requests.[6]

The interview scheme not only helps the health worker formulate the appropriate questions and gather information but also helps highlight the possible determinants of the problem and their interconnection, thus placing them within the clients' cognitive grasp.

The theory applied here is that of *interventive questioning* as put forward by K. Tomm (1987a, 1987b, 1988) on the basis of a concept previously elaborated by the *circular interview* group of Milan (Boscolo et al., 1987). According to this theory, the very act of putting the questions to the client is not a mere collection of neutral information but a technique that contributes to structuring a cognitive context capable of modifying the client's (or the family's) perception of the problematic situation.

The circular procedure consists in listening to and equally considering all of the participants' opinions so that the most frequently ignored viewpoints are given the chance to be included in the discussion. Posing questions according to this procedure, while putting up for discussion the implicit positions (prejudices) in each participant's way of thinking through a process of deconstruction of the conversation up to that time, helps clients out of the static and limited positions so far maintained (Mosconi, Gonzo, Sorgato, Tirelli, & Tomas, 1995).

The first step in the direction of helping pregnant immigrant women who ask for abortion and of reducing the incidence of the problem of abortion was to come to an agreement with the hospital's departments of gynecology and obstetrics. It was determined that all women with this problem should be sent to the Family Advisory Center so that a more specific type of intervention in favor of contraception and anti-abortion measures could be implemented. The resulting

---

[6] The case studies starting on p. 257 will illustrate other examples of how client dialogue can be improved with the introduction of new hypotheses and points of view.

influx of foreign women to the center gave rise to the necessity for the health workers to modify their usual method of intervention, which involved adopting an intercultural approach, as shall be presented below in the interview scheme.

From the psychological point of view, the situation of the immigrant woman who comes to the center for an abortion is quite different from that of the Italian woman who makes the same type of request (Kleinmann, 1980). In the case of Italian women, the root problem behind the decision is often psychorelational— for example, a subordinate type of relationship with the husband or discomfort experienced within the couple, or a tendency to become depressed that has prevented her from adopting all of the precautions available to safeguard her health. In the immigrant woman's case, there are often different determinants of psychological, social, and cultural order. Lack of information, cultural and religious prejudices, social marginality, psychological disturbances caused by the shock of acculturation, loss of significant relationships as a result of leaving one's country—all of these factors can make the woman more vulnerable and less sensitive to health protection concerns.

It is possible for the woman to accept behavioral change and to think in terms of prevention only if the health worker fully understands the way she feels and if there is real dialogue between the two cultures. To facilitate the communication between health workers and users, a scheme has been designed to serve as an outline for semistructured interviews in cases of abortion for the benefit of the health workers (who can be psychologists, gynecologists, nurses, social workers, and so on, but preferably trained in interviewing techniques). Such a scheme has the double objective of gathering data on the phenomenon so as to understand better its socioeconomic determinants and of carrying out a survey on the cultural models surrounding procreation and relationships (Gonzo, Tirelli, & Visotti, 1999). The areas explored in the interview are the following:

- personal data, country of origin, cultural background;
- level of education, profession, work situation;
- plans relative to immigration;
- housing situation;
- geneogram (family composition, children who have remained in the country of origin, family of origin);
- expectations and values relative to the family and the couple;
- level of information about contraceptives and willingness to use them, and number of previous abortions, if any; and
- reasons and circumstances behind the request for an abortion.

The questions posed to the women enable them to talk about their own individual way of thinking, feelings, expectations, and fears as well as stories, myths, and specific problems in a free and empowering dialogue in which both therapist and client explore new ideas (Anderson & Goolishan, 1988).

The decision to have an abortion is examined in relation to socioeconomic factors as well as psychological aspects connected with the family of origin and its internal image, with the relationship of the couple, and any other individual experiences before and after migration without neglecting the factors derived from the specific culture to which the woman belongs.

Then, on the basis of the data that emerge, the psychologist or health worker introduces within the conversation hypotheses and links that have not been considered yet by the client (or the partner or other family members or people accompanying the woman who are possibly close to her). This enables the client to elaborate a new and alternative interpretation of the problem and of her personal relational history.

For example, during the interview, a Serbian woman might give specific and accidental reasons for the abortion such as not having taken the pill for the few months following her recent pregnancy because she had been too busy with family responsibilities to go to her gynecologist. Later in the interview, however, a strong—but hidden—link to the family in her home country, particularly her mother and sisters, may emerge. The psychologist or health worker could come to this hypothesis by noticing a change in tone of voice when the woman speaks of these distant family members when reconstructing her geneogram. She also might reveal an unsatisfactory relationship with her husband.

Further focused questioning might reveal a certain dependency on the mother and sisters with whom she normally discusses problems regarding her husband. This could lead to the hypothesis that the woman (in addition to issues related to the new family formed after giving birth) has not resolved issues related to her family of origin and could, therefore, be unconsciously using abortion as a way of reconnecting with her mother and sisters. An additional hypothesis could be that the unsatisfactory relationship with her husband is making this detachment from the family more difficult and is hindering her emotional acceptance of the new culture in which she lives.

Through questions on family relationships and on the reasons for abortion, the psychologist or health worker can encourage connections between various aspects of the woman's life that previously she had held separate. For example, the hypothesis of a connection between the two problems could be confirmed by asking if the mother knows about the abortion and how she reacted. The interviewer could ask if the mother has accepted her daughter's emigration. Was it the woman's husband who insisted on emigrating while the woman herself was less certain? In this way, the information related to the family and her personal background can be connected in a new and different way for the client, allowing her to become aware of aspects of her emotional life that she had previously denied.

The context of the conversation changes so that the clients can be somehow helped in a therapeutic manner about thinking over their life choices and constructing different ways of looking at themselves in which the sorrow of abortion is not necessary any more (White & Epston, 1990).

TWO CASE STUDIES

The first case study consists of an interview with a Serbian woman who has requested an abortion. The therapist and the woman discuss the decision, the woman's social and psychological background is defined, and the woman is asked to consider future preventive measures. The second case study concerns a Ghanaian adolescent and her mother, who is requesting an abortion for her daughter.

CASE 14.1 | MILICA

Milica is 28 years of age and comes from Serbia. After separating from a previous partner of the same nationality, she began to live with her new partner, who is a Muslim. On her part, she is a nonpracticing orthodox Christian, and this could create various problems within the couple, especially in view of what has been happening in her country of origin. The man she cohabits with is not present at the interview, in spite of being explicitly invited to attend in order to understand better the relationship within the couple, a common practice in these cases. After all, this relationship represents the context that gives meaning to the decision to have an abortion; therefore, it is of prime importance for the therapist to analyze it.

At the beginning of the interview, the psychologist first examines more closely the general data relative to Milica's arrival in Italy, her job, the couple situation, the number of children, and so on. The woman relates the story of her arrival 6 years earlier. Spontaneously, she volunteers information relative to the separation from her husband 2 years ago because of his extreme jealousy: He did not allow her to meet her women friends and made it difficult for her even to go to work. He accused her of being "too free," and this provoked intense and continuous arguments between them. The psychologist encourages Milica to talk more about this relationship, and then she tells him about the violent rows and the thousand questions and threats her ex-husband subjected her to when she came back from work. In telling her story, she still shows great emotional involvement, including in her nonverbal communication, which supplies new information to the psychologist. Based on this new information, the psychologist builds one of the therapeutic hypotheses that she has not overcome the loss of the previous relationship.

When asked by the psychologist for an explanation of her ex-husband's behavior, Milica puts forward the idea that perhaps he was "psychologically disturbed" or perhaps simply "nasty." The psychologist encourages the first interpretation to facilitate her psychological "mourning" in relation to the breakdown of this relationship. The client accepts the redefinition.

From this marriage, Milica had a daughter, age 5, who lives with her. Her ex-husband seems to have finally accepted the separation, even though he does not always contribute to his daughter's maintenance. He visits the girl but irregularly. Milica maintains that it perhaps better so, given that when in the past he went to see their daughter more often, the couple always argued. She talks about how she felt neglected by this man: When they went on holiday together to Yugoslavia and stayed with his family, Milica no longer existed for him. That was something she really could not bear and became the main reason she decided to separate.

Milica's relationship with her first partner was certainly found to be difficult and unbalanced in favor of her partner. However, this type of relationship is not unusual in couples who have emigrated from Serbia. In my experience, these relationships are often characterized by commanding behavior of the man during the relationship and by aggression and resignation after the separation.

The psychologist tells Milica about the Italian laws concerning abortion and reminds her that in Italy this is permitted free of charge within the first 3 months, even though it is seen as something to be avoided for health reasons. Besides, the health and social care personnel are requested by law to try and avoid such a solution.

It is critically important for the health worker—who is in a position of greater power in the relationship—to make these contextual assumptions clear. The psychologist, by explaining that his role gives him the responsibility of looking for alternatives to abortion, allows Milica to become aware of the differences in significance given to abortion in the two cultures—that is, between her own culture and that of the health worker.

The health worker inquires about what motivates the request. The couple wants an abortion because they currently do not wish to have a child because they have housing problems and, more important, their relationship is not yet stable and they are not sure whether they will stay together. The problem is that they have been together for such a short time that Milica does not feel sure about him or trust him sufficiently. She does not even know whether they will go back to Yugoslavia or settle down in Italy, and this

(continued)

could be a serious problem. To the psychologist's question about why they did not use contraceptives, she says that "the pill does not agree with me. It gives me a headache."

The answer, not unlike those we frequently hear from other Serbian women, highlights how contraception is looked down upon despite the psychological and social precariousness of the relationship. Contraception receives little acceptance from the male partners and, at the same time, probably interferes with the image of the woman in the culture of origin, which is centered on the idea of motherhood.

To understand better the relationship within the couple in question, the psychologist asks why Milica has not invited along her partner. She replies that he had "to go to work" and it was "difficult for him to come to the center." Besides, she prefers to "handle these matters" (i.e., matters over which the woman traditionally has a certain amount of control) on her own.

The psychologist tries to broaden the context of the conversation and inquires about Milica's own family. She says that they have come to Italy a long time ago and now live in Vicenza. She had stopped seeing them for awhile when she was with her husband, who did not like her talking to them about confidential matters, although "with his own family he did that much more often" than she did. After the separation, she has reestablished contact with her family, although she does not see them often now. There appears to be no special relationship with them—that is, a relationship of a more intimate type as if she were still living at home with her mother or father or sisters. It looks as if Milica has effectively detached emotionally from her family of origin.

This is, in fact, a complicated point. It is essentially true if we look at the relationship with the family of origin from a "Western" point of view in which detachment from the family is quite evident and is a necessary step in one's psychological development. It is somewhat less true in the case in question in which it is perhaps more a symptom of a certain lack of support in the relationship and of Milica's solitude—that is, in the sense that after marriage she no longer receives support from her family of origin.

The psychologist decides not to ask any further questions on personal and relational matters, especially given the limited time available for the interview. He encourages Milica to embark on the relationship with her new partner and explore new life opportunities for herself and for her daughter. He advises her not to hold back in fear that the same traumatic events she experienced in her first marriage may repeat themselves.

Despite this concretization of her fear of relationships with men, particularly her lack of faith in her new relationship as evident in the discussion that followed this topic, Milica stays with her decision to abort, showing that she was still unable to overcome her problem. However, she shows greater awareness in the use of contraceptives, as evidenced by subsequent gynecological examinations.

Throughout the interview, the psychologist identifies many gender-related difficulties that Milica experiences with regard to adopting "appropriate preventive measures" against an unwanted pregnancy. He describes them as having the same origin as her difficulty in getting involved emotionally with her new partner. Her relationships with men appear to be influenced by traditional ideas of the latter's superiority and by the need to adopt a complementary behavior. These ideas were confirmed in the past by her relationship with her husband. As for pregnancy and contraception, she seems bound to a traditional concept that sees them not so much as an experience to be shared by both partners but more exclusively a female condition through which the woman defines her own space and sphere of action.

In the cases reported here, and in many others with which the center has dealt, it is essential that the health worker who is conducting the interview actively attempt to establish a dialogue that transcends all cultural differences. It is also recommended that she or he try to get close to the different situations through an understanding of the specific context from a cultural, social, and psychological perspective. The client and her family are, in fact, immediately aware if the health worker is trying to understand their cultural background and

CASE 14.2 | ELIZABETH

This second case study concerns a younger woman, an adolescent of Ghanaian nationality. Her name is Elizabeth, and she is 16 years old. She comes to the Family Planning Center with her mother. They are both accompanied by an acquaintance of the mother's, a Ghanaian man in his mid-30s who acts as an interpreter. They are requesting an abortion for Elizabeth.

During the interview, Elizabeth seems to have problems expressing herself in Italian, so all those involved—that is, the two psychologists of the center (a man and a woman), Elizabeth's mother, and the mother's male acquaintance—decide to conduct the interview in English instead. But, even then, Elizabeth sits quietly, with her head down, uttering hardly any words.

MALE PSYCHOLOGIST (MP), ASKING THE GIRL: Elizabeth, we are going to ask you some questions before speaking about your pregnancy and about what to do. When did you arrive in Italy?

ELIZABETH (E), SPEAKING ONLY AFTER THE QUESTION HAS BEEN REPEATED MANY TIMES: I have been in Italy for 8 months and at present, I'm attending secondary school.

MP: Which school?

E: Chemistry.

MP: And before, where were you, please? In your country?

MOTHER (M), ANSWERING FOR HER DAUGHTER, WHO IS SILENT: Up until her arrival in Italy, she lived in Ghana, and had not seen us, the parents, for 9 years. She was with her grandparents. Her sister, 2 years younger than Elizabeth, lives in Ghana with them, too.

FEMALE PSYCHOLOGIST (FP): And your father? Where is he now? Is he in Italy?

E. DOESN'T ANSWER.

M: He is traveling in Ghana at the moment. He is visiting a relative concerning some family business, but he doesn't know anything about the pregnancy. He would be very angry if he did! He doesn't know. He is here [indicating the friend who has come with them] to help us. He is very kind.

MP: Do you agree, Elizabeth? Is what your mother said correct?

E. DOES NOT ANSWER.

MP TO THE ACQUAINTANCE: And you?

ACQUAINTANCE (A): That's right, Elizabeth's father is very strict. But he's right. He wouldn't like such behavior.

The interview begins by collecting significant data about the life of the family, asking questions of the people present and, when possible, asking the others about issues regarding each person. It is important *who* is actually attending the counseling session. It is normally the person most concerned about or most involved in the problem—and often the one closest to the pregnant woman—who agrees to take part in it.

Finding out who is more involved in the situation (and, conversely, who is less involved) allows us to formulate a hypothesis on any relational factors that may cause or permit the problem (the girl's early pregnancy) to occur or to reoccur in the future. For example, the observation that, in addition to her father, the girl's partner has not attended the interview or is unaware of the pregnancy is information crucial to understanding that there are relationship problems within the couple and that the girl is alone or is only receiving support from her family of origin.

In this case, it appears that, although the girl has come to the center with her mother, there is also a father in the background, who has lived in Italy together with the mother and four other children for the last 10 years. The father might seem to be a "marginal" figure in the family, but this could either be temporary or a normal and accepted situation within the family. It could also be a factor that creates problems between the mother and the father and with the children. It will therefore be one of the hypotheses to return to later in the interview. The mother, on the other hand, has attended the interview, although it would appear that for 10 years there was only a distant relationship between Elizabeth and her mother.

(continued)

MP: What part of your country do you come from?

A: From Kumasi, in the southwest. Are you familiar with it?

MP: Kumasi. I have it here on the map on the wall. A lot of Ghanaian immigrants here come from there. So you are Ashanti perhaps? Which ethnic group are you from, and what is your religion?

They reply they are Ashanti and evangelical Christians. As for their housing situation, they live in a three-bedroom flat. Elizabeth sleeps with her 11-year-old sister. After collecting this social and cultural data, the psychologist explains the procedures and the laws relative to abortion. Because Elizabeth is underage, by law the parents must give their consent to the abortion or the case will have to be taken to a tribunal. This is the case also when one of the parents is absent or in disagreement. The mother, in fact, says she would prefer not to ask him about the abortion, because he would get angry and violent. She is worried about the danger that may result.

Elizabeth's mother, too, appears to be quite angry with her daughter over this pregnancy. There seems to be a sort of "symmetrical conflict"[7] between mother and daughter: a conflict that probably goes beyond the current situation.

MP: So, you prefer not to tell your dad about the pregnancy, too? Is that right?

E. SHAKES HER HEAD BUT DOESN'T LOOK UP.

MP: But was it difficult to tell your mother, too? It seems that she's angry as well.

E: Mm-hmm. Yes, she is.

M: She doesn't know who the child's father is. She refuses even to say. Neither my other daughter who shares her bedroom with Elizabeth nor I knew that she was pregnant. At a certain point,

Elizabeth got ill and had to be taken to hospital, where we discovered she was expecting!

Having listened to the mother, the male psychologist turns to Elizabeth, who up to that moment has kept quiet without denying her mother's version of the facts in any way. He asks her whether she is happy to be in Italy, exploring the hypothesis that her problematic behavior—having unprotected sex at such an early age and, consequently, having to undergo an abortion—may be the result of an existing disagreement between her and her mother over the decision that she should come to Italy, or perhaps about earlier staying in Ghana for 9 years without her parents. The hypothesis is that perhaps the daughter does not like these choices and feels uprooted from her environment. The mother's anger may also be explained on the base of an existing conflict between generations. More elements are needed, however, to check these hypotheses.

MP: Are you happy, Elizabeth, to be here in Vicenza? How do you feel here? Have you made some friends at school? Are they Italian?

E: Yes, I feel okay. Yes. I've got friends, some. They're mostly Italian. Some are Ghanaian.

MP: And you, ma'am, what do you think?

M: Elizabeth was happy when she first arrived. She adapted very easily. Really, I'm sure.

FP: So you both agree. And what do you do with these friends? Do you go out during the day or in the evening?

E: I go out when my mother goes to work, sometimes with my brothers and sisters, sometimes alone with Italian friends.

MP: Would your brothers and sisters agree that your relationship with your friends is good? What would they say if they were here?

E: Yes, I think so. They come with me as I've said. We go together.

MP: Your Italian friends accept your company?

E: Yes, of course.

FP: Do you agree, ma'am?

---

[7] *Symmetrical* and *complementary*—in systemic language—are two relationship schemes. In a symmetrical relationship, the conflict between the two people originates from similar and opposing behavioral modes, whereas in a complementary relationship their behaviors tend to compensate each other. Both of these behavioral models can normally be found in relationships, except in the most extreme cases.

M: Yes, I think so. She's never told me anything like that.

MP: What do you do when you're out? What time do you come back home?

E: Nothing, only walking with friends around town, listening to music. But I never come home very late.

FP: What time?

M: Yes, it's true, not very late, at 11.

The psychologist asks both mother and daughter (always with circular questioning to bring out differences) whether Elizabeth knew about contraception. No, she did not, says the mother, and the daughter confirms. The mother says that it is difficult for her to discuss contraception with her daughter because these are "delicate matters."

FP: Does it happen that girls accidentally get pregnant in your country? And can you explain please what happens to them?

A BEGINS TO LAUGH.

M: Yes, of course it happens! They get married sometimes. It depends.

FP: And normally the parents get really angry?

M: I think so. Maybe. It depends.

The answer is not clear. The psychologist's aim here is to see how the behavior in question is perceived in the different culture. However, so far no specific differences have emerged from the conversation on the basis of which specific hypotheses could be formulated.

MP: You've said the father doesn't know about the pregnancy. Do you think Elizabeth is very worried about what her father will say and do on his return?

M: Yes, she is. He will be very angry, I think. He will go into a rage. Elizabeth—she's very worried about being pregnant and everything.

FP: Was it your first time, Elizabeth?

E (CRYING): It was the first time—I had sexual intercourse—yes.

Then the possibility the girl was forced into having sex is also investigated, but both mother and daughter confirm there was no coercion. If the daughter had been raped, she would have told her, says the mother.

At this point, after asking permission to leave the room, the two psychologists leave and discuss the case with the gynecologist. Several hypotheses are put forward, one of which is that the girl has been raped, or even that she has prostituted herself with her mother's connivance. The man who has accompanied them arouses suspicion. The girl's behavior is so subdued, so dejected, and so timid that she looks just the type of person who could easily fall prey to manipulation.

The male psychologist does not agree. He is convinced that this is a simple psychological problem, that Elizabeth has been neglected, having lived in Africa for many years without her parents. Now she probably feels unsure of herself in her new environment and, in order to be accepted, she has allowed a certain sexual promiscuity between herself and her friends. Perhaps she is also angry with her parents, the mother mainly, as shown in the dialogue. The woman psychologist observes that in the girl's culture the problem appears to be her pregnancy rather than her "easiness" or the fact that she has had sexual intercourse. People from this country appear not to be as worried about their children as Italian parents are. Perhaps even abortion is not considered as morally wrong as it is in Italian society. This girl's relatives, in fact, seem angry with her as if she had "made a mess" of something, as if she had crashed a car or the like. The mother does not talk in moral or psychological terms about her daughter's pregnancy. The last two explanations are rather compatible with each other, and concur to elaborate a more complex hypothesis, according to which the girl has not been told about contraception, is not being sufficiently cared for by her family, may have negative feelings toward her mother, and is experiencing problems with feeling accepted in the new society.

The health workers then went to the clients. They summarized what they have discussed outside and asked them for their opinion on the varying hypotheses, taking care to explain the different points of view without giving them the idea that there is a right one or that they have to come up with just one truth.

The family doesn't accept the idea that Elizabeth had been abandoned, saying—consistent with their

(continued)

culture—that they gave the child to the grandparents, who cared for the daughter. Elizabeth, who has gradually become more talkative and expressive during the interview (even to the point of crying), appears receptive to this idea. This new formulation of her situation, done—even if reluctantly—with her help, helps her to feel more aware of certain personal psychological aspects (such as the pain she feels for the distance from her home country and the need to feel accepted in her new environment).

The discussion continues on the choice of abortion, which is preferred by both the family and Elizabeth. The health workers did not reject this option because of the difficult age of the girl and, in the end, because it is the woman's right to choose (with the family's consent in the case of minors). Finally, an abortion is granted by the service, by asking the authorization of the tribunal through the social worker's intervention. By this stage, the time of the interview is almost up. The conclusion reached is that a report will be written out and presented to the tribunal, and, furthermore, that the girl needs psychological assistance, as well as more information about contraception. The family is requested to come back with Elizabeth for further counseling after the abortion in order to help her and to increase the family's consciousness.

whether she or he respects them. The health worker's respectful attitude surely encourages the clients to act in a cooperative manner throughout the interview by using other languages or helping out in a variety of ways, such as volunteering information and the like.

By posing questions to all those who are taking part in the interview independently from their linguistic and social abilities, a new situation is established that allows all parties to equally participate. Furthermore, the strategy of asking about the culture of origin as well as about experiences before the client's arrival in Italy aims not only to shed light on the problem in question but also to give the client a chance to speak. This is especially important for immigrant women who are often silenced by virtue of being treated as outsiders in most aspects of their daily lives.

PERSONAL REFLECTIONS

My experience meeting with immigrant women requesting abortions over the last 12 years—or in the period when immigration in Italy has become much more common—has been important to me because it has given me the opportunity to work with different cultures and to leave the more familiar path of working with clients of my own nationality.

CONCLUSION

The very idea of "psychological help" or "therapy" when dealing with these immigrant women needed to be reconsidered. The idea of "prevention," rooted in the Western concept of modern medicine, health care, and planning for our own futures and that of our families, was challenged by contact with different cultural premises. In this way, the responsibility of the psychologist, and the health worker in general, became not that of providing help and assistance but of comparing and communicating for the purpose of finding a common idea as to what health and wellness are. Just as I hope the women and their families expanded their understanding, so did I as a result of these experiences. Contact with different worlds, both individual and collective, stimulated in me an interest in cultural and social issues such that I became increasingly involved in these themes and with other colleagues who are sensitive to this new situation into which I have broadened my experience and focus. I have continued to develop specific projects targeted at immigrant women and families.

On a personal level, I am finding that I can identify more and more with these people that our society and the public service system find difficult to accept, and at the same time I have come to the realization that we need to approach these matters from more than a psychological or health care standpoint directed at the individual, which ignores the social context of the client. Otherwise, we run the risk of oversimplifying and distorting these social relationships. I have come, then, to formulate a new idea of my profession that I hope is nearer to a more social view.

In sum, the fundamental approach to the problem of the high incidence of abortion among foreign women is the employment of the therapeutic dialogue within the interviews that are carried out to assess the motivations for the abortion requests. The therapeutic use of dialogue requires a preliminary systemic analysis of the context, which is not therapeutic in itself but becomes so only as a result of a process in which the client agrees to widen the scope of the interview and include her personal history.

An analysis of the possible factors that concur in determining the specific case that I am presented with involves first examining the relationship with the family and within the couple—for example, assessing which are the most important relationships, which are the preferential and most problematic ones, and what the relationship with the partner is like. Afterward, it will be necessary to consider the cultural and gender aspects to discover, for example, how the woman is seen in that particular culture and what degree of importance is given to maternity. Then it will be often useful to consider the experience of migration and investigate in what phase of migration the woman or couple is in—for example, whether the couple has just settled in the host country, whether it is the first or second generation to immigrate, for what reasons they have embarked on migration, and what their work and housing situations are like. Each time, these factors will exert a different degree of influence on the problem.

By asking questions about the significant aspects of the client's experience and her relations,[7] the circular procedure of interview produces a cognitive change in the client, introducing new information and new hypotheses and enabling her to elaborate a personal history that is more satisfactory and better adjusted to the circumstances.

---

[7] This is achieved by following a precise pattern of themes concerning her individual history, her family, her culture, her relationship with her partner, and finally her decision to have an abortion.

KEY CONCEPTS

- systemic analysis of the context
- therapeutic dialogue
- semistructured interview
- interventive questioning
- circular procedure of interview
- varying and different hypotheses
- examining the relationship with the family and within the couple
- consider the cultural and gender aspects

QUESTIONS FOR REFLECTION

1. What is the health worker's responsibility within the abortion-request interview? (Consider specific legislation in your country.)
2. Why does abortion evoke emotional reactions and ethical questions that make it more difficult for a health worker to make decisions on a specific case?
3. Can you describe the difference between "evaluation" and "assistance or therapy" contexts in the case of abortion?
4. What are the most important stages of the interview, and which aspects of the client's life do they investigate?
5. What are the social, psychological, cultural, and other factors that can influence the tendency of the woman to refuse contraception and to resort to abortion?
6. In what way can the interview change the client's perception of the problem and her life experiences?
7. How is it possible, through the interview process, to change the attitude of the client toward abortion and contraception in such a way that she would adopt less harmful birth-control strategies?
8. Which of the suggestions or procedures proposed in this chapter do you think could be applicable and useful in your specific profession?
9. What is the law in your country regarding voluntary abortion? Is it similar or different in respect to the quoted Italian law? In which points?
10. How would you manage the cases of Milica and Elizabeth taking into account the laws in your country?
11. Which of the suggestions or procedures proposed in this chapter do you think could be applicable and useful in your specific country, with attention to the specific cultural context?

EXERCISE

Think about your agency and work setting and one main population that your agency or work serves. Think about the social context of the agency and which professionals you are in contact with in helping your clients. Write a list of the goals of the agency or setting. List three problems that often occur within this context and tasks met by other helpers to handle these problems. Think about whether all the roles played by different helpers meet the goals of the agency or setting—or are these contradictions? How might the social context of your agency or setting or interactions between the professions impact the client population you selected? Create a questionnaire that could be used by all helpers for interviewing clients. The questionnaire should relate to the client's problems and the goals of the agency or setting. The questionnaire should be aimed to help focus on areas of concern to the agency or setting and its goals while aiming also to gain information that would be useful to helpers with these clients and their problems.

References

Anderson, H., & Goolishian, H. (1988). Human systems as linguistic systems: Preliminary and evolving ideas about the implications for clinical theory. *Family Process, 27*(4), 371–393.

Bateson, G. (1972). *Steps to an ecology of mind.* San Francisco: Chandler.

Bondi, C., Neri, C., & Bonfirraro, G. (1997). Interruzione volontaria di gravidanza. L'osservazione del fenomeno. La prevenzione. In Atti in press del Convegno "Immigrazione e salute. L'esperienza di Firenze" Firenze, 24 ottobre 1997.

Boscolo, L., Cecchin, G., Hoffman, L., & Penn, P. (1987). *Milan systemic family therapy: Conversations in theory and practice.* New York: Basic Books.

Bollettino Ufficiale Regione Veneto. (2002, September 4). n. 38.

Giorio, M. P. (1992, May). Problemi ostetrico-ginecologici nella donna immigrata. In R. Malatesta (Ed.), *Aspetti sanitari dell'immigrazione extracomunitaria, II° Convegno, Treviso, 21 maggio 1992* (pp. 84–88). Stampato in proprio.

Gonzo, M., Tirelli, M., & Visotti, V. (1999). Il colloquio per interruzione volontaria della gravidanza con le donne immigrate. In M. Gonzo et al. (Eds.), *L'intervista nei servizi sociosanitari. Un strumento conoscitivo e d'intervento per gli operatori* (pp. 83–105). Milano: Raffaello Cortina.

Kleinmann, A. (1980). *Clients and healers in the context of cultures.* Berkeley: University of California Press.

McLeod, M. D. (1981). *The Asante.* London: British Museum Publications.

Mosconi, A., Gonzo, M., Sorgato, R., Tirelli, M., & Tomas, M. (1995). From "paradox" to "therapeutic conversation." *Human Systems, 6*(1), 3–19.

Morokvasic, M. (1981). Sexuality and control of procreation. In K. Young, C. Wolkowitz, & R. McCullagh (Eds.), *Of marriage and the market: Women's subordination internationally and its lessons* (pp. 193–209). London: Cse Books.

Puzzi, P. (1998). Donne immigrate e IVG. In U.I.C.E. M.P. (Eds.), *Immigrati e salute sessuale e riproduttiva: le risposte dei servizi, U.I.C.E. M.P., Milano, 26–27 Novembre 1998.* Milano: Author.

"Relazione ministro della sanità sull'attuazione della Legge contenente norme per la tutela sociale della maternità e per l'interruzione volontaria della gravidanza (Legge 194/78) Dati preliminari 1999 dati definitivi 1998, 2 agosto 2000."

Sarpong, P. (1977). *Girl's nubility rites in Ashanti.* Accra-Tema, Ghana: Ghana Publishing Co.

Tognetti Bordogna, M. (1991). I reticoli della migrazione. In G. Favaro & M. Tognetti Bordogna (Eds.), *Donne dal mondo.*

Strategie migratorie al femminile (pp. 137–147). Milano: Guerrini e Associati.

Tomm, K. (1987a). Interventive interviewing, Pt. I : Strategizing as a fourth guideline for the therapist. *Family Process, 26,* 3–13.

Tomm, K. (1987b). Interventive interviewing, Pt. II: Reflexive questioning as a mean to enable self healing. *Family Process, 27,* 167–183.

Tomm, K. (1988). Interventive interviewing, Pt. III: Intending to ask linear, circular, strategic or reflexive questions. *Family Process, 27,* 167–183.

White, M., & Epston, D. (1990). *Narrative means to therapeutic ends.* New York: Norton.

VIOLENCE AGAINST WOMEN IN THE FAMILY

15

Immigrant Women and the U.S. Health Care System

SUSAN L. IVEY,
ELIZABETH KRAMER,
AND MARIANNE YOSHIOKA
UNITED STATES

OVERVIEW

This chapter will examine intimate partner violence (IPV) as it impacts immigrant women in the United States. Other terms such as *domestic violence* or *family violence* could broadly include child abuse or violence against men. Accordingly, we will use the term *intimate partner violence* to more specifically focus on violence from one's intimate partner. We will also discuss correlates of IPV and interventions among immigrant women in the United States. Case studies and vignettes drawn from Asian immigrant communities will be used to illustrate these concepts.

DESCRIPTION OF THE PROBLEM: PREVALENCE

According to the U.S. Department of Justice, American women are the victims in 85% or more of reported cases of family violence (U.S. Department of Justice, 2000, 2001). The lifetime risk of IPV is estimated to be as high as 1 of every 4 women in the United States (Schornstein, 1997). The National Crime and Victimization Survey (NCVS) indicates that women of all races and ethnicities in the United States are equally vulnerable to attacks by intimates, with reported overall attack rates of approximately 6 victimizations per 1,000 females age 12 and older (U.S. Department of Justice, 2001). However, this number hides some types of variation that are visible when data are stratified by age or socioeconomic status (SES). For instance, in 1999,

TABLE 15.1 | PREVALENCE OF DOMESTIC ABUSE AMONG ASIANS (%)

Abuse Exposure	Chinese	Korean	Vietnamese	Cambodian	South Asian
Know a woman who has been physically abused or injured by her partner	24	32	39	47	44
Hit regularly by their parents when they were growing up	61	80	72	70	79

Source: M. Yoshioka and Q. Dang, *Asian Family Violence Report* (2000).

black and white females experienced IPV at similar rates except for those aged 20 to 24, in which black women had significantly higher rates of IPV than white women (29 versus 20 victimizations per 1,000 for white and 22 per 1,000 for Hispanic women, respectively).

Although the status of women may be perceived as higher than in other countries, U.S. society is an especially violent one (Acierno, Resnick, & Kilpatrick, 1997). Most studies have found that IPV cuts across racial and ethnic lines but varies significantly by age, socioeconomic status, and alcohol use by a partner (U.S. Department of Justice, 2001; Barnett & Fagan, 1993). Tjaden and Thoennes (1998) reported that 19% of the 8,000 women they surveyed in the United States had been victimized by an intimate partner. In contrast to the NCVS statistics, there was tremendous variation across ethnic or racial groups (American Indian, 30%; black, 22%; white, 18%; Hispanic, 14%; Asian, 13%) in their survey, indicative of the influence of sociocultural factors.

Although there have been no national studies conducted in the United States that address the prevalence of IPV among immigrant populations, there is evidence that documents the seriousness of the problem. Raj and Silverman (2002) found that among immigrant South Asian women in the United States, 40% reported having experienced physical or sexual abuse from an intimate partner. In their sample of 607 immigrant Chinese, Cambodian, Indian, Korean, and Vietnamese adults in the Massachusetts area, Yoshioka and Dang (2000) found that 24% to 47% of participants reported that they personally knew a woman who had been shoved, pushed, slapped, or kicked by an intimate partner (Table 15.1). It is interesting to note that 61% to 80% of these same participants reported being hit as children by their parents.

Past research has shown that people who witness family violence as children or are hit as children are more likely to have attitudes that support family violence as adults. These figures are similar to those from studies of women in Asia. Based on a stratified random sample of the national population of Korea, Kim and Cho (1992) found that 38% of Korean wives reported physical abuse by their spouses within the last year. Likewise, in a sample of 600 Chinese women residing in Fujian province, 26% reported having been physically, emotionally, or sexually abused by an intimate partner within the last year (Xu & Campbell, 2000).

DESCRIPTION OF THE PROBLEM: THEORETICAL UNDERPINNINGS

Historically, there has been little public discussion of IPV. The topic has only been labeled a problem within the past few decades when feminist activists first described the power imbalance in society that would allow for this behavior to be viewed as acceptable (Mehrotra, 1999). Within a feminist framework, IPV is a marker of the low status that supports violence and discrimination against women in general. In most social systems, women occupy positions that assume that men have privilege and, in many cases, that women can be disciplined by their spouses and, in some cultures, by the man's extended family (brothers, in-laws, sons). In many societies, men historically have had the right to beat their female dependents.

However, within the mainstream feminist movement, the perspective of ethnic minority women was often overlooked (Merchant, 2000; Sharma, 2001). Further, while feminist theory has informed treatment and counseling of abused women and sought to empower them, it has often provided a narrow framework of options. A more inclusive view is needed that allows for more culturally acceptable treatment options across diverse cultures.

Within every culture, there are intricate connections among race, class, gender, and religion that influence IPV. For immigrant women, visa status and residency are additional complicating factors. Immigrant women may be at higher risk of staying in violent relationships because of cultural interpretations of status, gender, and family dynamics. For most cultures, the family unit takes priority over individual status. Immigrant women may believe their ability (and that of their children) to remain in the United States is related to the immigration status of their significant other or sponsor, or to their relationship with an employer. Stresses of immigration, limited English proficiency, underemployment, a lack of informal support networks, and discrimination and racism may all contribute to family stress, thus increasing a women's risk for IPV (Ayyub, 2000; Yoshioka & Dang, 2000). In cultures where family structure and dynamics are patriarchal, what is perceived as abuse by American standards may appear prevalent and sometimes even normative within immigrant communities.

The U.S. model for domestic violence services has been to encourage abused women to leave their abusive partners. However, this option assumes that leaving will improve the woman's life. In a traditional culture, for a woman to focus on her individual betterment may seem antithetical to the value of being a good wife who sacrifices personal freedom for her family. Discussion of leaving one's marriage or family challenges the notions of the collectivist model that most Asian and many other cultures value.

DEFINING ABUSE

Clear definitions of IPV are difficult to find because of cultural differences in what is considered appropriate and justified behavior. Drawing upon violence research in the United States, IPV has been identified as taking three main forms:

1. psychological—social isolation, use of threats and intimidation, economic deprivation, social humiliation, and verbal assaults including belittling language;
2. physical—slapping, pushing, beating, use of any weapon to inflict physical pain or injury; and
3. sexual—coerced and forced sex or rape.

Violent acts are often categorized in terms of their intensity, with minor being distinguished from severe abusive behavior. Although there is more agreement cross culturally that severe physical abuse (e.g., stabbing, using a gun, burning) is unacceptable, there is cultural variation in terms of women's tolerance of the use of minor forms of abuse (e.g., threats, slapping, pushing). Much of this is related to gender and marital role expectations and the relative power of women in the society. Studies across several cultures have found that those in which the use of minor violence is more tolerated are more likely to have high levels of IPV, whereas cultures in which violence is not normative have lower rates (Bui & Morash, 1999). For example, Torres (1991) compared Mexican American women to Anglo American women and found that Anglo women perceived more violent incidents as abusive than did their Mexican American counterparts, and that Hispanic values about gender roles shaped their definitions of IPV. Song (1996) demonstrated that Korean American women who held more traditional attitudes in marriage experienced more abuse than those who were less traditional, and that couples who adhered rigidly to traditional and patriarchal Korean sex roles tended to be more violent than couples with less rigid gender roles.

In cultures influenced by Confucianism, obedience of women to men is stressed (Yick, 2001). For many Chinese women, men have final authority in the household (Yick, 2001). Similarly, while Vietnamese women may have economic and property rights, and sometimes are referred to as "chief of domestic affairs," their role is subordinate to men in many aspects of social life. Cultural norms may encourage self-sacrifice, traditional sex roles, modesty, and obedience to men (Bui & Morash, 1999).

Contrary to the popular myth of Asians being the "model minority," there is a high prevalence of woman abuse in some Asian countries. Male abuse also appears to be widespread, particularly among Vietnamese and Cambodians. A fear of bringing shame on one's family adds to the reticence of certain women to reveal to anyone that IPV is a problem in their marriages or relationships. There is a real fear of retaliation and increased abuse if they disclose the violence or attempt to leave.

The life context of immigrant women is important to understanding their experience of IPV. The abusive partner may withhold legal or civil rights, including withholding a woman's passport or threatening to report her or her family member to the immigration service (the Immigration and Naturalization Service, or INS, in the United States). In addition, some authors report that use of purposeful isolation from family, friends, and the outside world can be an important factor in nonphysical abuse (Abraham, 2000). Failure to grant a woman access to other important papers or documents (such as children's birth certificates or bank account information) has been seen as a form of abuse that specifically affects recent immigrants. Each of these acts signals a woman's lack of control in a relationship and can be considered a form of psychological abuse.

ASSESSMENT AND INTERVENTIONS: UNDERSTANDING THE CULTURAL CONTEXT

Fear of bringing shame on one's family adds to the reticence of women to reveal to anyone that they are living with IPV. There is a real fear of retaliation and increased abuse if they disclose the violence or attempt to leave. A study of Asian immigrant adults in Massachusetts found that 18% to 29% of the Chinese, Cambodian, and Korean samples felt that a battered woman should not tell anyone about the violence (Yoshioka & Dang, 2000). Individuals may prefer to involve family and friends rather than seek formal services.

However, for many immigrants, nonkin members will be constrained in their ability to help. Marriage in most societies brings with it social standing for women. Thus, divorce and separation are not seen as positive alternatives to the abusive relationship. Yoshioka, Gilbert, and El-Bassel (2003) found that immigrant women were more likely to be told to stay in their marriages when they disclosed abuse to their family members than were American-born women. In addition, for immigrant women who lack fluency with the social systems of the host culture, the process of acquiring housing, employment, and child care may seem insurmountable.

Most cultures of the world are collectivist in orientation and characterized by a respect for authority. As such, the interests of the family take precedence over those of the individual. Shame creates an emphasis on interdependence between group members in place of individual desire and can be a primary obstacle to seeking services or reaching out for help when needed (Yoshioka & Dang, 2000; Crites, 1991).

Over the past decade, community-based organizations have sprung up in urban centers to address partner abuse in ethnic immigrant communities. Most of the programs are small and struggle to identify professionally trained bilingual staff. In Asian communities, only three organizations target multiple Asian ethnic communities. One of the most notable model programs is the Asian Task Force Against Domestic Violence in Boston, which is discussed in Case 15.1. To better design programs for immigrant women in the United States, it may be important to deliver services within a client-defined and family-oriented model. Those that are not culturally syntonic with clients' backgrounds and

CASE 15.1 | ASIAN TASK FORCE AGAINST DOMESTIC VIOLENCE

The Asian Task Force Against Domestic Violence in Boston provides victim services, a 90-day emergency shelter, a 14-day safe house, a 24-hour bilingual hotline with staff members who speak eight languages, a community-based advocacy program, and community outreach to 254 community-based and 57 residential Chinese, Japanese, Korean, South Asian, Vietnamese, Cambodian, Thai, Filipino, and occasional other Asian clients. The majority of the clients are Cambodian and Chinese.

The task force operates on the strong premise that there should be dedicated organizations specifically for immigrant women and their families who are victims of IPV. There are several reasons for this. First, immigrants and refugees require staff who know victims services as well as how to integrate immigrants into mainstream society and how to serve the extended family. Sometimes there are multiple victims; sometimes there are multiple perpetrators.

Immigration status is always a complication, and it is the major reason why the women don't leave their perpetrators. They may be afraid to leave the community because they haven't integrated. But if they leave

their husbands, then they may feel they can't even go to the grocery store anymore because the perpetrator may find out. The constant concern about day-to-day survival issues is a barrier to leaving the closed community. The tightness of the community and a lack of community level education about why domestic violence is a crime in this country are major cultural issues, as is women's distrust of law enforcement.

To fulfill its mission, the organization uses both paid and volunteer workers. A paid staff of 25 includes three outreach workers, six shelter workers, two financial workers, a grants manager, eight advocates, one program director, and two operations personnel. The agency has an active volunteer program with 35 hours of training for volunteers. Approximately 40 to 50 volunteer workers, some of whom are men and many of whom have professional backgrounds, do fund raising, work with children, teach English as a second language, and do other needed tasks. A volunteer coordinator sets the program. The Asian Task Force networks with providers of other services needed by their clients and their families by heightening community awareness and raising consciousness by going to events and festivals and doing community outreach. In addition, the agency facilitates medical care by encouraging clients to enroll in the state's insurance plan so they cannot be traced through their spouse's insurance. The agency also refers clients to culturally and linguistically competent mental health care.

---

needs are not likely to attract much less retain potential users, and they could cause more harm than good. Comprehensive programs of coordinated care include delivery of social, health, legal, and community services in one setting. If all services cannot be delivered in one setting, it is important that programs explicitly address with immigrant women how they can reach appropriate and available services.

ASSESSMENT AND INTERVENTION: BATTERED IMMIGRANT WOMEN AND HEALTH CARE SERVICES

The growing immigrant and refugee population in the United States has presented many challenges to health care providers. Refugee women are especially vulnerable to violence during their flight. Refugees suffer from higher rates of posttraumatic stress disorder and depression (Frye & D'Avanzo,

1994; Chung Kagawa-Singer, 1993). Their postmigration adjustment can be aggravated by the use of violence as a problem-solving mechanism within the family and by the stressors of immigration and resettlement, linguistic isolation within the community and from service providers, and fear of discrimination (Sharma, 2001).

In the United States, systems level barriers can be enormous. Immigrant and refugee women are faced with barriers to receiving both general medical and mental health care. These barriers include poverty, unemployment, and inadequate insurance coverage. Victims may not understand Western biomedicine and their medical rights within the U.S. health system, and they may be afraid to seek public assistance or public health coverage because of the perception that it could lead to deportation (Mayeno & Hirota, 1994). Given these barriers, it is recommended that health care systems and providers be culturally sensitive to those who do seek assistance. Cultural competence training about IPV must be included in curricula for agency staff and made mandatory for professional students and trainees. This is particularly important because needed services in the United States are often fragmented rather than having specific dedicated IPV agencies, where all services are offered or coordinated under one umbrella. Coordinated services and case management are particularly important for immigrants and refugees.

ASSESSMENT AND INTERVENTION: SCREENING FOR IPV IN THE CLINICAL SETTING

Given the high prevalence of IPV, all health care providers must be trained to screen for domestic violence and to be culturally competent when eliciting a history of abuse from immigrant women. The lack of community-based services for IPV has resulted in an increased responsibility of U.S. health care providers in the identification, screening, and referral of victims of IPV. Use of standardized protocols in some hospitals has been shown to increase the accurate identification of physical abuse of women by their husbands, boyfriends, or other intimates (McLeer & Anwar, 1987). In the United States, the Joint Commission on Accreditation of Healthcare Organizations has required such protocols since 1992. The Association of American Medical Colleges requires education of medical students in the recognition of family violence (Kassebaum & Anderson, 1995) and residency curricula have been created for training physicians in several specialties, including emergency medicine and obstetrics and gynecology.

Screening instruments for IPV are widely used. However, they may be of limited value in victims who come from some cultures, not only because they may have been developed and validated in a white or English-only context but also because of the variations in values and beliefs related to IPV across cultures. Some English-language instruments appear to be valid in Spanish (Fogarty & Brown, 2002). Unfortunately, there are few if any universally adaptable screening protocols. A 20-item screening inventory, however, has been developed by the World Health Organization.[1] Although developed for research use, it could be formatted for clinical use. This instrument was developed in consultation with international agencies that address women's health and family concerns. It has been tested in many countries, including Bangladesh, Brazil, China, Namibia, Peru, Tanzania, and Thailand (World Health Organization, 2000) and found to be valid and reliable. Women must be assured of confidentiality in the provider–client relationship.

Linguistic accessibility is difficult but paramount in assessing for abuse. Disclosing violence in a health care or therapeutic setting is challenging if the abuser accompanies the woman wherever she goes and especially so in settings where few immigrants of a certain language group are seen. It also can be difficult to find private time with a patient who is a victim of battering. It is not uncommon for batterers to insist upon remaining with the victim the entire time, to relate the history, and to assume a "protective stance" in the presence of providers. When the index of suspicion is high, potential victims must be removed from all family company long enough to get unfiltered information. This can require a great deal of resourcefulness on the part of the clinician and staff. Training of staff ensures that a mechanism for separating suspected victims from partners is in place.

There are significant sequelae from all types of abuse. These include a range of somatic complaints such as headache and migraine, abdominal pain, back pain or other chronic pain, and sleep disruptions. Behavioral problems include anxiety and depression, suicidality, posttraumatic stress disorder, and substance and eating disorders (Acierno et al., 1997). Thus, multiple clues may guide the provider to suspect that a patient is experiencing violence in her home. Many of the sequelae of domestic violence result in loss of time from work and loss of productivity (Dunham & Leetch, 1996). As there has been greater understanding of the consequences, this problem has been shifted into public view by women's organizations, the United Nations, and the World Health Organization.

In Case 15.2, the physician provided linguistic access for the client. In these situations, it is critical to avoid the use of spouses, children, or other relatives who may accompany the patients to medical care. It is important to establish a supportive context for the screening. This can be accomplished by educating women about the high prevalence of violence in the home—for instance, by saying "Violence is common" and noting the response of the woman to this information (Acierno et al., 1997). To be most effective, screening must be universal and brief to be easily incorporated into care routines. Screening needs to avoid stereotypical wording and stigmatizing language and must be conducted privately (away from those who accompany the patient). When on-site interpretation is unavailable, remote interpretation via telephone may be necessary (Kramer, Ivey, & Ying, 1999).

---

[1]More information about the WHO questionnaire may be found by contacting the World Health Organization, Dr. Claudia Garcia-Moreno, GPE/WHO, 20 Ave Appia, Geneva 1211, CH (garciamorenoc@who.ch).

CASE 15.2	ASHA

Asha is a young Punjabi woman who arrived from India for an arranged marriage. She lives in a community in which many South Asian marriages are arranged, and where it is expected that a bride will live with an extended family where she may be subject to discipline not only by her husband but also by her in-laws. Asha is beaten when she does not comply with her husband's wishes. The abuse has included both physical and sexual violence depending on the event. During one episode, she was pushed down the stairs by her husband and injured her wrist.

Her husband brought her to the emergency department for assessment and treatment of the injury. The physician who saw her did not speak Punjabi nor was there a Punjabi translator available. The physician did, however, recognize that the husband steered the entire history toward the clumsy accident that occurred and did not allow his wife to speak at any time. Asha nodded when the physician addressed her directly, looking at the ground the entire time. The physician told the husband she would need to obtain an X-ray of the wrist. The husband prepared to come

with his wife to the X-ray suite. The physician told the husband that X-ray exposure is dangerous and that he could not be in the suite with his wife because too many X-rays could result in infertility. The husband acceded, and a radiology technician escorted Asha to the radiology suite.

In the suite, the emergency nurse met the patient and obtained an immediate line for translation via a telephone interpretation service. The interpreter was specifically trained in medical interpretation. The patient was reassured that her information would be completely confidential and was provided with information on the availability of counseling and safe housing resources in the community. Armed with an adequate history now, the physician offered immediate access to resources, but the patient refused. A discreet phone number was provided for the patient's future use and she was informed that battering, while common, is not acceptable and can escalate. After the physician was assured that the patient had successfully communicated her concerns and knowledge of other injuries to the physician through the interpreter, and that the patient understood her resources, she was treated for her injury. Although not a completely successful outcome in the physician's eyes, the patient no longer looked dejected and accepted treatment of her injury.

INTERVENTION: ADDRESSING IPV IN IMMIGRANT COMMUNITIES

In addition to screening, public and provider education in the area of IPV prevention is needed in immigrant communities. Many myths regarding IPV must be overcome, including:

- Family violence does not happen.
- Family violence is acceptable.
- It is a woman's fate to be abused.
- Men are the rulers of the home and can discipline their wives (or use corporal punishment).
- Battered women have no alternatives but to live with the violence.
- Family violence is a problem for only one subsection of the community such as recent immigrants or those with less education.

To address these myths, it is necessary to educate the community about services, and to address the shame, stigma, and mistrust associated with obtaining IPV services. Linguistic accessibility must be improved, and social service and medical providers must be educated about IPV and cultural sensitivity in an

CASE 15.3 | NEW YORK ASIAN WOMEN'S CENTER

The New York Asian Women's Center (NYAWC) is the only New York City IPV program that serves multiple Asian immigrant communities and the only Asian women's shelter program in New York state. The NYAWC has taken a lead role in public education about IPV in Asian communities by publicizing domestic violence issues through a variety of media and forums, including workshops, conferences, public hearings, rallies, radio programming, and advertising. Workshops are conducted at social service, health, employment and city agencies, schools, police precincts, and corporations. Presentation topics have covered domestic violence in Asian communities and barriers that immigrant women encounter when seeking help. By teaching about how specific cultural issues affect Asian women's lives, these workshops sensitize many people to the unique situations that battered women face.

In keeping with East Asian tradition, community education programs focus on family harmony, good communication, and legal rights rather than family violence. NYWAC partners with two police precincts and the district attorney's office to train police officers in how to handle abused women and how to obtain orders of protection. Vietnamese, Cambodians, and Laotians don't cooperate with the police and try to keep things private.

The center also produces radio programs in different Asian dialects during which counselors hold interactive discussions about battered women's rights, self-petitioning for green cards, the effects of domestic violence on children, welfare reform and its effects on battered women, and safety plans. The radio shows have mass appeal because listeners can learn about domestic violence in their native languages—regardless of their literacy levels—and access valuable information. Listeners can also call in with questions and remain anonymous. The center also sponsors an annual walk against domestic violence. Although radio is the preferred medium for Chinese women, Koreans and South Asians tend to prefer newspaper articles.

---

effort to increase awareness and improve response to family violence. Service providers may need to be taught about victims' rights and the role of police and courts both here and in native countries in order to assuage fears on the part of victims.

INTERVENTION: LEGAL AND POLICY PREVENTION STRATEGIES

Many immigrants are not aware of the changes in U.S. immigration law that resulted from passage of the Violence Against Women Act (1994), which allows victims of domestic violence, even if they are undocumented, to seek suspension of deportation and lawful permanent resident status through self-petitioning. Another change is the memorandum issued by the INS in 1995 that allows women to seek political asylum in the United States because of gender or gender-specific persecution (Orloff & Kelly, 1995; Schornstein, 1997). Finally, a new procedure called the "U Visa" was created in the VAWA 2000 renewal. This is a new nonimmigrant visa for crime victims not protected by the original 1994 VAWA. The U Visa was designed to help noncitizen crime victims who have suffered substantial physical or mental abuse and who are willing to cooperate with government officials investigating or prosecuting the criminal activity (National Network on Behalf of Battered Immigrant Women, 2002). Unfortunately, many immigrant women have no information about these protections. This lack of knowledge is compounded by fear and distrust of governmental authorities and legal channels (Bui & Morash, 1999).

MANDATORY REPORTING

Mandatory reporting is a laudable step toward the recognition and criminalizing of domestic violence. However, given the reticence of immigrant women to report violence against them and in their families, mandatory reporting may have serious negative repercussions and potentially discourage women from reporting the violence (Hyman, Schillinger, & Lo, 1995; Rodriguez, McLoughlin, Nah, & Campbell, 2001). It is not uncommon that a woman who meets behavioral criteria for physical victimization does not perceive herself as being abused. Furthermore, depending on the police or legal action that is taken, she may be vulnerable to more abuse. Many immigrant and refugee women come from war-torn areas, and they have witnessed political, economic, and social strife. They mistrust the government and its various arms, so the consequences of the reporting and the threats of deportation can result in more tensions within the family and potentially more abuse of the women. If men who are not lawful residents are deported as a result of reporting through this mandate, then women encounter the added burden of family breakup and the issues relating to custody and sharing of the children across international boundaries.

It has been argued that asking a woman about the abuse is in and of itself an intervention (Heise, 1994). However, given the issues with which immigrant women are confronted, even the chance to share their experiences is denied. The "choice" to report the violence to the police or governmental authorities has to be made by the woman. To avoid compounding her trauma, it is important that she is not pressured to sign a consent decree to disclose the violence. She has to be given sufficient time, resources, support, and information before she can arrive at such a decision.

Policies that focus on improving access generally might also be expected to improve access to medical, mental health, and social services. An example of this is the recent federal health policy in the United States that established a patient's right to interpretation services in a hospital setting for those with limited English proficiency. It remains to be seen if this policy will be expanded to include office settings in private practice. Similarly standards for curricula and training of providers can help ensure that immigrant women receive the best possible services for IPV. Clinicians must be trained to ask about domestic violence routinely via curricula in medical, psychology, social work, and nursing schools and in all residencies.

Although not all of these policies have been assessed in terms of efficacy in detection and prevention of IPV, it is important as policies change that outcomes be assessed by advocacy organizations and that the findings are communicated back to policy makers.

PERSONAL REFLECTIONS

In our experience, it is rare to find a woman whose life has not been touched in some way by intimate partner abuse through firsthand experience or through the experience of a family member, friend, neighbor, or co-worker. Each of us has worked with immigrant women and been deeply affected by their struggles to survive and to keep their families together, as well as the overwhelming barriers they face when trying to get the help that they need. Susan worked many years as an emergency physician, caring regularly for women who had experienced domestic violence. The frustrations of that experience led her to incorporate routine screening and referral as well as to advocate policy level changes for women. Liz researches and writes about immigrant health. Her areas of expertise include cultural competence and patient–provider communication. She specializes in East Asian cultures, particularly Chinese American, and she has worked extensively in the area of Asian American mental health. Susan and Liz coedited a book, *Immigrant Women's Health: Problems and Solutions,* in which they included a chapter about IPV. Marianne has worked with community agencies to design programs and services. She has conducted research with women from numerous Asian communities, providing them a voice to inform others of their experiences. She views her research and writing as a vehicle for advocacy.

An important part of our learning comes from listening to and validating the experiences of women across cultural lines. Women from all countries of the world are vulnerable to IPV. It is important for practitioners across all disciplines to be aware of the unique circumstances that confront immigrant women in terms of its high prevalence and its attendant physical, emotional, and economic consequences.

CONCLUSIONS

One of the important lessons that can be drawn from research with immigrant women is that domestic violence screening protocols should be incorporated into all intake assessments. Although care should be taken to approach the issue in a culturally sensitive manner, it is important that every woman be given the opportunity to have private time with an appropriate interpreter away from family members in order to fully assess her risks and inform her of her options for receiving care, support services, and asylum. Practitioners need to be especially cognizant that somatic symptoms of all types can be a manifestation of battering and sexual violence. Ruling out appropriate medical causes is important, but because of the high prevalence of IPV, the provider should be prepared to obtain appropriate consultations with therapists who have experience dealing with the sequelae of long-standing abuse as soon as is feasible.

If the clinician establishes that a patient has a history of victimization, concern should be evidenced for the patient and the patient reassured that help is available. Safety needs should be addressed first, including the safety of dependents such as children. In the context of the immigrant woman, it is important to identify those resources in the community that are likely to have language interpretation skills available. In addition, the need for family-centered treatment should be determined because it may be more acceptable to immigrant women from cultures in which the family is supreme. In the United States, the patient should be told that protection exists under current law, even if she is a recent or undocumented immigrant. Laws that mandate reporting of injuries from domestic violence vary from state to state in the United States and certainly cannot be expected to be the same across countries. Clinicians should be familiar with the laws on domestic violence in their states and respective countries (Hyman, Schillinger, & Lo, 1995).

Finally, working with women from other cultural contexts will require clinicians to reexamine their convictions about the need for culturally competent practices and feminist principles that call for the end of patriarchal structures that oppress women. There is a dilemma inherent in the work that raises difficult questions about what constitutes ethical practice that each of us must answer individually. It is also an area of collective concern that clinicians and researchers must begin to discuss.

KEY CONCEPTS

- high prevalence of IPV among immigrant populations
- factors unique to immigration elevate a woman's risk for violence
- cultural differences in acceptability of minor violence within intimate personal relationships may present a difficult cross-cultural void for providers
- immigrant women face multiple barriers to receiving help
- immigrant women may be at higher risk of staying in violent relationships because of cultural expectations
- most immigrant women concerned with issues of family solidarity more than their individual freedom
- universal screening for intimate partner violence increases detection
- certain patterns of injury, somatic complaints, and behavior are associated with IPV
- providers must provide culturally competent resources and services whenever feasible
- community services that highlight family-centered treatment may be more acceptable in some cultures; individual approaches may serve other women
- policy approaches to IPV include asylum provisions for IPV victims, mandatory reporting of injured persons, and mandates for provision of linguistically and culturally appropriate services

QUESTIONS FOR REFLECTION

1. What messages have you received from your upbringing, media, and your peers about intimate partner violence?
2. In your cultural background, what is the stereotypic "role" for a woman in a marriage?

3. If a woman slaps a man across the face after he says something that she finds offensive—is that partner violence? If yes, why? If not, why not?
4. How do you define abuse?
5. A woman tells you that it is a man's place to discipline his wife. How do you react?
6. You are working with a woman from a different cultural background than yours. She complains of headaches, stomach aches, and difficulty sleeping. You notice bruising on her arms. What do you do next?

EXERCISE

Imagine the following situation. Within the context of your own agency, your work leads you to suspect that violence is commonly used against women in one of the client populations. You discover that this use of violence is culturally sanctioned by the elders of the community and is considered to be necessary in maintaining the traditional respectful position with regard to males in this culture.

With a partner who works in a different kind of agency, discuss the following general and practical issues:

1. What does the law say about this issue?
2. What are your specific hesitations about revealing this situation?
3. What are some of the strategies you could both come up with for protecting women in this culture but not alienating them from their community? What policy changes need to be made in your agency to do this? What skills would helpers need to learn? What would be the first step in changing the situation?

References

Abraham, M. (2000). Isolation as a form of marital violence: The South Asian immigrant experience. *Journal of Social Distress and the Homeless, 9*(3), 221–236.

Acierno, R., Resnick, H., & Kilpatrick, D. (1997). Health impact of interpersonal violence 1: Prevalence rates, case identification, and risk factors for sexual assault, physical assault, and domestic violence in men and women. *Behavioral Medicine, 23,* 53–64.

Ayyub, R. (2000). Domestic violence in the South Asian Muslim immigrant population in the United States. *Journal of Social Distress and the Homeless, 9,* 237–248.

Barnett, O., & Fagan, R. (1993). Alcohol use in male spouse abusers and their female partners. *Journal of Family Violence, 8*(1), 1–25.

Bui, H., & Morash, M. (1999). Domestic violence in the Vietnamese immigrant community: An exploratory study. *Violence Against Women, 5*(7), 769–795.

Chung, R. C., & Kagawa-Singer, M. (1993). Predictors of psychological distress among Southeast Asian refugees. *Social Science and Medicine, 36*(5), 631–639.

Crites, L. (1991). Cross-cultural counseling in wife battering cases. *Response to the Victimization of Women and Children, 13*(4), 8–12.

Dunham, N., & Leetch, L. (1996). *The health care components of domestic violence* and abuse: Implications for Wisconsin providers and health care systems. Madison: Wisconsin Network for Health Policy Research.

Fogarty, C., & Brown, J. (2002). Screening for abuse in Spanish-speaking women. *Journal of American Board of Family Practice, 15,* 101–111.

Frye, B. A., & D'Avanzo, C. D. (1994). Cultural themes in family stress and violence among Cambodian refugee women in the inner city. *Advances in Nursing Science, 16*(3), 64–77.

Heise, L. (1994). *Violence against women: The hidden health burden.* World Bank Discussion Papers. Washington, DC: World Bank.

Hyman, A., Schillinger, D., & Lo, B. (1995). Laws mandating reporting of domestic violence. Do they promote patient well-being? *Journal of the American Medical Association, 273*(22), 1781–1787.

Kassebaum, D., & Anderson, M. B. (1995). Proceedings of the AAMC's Conference on the Education of Medical Students about Family Violence and Abuse. *Academic Medicine, 70*(11), 961–1001.

Kim, K., & Cho, Y. (1992). Epidemiological survey of spousal abuse in Korea. In E. C. Viano (Ed.), *Intimate violence: Interdisciplinary perspectives.* Washington, DC: Hemisphere.

Kramer, E., Ivey, S., & Ying, Y. (Eds.). (1999). *Immigrant women's health: Problems and solutions.* San Francisco: Jossey-Bass.

Mayeno, L., & Hirota, S. M. (1994). Access to health care. In N. W. S. Zane, D. T. Takeuchi, & K. N. J. Young (Eds.), *Confronting critical health issues of Asian and Pacific Islander Americans.* Thousand Oaks, CA: Sage.

McLeer, S. V., & Anwar, R. (1987). The role of the emergency physician in the prevention of domestic violence. *Annals of Emergency Medicine, 16*(10), 1155–1161.

Mehrotra, M. (1999). The social construction of wife abuse: Experiences of Asian Indian women in the United States. *Violence Against Women, 5*(6), 619–640.

Merchant, M. (2000). A comparative study of agencies assisting domestic violence victims: Does the South Asian community have special needs? *Journal of Social Distress and the Homeless, 9*(3), 249–259.

National Network on Behalf of Battered Immigrant Women (2002). *Legal opinion on U-visas.* Available at www.nationalimmigrationproject.org/domestic-violence/Uvisas/UVisa_index.htm.

Orloff, L., & Kelly, N. (1995). A look at the Violence Against Women Act and gender-related political asylum. *Violence Against Women, 1*(4), 380–400.

Raj, A., & Silverman, J. (2002). Intimate partner violence among South Asian women in greater Boston. *Journal of the American Medical Women's Association, 57*(2), 111–114.

Rodriguez, M. A., McLoughlin, E., Nah, G., & Campbell, J. C. (2001). Mandatory reporting of domestic violence injuries to the police: What do emergency department patients think? *Journal of the American Medical Association, 286*(5), 580–583.

Schornstein, S. L. (1997). *Domestic violence: A primer for health care professionals.* Thousand Oaks, CA: Sage.

Sharma A. (2001). Healing the wounds of domestic abuse. *Violence Against Women, 7*(12), 1405–1429.

Song, Y. I. (1996). *Battered women in Korean immigrant families: The silent scream.* New York: Garland.

Tjaden, P., & Thoennes, N. (1998, November). *Prevalence, incidence, and consequences of violence against women: Findings from the National Violence Against Women survey.* Research in Brief, NCJ 172837. Washington, DC: U.S. Department of Justice, National Institute of Justice.

Torres, S. (1991). A comparison of wife abuse between two cultures: Perceptions, attitudes, nature and extent. *Issues in Mental Health Nursing, 12*(1), 113–131.

U.S. Department of Justice. (2000). *Intimate partner violence: A special report from the Bureau of Justice Statistics.* Available at www.ojp.usdoj.gov/bjs.

U.S. Department of Justice. (2001). *Intimate partner violence and age of victim, 1993–1999* (pp. 1–2). Available at www.ojp.usdoj.gov/bjs.

World Health Organization. (2000). *WHO Multi-country study on women's health and life events.* Geneva: Author.

Xu, X., & Campbell, J. (2000). Intimate partner violence against Chinese women. *Trauma, Violence, and Abuse, 2,* 296–325.

Yick, A. (2001). Feminist theory and status inconsistency theory: Application to domestic violence in Chinese immigrant families. *Violence Against Women, 7*(5), 545–562.

Yoshioka, M. R., & Dang, Q. (2000). *The Asian family violence report: A study of the Cambodian, Chinese, Korean, South Asian, and Vietnamese communities in Massachusetts.* Boston: Asian Task Force Against Domestic Violence.

Yoshioka, M. R., Gilbert, L., & El-Bassel, N. (2003). Social support and disclosure of abuse: A comparison of African American, Hispanic, and South Asian battered women. *Journal of Family Violence, 18*(3), 171–180.

THE THERAPEUTIC VALUE OF ACTIVISM

Albanian Women in Postwar Kosova

**MELISSA STONE AND
VJOSA DOBRUNA
UNITED STATES AND KOSOVA**

OVERVIEW

This chapter will describe one of the most ancient and prevailing social structures or custom laws in Europe—the Kanun of Lekë Dukagjini—and how it still influences the women and men of Kosova in their private and public lives, especially in rural agrarian communities, the last place in every society where new social change takes root. Some of these traditional influences continue to hinder women's capacity to reach their full human potential, as well as contribute negatively to the postconflict stresses that affect them disproportionately. Furthermore, the reintroduction of the Kanun, as new translations and interpretations are currently appearing and becoming widely available, could pose a serious challenge to the development of democratic structures and the rule of law according to international human rights standards, which require a dramatic change in the historical treatment of women in Kosova.

The chapter will explore the Kosovar population's increased willingness after the 1998–99 war to change particular aspects of Albanian cultural identity associated with custom law that may have outlived their usefulness. Examples will include women's responses to a series of internationally facilitated participatory group processes in Peja, Klina, and Istog; and women organizing around missing persons and prisoners of war in Gjakova. The women's responses will be analyzed to identify behavioral distinctions between women in rural and urban areas, and those who have had access to international experiences compared to those who have not. This analysis shows how increasing Kosovar Albanian women's options for self-expression through social activism can serve as a foundational intervention for addressing gender discrimination.

The chapter will also identify new opportunities for women's participation and decision-making authority in public as well as private life, particularly in democratic self-governance systems currently developing in Kosova. These opportunities can provide a form of therapeutic healing in a postapartheid environment for the ethnic Albanian population, particularly women who are new participants in numerous community development projects. Such intervention has inherent therapeutic value because of the similarities in the personal growth and empowerment that women experience whether they are engaged in social activism or are involved in rehabilitation methods prescribed for those suffering posttraumatic stress syndrome.

THE PROBLEM

The underprivilege of Kosovar Albanian women is characterized by:

- unequal access of male and female offspring to family inheritance;
- the highest maternal mortality rates in Europe at 152 per 1,000 live births (United Nations Population Fund, 2002);
- child custody disputes, whereby the husband's family gains custody by default according to custom;
- domestic violence, in an environment where women encounter difficulty finding safety in public or private life; and
- widespread posttraumatic stress syndrome because of war, including rape, injury, and loss of family members and property.

Few of the examples above of structural gender-based discrimination are unique to Kosova. To the contrary, discrimination along gender lines occurs on every continent. However, the normalization process experienced by formerly isolated or postconflict societies as they work to rebuild their political, economic, and social lives includes the integration of their current realities into the larger global context. During this process, invariably traditional ways clash with rapidly evolving international regulatory structures, including human rights law, which promotes egalitarian values while discouraging gender-based discrimination.

Specifically, there is a clash between the Kanun, the traditional code of laws that is highly patriarchal, and the international human rights laws developed by the world community through the United Nations to protect equality between the sexes. As a comprehensive legal system, the Kanun is complete with a code of conduct for every family member and remedies for addressing nearly every aspect of noncompliance with its tenets. The U.N. Convention on the Elimination of All Forms of Discrimination Against Women (CEDAW) of 1979 is designed to ensure equality between the sexes and to protect the rights of women. CEDAW is the most comprehensive human rights instrument ever devised to support equal human rights for women; it was ratified by 171 of 190

United Nations member states (United Nations, 2001). As of May 2001, the constitutional framework of Kosova ensures the rights and freedoms of this convention as applicable domestic law in Kosova.

To reconcile the fundamental differences between local customs and global standards, strategies and mechanisms for increasing women's advocacy for gender equality are needed in a variety of sectors: from reproductive health care, to legal and judicial systems addressing parental and property rights, to enforcement of criminal codes on assault, and to social services. CEDAW addresses all of these sectors in an effort to reduce and eventually stop discrimination against women.

THE KOSOVAR ALBANIAN POPULATION[1]

The Albanians of Kosova practice an unusual blend of Western and Eastern cultures, influenced by the Kanun and Catholic and Muslim religions combined with socialist ideology.[2] They have adapted to a particularly complex, and historically conflict-ridden environment, compounded now by a dependence on international support with no answer in sight to their plea for independence. This situation is unlike the four other former Yugoslav states that were internationally recognized as independent nations a decade ago. For the Kosovar populations, these complexities have accumulated gradually, over many generations, each seemingly with its own tale of conquest and creation.

Aside from vague memories of tax breaks for Muslims, not many people living in Kosova today remember exactly how the majority of Catholic Kosovar Albanians became Muslims under the Ottoman rule, which began in 1389 when the Ottomans (Muslims) defeated Serbs, Albanians, and other Christians in the "Blackbird Battle" of *Kosova Polje* (Serbian) or *Fushe Kosove* (Albanian). Soon after, Lekë Dukagjini (1410–1481) codified a custom law known as the Kanun, some elements of which may predate mass Indo-European migration, while others evolved as compromises between the Catholic Church and the Turkish government that was imposing Islamic Sharia, or religious law.[3] Nevertheless, the Kanun forms the core of traditional Albanian social organization, ritual, legend, and folksongs from Albania to Montenegro, Serbia, Macedonia, and, of course, Kosova. It is one of the oldest and most enduring self-administered legal systems anywhere in today's Europe.

---

[1] The total population of Kosova comprises 90% to 95% ethnic Albanians in addition to Ashkali, Bosnian, Croat, Egyptians, Gorani, Roma, Serb, and Turkish populations, whose numbers vary between municipalities.

[2] In addition to Catholic and Muslim influences, there is a significant Albanian population in the south of Albania and diaspora that is Christian Orthodox and also influenced by the Kanun.

[3] Given the strong Catholic influences on the Kanun, questions remain about how, when, and where the Islamic Sharia came to influence Albanian practices. These nuances would require significant comparative research of different versions of the Kanun and are beyond the scope of this document, which concentrates on the version of the Kanun that is currently the most widely available in Kosova, Macedonia, and Albania and translated into at least four languages.

After World War II, there was one 40-year wind of change when Kosova was an autonomous province of Yugoslavia, and the state prospered, developed modern infrastructure, and provided many residents with advanced education and relative freedom of movement within and beyond Europe. During that period, the number of Kosovar Albanian men and women who became doctors, lawyers, scholars, engineers, architects, and nearly every other profession increased exponentially. Albanian Kosovars participated actively in government, were free to speak Albanian, and studied its unique and wealthy literature, which dated back to the Illyrian civilization.

However, the direction of this wind was suddenly reversed when the former Yugoslav regime, led by Slobodan Milosevic, ended most rights for Albanian Kosovars by revoking Kosova's autonomy in 1989, enforcing a mass expulsion of ethnic Albanians from state jobs in 1990, and subsequently dividing public schools and health care along ethnic lines. In response to these precedent-setting ethnic divisions, within two years Slovenia, Croatia, Macedonia, and Bosnia and Herzegovina had declared independence, and war raged in the western part of what had once been the Federal Republic of Yugoslavia (U.S. Department of State, 1995).

During the 1990s in Kosova, the dominant Yugoslav state escalated policies of forced ethnic apartheid, using the rule of law as the self-legitimizing regime's tool for colonial domination over its own citizens (Malcolm, 1999, p. 349). In 1998, the Serb-led Yugoslav dominance turned violent. Despite Kosovar Albanian armed resistance, more than 1.5 million people were forced out of their homes, most exiled to neighboring states before and during a NATO-led air strike campaign in 1999 that ended when the Yugoslav military withdrew from Kosova in June (North Atlantic Treaty Organization, 1999). Shortly thereafter, the United Nations initiated an interim administrative mission, which has engaged in the development of provisional democratic institutions with gradual transfer of authority to Kosovars and reform toward a market economy.

In the absence of reliable state institutions in Kosova during the 1990s, particular aspects of Kanun custom law were again the default, which reinforced the extended family as the foundational economic support network that linked rural and urban Kosovar Albanians to a lifeline offered by their kindred, albeit distant family Diaspora. New translations and interpretations of the Kanun, which are now widely available in Kosova, suggest that the code is being reintroduced.[4] This recent reinforcement of patriarchal values and tradition-based gender discrimination from the Kanun may be a direct challenge to new developments of democratic structures and the rule of law.

At the same time, there have never before been so many reasons for Kosovar Albanians, particularly women, to consider revisions toward democratically and legally based gender equality. Regardless of its many merits, Kanun law is simply not serving many women's needs, especially women in rural areas—not

---

[4] The version of the Kanun discussed in this chapter was translated and interpreted from the original Albanian text by Shtjefën Gjeçov and published in 1989.

compared to the rights they would have according to CEDAW, which obligates states parties to "take all appropriate measures to modify the social and cultural patterns of conduct of men and women." The purpose of modifying these patterns is to achieve "the elimination of prejudices and customary and all other practices which are based on the idea of the inferiority and superiority of either of the sexes or on the stereotyped roles for men and women" (CEDAW, Article 5a).

THE KANUN

Without contracts, lawyers, or formal courts, the Kanun has several virtues that Western "rule of law" does not offer, such as *besa* (word of honor) or belief, which means that a man's word is worth his life.[5] If he breaks his word, the person who he has deceived has the right to kill him. Thus, one's personal accountability is regarded as one of the highest virtues.

Marriage is the most magnificent ritual that any person could ever experience, requiring months of celebrations, weeks of family gatherings, and the biggest life change of all for women. A new wife joins her husband in his family's home, where the fruits of their labor, including children, become the responsibility of the husband's family. The economic sustainability of the family, as well as its representation in public life, is thus the responsibility of the males. Fathers pass their land to their sons. Male heirs, specifically the eldest son, provide for the elderly until death takes them. The division of labor by gender enables women to birth many children, as is common in agrarian societies.

For almost six centuries, Kanun custom law has provided ethnic Albanians with a reliable and stabilizing system for social organization and self-governance. Despite the abolition of custom law in 1912, Kanun-based practices of responsibility to the family and rituals around birth, death, marriage, and property ownership are still widely exercised (Gjeçov, 1989, p. xvii).

In the 20th century, there have not been many enduring reasons for Kosova Albanians to stray far from the teachings of the Kanun. Numerous severe traumatic events may have created a need to hold onto tradition and strengthen the collective patriarchal community and family structures. These events include Balkan wars, the massive devastation of two world wars, two major redefinitions of national boundaries, multiple attempts to force Kosova Albanians out of Kosova, and 40 years of socialist rule that were followed by ethnic apartheid and yet another war. Because of this tumultuous history, there is not a person over the age of 5 alive in Kosova today who does not remember from one to a dozen of these human-made, life-threatening, or severely life-altering events.[6]

Of course, Kosovar Albanians experienced the effects of trauma that are usual for individuals to experience during and after war, violent territorial redivisions,

---

[5] The concept of *besa* is not equally applicable to women.

[6] Given the strong domination of males in all of the regimes that were responsible for the decision making associated with these events, the gender specificity of this terminology is deliberate.

and policies of exclusion and forced assimilation. However, because there were so many of these devastating events in a short time, the usual trauma experienced by Kosovar Albanians as individuals is further compounded by the repeated challenges to Kosovar Albanian identity.

COMPARISON OF THE KANUN AND CEDAW

This section compares some of the social and cultural patterns codified by the Kanun with the provisions of CEDAW as they relate to the most significant problems that Kosovar Albanian women are currently experiencing. It will show how the domination of the Kanun's traditional law contributes to these problems rather than enabling social evolution for problem alleviation.

Maternity and Maternal Mortality Rates

Because marriage is a precondition for socially acceptable reproduction, maternity, and maternal mortality, marriage and the constraints it imposes upon women are inextricably linked to the conditions under which maternal mortality is prevalent. For example, if a woman does not have the right to choose her own husband, then it is unlikely she will have the right to choose when and under what conditions she engages in reproductive behavior within her marriage. Although many factors contribute to maternal mortality, including access to professional health care and general nutrition, the number of children and intervals between pregnancies are the critical issues to consider that are related to women's participation (or lack of) in decision making about reproduction within marriage.

According to the Kanun, marriage is a requirement of young women, not an option:

> The young woman, even if her parents are not alive, does not have the right to concern herself about her own marriage; this right is held by her brothers or other relatives. The young woman does not have the right: (a) to choose her own husband; she must go to the man to whom she has been betrothed; (b) to interfere in the selection of a matchmaker or in the engagement arrangements. (Gjeçov, 1989, p. 22)

"If the girl refuses to submit to her fate under any circumstances, and her parents support her, she may never marry another man" (Gjeçov, 1989, p. 26). According to the Kanun, a woman's rejection of her fiancé could be *de facto* suicide. Thus, not only are village women's marriages arranged without their choice of husband but also the rejection of the husbands chosen for them could leave them either as lifelong burdens to their parents, without husbands at all, or dead. This aspect of forced marriage, combined with the wife's duties[7] toward her husband "to submit to his domination" and "to fulfill her conjugal duties" may explain why Albanians have the highest fertility rate in Europe. The combination of high fertility rates and poor reproductive health care has consequences

---

[7] In the Kanun tradition, women have duties rather than rights.

for Kosovar Albanian women and children, including the highest maternal mortality and one of the highest infant mortality rates.

CEDAW proposes a different set of rights regarding women's participation in decision making within marriage and family life that are likely to affect women's fertility rates. States are required to "ensure, on the basis of equality of men and women" the same rights to "enter into marriage" and "freely to choose a spouse and to enter into marriage only with their free and full consent"; as well as "the same rights and responsibilities during marriage and its dissolution." Further, states must ensure men and women "the same rights to decide freely and responsibly on the number and spacing of their children, and to have access to the information, education and means to enable them to exercise these rights" (CEDAW, Article 16a, 16d).

Male and Female Offsprings' Access to Family Inheritance

Kanun law does not permit women under any condition to inherit land or houses. The Albanian woman does not inherit anything from her parents—neither possessions nor house; the Kanun considers a woman as superfluity in the household. Her parents are not concerned about their daughter's trousseau or about anything else; the man who has become engaged to her must take care of such matters:

> [Even] if there may be a hundred daughters, none of them have the right to any share in the inheritance of their parents, nor do any of their sons or daughters. . . . A father who does not have sons may leave his daughter neither land nor property nor house. If a house has only female heirs, the closest relative either goes to live with them or takes them into his home, and from that time he takes ownership of the property and wealth. (Gjeçov, 1989, pp. 52, 56)

The 1984 Yugoslav Law on Marriage and Family Relations contains some of the most progressive provisions in Europe for equal property ownership rights between spouses, despite the fact that there was less than three years of implementation between the passage of the law and the beginning of the Milosevic campaign promoting ethnic divisions in 1987.[8] Nevertheless, CEDAW reinforces women's equal rights to property ownership and inheritance as men, including "the right to family benefits" (CEDAW, Article 14a).

Child Custody

According to the Kanun, "the wife who is left, in leaving her husband's house, has no right to take anything with her" (not even her children)—

> except the clothes she is wearing. The wife does not have any rights over either the children or the house. A young woman who becomes a widow, but who has children, and who wants to remain in her husband's house with her children must be

---

[8] Articles 51, 54, 306, and 307.

> guaranteed by two local guarantors . . . who must state that she will not separate from her children, or that she will not ask to separate from them and remarry. (Gjeçov, 1989, p. 40)

It is implied that if she wants to remarry or do anything else not explicitly permitted by the head of the husband's household, then she has to leave her children in that household when she departs it. "The wife does not have any right over either the children or the house" (Gjeçov, 1989, p. 34).

However, CEDAW requires states that are party to the convention to "ensure, on a basis of equality of men and women . . . the same rights and responsibilities as parents, irrespective of their marital status, in matters relating to their children; in all cases the interests of the children shall be paramount." Also ensured are "the same rights and responsibilities with regard to guardianship, wardship, trusteeship and adoption of children, or similar institutions." Regarding the property of a marriage, CEDAW provides for "the same rights for both spouses in respect of the ownership, acquisition, management, administration, enjoyment and disposition of property" (United Nations, 2001; see Article 16d, 16f, 16h).

Currently, in postwar Kosova, there are many cases of women who are victims of this interpretation of the Kanun, including several women at the Safe House in Gjakova. In the Drenica region, where much fighting and loss of male lives occurred during the 1999 war, young widows were forced to leave their children and to go back to live with their parents without their children because neither their in-laws nor parents will allow the mothers to care for their children. In addition to expulsion from their late husbands' houses, these women are forbidden to contact their children. In order to remarry, any of these women will have to have permission from her parents and from her in-laws.

Domestic Violence

According to Kanun law,

> a woman is known as a sack, made to endure as long as she lives in her husband's house. Her parents do not interfere in her affairs, but they bear the responsibility for her and must answer for anything dishonorable that she does. . . . The husband has the right to counsel and correct his wife, to beat and bind his wife when she scorns his words and orders, . . . [whereas] the duties of the wife are to submit to his domination. (Gjeçov, 1989, pp. 28, 38, 44)

In Kosova, gender-based subordination is deeply rooted in the mentality of men and women and is regarded as a natural biological difference between them. "If a husband beats his wife, he incurs no guilt," according to the Kanun, and her parents may not make any claims on him because of the beating.

In addition to a woman's vulnerability to the wrath of her father and husband, she is vulnerable to expulsion from the house by her son, with no right to self-defense, and without the perpetrator of violent acts against her holding any responsibility for the guilt of causing her damage. "If the mother is vexatious (causing disorder in the house), her son expels her from the house empty-handed except for giving her bread (three loads of grain) for the first year, and nothing else" (Gjeçov, 1989, p. 44).

Under such conditions, where violence is permissible by fathers against their children and husbands against their wives, violence against women remains an acceptable part of the deeply entrenched tradition. This is blatant noncompliance with human rights standards according to the Universal Declaration of Human Rights, which states:

> Everyone has the right to life, liberty, and security of person. No one shall be held in slavery or servitude; slavery and the slave trade shall be prohibited in all their forms. No one shall be subjected to torture or to cruel, inhuman or degrading treatment or punishment. (United Nations, 1948, Articles 3–5)

POSTTRAUMATIC STRESS SYNDROME

War created a situation that made the Kanun inoperable, paving the way for social change as well. In stark contrast to the Kanun's provisions for the protection of women by men, Albanian women in Kosova have often been subjected to threats of abuse, whether from domestic violence within the home or from Yugoslav state-led violations in the public sphere. For example, in the recent postwar period, evidence of rape as a war crime propagated by the Yugoslav state has been gathered for use at the International Criminal Tribunal for the Former Yugoslavia (ICTY) (Human Rights Watch, 2000).

Albanian women who have endured this inhumane violation experience double, sometimes triple jeopardy. First, she suffers from the experience, physically, emotionally, and psychologically—perhaps economically and socially as well—for the rest of her life. Second, if she is unmarried, the Kanun may consider her rapist to be her husband, considering that "abducting a woman or girl" and "keeping a woman outside of marriage" are both "types of marriages" defined by the Kanun (Gjeçov, 1989, p. 20). If she is already married, the insult to her husband remains forever without forgiveness, "A man is dishonored if his wife is insulted or if she runs off with someone" and "an offense to honor is never forgiven" (Gjeçov, 1989, p. 130). Because a woman may be shot in the back for adultery, presumably whether the adultery was consensual or not, rape is considered as adultery according to this tradition. In addition to the horror of rape and the accompanying trauma, these women's honor is ruined forever, and consequently they may experience rejection and shame from their communities.

Self-perceptions of potential worthlessness in family life can serve to further silence women. If they provide public testimony against rape as a war crime, they admit their own dishonor and that committed against their husbands and families. Because rape as a war crime perpetrated by Yugoslav military and paramilitary in Bosnia received so much global media coverage, by the time war came to Kosova, most women were afraid of being raped whether or not they physically experienced it. The real threat of rape, compounded by a natural fear of violation, has made many girls and women—as well as their families—hyper-vigilant about security. This vigilance has not ended with the cessation of war, and the entry of 50,000 foreign troops has not dispelled the widespread fear of male-perpetrated sexual violence against women. In addition, the fear of living under apartheid and being oppressed again by a discriminatory and violent regime has not permanently subsided as Kosova awaits a final determination of statehood.

Posttraumatic stress syndrome results when women and men continue to experience fear responses repeatedly after the fear-provoking stimulus is no longer present. Western psychotherapists sometimes consider traumatic response to be a mental disorder. However, Levine makes a distinction between normal and healthy responses (i.e., as an initial response to danger, during and imme-diately after a traumatic episode) and problematic responses (i.e., when the responses continue in circumstances where there is no perceivable danger) (Levine & Frederick, 1997).

The silence of Kosovar Albanian women about domestic violence and rape in war may prevent traumatic responses from ever being processed or subse-quently resolved. Further, culturally sanctioned women's silence in public life, especially in rural areas, may also preclude the gathering of evidence such as wit-ness and victim testimonies in legal prosecution of those who committed atroc-ities in the recent war, including rape, at the ICTY. However, over the past 15 years, there have been numerous indigenous Albanian Kosovar women's rights advocates who have made leaps forward in providing new culturally acceptable models for addressing domestic violence and crimes against women in war.[9] Furthermore, there are indications that some of the postwar international inter-ventions that pay attention to women, promote their expression in public life, and encourage their active engagement in social change efforts may offer some therapeutic relief from posttraumatic symptoms. Below is an explanation of how this takes place.

THE MEANINGS OF AUTHORITY AND PARTICIPATION IN PUBLIC LIFE

The impact of the women-only groups resulted in epistemic differences in per-ceptions of authority between self and other. This fits well with Paolo Freire's four-stage model of culturally conditioned consciousness. It shows the movement from intransitive to transitive modes. The *transitive* is the ability to take action in the face of crisis, and moving into this mode involves becoming an active agent

---

[9] For example, consider the following: the Center for the Protection of Women and Children founded by Dr. Vjosa Dobruna and now directed by Sevdie Ahmeti in Pristina, with branches in more than five locations around Kosova; the Women's Shelter, also founded by Dr. Dobruna, and directed by Sakibe Doli in Gjakova; Motrat Qiriazi, led by two sisters, Igballe Rogova and Safete Rogova in Pristina with activities around Prizren, Has, and Mitrovica; and the Women's Wellness Center, led by Lumnije Decani in Peja.

THE DUKAGJINI VALLEY AFTER THE WAR

The following is a summary of observations of how Kosova Albanian women's participatory behavior in public settings differs between rural and urban populations and the healing potential in breaking the code of silence. All observations were made within three municipalities: Peja, Klina, and Istog, which are clustered in the Dukagjini Valley (named after the one and only Lekë Dukagjini, founder of the Kanun). As the massacres and village burnings started in 1998 in the municipality just next to Klina, these three municipalities were among the most war-ravaged. By June 1999, when NATO troops entered, between 70% and 90% of all building structures had been burned, shelled, or otherwise damaged, many of them beyond repair. Dead livestock and humans had been deposited in wells to poison the water supply. The fields were barren, except for those seeded with landmines. Many inhabitants of this area had spent 1 to 6 months of winter and spring living in forests without shelter or food before fleeing Kosova—if they had been able to leave at all. Members of every village and town spoke of their dear ones who were missing, dead, imprisoned or otherwise injured and devastated during the period leading up to NATO entry into Kosova in June 1999.

Immediately after the war, the U.S. Agency for International Development's Office for Transition Initiatives (USAID–OTI) initiated community meetings in townships and villages across Kosova to assist local community members in identifying their areas of greatest unmet needs. Equipment, supplies, building materials, and technical assistance were donated to project activities that were organized according to democratic standards, meaning that the basic requirement for the USAID donations was that each community achieved reasonable consensus about which projects would be addressed and how they would be organized. Women's participation was named a key objective in determining the success of community decision making, as more than half of the population (i.e., beneficiaries) of each project are female.

Between July 1999 and February 2000, as the co-director of the USAID–OTI Office in Peja, Melissa Stone attended and facilitated more than 300 community meetings in the municipalities of Peja, Klina, and Istog with approximately 35 different groups of Kosovars, mostly Albanians, to assist each community in organizing projects to be supported under this USAID program. After long attempts to establish gender balance in the representation and participation at such meetings, noticeable differences between rural and urban women's participatory behaviors in public space became predictable. Rural women from villages did not often attend community meetings. When they did, they remained silent and deferred to the men in alignment with the Kanun's duties of the wife toward her husband: to preserve the honor of her husband, serve her husband in an unblemished manner, and submit to his domination. Urban women attended community meetings as often as men, but usually in significantly lower numbers—there were often more than twice as many men as women in attendance, and the men were twice as likely to speak.

Part of this difference in rural and urban women's participation levels may have been the result of diversity in levels of knowledge or education or variations in the relationships between participants at village compared to town meetings. Participants at village community meetings were often members of the same family, with women participants having a secondary school education or below. Traditional village councils that deal with community issues are exclusively male, according to the Kanun requirements of the head of the house: "He must participate in every conference of the village" (Gjeçov, 1989, p. 18). Combined with the male-dominated professions related to construction and public utilities, it is common that community organizing of building and infrastructure rehabilitation would be customarily left for male intervention.

However, participants at the more urban town community meetings, male or female, were often professional colleagues rather than members of the same family or community. In most cases, participants at the meetings in these urban settings had university or advanced degrees and were assigned to attend the meetings by their employers—the local municipality and local and international nongovernmental

(continued)

organizations—rather than turning up as volunteers, like the rural village participants did.

Development of Women-Only Groups

Because of the poor attendance of women, each group at its own initiative divided into two different types of groups: a mixed-sex group, and a women-only group.[10] The women-only group was formed in the Novoselo and Jablonica e Vogel villages, because whenever women attended mixed meetings, they did not speak. Although the men were engaging well in community decision making in the mixed meetings, urban women from Pristina advised USAID–OTI that rural Kosovar Albanian women might be more inclined to participate more actively in a women-only setting that was in alignment with their culturally determined division of labor. When approached after the fifth meeting to speak in the mixed meeting, the rural women reinforced the advice from female urbanites and asked USAID–OTI to set a meeting time for women only where they would feel more comfortable.

The Well of Grief in Novoselo and Jablonica e Vogel

As soon as the women-only meetings were formed, women's community participation increased exponentially from two women at the mixed-sex meeting to more than 50 women in the women-only meetings. The village elder agreed to permit the women to hold their meetings in the room in his home where the village council usually met. In preparation for the meetings, the village women always had the wood stove ablaze and refreshments ready in advance for the guests—but not always for the women themselves. Suddenly, the same village women from Novoselo and Jablonica e Vogel who declined to speak in community meetings with men present were far more vocal in women-only meetings. Women and girls of all ages attended, with approximately half of school

age but clearly not enrolled in primary or secondary school.[11]

At the first meeting, there were two women USAID–OTI facilitators, a woman from an international NGO, and a room full of Kosovar Albanian women. We started by shaking the hand of each woman present, saying hello to each one directly, personally, and with eye contact. After sitting, we started introductions by introducing ourselves. Of the Kosovar Albanian women, many shared the same last names, and when they went around the introduction circle, each saying her name, altogether it sounded like a softly sung song. It was so beautiful that one of the facilitators asked them to "sing" their names again, which they did gladly.

Soon after, the women asked us if we wanted to know their story, and they nominated one of the young unmarried women to read her diary aloud about what the members of Jablonica e Vogel had experienced during the war. The reading lasted nearly two hours as she recounted in Albanian and then was followed by an English translation the details of how the conflict had escalated in their area; how she, her family, and her neighbors lived for months in the nearby forest; and how she felt when the men and women of the village were separated by Serb paramilitaries. She ended by reading each name of the boys and men from the village who were still missing. During the story, many women nodded in agreement, and some wept.

For these women, community development meant telling the stories of their lives. Every meeting continued similarly, first with introductions, then their "song." On the third meeting, their rhythmic saying of names was so lovely that a facilitator offered to bring a tape recorder for the next session, to record them and then play back the song so that the women could hear it for themselves. Upon arrival of the tape recorder, on the first go-round of the song, the women

---

[10] The ideal meeting model identified by the USAID–OTI project director in Washington, D.C., was one of mixed-sex integration, but in Kosova the model simply was not working well because women from rural areas were not participating equally. Having women-only meetings as a transitional step was the only alternative that could address the priority of women's inclusion in democratic decision making and the equitable distribution of resources.

[11] The issue of girls' attendance in schools is significant in Kosova, where the nongovernmental organization Women Artists and Veterans of Education reported in late 2002 that only 75% of Kosovar school aged girls are attending schools. They identify many reasons for girls' absence, including: the high cost of transport, books, meals, and clothes; and outdated assumptions that girls do not need education as much as boys if their destiny is to marry and become full-time homemakers. In the period immediately after the war, however, many schools were still under reconstruction—including the school in the Novoselo village.

passed the tape recorder from hand to hand. The song came out slower than usual. Then to retain their natural speed while accommodating the necessity for the recorder to be in microphone range, they appointed a holder of the tape recorder who went from person to person; and they worked on their cues so that each woman spoke her name immediately after the last speaker. Everyone loved it.

By the fifth meeting, the "song" itself had become a therapeutic exercise, and discussions emerged about what it means when a woman says her name softly or loudly or with hesitation. We practiced saying different phrases as a group, some softly, poetically, like "the wind is blowing"; some with confidence, like "I am free!" After experiencing the group-spoken phrase of freedom—so poignant right after 10 years of apartheid and state-led oppression that ended in war—each woman had far more confidence and energy when saying her own name.

In every meeting, there were announcements, particularly about the status of the rebuilding of the village community center, where women used to go to sew or do other community activities. Questions were answered about whether the estimate for the cost was finished, if the proposal had been translated, to which donors it had been submitted, when an answer might be expected to arrive, and other logistical issues. Then the floor was open to anyone who had an issue to raise. The only time there was a prearranged agenda was when a guest donor came to talk about how the village could gain more support, and the donor would explain the process. In all of the meetings with an open agenda, the women needed to talk about their dead and missing and how to get their husbands, sons, and brothers out of Serbian prisons. At about the fifth meeting, a woman shared a letter that she had just received from her brother, who was incarcerated in a Serbian prison and in poor condition. Some women cried, while others held them.

Thus, while the mixed-sex groups talked about topics that were determined by the men and reflected the male interests in the gendered division of labor (such as restoring buildings or upgrading power lines), the women's group discussed community, family cohesion, personal experiences, and relationships and told stories of pain and suffering. For some of the women, it was clear that they had never spoken to a foreigner

before—and especially not in the home of the head of the village and in front of all the other women. However, there was an urgent matter at hand with the missing persons, and the women were compelled to do whatever they could to find out what had happened to all of them and to free the prisoners. In the matters of basic caretaking for children and men, they were speaking out in their culturally appropriate domain. These women may have been accepting of their husbands' authority as family spokespersons in public meetings, but they refused to accept the Serb authority's view that their family members in prison had done anything wrong.

The women of Jablonica e Vogel wanted to remedy the missing persons and prisoner problem. It was in their interest to identify the social action activities of advocates in other parts of the world. The facilitators thus shifted the discussion to stories of social change and ways of getting political leaders' attention. They made a logo, which was a black and white circle to symbolize solidarity with those who were not yet free. Several of them attended meetings with urban women in Peja to solicit the support of women in the township. They developed a plan, and they carried it out.

After eight meetings, the women of Novoselo and Jablonica e Vogel had organized a silent candlelight march for All Hallows' Eve in the center of Peja to raise the attention of public officials to the need to honor the dead, to take action to find missing people, and to have Kosova Albanians released from prison. They had knitted hundreds of logo pins, with their two interlinking black and white circles, to give to people to pin on their lapels in a show of solidarity, rented a bus to drive them from the village to the outskirts of town, and invited the mayor and the U.N. regional administrator to attend the event.

On the night of the event, at 7:50 P.M., the town center was in still darkness except for a few early arrivals who brought candles for others. A single flame, lit by one match, was distributed from candle to candle in silent wait for the distant glowing procession approaching from the town's edge. As the village women arrived with their husbands and children, all holding burning candles, they were greeted with slow nods and knowing gazes. Soon the mayor and U.N. regional administrator arrived and were given

(continued)

candles by the village women. Each woman made an effort to approach these policy makers, to stand before them and look into their eyes, sending a wordless but powerfully unified message requesting immediate political action.

After one hour, a senior woman leader walked to the circular stone border that frames the flower bed in the town center and posted her candle on the edge of it. Without any premeditation, or instruction, every person in the crowd did the same. When the last candle was mounted on the wall and a ring of fire burned brightly in the center of the town's roundabout, the woman nodded her farewell and turned to go home. Without a sound or word, her message was loud and clear. The group disbanded as quietly as it had come together.

---

rather than a passive observer. The model of culturally conditioned consciousness includes the following stages:

1. intransitive—absence of awareness beyond biological survival;
2. semi-intransitive—perceptive association of living environment with fate or destiny;
3. semitransitive—naïve understanding of human influence on sociocultural factors; and
4. transitive—capacity for critically thinking about and intentionally influencing social change (Freire, 1970).

The observable differences in the willingness of rural and urban women to participate in public life, defined in particular by their willingness and courage to vocally express ideas publicly, may be connected to environmental factors that influence transitivity. For example, women from rural agrarian areas have often lived isolated in their communities, where access to formal education and diverse European and International cultural inputs have been lacking. Thus, in rural areas, traditional cultural values, including those of the Kanun that permit women little voice, have been socially reinforced and encountered fewer challenges from alternative social models than in urban settings. Women from urban areas are more likely to have had more access to formal education, especially if they were at university level before the troubles began in 1989, as well as opportunities to question authority and gain exposure to a wider array of cultural influences.

For a rural woman to feel comfortable enough to speak out in a group, she has to believe that she has a worthwhile contribution to make. To find her voice, she has to find her own sense of agency. Thus, behavioral differences related to vocalization in public space between urban and rural Kosovar women show direct correlation with differing levels of conscious awareness and self-perceptions of authority as defined by Freire. Further, any individual woman's willingness to speak or not appears to be indicative of her personal concept of permeability of culture and her ability to influence the views of others.

For example, wives of missing persons in the town of Guska have been helped through activism to cope with their own losses. In their highly patriarchal environment and according to the Kanun, these women are not supposed to work outside of the home. Had this continued, they would have been silenced about their losses because of a lack of forum in which to speak. However, they exercised their right to work by building a mushroom production facility. For the first time in their lives, they have earned the right to work from the local community. They found therapeutic benefit through participation in public life, in earning income for themselves, and in communicating with the outside world. Through their activities, the women of Guska have gained the strength not only to challenge ancient rules but also to change their community's view of the role of women.

The concept of transitivity, or the ability to take action in the face of crisis, is a critical factor that also determines how well a person can overcome hardship free of posttraumatic stress symptoms (Levine & Frederick, 1997). Siebert describes the *"survivor personality"* who is able to utilize resources and has an ability to act appropriately to survive and thrive after trauma (Siebert, 1999).

In this way, the participation in community action projects with international partners can help to create a "safe" space that can ultimately help women who have lived in fear to open themselves up to the world. This type of engagement can stretch the boundaries of women's comfort levels and their willingness to interact with people they have not known all their lives—and ultimately to determine new barometers for themselves of who is safe company and in what kinds of situations. Ultimately, women's willingness to engage in such new activities may create or restore a sense of confidence in their changing environments, as well as in their own abilities to determine for themselves what constitutes appropriate behavior within the new space. This influences their transitivity or ability to take action in the face of crisis, and it can have a direct influence in healing trauma they have experienced.

Clearly, awareness of the conditions that determine safety is an important skill for women to learn. Through testing their cognitive understanding of what constitutes a safe environment, women are able to consciously identify, choose, and gravitate to safe conditions. For women who encounter posttraumatic stress symptoms, such as hyperarousal in group settings, access to new and safe community environments enable them to channel their hyperarousal response into positive and appropriate responses. Repeated affirmations of their capacities to succeed at interactions in such group surroundings may enable such women to recalibrate their sensory perceptions to at first tolerate and, then with time, participate in and even enjoy group processes that may have initially triggered states of hyperarousal.

PERSONAL REFLECTIONS

Melissa Stone is a social psychologist and Ph.D. candidate at the California Institute of Integral Studies, who became involved in promoting women's human rights in Kosova in her association as a board member and acting executive director of the Network of East–West Women. She began living and working in Kosova after the entry of NATO peacekeeping troops in mid-1999. Before, during, and since the postwar emergency phase, she co-directed a community development project (U.S. Agency for International Development, Office of

Transition Initiatives) in Peja. From 2000 through 2002, she was an advisor to the Equal Opportunity Bureau within the Department for Democratic Governance and Civil Society of the Joint Interim Administrative Structure created by the U.N. Administrative Mission in Kosovo, and later an advisor to the first prime minister of Kosova. Her major lesson learned from her 3.5 years in Kosova is that women's human rights include the right to learn, grow, and evolve at their own pace and according to their own agenda.

Dr. Vjosa Dobruna is a Kosovar pediatrician and founder of the Center for the Protection of Women and Children in Pristina, Kosova (1992); the Safe House in Gjakova, Kosova (2000); and the Women's Center in Tetova, Macedonia (1999). She is also a founding steering committee member of the Network of East–West Women and a witness to many of the cases included in this article. During the recent war in Kosova, she was an outspoken advocate for human rights. For more than a year, she was the co-head of the Department for Democratic Governance and Civil Society in the Joint Interim Administrative Structure initiated by the U.N. Mission in Kosovo. Dr. Dobruna is currently a fellow at the Carr Center for Human Rights Policy, Kennedy School of Government, Harvard University.

CONCLUSION

The project example elaborated in this chapter is only a drop in an ocean of projects in Kosova and elsewhere. Such social activism that promotes women's participation is encouraging women to be more vocal, active, and political social change makers in public life. Social activism has enabled women to shed some of the outdated cultural traditions that even now keep them in positions of political underrepresentation and economic and social disadvantage.

Clearly, the increase of new projects promoting women as active social change makers are critical for the development of egalitarian democratic institutions—guarantors of human rights, including women's rights ensured by CEDAW. The process of voicing the views, needs, and interests that the women encounter while creating conditions and opportunities for social action has a therapeutic effect. This confirms the effectiveness of developing personal perceptive awareness of transitivity as a therapeutic form of psychosocial healing for those suffering from posttraumatic stress symptoms. It points to the need for community-level healing for women (and men) who are undergoing cultural change and have suffered from trauma. Hopefully, the methods identified in the context of Kosova can be adapted and applied elsewhere.

KEY CONCEPTS

- transitivity and survivor personality
- Paolo Freire's model of culturally conditioned consciousness
- conflict between traditional customs and international human rights law
- externally imposed aspects of globalization on the lives of individuals, especially disproportionate effects on women

- importance of understanding and respecting cultural norms in maximizing the effectiveness of development investment
- telling of stories as a prerequisite for social activism and posttraumatic stress healing

QUESTIONS

1. Describe the traditional family structure with regard to women's role and rights in Kosova.
2. How is your culture's traditional family structure similar to or different from women's role and rights in Kosova?
3. How does your family respond to your culture's traditional family structure related to women's role and rights?
4. How does your culture's traditional family structure pertaining to women's role and rights affect you as an individual? How do you react to these structures?
5. Where do you believe that you are in Freire's model of culturally conditioned consciousness?
6. If you worked with a population similar to that in Kosova, how would you feel toward a community with such a family structure? How might that structure impact on your work?

EXERCISE

Together with a partner, share the following experience related to transitivity: Identify three individuals from your family or circle of friends who share your cultural traditions and who you believe have levels of cultural transitivity that are different from the level you assigned yourself. Could they be models for you—or you for them? Who are your models for transitivity? What might be some issues that would arise for you individually as you strive to create social change within a society that might have different traditional family structures than those that are familiar to you? Can you think of a time in your life when you created change in some traditional belief about gender roles for yourself? Describe what happened and the results of this change. If possible, utilize the idea of transitivity in your description.

References

Freire, P. (1970). *Pedagogy of the oppressed.* New York: Herder & Herder.

Gjeçov, S. (Ed.). (1989). *The code of Lekë Dukagjini.* New York: Gjonlekaj Publishing.

Goleman, D. (1995). *Emotional intelligence: Why it can matter more than IQ.* New York: Bantam Books.

Human Rights Watch (2000). *Recommendations to the International Criminal Tribunal for the Former Yugoslavia.* Available at www.hrw.org/reports/2000/fry/Kosov003-01.htm.

Levine, P., & Frederick, A. (1997). *Waking the tiger: Healing trauma.* Berkeley, CA: North Atlantic Books.

Malcolm, N. (1999). *Kosova: A short history.* New York: New York University Press.

North Atlantic Treaty Organization. (1999). *NATO's role in relation to the conflict in Kosovo.* Available at www.nato.int/kosovo/history.htm.

Siebert, A. (1999). *The survivor personality: How to thrive and survive any life crisis.* London: Thorsons.

United Nations. (1948). *Universal Declaration of Human Rights (UDHR).* Available at www.udhr.org/UDHR/default.htm.

United Nations. (2001). *Convention on the Elimination of All Forms of Discrimination against Women (CEDAW).* Available at www.un.org/womenwatch/daw/cedaw/cedaw.htm.

United Nations Population Fund. (2002). Personalizing population: Background on Kosova. Retrieved on 30 September 2002 from www.unfpa.org/modules/focus/Kosova/ background.htm.

U.S. Department of State. (1995). *Bosnia: Chronology of the Balkan conflict.* (Fact sheet). Available at http://dosfan.lib.uic.edu/ERC/bureaus/eur/releases/951101Bosnia Chronology.html.

THE ROAD TO MULTICULTURAL SENSITIVE STUDENT SUPERVISION

17

Ethiopian Social Work Students in Israel

NAVA ARKIN
ISRAEL

OVERVIEW

This chapter focuses on the supervision of students from other cultures, specifically from Ethiopia, and supervisors from the majority culture in Israel. It also explores the difficulties in the supervisory process from two approaches. One approach minimizes and the other magnifies cultural differences. Clinical examples are presented, and culturally sensitive ways of working through these issues are suggested. Implications for training and supervision are also discussed.

INTRODUCTION

Demographic changes in Israel—as a result of the immigration waves in the past decade, especially from the former Soviet Union and Ethiopia—have created a challenge for professional helpers, instructors, and supervisors in the field of the helping professions. The basis of this challenge lies in understanding that professional education must develop a multicultural concept and focus on therapy that is sensitive to culture, ethnic diversity, racism, oppression, and discrimination (Cnaan, Goodfriend, & Neuman, 1996; Devore & Schlesinger, 1987; Ford & Jones, 1987; Harper & Lantz, 1996; Jaffe, 1995). The integration of students from these immigration waves into academic faculties of the helping professions (schools of social work, psychology, occupational therapy, etc.) has raised the need for coping with dilemmas, challenges, and difficulties in the professional education of students from different cultural backgrounds in general and the supervision of these students in particular. However, insufficient effort has been devoted to developing a multicultural approach within the training course for supervisors in order to meet these needs.

Regarding the development of a multicultural approach, the literature has tended to focus in recent years on developing and practicing multicultural competency models for therapists (Fukuyama, 1994; Hoag & Beckler, 1996; Ibrahim, 1991; Leong & Kim, 1991; Pedersen, 1991). These models focus on the phases of gradually developing cultural sensitivity in the therapist as well as on the various elements that were identified as important in achieving multicultural competency: awareness of beliefs, attitudes of the therapist toward cultural diversity, knowledge of the cultural context of the client, and the skills that the therapist must learn to apply (Ben-David, 1998; Christensen, 1989; Harper & Lantz, 1996; Heppner & O'Brien, 1994; Leong & Kim, 1991; McRae & Johnson, 1991; Midgette & Meggert, 1991; Solicido, Garcia, Cota, & Thomson, 1996; Sue, 1991). In comparison with the abundance of professional literature that deals with developing competency for multicultural therapy as part of a professional education in psychology, counseling, and social work, relatively little attention has been paid to applying this knowledge in multicultural supervision situations where the supervisor and the supervisee come from different cultural groups (Batten, 1990; Bernal, Barron, & Leary, 1983; Bernard & Goodyear, 1992; Fukuyama, 1994; Leong & Wagner, 1994).

The available literature on supervision and multicultural issues of race, ethnic minority, sect, and religion refers mainly to the cultural differences between the supervisee or therapist and the client, the difficulties and dilemmas that may arise as a result of these differences, and their effect on the therapeutic process (Bernard & Goodyear, 1992; Black, Maki, & Nunn, 1997; Carney & Kahn, 1984; Cook, 1994; Petterson, 1991). The emphasis is placed on the responsibility of the supervisor to work on these issues during supervision in order to increase the effectiveness of the therapy for the client (Bernard & Goodyear, 1992; Carney & Kahn, 1984; Fukuyama, 1994; Lago & Thompson, 1997; Leong & Wagner, 1994; Lopez, 1997; Newfeldt, Iversen, & Juntumen, 1995). Another reference to cultural diversity in supervision is in regard to different factors that should be fostered by supervisors among their supervisees in order to increase their cultural sensitivity. These include awareness of stereotypes in order to decrease bias toward clients that could lead to a misguided selection of intervention goals, as well as the development of knowledge and skills that are sensitive to cultural diversity (Bernard & Goodyear, 1992; Leong, 1994; McRae & Johnson, 1991; Priest, 1994; Solicido, Garcia, Cota, & Thomson, 1996).

Little mention is given in the literature to cross-cultural supervision, which develops cultural competency among supervisors and develops their sensitivity toward their culturally different supervisees (Davidson, 1987;

Ibrahim, 1991; Midgette & Meggert, 1991; Watson, 1993). Moreover, there is a lack of theoretical and empirical material that examines cultural diversity between the supervisor and the supervisee and the effect of this diversity on the supervisory relationship (Black et al., 1997; Cook, 1994; Hilton, Russell, & Salmi, 1995; Holloway, 1997; Leong & Wagner, 1994; Priest, 1994; Ryan & Hendricks, 1989).

Study of the difficulties that arise in the supervisory relationship—from both the supervisor's and the supervisee's perspectives toward cultural diversity—may contribute to developing cultural sensitivity among supervisors and reducing the ineptitude of students from different cultural backgrounds. This chapter describes the difficulties found in the context of supervision between social work supervisees from Ethiopia and supervisors from the mainstream Israeli culture. It examines the difficulties according to the two approaches of the supervisors toward cultural diversity in supervision and presents examples based on students' and supervisors' narratives, experience, and observation. In addition, the chapter discusses the solutions that were designed to improve cross-cultural interaction in supervision.

The chapter is conceptually based on postmodern notions that deal with the implication of the strengths perspective to supervision (Cohen, 1999; Saleebey, 1994, 2002; Stewart, 1994). The strengths perspective encourages supervisors to use the existing strengths and resources of the supervisees' culture to promote multiculturally sensitive student supervision. Likewise, it helps the supervisees to discover within themselves their cultural power, and it inclines to focus more on contextual variables that are unique to the therapeutic and supervisory contexts than on personal issues of the supervisee. Those notions enhance the supervisors' and supervisees' abilities to learn the many ways of knowing, to develop multiple "truth" in cultural diversity supervision, and to adopt the position of collaboration in supervision.

In line with this perception, the chapter is built on the writer's practice experience with supervisees from diverse cultures—immigrant supervisees as well as supervisees who are not from the mainstream Israeli culture (i.e., Israeli Arab students). Another professional experience comes from an ongoing mutual open dialogue with many supervisors in the training course of supervision. This experience provides the writer a rich source for learning how to promote multicultural sensitivity in supervision of the helping professions that transforms the meaning of the theoretical and empirical knowledge to practical knowledge.

EXPECTATIONS VERSUS DIFFICULTIES

Fieldwork supervisors in an Israeli school of social work were asked to supervise students from Ethiopia without receiving prior training. The process of assigning fieldwork took into consideration geographical proximity, the needs of the Ethiopian population, and the required academic standards for matching supervisors with students. The supervisors, who had not been trained for culturally diversified supervising situations, expected to meet supervisees to whom they could contribute in terms of growth and development, awareness, interpsychic processes of identification, transference, and parallel processes. Moreover, they expected to develop depth and understanding in the supervisees' use of various skills and to improve their therapeutic reactions, problem-solving abilities, and working skills in community systems.

In the supervising sessions between the supervisors and the Ethiopian students, expectations were shattered. It did not take long for the supervisors to realize that time, pace, knowledge, abstract ability, professional functioning, and initiative were different from their expectations. Confronting emotions and working with projection-identification processes or parallel processes led to a dead end. For example, showing emotions in public is considered in Ethiopian culture as both inadequate and unacceptable. Grownups are required to internalize all their emotions. The Ethiopian's language is missing words of emotions. When a supervisor tries to ask an Ethiopian student to describe his feelings toward immigrating to Israel as a way to understand his client's feeling as an immigrant, the reaction was silence without any expression of emotions.

In the supervisory dialogue, the main issues raised were concrete assistance, the presence of silences, and the unconditional acceptance of authority. Lack of the Ethiopian students' technological tools made it difficult to function at work and to be in contact with community systems. Their inability to express independent opinions in front of the supervisors results from the cultural obligation to respect the authoritative figures. In such cases, the supervisor could not know whether the student has no original opinion or he did not understand his question. Such a situation may not lead to progress.

The reactions of the supervisors toward their shattered expectations were emotional: disappointment, frustration, and anger. These reactions characterized the supervisors who adopted a more dynamic supervising style as well as those who adopted a problem-solving style. Examination of their cognitive, emotional, and behavioral expressions distinguished between the two major approaches to supervising students from different cultural backgrounds: one that minimizes cultural differences in supervision, and the other that magnifies them. These varying approaches are only barely addressed in the literature dealing with cultural issues in therapy (Falicov, 1988; Lopez, 1997; Pedersen, 1991).

TWO APPROACHES TO CULTURE

Minimizing Cultural Differences in Supervision

The supervisors who minimize cultural diversity in supervision are those who adopt a universal outlook (Fukuyama, 1990; Leong & Kim, 1991; Pedersen, 1991). According to this concept, there is a general professional basis, shared by all cultures, to which individuals must adapt. Difficulties confronted by ethnic minorities in their attempts to integrate into society and the social work profession are therefore minimized insofar as they are common to all cultural groups.

The supervisor's behavior demands, both explicitly and implicitly, that the student adopt values, cognitive modes, and professional behavior that are in accordance with the standards of the mainstream culture. For example, the student is expected to establish a professional relationship with boundaries and emotional exposure, openly discussing and analyzing the client's problems. However, this style of intervention does not reflect the Ethiopian cultural system, which does not condone the disclosure of emotions. Rather, their cultural code requires protecting and helping other members of their community.

Thus, the conflict that emerges is between a Western intervention style, with its professional mode of communication, and the specific communication style of the Ethiopian culture. As a result, the supervisee becomes an interpreter, instead of a social worker, an escort without boundaries, rather than a therapist who establishes a professional relationship with the client. By avoiding the cultural aspect of supervision, the supervisor represents only the point of view of the mainstream culture, and thereby limits the possibilities of transforming the personal interaction into a professional one. Failure to live up to expectations may evoke anger, tension, frustration, disappointment, guilt, and denial in the supervisory relationship and may create an obstruction to real and effective communication during supervision.

Difficulties that emerge as a result of minimizing cultural diversity are often manifested in the issues, which are brought to or withheld from the supervision process recording. This derives from the fact that the supervisee shares the same language and culture with his or her client, a language and culture that is different from that of the supervisor. The supervision is carried out in a language different from that used in the therapy, and the material presented during the supervision session is translated into a short report and a series of concrete questions. Although the student's verbal report may indicate that the dialogue with the client is open and flowing, the subtleties of the language may be difficult to convey, and the supervisor may find it hard to obtain a clear picture of the session, the therapy, or the client. Feeling isolated and frustrated, the supervisor is thus unable to share the whole process with the student. This presents the danger of a potential conflict that can affect the supervisee, the client, and the relationship. When examining the process recordings of the Ethiopian students, it seems that the issues that the students found hardest to report were those connected with aspects involving conflicts with their cultural values.

The following example demonstrates the problems that may emerge as a result of minimizing the cultural differences in supervision. A student supervisee, who had immigrated to the country during adolescence, was assigned for therapy to a family who had just arrived from Ethiopia a few months earlier. The family included a 17-year-old boy with cerebral palsy and a father who was not cooperating with the rehabilitative therapy offered to his son (physical and occupational therapy). The purpose of the therapy, as defined in the supervision, was to support and accompany an adolescent boy, with cerebral palsy and to promote his rehabilitation program. It was decided that, in order to do so, the supervisee would first talk with the father regarding the importance of the rehabilitation program. Although the father reportedly agreed to cooperate, he did not actually send his son to therapy. This infuriated the supervisor as well as the agency that was providing the therapeutic services. Further adding to the supervisor's frustration was the fact that the student did not report on any difficulties or involve the supervisor in any issues of resistance or ambivalence expressed by the father toward the proposed rehabilitative therapy.

The student felt a conflict between the father's authority, which, according to the cultural code, must be respected, and the authority of the supervisor, whose teaching and advice must also be followed. The goal of the therapy also created a conflict between Western-style intervention, which aims to develop the adolescent's independence through rehabilitation, and the values of the Ethiopian culture, which dictate that the boy must rely on his father's authority and not disobey him. The student was therefore caught in the middle of a conflict between the father, the boy, the supervisor, and the goals of the therapy. Denying the cultural issues only increased the difficulties and created a gap in the supervision process.

Analysis of the process indicated that the student had not reported her attempts to convince the father, as these evoked feelings of guilt. In addition, she had neither encouraged the boy nor offered to accompany him to the rehabilitation treatment, identifying with his passivity and dependence on his father's authority. This identification prevented her from dealing with independence issues and from bringing them to the supervision session. Further contributing to her silence was the cultural expectation that the authority figure (in this case, her supervisor), who "knows all," would realize her emotions and difficulties without having to bring them up in the session.

When cultural differences and the need to develop modes of analysis suitable to another culture are ignored, the ability of both the supervisor and the supervisee to function is severely impaired. If the authority and the cultural context of the student are not taken into consideration, then the student can be perceived as passive and incapable of internalizing the supervision. This denial of cultural diversity is also expressed by the tendency to regard the supervisee as an extension of the supervisor's ego, termed in the professional literature as the "theoretical myth of sameness" (Hardy, 1989). It leads the supervisor to wrongly assume that if the supervisee demonstrates motivation to learn and expresses a sense of connection with the profession, then this also indicates identification with the mainstream culture and willingness to relinquish one's own cultural foundation.

For example, an Ethiopian student found it hard to deal with the emotional processing of the death of a client's wife. He dealt strictly with the client's concrete needs, accompanying him to medical checkups and serving as his translator at the hospital. Despite the student's motivation to read theoretical material on bereavement, the supervisor concluded that the student was incapable of internalizing and applying the lessons learned and thus reproached him for inadequate intervention. In this case, the precedence of the student's cultural codes (the prohibition to express and talk about emotions) over professional demands led to the supervisor's excessive criticism and bias in judging and assessing the student's capabilities. This highlights the need to understand the emotional component from a cultural point of view that is so essential to the therapeutic process (Bernard, 1994; Leong & Wagner, 1994; Watson, 1993).

Magnifying Cultural Differences in Supervision

The supervisors who magnify cultural differences in supervision are those who adopt a relative outlook (Ibrahim, 1991; Pedersen, 1991). According to this approach, excessive emphasis is placed on unique cultural differences while the common factors are neglected. This approach reinforces the social stereotype of deprivation, disadvantage, and discrimination inherent in being a member of a minority group. As such, a person who is culturally different and comes from a minority group is seen as oppressed and in need of protection.

The behavioral expression of this approach, which requires the supervisor to serve as the social conscience, includes being patronizing, overprotective, feeling pity, feeling guilt, and continuous compensation in supervisory relations. The supervisor overlooks the supervisee's incomplete assignments and downplays criticism of professional performance, which can undermine the supervisee's self-confidence and lead to frustration, confusion, anxiety, and overdependence on the supervisor (Bernard & Goodyear, 1992; Leong & Wagner, 1994; Watson, 1993).

The following example demonstrates the difficulties that can emerge as a result of magnifying the cultural differences in supervision: An Ethiopian student was treating a young couple who had a baby suffering from a developmental disability. The parents' difficulties and anxieties regarding the birth of a baby with a developmental disability were not brought up in the course of the treatment. The supervisor ascribed this omission to cultural diversity and told the student that it was not necessary for him to deal with such culturally unacceptable issues. She also exempted him from process recordings and prepared the required report for the center of child development for him. Likewise, when it came time for a staff meeting on the family, the supervisor presented the case instead of the supervisee.

The supervisor's patronizing and overprotective behavior resulted from her own feelings of pity and guilt. She said to her supervisor, "I am the student's crutches, and I am doing all the professional tasks instead of him. All the time I have to push him, otherwise nothing will move." She attributed all of the student's difficulties to his cultural background, causing her to compensate for his shortcomings and withhold constructive criticism. In so doing, she deprived the supervisee of an opportunity to learn more in depth and left him feeling isolated and helpless in his overdependency on the supervisor.

Another difficulty that may emerge as a result of magnifying cultural differences is turning the supervisee into an "expert" on his or her culture. Such an expectation can create undue pressure to explain the culture and places the responsibility of understanding the client on the supervisee, who ends up feeling trapped and alone. This process reflects the danger in viewing the Ethiopian student as a spokesperson for the entire Ethiopian culture. In effect, the supervisee represents his or her own individual personality, maturity, and cultural identity. The unawareness of the supervisor of the whole complex reduces the quality of supervision. The supervisee is prevented from having a multidimensional view of the client and is caught in a cycle whereby any objection may be interpreted by the supervisor as uncooperative behavior.

A MULTICULTURAL APPROACH TO SUPERVISION

By adopting either of these two approaches to supervision—minimizing or magnifying cultural differences—the supervisor is demonstrating ethnocentric behavior that derives from stereotypical and judgmental attitudes toward foreign cultures (Ben-David, 1996). Both can lead to estrangement from and feelings of arrogance toward the supervisee, as well as a lack of understanding of individual academic needs, part of which are the same among all students and part of which are unique to each particular culture. Furthermore, both approaches have a negative impact on many aspects of supervision: The evaluative conclusions toward the supervisee are biased, the professional progress of the supervisee is hindered, and the overall supervision program is rendered inadequate (Petterson, 1991). Those two approaches of the preferable stories of the supervisors excluded the Ethiopian students from the profession, whereas one of the goals of the supervision process is to help them to be included in the social work profession.

The multicultural approach to supervision must develop a broad-based conceptual framework that will recognize the complexities of a pluralistic society and, at the same time, create a bridge between the different cultural backgrounds of the supervisor and the supervisee (Cook, 1994; Fukuyama, 1994; Leong, 1994; Leong & Wagner, 1994). An integrated supervision approach should be based on the universal aspects of the profession as well as on the cultural uniqueness of the student, stemming from the understanding that culture molds behavior and that in behavior there is a reaction to culture (Bernard & Goodyear, 1992; Petterson, 1991; Priest, 1994). In a truly multicultural approach to supervision, it is essential to develop an acceptance and respect for cultural diversity without using the ethnic identity of supervisees as the rationale for providing reduced supervision.

Analysis of the supervision process, which did succeed in overcoming the difficulties and in which there was professional development, shows that the supervisors in these dyads tried to achieve a balanced approach between minimizing and magnifying cultural differences—that is, taking an approach that sensitively integrates and makes use of both approaches. The next example demonstrates a culturally sensitive supervision process that reflects the attempt of the supervisor to provide a supportive atmosphere by recognizing cultural differences and addressing the ideological conflict between the unique culture of the supervisee and the common culture of the profession.

An Ethiopian student, aged 23, who had immigrated to Israel two years previously was assigned for therapy to a client whose wife had abandoned him and run away to her family in another city. The father remained with his 11-year-old son, who was frequently absent from school in order to help the father by preparing *Ingara* (Ethiopian food) and acting as his interpreter with the establishment when problems arose. In this supervisory process, the need to confront the father's anger, dependence, and helplessness were discussed. In therapy, the student managed to convince the father to send his son to school. The father agreed, and said *Ishy*, a word used to satisfy authority, but he continued to keep his son at home, complaining that he could not manage the household affairs and other arrangements by himself. The student's assessment was that there did not seem to be any progress or change induced by the treatment.

Taking into consideration the supervisee's knowledge of the culture, the supervisor helped him cope with the cultural conflicts involved in treatment, including issues of authority and respect for elders, as well as appropriate roles for the supervisee and the father. This process helped to develop the supervisee's self-awareness and the realization of how those issues affected his intervention. The supervisor continued to examine the difficulties together with the student, rather than attributing all of them to cultural dilemmas. Some were attributed to a lack of interviewing skills, which were improved by practicing during the supervision sessions. In addition, the father was given assistance with domestic responsibilities in order to bolster his trust and facilitate a change in the boy's school attendance. The support, sensitivity, practice of skills, and concrete assistance created a change in the supervisee's capability to become more authoritative, more focused, and more self-confident while helping the client become more open as well. At the same time, the supervisee improved his ability to involve the supervisor in his difficulties without reservations.

It is easy to see how the supervision process became multidimensional in this case, involving the dimensions of awareness, knowledge, relations, and skills based on mutual respect for cultural differences between the supervisor and the supervisee. Supervisors who succeed in implementing a multicultural approach must be willing to accept cultural diversity and to discuss cross-cultural issues with their students without fear of being perceived as racists. While showing empathy for the students' difficulties, they cannot permit themselves to be drawn into the students' helplessness, dependence, or lack of skills. They must work in a structured way by clarifying and focusing on the demands and suitable pace for each individual student, while being careful not to neglect the needs of the clients. Evaluation of students' functioning should be carried out within a cultural context, sensitively considering the conflict of values between the common culture of the profession and each individual student's culture. This approach will enable a genuine supervisory relationship that facilitates the growth and development of the supervisee coming from a different minority culture (see Table 17.1).

TABLE 17.1 | APPROACHES OF SUPERVISORS TOWARDS SUPERVISING CULTURALLY DIFFERENT STUDENTS

	Minimizing Cultural Differences	Magnifying Cultural Differences	Balancing and Respecting Cultural Differences
Outlook	The supervisor embraces a universal outlook.	The supervisor embraces a relative outlook.	The supervisor embraces a multicultural integrative outlook.
Attitude	There is sufficient room for all cultures because behavior is universal.	There are cultural differences and discrimination. Anyone who is culturally different and a member of a minority group is unfortunate and should be pitied. One should protect their rights and serve as a social conscience. Overemphasis on uniqueness. All behaviors are the result of a cultural cause.	There are benefits and gains from the existence of various cultural groups. Interaction is important.
Behavior	Denial; minimizing of difficulties confronted by the ethnic minority when attempting to integrate into society and the profession. The supervisor makes demands according to the professional standards of the cultural majority. Demands adaptation and is critical.	Strengthening of social stereotypes. It is unfortunate to belong to a minority group as they suffer from deficiency and disadvantage. The supervisor acts as a patron. Overprotective reaction. Does not insist on completion of assignments and professional depth. Lessens criticism.	Acceptance of cultural differences, respect for different values, cognitive styles, and communication. Is interested in understanding the culture while ensuring that the cultural diversity does not serve as a rationale for reduced supervision.
Emotions	The supervisor reacts in anger, frustration, disappointment, guilt, denial, avoidance, and fear.	Reacts with pity, guilt, reaction formation, frustration, fear, and attrition.	Emotional reactions are empathic and balanced. High level of awareness in accordance with the circumstances of the supervision.
Conclusion	Evaluative conclusions about the supervisee: Incapable; does not develop. The difficulties are mainly personality-dependent.	Evaluative conclusions about the supervisee: Cultural diversity and cultural conditions have created the difficulties. Lack of professional advantage is the main cause for the situational problems.	Evaluative conclusions about the supervisee: Integration between the common culture of the profession and the cultural uniqueness of the student. Critical evaluative perception of personality and situation.

CASE 17.1	STUDENTS' NARRATIVES AND SUCCESSFUL SOLUTIONS IN THE SUPERVISORY PROCESS

Student narratives are used here as case examples for successful solutions in the supervisory dialogue. These examples promote multiculturally sensitive student supervision and can be used in class to analyze the elements of the multicultural competency.

> When our relationships were opened and I felt secured and trusted, I could tell my supervisor my hard experience about the racism in the neighborhood I made home visits. Few children called me "Negro—black" "Ethiopian is AIDS". . . . I got very silent, and very angry. My supervisor react very sensitive, she did not ignore the problem. She asked me about this experience and my meaning. She listened to my experiences of feeling powerless rejected. We were talking how this experience affects my attending skills. She helped me to see what does another client identifies in me that cause him to be willing to talk with me, to be in professional relations with me. This session was a turning point for me. I stopped being afraid of being rejected and accept my dark color. I asked her to tell me what it is for her to supervise me, so culturally different from her. Those open relations, so authentic, enable me this meaningful experience.

> My supervisor talked with me on my experience of being different. We were talking about the meaning of my name. I came to the conclusion that I have my Ethiopian name Maharat and my Hebrew name Mordehai. It is o.k. with me. I am lucky. I have grown between two worlds: The Ethiopian and the Israeli. I have the two identities. I want to feel like Ethiopian and to think like an Israeli. My supervisor explained me that this is the biculture solution. This open session between us affect me very much. I feel she helps me to construct my self-identity and to find a solution for my self that balance my function.

> When my supervisor sent me to use my culture to help my clients, she showed me the power of my culture, she suggested me to ask my mother what families did in Ethiopia when a retarded baby was born? How they rear crippled children? I understood that in a spiritual meaning the family used such a child for luck and they will not cooperate with any program of his individuation. This experience gave me back my relationship with my mother. Suddenly she knows what I am doing and learning. . . . I understand that there are many ways of knowing, many ways of learning . . . and I need my culture to help people from my culture . . . otherwise my intervention will not be effective

The experiences of the Ethiopian students can provide a rich source for learning and a framework for understanding the meaning of being different and supervised in a multiculturally sensitive approach.

CONSTRUCTING MULTICULTURAL SENSITIVE SUPERVISORY DISCOURSE

The literature review, the study of the dynamics of the supervision process, and the case examples as described in this chapter certainly indicate that the meeting point between a supervisor from the mainstream culture and an Ethiopian supervisee evokes many difficulties. Nevertheless, cultural diversity can be changed from an obstruction in the supervision process to an uplifting of the professional development of both the supervisee and the supervisor. Supervisors must be trained in multicultural competency based on four main dimensions (also see Figure 17.1):

1. *The awareness dimension*—The supervisor must be aware of his or her own cultural and personal values (self-awareness as a cultural entity), stereotypes, prejudices, and biases, as well as differences with the supervisee in terms of

FIGURE 17.1

The dimensions
of multicultural
competency in
supervisor training

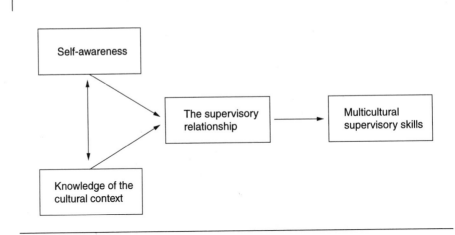

values, styles of communication, cognitive orientations, and emotional reactions. Awareness must also be high regarding potential conflicts, the extent of resistance, and the need for empathy, identification, defense, or criticism.

2. *The knowledge dimension*—Facts and information about the culture should be acquired, including the political, social, and economic history of the culture; research and theories that have been developed about the culture; attitudes, worldviews, and cultural codes; and specific knowledge connected to difficulties that emerge during supervision, such as the significance of passivity, silence, verbal and nonverbal language, and emotional expression.

3. *The relationship dimension*—This requires examination of supervisory relations in cultural terms, namely, how differences in the cultural variables of the supervisor and the supervisee—such as cultural identification, expectations, criticism, initiative, passivity, and roles—affect the supervisory relationship.

4. *The skills dimension*—The supervisor must work on developing skills that facilitate multicultural competency—that is, the ability to intervene in a culturally sensitive way without detracting from the quality of the professional training. This entails defining skills in a culturally diversified setting, addressing cultural issues with focus and empathy, and encouraging risk taking in cultural issues in order to develop suitable dialogue skills. The culture must be legitimized by showing a keen interest in it and by respecting the fact that supervisees know how to deal with their own group members, even though the supervisor has more professional knowledge. Here flexibility is required in applying intervention skills, which are different from the traditional skills used in psychosocial therapy. Case studies that require initiative and professional writing should be constructed, taking into account the different pace and behaviors that are culturally specific. The supervision demands can be raised in accordance with the improved abilities and skills of the supervisee, while the supervisor at appropriate points provides flexibility, support, and reinforcement.

CONCLUSIONS

In conclusion, the success of the supervision process within a context of multicultural diversity demands effective preparation of the supervisors, who not only have to be aware of the different cultural variables and their effects but also must be able to establish empathic and authentic relations with their supervisees. Supervisors must demand professional quality as well as cultural relevancy from their students while developing their own competency in culturally sensitive supervision through guidance and counseling. Further investigation is needed to explore other factors required for reducing the complexity of the supervisory process in culturally diversified situations and for meeting the many challenges faced by professional helpers in every immigration-absorbing country around the globe.

PERSONAL REFLECTIONS

Two decades of social work intervention, teaching, and supervising people from diverse cultures has affected my way of looking at students, supervisors, and the supervisory process. I learned that my culture is an integral part of my identity like other context variables. I became aware of the dynamic power of the cultural issues on the way in which supervisee and supervisor interact. I learned to appreciate the strengths of the Ethiopian students and respect their struggle for empowerment as a minority group in Israel, their effort to preserve their own cultural codes, and their desire to belong to the professional culture at the same time. I understood that I have to let go of many of my traditional supervision concepts, because in multicultural contexts they may exclude the students from diverse cultures instead of including them in the profession.

This experience directed me to emphasize racial and cultural strengths perspective in my practice, which means listening to and integrating into the supervisory process the racial and cultural themes that are brought to the supervisory dialogue and to view them as a power. It requires that supervisors will be open-minded enough to respect and listen to the racial and cultural themes by which supervisees define themselves and to see the impact of those themes on their professional behavior. I adopt the position of "not knowing" in the cultural diversity supervision, which means knowing more because it enables the supervisees to bring their knowledge and their culture in constructing and empowering their understanding and meaning of their clients. This is my own complex road to multiculturally sensitive student supervision.

KEY CONCEPTS

- cultural diversity in the supervision of social work students
- developing competency in culturally sensitive supervision
- minimizing versus magnifying cultural differences
- the supervisor's discourse and its implications

- deconstructing supervisors' meanings of the process of multicultural supervision
- from paternalism to collaborative relationships in supervision: looking at unique outcomes with transparency and mutuality
- accessing strengths in the supervisees' culture
- personal and professional knowledge
- skills of multiculturally sensitive supervision
- learning from success

EXERCISES

This is a guideline for discussion between supervisors who work with minority and culturally diverse supervisees. Alternatively, minority students who have supervisors of different cultural backgrounds can use this exercise to evaluate their supervision experience and help them bring up multicultural issues with their supervisors.

The Awareness Dimension: My Cultural Foundation

Relaxing and Feeling Your Culture   Sit comfortably, breathe as deeply as you can, and forget your concerns. Try to concentrate on your culture, on your social group, on your ethnic identity. Try to identify for yourself something from your cultural foundation: things that connect you to your patterns in interpersonal relationships; to your verbal and nonverbal communication; to your relationships with authority, trustworthiness, work, commitment, time, power, and role. Try to clarify to yourself how the cultural foundation that you have chosen influences you today—what it means for you now. Please write it down.

Bring an object (or a picture) that represents your cultural foundation. What does it mean for you? How does it influence you today? Tell its story.

Work on the material will take place in group sharing and group reflections. What is the resonance that came out of your exercise? Which themes were revealed? (For example, individualism, concern for the community or the social group, achievements, activities, actions, reactions). Legitimize the different feeling and thoughts. Tell the meaning of the culture and the influence on you as a human being, and as a professional social worker.

Feeling, Thinking, and Behaving   Write about how you interact with someone from a different culture or ethnic group. How do you feel, think, and behave when in such a situation?

Write a letter (that will not be sent) to someone from a different culture or ethnic group.

Draw a picture that shows the obstacles you feel when you interact with someone from a different culture. Why are the obstacles there? What do they mean? What will help remove them?

The Influence of Cultural Diversity on Supervision   Discuss or write about the following: The influence of my cultural foundation, my feeling, thinking, and behaving, on the process of supervision. Describe difficulties, challenges, and dilemmas; my expectations from the supervisee as helper or as a supervisee.

The Knowledge Dimension   *Knowledge about the client's culture* (group discussion and self-assignment)

What is your way of knowing about the different culture of your supervisee?

Did you read about the culture?

Did you talk with people from your supervisee's culture?

Do you know what your supervisee's cultural outlook or attitude is?

How does your supervisee handle the cultural codes?

Do you know his or her meanings of silence, feelings, passivity, and authority in relation to culture?

The Relationship Dimension

To examine the supervisory relationship in cultural terms, answer the following questions:

Do you feel competent and brave enough to talk about how the differences in cultural variables between you and your supervisee affect the supervisory relationship? Think of issues such as cultural identification, expectations, criticism, initiative, passivity, and roles.

What factors restrain you from raising the cultural difference between you? The fear of offending his or her feelings? The fear of being offended? The fear of being determined to be a racist when dealing these issues? Do you feel in danger?

How are you more tempted to deal with concrete content? Case examples? Skills?

How difficult is it for you to speak on a subject such as relationships in supervision?

The Skills Dimension

The supervisor must work on developing skills that facilitate multicultural competency—that is, the ability to intervene in a culturally sensitive way. The teacher can work on case examples that the group members bring in.

Supportive Skills

Acceptance, reassurance, and encouragement to take risks while dealing with cultural issues to develop. For example, a supervisor: "I feel that you and I have different cultures and different colors and that can influence what is going on in supervision. Is it okay for you to talk about it now?" or "When we decide something about your client and it is not accepted in your culture would you please let me know? I will also ask you from time to time."

The expert power of the supervisee to his culture: Legitimization of his knowledge and showing a keen interest in his culture. Appreciate that he knows how to talk with a person from his culture although you are the expert in terms of professional knowledge. For example, a supervisor: "In your process recording I saw that there is a tension every time you try to talk with the boy's father about his son and his rehabilitation. What is accepted behavior in your culture toward the disabled? We will talk about it and learn the case together."

Skills From the Strength Perspective

Encourage interventions and development and not deficits. Together, explore the strengths of the culture and in a flexible way find creative ways to intervene that respects culture. Focus more on context than on problems within the individual.

References

Batten, C. (1990). Dilemmas of cross-culture psychotherapy supervision. *British Journal of Psychotherapy, 7*(2), 129–140.

Ben-David, A. (1996). Therapists' perception of multicultural assessment and therapy with immigrant families. *Journal of Family Therapy, 18*(1), 23–41.

Ben-David, A. (1998). Teaching awareness of cultural pluralism: The Israeli experience. *Social Work Education, 17*(1), 101–109.

Bernal, M. E., Barron, B. M., & Leary, C. (1983). Use of application material for recruitment of ethnic minority student in psychology. *Professional Psychology: Research & Practice, 14,* 817–829.

Bernard, J. M. (1994). Multicultural supervision: A reaction to Leong and Wagner, Cook, Priest and Fukuyama. *Counselor Education and Supervision, 34*(2), 159–171.

Bernard, J. M., & Goodyear, R. (1992). *Fundamentals of clinical supervision.* Boston: Allyn & Bacon.

Black, J. E., Maki, M. T., & Nunn, J. A. (1997). Does race affect social work student–field instructors relationship? *The Clinical Supervisor, 16*(1), 39–54.

Carney, C. G., & Kahn, K. B (1984). Building competencies for effective cross-cultural counseling: A developmental view. *The Counseling Psychologist, 12*(1), 111–119.

Christensen, C. P. (1989). Cross-cultural awareness development: A conceptual model. *Counselor Education and Supervision, 28,* 270–287.

Cnaan, R. A., Goodfriend, T., & Neuman, E. (1996). Jewish ethnic needs in multicultural social work education. *Journal of Teaching in Social Work, 13*(1–2), 157–174.

Cohen, B. Z. (1999). Intervention and supervision in strengths-based social work practice. *Families in Society, 80,* 460–466.

Cook, D. A. (1994). Racial identity in supervision. *Counselor Education and Supervision, 34*(2), 132–141.

Davidson, L. (1987). Supervision of psychotherapy, East and West. *American Journal of Psychoanalysis, 47,* 230–236.

Devore, W., & Schlesinger, E. (1987). *Ethnic sensitive social work practice* (2nd ed.). Columbus, OH: Merrill.

Falicov, C. J. (1988). Learning to think culturally. In H. A. Liddle, D. C. Breunlin, & R. C. Schwartz (Eds.), *Handbook of family therapy training and supervision* (pp. 335–357). New York: Guilford Press.

Ford, K., & Jones, A. (1987). *Student supervision: Basic practical social work.* London: MacMillan Education.

Fukuyama, M. A. (1990). Taking a universal approach to multicultural counseling. *Counselor Education and Supervision, 30,* 6–17.

Fukuyama, M. A. (1994). Critical incidents in multicultural counseling supervision: A phenomenological approach to supervision research. *Counselor Education and Supervision, 34*(2), 142–151.

Hardy, K. (1989). The theoretical myth of sameness. In G. Saba, K. Hardy, & B. Karrer (Eds.), *Treating minority families.* New York: Haworth.

Harper, K. V., & Lantz, J. (1996). *Cross-cultural practice: Social work with diverse populations.* Chicago: Lyceum Books.

Heppner, M. J., & O'Brien, K. M. (1994). Multicultural counselor training: Students' perceptions of helpful and hindering event. *Counselor Education and Supervision, 34*(2), 4–18.

Hilton, D. B., Russell, R. K., & Salmi, S. W. (1995). The effect of supervisors' race and level of support on perception of supervision. *Journal of Counseling and Development, 73*(5), 554–563.

Hoag, K. M. H., & Beckler, P. S. (1996). Educating for cultural competence in generalist curriculum. *Journal of Multicultural Social Work, 1*(3), 37–56.

Holloway, E. L. (1997). Structures for analysis and teaching of supervision. In C. E. Watkins, Jr. (Ed.), *Handbook of psychotherapy supervision* (pp. 249–276). New York: Wiley & Sons.

Ibrahim, F. A. (1991). Contribution of cultural worldview to generic counseling and development. *Journal of Counseling and Development, 70,* 13–19.

Jaffe, E. D. (1995). Ethnic and minority groups in Israel: Challenges for social work theory, value, and practice. *Journal of Sociology and Social Welfare, 22*(1), 149–171.

Lago, C., & Thompson, J. (1997). The triangle with curved sides: Sensitivity to issues of race and culture in supervision. In G. Shipton (Ed.), *Supervision of psychotherapy and counseling: Making a place to think* (pp. 119–130). Philadelphia: Open University Press.

Leong, F. T. L. (1994). Emergence of the cultural dimension: The roles and impact of culture on counseling supervision. *Counselor Education and Supervision, 34*(2), 114–116.

Leong, F. T. L., & Kim, H. H. W. (1991). Going beyond cultural sensitivity on the road to multiculturalism: Using the intercultural sensitizer as counselor training tool. *Journal of Counseling and Development, 70,* 112–118.

Leong, F. T. L., & Wagner, N. S. (1994). Cross-cultural counseling supervision: What do we know? What do we need to know? *Counselor Education and Supervision, 34*(2), 117–131.

Lopez, S. R. (1997). Cultural competence in psychotherapy: A guide for clinicians and their supervisors. In C. E. Watkins, Jr. (Ed.), *Handbook of psychotherapy supervision* (pp. 570–588). New York: Wiley & Sons.

McRae, M. B., & Johnson, D. S., Jr., (1991). Toward training for competence in multicultural counselor education. *Journal of Counseling and Development, 70,* 131–135.

Midgette, T. S., & Meggert, S. S. (1991). Multicultural counseling instruction: A challenge for faculties in the 21st century. *Journal of Counseling and Development, 70,* 136–141.

Newfeldt, S. A., Iversen, J. N., & Juntumen, C. L. (1995). *Supervision strategies for the first practicum.* Alexandria, VA: American Counseling Association.

Pedersen, P. (1991). Multiculturalism as a fourth force in counseling. *Journal of Counseling and Development, 70,* 6–12.

Petterson, F. K. (1991). Issues of race and ethnicity in supervision: Emphasizing on who you are and not what you know. *The Clinical Supervisor, 9*(1), 15–31.

Priest, R. (1994). Minority supervisor and majority supervisee: Another perspective of clinical reality. *Counselor Education and Supervision, 34*(2), 152–158.

Ryan, A. S., & Hendricks, C. O. (1989). Culture and communication: Supervising the Asian and Hispanic social worker. *The Clinical Supervisor, 7*(1), 27–40.

Saleebey, D. (1994). Culture, theory, and narrative: The intersection of meaning in practice. *Social Work, 39*, 351–359.

Saleebey, D. (2002). Power in the people. In D. Saleebey (Ed.), *The strengths per-spective in social work practice* (3rd ed., pp. 1–47). Boston: Allyn & Bacon.

Stewart, K. (1994). Postmodernism and supervision. *Supervision Bulletin, 7*, 6.

Solicido, R. M., Garcia, J. H., Cota, V., & Thomson, C. (1996). A cross-cultural training model for field education. *Arete, 20*(1), 26–36.

Sue, D. W. (1991). A model for cultural diversity training. *Journal of Counseling and Development, 70*, 99–105.

Watson, M. F. (1993). Supervising the person of the therapist: Issues, challenges, and dilemmas. *Contemporary Family Therapy, 15*(1), 21–31.

INDEX